# Stone Walls and Men

# STONE WALLS AND MEN

Robert M. Lindner

Author of *Rebel Without a Cause*

**ODYSSEY PRESS**          New York

For

*Marged and Dan*

Here is the Green Book
I Promised You

# Table of Contents

# A Note to the Reader

WRITING a book like the one you have in your hands is a polite form of plagiarism or, better, a kind of mental kleptomania. Into it goes a distillation of ideas and facts from every conceivable source, from conversation and reading, and from study and observation. To assign credits for ideas, opinions, or expressions would be alien to the purpose of this volume, which is to bring alive and make challenging one of the most pressing aspects of our common life.

What I have to say in this book is the result of some years of observation and experience among criminals and with crime. For more than six years I have lived with a vivid awareness that our current techniques for handling the problem of crime are pitifully inadequate, that we have been bogged down by misconceptions about crime and criminals, that these inadequacies of technique and these misconceptions are endlessly perpetuated through the usual textbooks and other vehicles of expression. The trouble has been, I think, that writers about crime have approached it from an academic and theoretical standpoint and have rarely, if ever, plunged into the deeps of the offender's very being with him. This I have done, many times.

The orientation throughout this volume is both practical and analytical. While most of it is unoriginal—the plagiarism and kleptomania mentioned before—some of it is novel, at least in the sense that it has not before appeared in a work on crime. Particularly is this true about my ideas relating to the role of the ego and allied matters with which the practicing psychoanalyst will either agree or disagree, depending upon his training, his own experience in the treatment of criminotics, and what he knows from direct observation about the psychology of the ego and the psychogenetics of crime.

If this book makes you think about the matters on which it touches, I shall have to thank my students of the years from 1940 to 1943 at Bucknell University. It was at their suggestion that I first began to entertain seriously the idea of writing such a work. What they wanted me to do was, essentially, to transcribe the highly illustrated lectures they heard and to put them into such a form that the student or his father or his friend could follow without the interruption of graphs and figures that become outdated as the ink dries or of distracting pedagogical obeisances, such as those made to the dubious immortality of a footnote. They wanted, in brief, to know about crime and those people whom I call, after the suggestion of Arthur N. Foxe, criminotics. They wanted to know about it and them because they perceived, as I think we all do, the paradox of crime and the menace. Some of them even saw its meaning in terms of its cancerous spread from criminotic individuals to criminotic nations. And some of them will not be able to read this book because of it.

You will find herein an approach to crime which at first may frighten you a bit because the experience of confronting criminosis may seem a little like standing before a mirror. That is because, whether you know it or not or whether you admit it or not, the crime problem is your problem, and crime exists because you permit it to exist.

*You*, reader, have it in your power to wipe out crime. If you wanted to—and in the chapter on punishment you will find some reasons why you don't want to—if you wanted to you could make this book as much of a curio and a relic as the pyramids or the strange figures on Easter Island. But the first thing that you must do about crime is to learn about it.

ROBERT M. LINDNER

Lewisburg, Penna., June, 1945

# Stone Walls and Men

# 1. An Orientation

AMONG the most pressing and challenging problems confronting civilization are those produced by the phenomenon called crime. When we consider the technical achievements man has scored against the unfriendly fragment of the universe which stages both his birth and his burial, the persistence of a kind of behavior so opposed to his best interests appears strange and even terrifying. To understand such a variety of behavior and to develop techniques for controlling it, is the task of criminology, a slightly retarded child of the social and biological sciences.

The reason for the retardation of the study of crimes and criminals is to be found in the fact that, unlike such independent sciences as physics and chemistry, progress in criminology is utterly dependent upon advances in related disciplines. Until from psychology he can obtain reliable explanations for human behavior, the criminologist is at a loss to explain any given instance of crime. Until sociology provides a valid descriptive terminology with which to depict the anatomy and mechanics of the social organism, the criminologist cannot estimate the role in crime of the social setting.

This crippling dependence seems to have fostered among some students of criminology an attitude of resigned despair and a fearfulness which is expressed by desperate clinging to ideological life rafts. So, for instance, one criminologist will exploit the shoddy remnants of Association Theory (transposing ways of behaving for ideas) to construct an inclusive explanation of most if not all crime. Another, hopelessly bogged by an inability to admit even one economic termite, will hold out to the bitter end for an entirely physical interpretation of crime. Then, opposed to the cautious, there are the faddists who crowd aboard any train that happens to be leaving the station. Depending upon the moment, they will ride the vitamin limited, the glandular express, the Freudian flyer, or the Lenin local.

In a sense, however, the dependence of criminology on other studies is a disguised blessing. Since the field encompasses almost every branch of knowledge, no one person could be expected to master even the basic principles and methods of all. Thus some of the burdens and responsibilities for development of the field are placed in the hands of individuals trained thoroughly in the practices and techniques of related subjects. The function of the criminologist, then, is to abstract the findings of sister studies and apply them to his own.

It is indeed difficult to think of a science or a branch of knowledge which in some way does not relate to criminology. Sociology surveys the social milieu in which crime occurs and criminals perform. It seeks to provide us with explanations of behavior originating in the social setting and due to forces resulting from man's interaction with man. From psychology we obtain concepts relating to the dynamic processes and functions of mind and human performance, both normal and abnormal. Of paramount importance for our study is the work of the psychologist in the realm of motivation. Anthropology illuminates the mist which surrounds primitive cultures and their modes of behavior with regard to crime, and sheds light on historical and ethnological considerations. One branch of anthropology is concerned with man as a purely physical organism, and its practitioners collect data in terms of human types which offer challenging propositions to the criminologist. Physiology, anatomy, medicine, and psychiatry offer information bearing upon the relationships of organs and bodily processes to behavior. Economics and political science seek to explain the immutable postulates which underlie the social structure. Law defines and fixes the framework of the permissible. Even physics and chemistry are utilized in the detection of crime and the settling of individual responsibility. This list could be extended indefinitely, but enough has been said to establish the dependency of criminology on other fields of knowledge as well as some of its relations to them.

Whether or not criminology itself can be considered a science is a question that need trouble no one but pedants. It is enough for us to note that our study has, through the years, collected a respectable store of knowledge in the form of unalterable facts; that on the basis of such facts predictions about individual or social behavior can be made; that statistical methods for gathering and interpreting data are employed; and that we have reached a stage where experimentation is regarded as feasible.

Science, pseudo-science, or intellectual gymnastics, criminology is the study of two kinds of behavior: individual and social. On the one hand it seeks to collect information about persons who commit crimes, as well as to comprehend their motives and the influences which caused such motives to be translated into action. On the other hand it attempts to examine society for information about the machinery which it has set up to deal with crimes and criminals, as well as for factors pertinent to crime-producing which originate in social situations. So criminology is really the study of man's behavior as an individual and also in groups as it relates to crime.

As one would expect, because of the midzonal position of criminology between the social and biological sciences, logic supports the criminologist's use of whatever tools and instruments these other disciplines employ. No method should be foreign to the student of crime so long as it offers the remotest possibility of getting at the facts. The important thing is to learn as much as we can about what are called crimes and the people who are called criminals. Whether this entails vivisection, immolation in formaldehyde, observation under a microscope, or filling in blanks on questionnaire sheets, is a matter of no great moment.

From a review of current as well as historical practices it would seem that techniques of collecting and treating information in criminology can be subsumed under about six general headings:

1. *The statistical method* has been a commonly accepted procedure since it was "discovered" by that amiable genius, Sir Francis Galton. It consists in reducing the facts of physique or circumstance or individual history to units which can be treated quantitatively for the establishment of norms, for the comparison of one person or group with other persons or groups, for the discovery of relationships of consonance or dissonance between and among items. This method has a language and laws of its own; and it has come to be regarded with considerable awe especially among individuals who feel insecure about anything unless it can be expressed and manipulated as a number. Latter-day knowledge has been so affected by statistics that today it is regarded as an essential research tool. It has served criminology by collecting a library of studies showing trends in crime, characteristics of persons who commit crimes, geographical distributions of unlawful acts and criminals, and countless other aspects of the problems in our field.

While this counting of both real and hypothetical noses has unquestionably contributed markedly to criminology, statistics is by itself a somewhat unreliable tool. In the first place it is coldly inhuman in its assumption that it can substitute a manipulable hieroglyphic for a subtle personality or social characteristic which, in any case, cannot be divorced from the total organism and situation. That is, the reduction of any feature of personality or aspect of behavior to a single number (or even a collection of numbers and symbols) tends to encourage one to forget that he is dealing with an item in a "frame of reference" from which it is impossible to separate it. We should always remember that any given personality feature does not exist by itself and can only infrequently be dissected out of the pattern. And we should also mention the remarkable ease with which statistical material allows itself to be handled. This point need not be stressed for we are all familiar with the numerical feats performed by modern advertisers who have learned this fact and exploit it to the limits of human credulity.

Behavior—even criminal behavior—is not and never will be resolvable to numerical formulae and signs. The personality is dynamic, and the patterns created, while they probably follow a master design, are ever-changing. The writer would go so far as to assert that one of the most potent agents for impeding progress in criminology is just this practice of abstracting non-living matter from the biography of an offender and comparing this lifeless stuff with similar detritus from the lives of other criminals.

The use of statistics has been justified on the grounds that, in spite of such criticism as we have indicated, they do give some information about crime in terms of its volume and trends, generally describe offenders of the law, and aid administrators in viewing and reporting the magnitude of their problems and the success of their methods. But even if the foregoing statements about the statistical method were entirely untrue, the fact would remain that statistics in criminology are notoriously untrustworthy. Take crime volume, for instance. No one would be so foolish as to maintain that our figures reflect the true number of crimes committed. Everyone knows that the majority of those who commit criminal acts "get away with them." Even if a criminal is caught, tried, and convicted, we have only one criminal act, one trial, and one conviction to record, regardless of the fact that the criminal may have been engaged in forty offenses before apprehension. And what confusion results in our figures on crime volume when a new law is passed, an old one abrogated, or an existing statute modified! Immediately a whole new set of criminals is created (or abolished) and our statements are scattered to the winds. We were recently provided with an excellent illustration of this when the Selective Service Act was promulgated. With its enactment, the evader and sometimes even the objector became a criminal, and our statistics again demonstrated dependency upon legislative activity.

Only the very naïve have no appreciation of the role politics plays in crime. Where the District Attorney is ambitiously eyeing the gubernatorial chair, convictions may mount as he sets out on a zealous campaign to impress the voters, and persons who otherwise would have evaded conviction are paraded in triumph through the headlines. In this connection the deals made in the privacy of the D.A.'s office or the judicial chambers are never reflected in our volume-and-trend statistics. To obtain a conviction without expense to the State or danger of reversal on appeal or lengthy and difficult trial procedure with the verdict in doubt, a D.A. or a judge may come to terms with an offender. He is, let us say, guilty on five counts or charges. He agrees to enter a plea of guilty to the least of the five, to "settle" for a three-year prison term, to refrain from contesting his guilt in return for immunity on the remaining charges. The D.A. gets his conviction, the public being duly informed. The State has been saved the expense and bother of a long, drawn-out trial. The offender is relieved with having to serve only a fraction of the time his offenses merit. Everyone is satisfied except the criminologist (who for five crimes can enter only one) and Justice (who is blind anyhow).

One important prerequisite for the treatment of data statistically is the obtaining of "representative samples"; that is, the statistician, before he can apply his formulae, must be assured that the group with which he is dealing accurately reflects the larger group which is not available but to which his conclusions will apply. To obtain a representative sampling in botany is relatively simple; to obtain a representative sampling in criminology is well-nigh impossible. Who would dare to maintain that our prison population is similar to the great mass of unapprehended criminals? As a matter of truth, the very fact that they have been *caught* suggests that they are in some way different. It is notorious that the higher-ups, the "big shots" and bosses, are rarely convicted, frequently never see the inside of a courtroom, much less a jailhouse.

Then there is the matter of the sources of criminal statistics. These are threefold. The first and most important reporting agency is the police, to whom a crime is first made known. But not every crime committed is entered or reported. From the side of the public, this may be because of fear of consequences, a natural reluctance to approach the authorities, or a shyness of publicity. From the side of the police, this may be because of negligence, ignorance, or corruptibility. In any case, such reports as are made to a central publication such as *Uniform Crime Reports* tend, quite naturally, to show up the best side of the police force in question. Reporting too many crimes (in spite of the inescapable fact that they happened) would reflect on police efficiency; reporting too few crimes would perhaps bring the budget shears uncomfortably close. So, in general, police reports must be regarded with suspicion.

A second source for statistics is the courts. Such figures as are available from the judiciary involve prosecution and methods of dispensing justice. The difficulty arises from the fact that minor courts do not enter figures, and that different courts handle their cases differently. The minor police and municipal courts are free in some instances to dispose of cases without supervision or obligation to record proceedings, and much material which is considered important for any bona fide survey of criminal activity is lost. When it is considered that there are about three thousand counties in the United States with trial courts and jurisdiction subject only to appellate review, the magnitude of this loss of valuable data can be appreciated.

A final source for criminal statistics is represented by the penal institutions. Even when we discount the fact that many smaller places of detention such as workhouses, city and county jails, as well as stockades and roadgangs do not collect information, figures obtained from penal sources are necessarily inaccurate. Much of the material is obtained from the prisoner himself and is usually unreliable because it cannot be verified. Such seemingly simple data as those involving age, residence, place of birth, etc., undergo miraculous transformation as the offender seeks to cover his tracks, avoid involving family or accomplices, or attempts to put himself in a more favorable light.

So much, then, for the method of statistics in criminology. Our final word regarding it is that it is a valuable tool which we seem not to have mastered as yet.

2. *The method of experiment* is only now finding a place as a technique in criminology. In general, four varieties of experiment seem feasible in the search for knowledge about crime. The first technique consists in subjecting the known offender to a variety of carefully controlled conditions, and from his performance under such circumstances formulating generally applicable principles or deducing pertinent information relative to criminals. It is, in short, a way of finding out

something about criminals. One typical experiment had for its objective the study of possible differences between the behavior of criminals and non-criminals in response to a situation designed to produce the emotion of fear. Changes in blood pressure, respiration, and electrical resistance on the skin were obtained and compared. This led to the formulation of hypotheses regarding emotional differences between convicted offenders and extra-institutional persons.

A second kind of experiment deals with the treatment of crime, concerning itself with the handling of criminals in institutions and with the discovery of satisfactory methods of rehabilitation and reform. Administrators and prison architects alike have devised various types of institutions for the custody of different penal groups, and such physical plants are, so to speak, themselves on trial with respect to their suitability for the keeping of men and women assigned to them. Treatment methods, ranging from the electric-shock therapy of psychopathic offenders to the psychoanalysis of compulsive thieves, are utilized by competent personnel in an experimental manner. Under this heading belongs the experimental usage of a hormonal preparation recently tried with certain sexually maladjusted offenders.

A third variety of experiment deals with the study of criminal attitudes, traits, or characteristics and has for its purpose the discovery and recognition of situations likely to produce crime and individuals likely to respond to such situations by criminal behavior. Of this general type was an experiment in which school children, all of whom had been explored psychologically and physically, were given money and sent to the corner store to make a purchase. They were told the article to be bought was a certain price, and that the teacher expected to receive a certain sum in change. By pre-arrangement, the storekeeper charged each child less than the child expected. The basic question became: What are the special characteristics (attitudes, traits, features of history, etc.) of those children who retain the extra money?

Finally, experiments on a grander scale are attempted. In this variation, persons and sometimes whole communities are observed under various conditions and both individual and group behavior charted. One such ambitious experiment undertook to record the behavior of a community purposely chosen from near an industrial center and another in a more rural situation. Here the physical environment rather than the individual was the variable.

There exist many minor variations in the broad four-pronged experimental schema sketched above. All of these methods are open to some general criticisms which echo the accusations we have applied against the statistical method of approach. Representative samples are almost impossible to obtain; situations are necessarily "cold" because they arise within laboratory walls or under controlled conditions and hence lack the warm reality of life experiences. Yet the very fact that experimental regard is directed on the pressing problems of crime and criminals speaks well for the future of our study, and what harvest has been gathered has been rich.

3. *The method of analysis* finds a place in criminology as one of two a priori techniques designed to uncover material relevant to crime. Operationally it is comparable to the procedure employed by a detective who is faced with the fact of a criminal event. It, too, begins with the fact of crime or criminal behavior, and then traces it warily to personal or social sources believed potent enough to have caused or contributed to behavior of the criminal kind. This is the method favored most by the philosophers and logicians of criminology, as well as by our social moralists and reformers. Generally this way of searching for knowledge suffers from one great fault: it is frequently guilty of violating the philosopher's own injunction to avoid ascribing causality to an event or situa-

tion just because it happens chronologically before the event under consideration.

4. *The method of synthesis* is the second of the a priori procedures in criminology. Here the reverse side of the coin appears: the social situation is examined and surveyed, and from this the fact of crime is induced. This method properly belongs to social prophets and planners. For the study of any single crime, however, synthesis as well as the method of analysis is a fruitful source of insights and clues to behavior.

5. *The method of individuation* in the study of crime is that procedure which regards each criminal and each crime as a separate social-individual phenomenon, and which has as its unequivocal premise the dictate that only by the study of single individuals can the field of crime be comprehended. This entails the isolation and painstakingly detailed study of crimes and criminals one by one. Those who practice this way of study are not bothered by the difficulties of sampling.

6. Finally there is *the method of conjugate samples*. This is similar to the method of identical twins in psychology. It consists in the comparison of criminals and non-criminals from similar ethnic and economic levels to discover where the blame for divergent behavior falls. Such a procedure calls for the keenest sociological and psychological observation and insight.

All of these ways of study have for their aim the accumulation of knowledge concerning crime and criminals. No one of them is ever used alone, nor is any one independent of another. They should be conceived of as guide-lines pointing toward a central goal. They are, loosely speaking, attitudes assumed by persons who are eager to learn more about the field of criminology. Each has its own offer to make, each its own high priests and champions. But all work toward a single end: a compendium of information useful in understanding, predicting, and controlling crime.

The question may arise why all this is necessary, why the gathering of such knowledge and its organization into study-form is felt by some persons to be important. Admittedly, crime is a "bad" thing; it costs money, endangers life and property. But beyond this economic aspect of the problem, larger considerations loom. Some of them are societal, dealing with man in the broader sense; some of them are individual.

One reason why we should study crime is because the knowledge gained thereby should aid in the development of a more satisfactory society—one in which the solution of the problem of crime may be possible. In spite of wars and personal, national, and international catastrophes of one variety or another, the impartial observer (the mythical man from Mars) cannot but remark what, for want of a better term, we call progress in human affairs. More people are coming to enjoy more of what life has to offer, are healthier and live longer than their ancestors. But modern social, political, and biological science imply that these advances and conquests are mere promises of what is to come when and if we ever develop the good sense to exploit them. Whether we like it or not, the social constellation of the moment is rapidly becoming historical. The entire world appears to be awakening to a new day. The artisan and the scientist are looking to their tools to envision the best usage of them in the giant construction our social architects have blue-printed. The plan of this new world includes more freedom, more safety, more opportunity. For all these "goods" to be realized, there must be less crime, less of the strange activity that makes of one human the stalker and another the prey, that results in the barbaric spectacle of one man brutalizing another, that leads to the sheer monstrosity of a society rocked by chronic civil war.

Yet another reason for studying criminology falls within the compass of knowledge and appreciation. Even in a democracy, where a share of government falls to each member who would claim it, too few persons are acquainted with the services rendered by the State. We take it for granted that the meat we eat at dinner is free from taint; but rarely if ever do we pause to consider the painful efforts and exertions of an anonymous but protecting officialdom. We read in the morning newspaper that a killer has been apprehended by police after a gun battle in a remote corner of the land; but our thoughts seldom turn to the immensity and complexity of the machinery which makes most of us safe from attack. Citizenship entails more than the half-hearted acquiescence to machine-politics at the polls; it necessitates more than "grousing" about governmental bureaucracy and high taxes and inefficiency, or derogating "that man in the White House." Good citizenship includes knowledge of the functions of the State, and one of the principal and necessary services of the State is the protection of its citizens from the criminal.

A reason for studying criminology that each day grows more and more strong relates to the crying need for a trained personnel in the field. The new philosophy of treatment—which we will discuss in an appropriate place—demands alert and informed persons to participate in realizing its goals. Our prisons no longer call for men of brawn alone to handle the refractory offender; our police no longer insist on beefiness and brogue; the ability to tell a good story and skill in using the brass spittoon are no longer regarded as the ultimate attributes of our legislative and judicial officers. The field needs men and women of vision, perspective and, above all, training. A career of service and personal satisfaction awaits the daring of spirit who enter this field.

Lastly, through the study of crime and of criminals, it is hoped that social tolerance and brotherhood can be fostered. This is a day when ruinously unhealthy social forces have been loosed on the world. We seem to have forgotten that a man differs from his fellows never in kind, always in degree.

As we make our way through the field of criminology, one great truth emerges: "There, but for the grace of God, go I."

So much for a general orientation in our study. We know now what the field encompasses, how it is to be investigated, and why we should be interested in attempting to understand it.

# 2. A History

THERE are very few areas of knowledge which are more youthful than the study of crime and criminals. This is not to say that man before recent times was unconcerned about the facts or results of crime; but it is a matter of record that the serious and *formal* concern with crime as a phenomenon both vital and interesting is a novel adventure of the human intelligence. The thunderous condemnations and injunctions of the Bible, the weighty evidence of historical and anthropological research, even our familiar if deep-rooted and archaic responsiveness to the subject—all of these testify to the antiquity of humanity's preoccupation with the offender and his offenses.

The First Man—that biped who initially walked somewhat erect and possessed the feeble glimmerings of what we now call intelligence—knew nothing of legal codifications or the prime motivants that lead to the commission of acts opposed to the general or special interests of fellow men. He lacked a sense of community with his fellows. The setting against which this creature enacted his primeval role was hostile. He was lonely, roving, and friendless. The majority of his "social" contacts—apart from those with his mates and children—were limited to such negative aspects as combat. For perhaps eons the minuscule family group in which he moved was self-contained and independent. He was a predatory animal, galvanized into action only by the insistent stirrings of biological urges and the need to defend his possessions. By

modern standards he was rapacious, thieving, incestuous, murderous, cannibal, parricidal, matricidal, and infanticidal. The
ultra-individualist, he fought fiercely in defense of his feeding-
grounds and for the continued possession of his mates. And
yet he made forays into his neighbor's territory when his
nourishment sources were depleted, or when he desired another's female. But when he appropriated, even when he killed
in such encounters, there was no remorse, no guilt. He merely
took over property (forage-ground and family) of his erstwhile opponent. And he did all these things simply and unself-
consciously.

So, among First Men, there was no crime in the sense in
which this complex word is used today. The development of
the notion of guilt, then of the notion of the individual's responsibility to others, and finally of the notion of property
were required for the creation of the peculiar constellation
"crime."

Somewhere during the millenniums that witnessed the slow
cooling of earth and nature's riotous experiments with forms,
the species undertook its own experiment in living together.
As to how this came about we can only speculate; but hereafter men roved in groups of families rather than in
small familial bands that consisted only of authoritarian
father, submissive mates, their children, and those hangers-
on who sought the protection of the powerful father. Now
the pack was dominated by the patriarch, the leader of the
clan.

It would seem that the first "crime" involved the sanctity
or inviolability of this powerful, all-supreme father. Modern
research, oriented in the direction of disclosing the wellsprings
of behavior following the lead of such original thinkers as
Freud, has been able to reconstruct a plausible if somewhat
startling semblance of the prehistoric ancestor, not alone
physically but also psychologically. It appears that the pa-

triarch was primarily the instrument through which the basic taboo, fundamental to a large area of future behavior, was formulated. Baldly stated, the patriarch was challenged in his authority and possessions by his sons. As they grew older and more powerful, they frequently disputed his absoluteness and his retention of the females of the clan. Motivated thus and by a consuming desire especially for the mother, as well as by an urge to assume the qualities of strength possessed by the patriarch, they sought his death. Because of their youthfulness, they often succeeded. Once successful, it is highly probable that, following the primitive logic in such matters, they indulged in a cannibalistic feast the succulent portions of which were the organs of the father where they believed were located those special attributes of which they were in need. By such "sympathetic magic," they conceived of themselves as now endowed with the qualities of dominance and leadership. But somehow, sometime, the murder of the father and his immolation in the body of his successor became forbidden, taboo. Perhaps the injunction to abstain from such acts originated with a powerful father who objected to his demise at the hands of a son; perhaps (and why not?) a group or union or fellowship of fathers decided to put a stop to such nonsense; perhaps, on the other hand, the sons awoke to the frightful prospect of their own risk in becoming fathers. In any case, the original intent was lost and the practice eventually was abandoned. Fathers were permitted to abdicate when their sons attained to the wisdom and strength necessary for ruling, and the original act of murder was displaced to a totem animal. It became taboo to murder the father; but the aggression was hereafter acted out upon the person of the totem animal on special occasions. This animal or tree or plant—whatever the case may have been—was chosen for a special attribute which had formerly been delegated to the father; and it, too, was inviolate except for special ceremonial occasions when the animal could be killed and eaten, or the tree or plant ritualistically used.

Thus guilt—the elemental requisite for the *subjective* concept of crime—arose more than likely from the injunction levelled against the attack on the patriarch. And hand-in-hand with this taboo went the correlative taboo immunizing the mother (and other clan females) from sexual assault. Fear, an integer in the guilt complex, restrained the sons from the commission of these ancient acts and gave birth to the first unwritten laws.

Primitive man,* then, knew "crime" as violation of taboo. But he did not know why men were driven to flout the stern and ancient injunctions; nor did he care. His life was governed and guided by taboo and myth, and he never inquired into causes. To his multitudinous gods and local rulers he relegated the authority of the patriarchal ancestor, quickly associating event and consequence, moving in a murky twilight compounded of awe of the elements and myth and taboo. He devised mechanisms and rituals to act out his aggressions and conflicts, or to sublimate his secret wishes. He became a creature continuously acting under compulsion, his existence ordered by "dos-and-don'ts," by things permissible and not permitted, resembling his modern counterpart, the tortured neurotic who is dependent upon the endless performance of minor rituals to avoid an impending (imaginary) doom.

Neither did the Man of Antiquity attempt to explain crime nor inquire why some of his contemporaries behaved in a criminal manner. He felt no great need to question. Supreme authority was vested in the godhead or the king, and all pronouncements came with a warranty backed either by the might of the State or the terrible power of the gods. Taboo

* The distinctions between "First Men," "Primitive Man," "Man of Antiquity," "Man of the Middle Ages," and "Modern Man" are of course highly arbitrary and made only for convenience.

and myth had crystallized to religion, formal and specific, in some places embodying written law. The notion of property had jelled to rigidity, and with it had come the displacement of certain original motivants into economic channels. Crime was conceived as an affront to the gods or the god-image, the king. Naturally, the powerful economic interests of those times capitalized on the situation and ranged themselves on the side of the gods. Retribution and vengeance for the commission of inter-individual acts such as wife-stealing, cattle-theft, and murder had heretofore been effected through the Blood Feud or by application of the *Lex Talionis*, "an eye for an eye, a tooth for a tooth." But now, "Vengeance is mine, saith the Lord": and the function of dealing with crime was taken over by the religious and kingly powers, who favored, as always, the powerful and wealthy. The written law exerted full force. In the third millennium B.C., the Code of Hammurabi outlined crimes and punishments in no uncertain terms. As an example: "If a votary, a lady, who does not live in the convent, has opened a wineshop, or enters one for drink, one shall burn that woman." The Salic Law, prevalent among the so-called barbarians, the Teutonic tribes, described the penalties to be imposed for certain acts, and these penalties were based upon a single criterion, the extent of injury. In Leviticus, XXI, 9, we read: "And the daughter of any priest, if she profaneth herself by playing the harlot, she profaneth her father: she shall be burned with fire." Similarly in Exodus, XXII, 19, "Thou shalt not suffer a sorceress to live." And then, of course, there is the Mosaic Law—the Ten Commandments.

With the rise of Christianity, however, a subtle but important change occurred. While man did not yet inquire into the causes for crime, the area of what is "criminal" was extended. Until now the act, the behavior, the actual doing of something or the omitting of something was "criminal." Henceforth, moral behavior, thought and inner belief itself became subject to the successor of the patriarch, the Church. Somewhat in the manner of modern Japan, where having "dangerous thoughts" is criminal, the Church in its majestic supremity assumed sway over the inner life of men, bringing belief, attitude, and personal philosophy into the framework of Canon Law as distinct from, but as important as, Civil Law. Subjective "crime"—guilt and fear and apprehension—increased the burden of the individual, and from this arose the tortured, demon-ridden Man of the Middle Ages.

This type lived in a black hell of mystery and demonology. Crime was to him devil-inspired, a form of cussedness motivated by supernatural, awesome forces. People behaved "criminally," robbed, murdered, uttered heresy, because they were possessed (literally occupied) by evil spirits doing the bidding of the dark hordes whose business was—in the divine order of things—to captivate as many souls as possible. Curiously enough, this universal madness not only defined crime but accounted for the horrible punishments exacted for criminal acts or beliefs. Punishment was severe: the rack, the thumbscrew, the deprivation of body-organs; but its intent was to exorcise, to drive out, the malignant spirit. The Inquisitors and their henchmen were not necessarily sadists bent on the destruction or disfigurement of a miserable offender: they were inspired men who resorted to drastic measures as—so they thought—the only means whereby to impress the fiend who was, after all, the cause for the offense. With his instrument, the offender, they were unconcerned. This notion of demoniacal possession as the responsible factor in crime became so widespread that animals and even inanimate objects—stones, trees, rivers—were tried and "punished."

Concern with understandable, discernible, logical and material causes of crime came with the general awakening of the Eighteenth Century. Out of alchemy and medieval philosophy came science. Men began to look for causes in everything. Inspired by the great Protestant awakening which successfully challenged the supremacy of the Church, men dared to tear from their eyes the fogging veil of mystery, and to employ their senses and intellects in an inquiring fashion. The great Humanitarian awakening began, led by such skeptics as Montesquieu, Voltaire, and the Encyclopedists. Like the waves from an under-sea earthquake, the influence of their thoughts and words rolled outward with such tremendous force that the very walls of medievalism were shaken.

If a date must be set for the time when the serious and formal study of crime can be said to have begun, that date should be the year 1767. In this year a young Italian nobleman, Cesare de Beccaria, published a pamphlet, *On Crime and Punishment*. The effects of this work were widespread, almost cataclysmic; it provoked argument and contributed generously to those forces that were rudely reshaping the temper of mankind. Moreover this work, like Newton's and Darwin's, had an influence extending over the centuries. It profoundly modified the later Napoleonic Code, had a distinct role in orienting the Reform movement in the English Parliament, and is today basic to our own Criminal Code.

Beccaria held that individuals have Freedom of Will. Persons are endowed with freedom to *choose* to do right or to *choose* to do wrong. If, therefore, they offend, commit a crime, they deserve to be punished. Punishment, however, should be just enough to prevent people from invading the liberties of other people. (This arose from Rousseau's doctrine of the Social Contract: in order to live together amicably, persons enter into an unverbalized but generally adhered to contractual arrangement whereby each party guarantees the safety and immunity of all the others from attack.) Beccaria further emphasized the necessity for persons who committed the same crimes to be punished with the same penalties. Finally, he urged that crimes be arranged in order of severity and punishments the same way, thus making punishment arbitrary and invariable.

Other postulates of Beccaria's position need not concern us. It is important, however, to note that crime now is no longer due to mystical causes. Beccaria made a special point of *deducing* Freedom of the Will. His is a rational, logical formulation of the problem: "Why crime?" Of course, in the light of our newer knowledge, we can criticize Beccaria's premises. But this would be unfair, since we should realize that Beccaria was a product of his time, reflecting the intellectual and philosophical climate of an era that had just thrown off the shackles of medievalism. Today we reject, almost wholly, the notion of Free Will. Although, for its own purposes, the Law necessarily retains the concept, and religion similarly draws heavily upon it, modern psychology and sociology have little patience with the notion that man is always free to choose what is right and to do it, or to select what is wrong and wilfully elect to travel along that path. We wonder whether Beccaria, were he alive today, would grant Free Will to infants, to maniacs. We wonder further whether he would continue to hold that the person who unintentionally kills the pedestrian who darts in front of his car, the person who murders while in an amnesic state, and the person who kills while holding up a bank, should all be meted out the same punishment.

The contributions of Beccaria and the so-called neo-classical philosophers of the Eighteenth Century may be summarized succinctly as outstanding in at least four respects. First, they influenced the orderly arrangement, classification, and definition of crimes and punishment. While their standards were arbitrary, they at least forced the acceptance of criteria by which to recognize and define crime. Second, they profoundly influenced the use of punishment as a deterrent to criminal behavior, aiming thus to reach beyond the criminal himself to the rest of the community. Third, their efforts brought order to chaos and led to the adoption of a uniform, orderly procedure in criminal law and enforcement. Finally, they were instrumental in abolishing the Ordeal as a method of proof, and exerted an effect upon the framing of rules of evidence which persists to the present day.

From the Eighteenth Century onward, Criminology, the serious and formal study of crime and criminals, was part of the general search for knowledge. The search for causes of crime, the attempt to explain crime and account for it, went hand in hand with the discovery and application of new tools and methods of research. The Eighteenth and Nineteenth Century thinkers were preoccupied with such subjects as the relation of mind to body, soul to matter. Phrenology and Physiognomy, pseudo-sciences which heralded their more exact successors, provided an impetus which cannot be underestimated. Searchers after knowledge and men concerned in their daily tasks with the immediate application of such knowledge became obsessed with the notion that the shape and contour of the body mirrored its contents and that—if only the code could be mastered—the inner workings, even the soul, could be read by the application of the principles which these immature "sciences" announced. They began to look for stigmata of criminality and other characteristics of man. This was the time of the caliper and the measuring stick, the day when the body began to be subjected to probing and examination. Concurrently, experimental psychology and psychiatry were born. Influenced by the Beccarian doctrine of Free Will, the vogue of knob-and-bump-and-contour from the hesitant pseudo-sciences, and the newly-arrived, lusty and blatant capitalism, these disciplines (psychology and psychiatry) brought to fruition the concepts of degeneracy and moral insanity as causes for crime. During this time, too, a supplementary stream in the flow of interest and knowledge relating to crime came from the rise of statistical science applied socially. Adolphe Quetelet represented the shift in emphasis away from the qualitative with his attempt to show the relation between crime and social phenomena. His quantitative measurements indicated such important co-variables as the rise of crimes of passion in Southern climes and during hot weather, and the preponderance of crimes against property in Northern climes during cold weather.

The mid-Nineteenth Century saw the flowering of exact science. Cesare Lombroso, of whom we shall have much to say later, drew upon all the influences already mentioned to formulate his bold thesis of the born criminal who differed measurably from his fellow men and behaved criminally not because he willed to do so, but simply because he was born to behave that way. Darwinism modified this view and soon attributed criminality to natural selection. Meanwhile two small voices, each destined to swell to roaring proportions, began to be heard. Under the impact of ideas derived from Marx and Engels, men began to doubt the world they inhabited. They looked about them perhaps for the first time with a clear and unobstructed vision, and saw the sorry state to which the great mass of humanity had been reduced by rabid greed and struggle for economic power. They saw disease and corruption, vice and poverty; and they pointed the accusing finger at a form of economy which held almost all men in slavery and oppression from the cradle to the grave. With revolutionary abandon they proclaimed a faith in a time when the festering slum and the begrimed industrial area would give way before a planned economy that would cut out the cancerous tissues that erupted in criminal behavior; when the provision of economic security for Everyman, achieved through mass ownership of the means of production, would guarantee against such monstrosities as criminal activities; when inter-class rivalry and hatred would vanish, and communal enterprise would become the essential motivator in the individual's pattern of life.

On the other hand, under the impact of the psychologists, a different trend in attitude toward and ideas about crime appeared. The dynamically-oriented among them, spurred by the Freudians, traced all aberrative behavior, including crime, to the influence of early life with its hazards and obstacles, and to the interaction of personality factors which produced internal conflicts generative of behavior that is criminal. They pointed out that the watershed of crime was in the nether regions of the "unconscious," which was approachable only by a special method; that all behavior was designed to fulfill certain instinctual (innate) needs that themselves were grafted into the individual personality by life-history as well as by a pattern peculiar to man from prehistoric times. Again, these deep-delvers were refuted by a body of psychologists who viewed the organism as pliable and amenable to a kind of automatic habit-training that left irremovable traces. Stemming from Pavlov and Watson, they loudly proclaimed the exclusiveness of the conditioning process in the determination of behavior. Latterly, this view has become less rigid with the admission of new data; but for almost twenty years it was fashionable and, indeed, it is still in a sense basic to penology, for much of modern "rehabilitative" philosophy is based on the as yet unproved hypothesis that training on the habit-level alone can undo the evil effects of earlier "conditioning."

We cannot leave this absorbing topic without describing a recent and disheartening transition in the history of human concern with crime. It will be recalled that our path of research has led us from the primeval jungle through the taboo-haunted culture of primitive man, through the time of emergent religion and its culmination in the shift of emphasis which extended the area of crime to moral behavior, then through the period of the rise of reason and into that of the triumph of scientific method. But now, in this day, we are confronted by the bleak terror of the fascist specter which represents a regression in the criminological field as well as in all other areas of life. As we ready our tools for scientific understanding and treatment, the concentration camp and the sociology of pogrom-making thrust us back into pre-history. In fascist lands the order of things has been reversed. Those who, by the standards of the rest of the world, are criminal, are sanctioned in their behavior by the laws and the might of the State. It is "criminal" to belong to an opposition group, to subscribe to certain religious faiths, to possess an ancestry that happens to be out of favor, to have "dangerous thoughts." In such lands it is the psychological deviate who is in power, and who decides upon the "criminality" of any facet of behavior. What was once "criminal"—slaughter, rapine, thievery —is the approved order of the day. For criminology, as for other fields of knowledge, this is a catastrophe the disruptive effects of which we must combat with every weapon of intelligence we can command.

With this rapid summary we have high-lighted the history of man's concern with crime and criminals. We have seen how crime arose and how it has been regarded from the dawn of humanity's habitation of earth to the present moment. Our task has been to focus on the main currents of thought and opinion, considered in the light of the reigning attitudes of the times. However, this summary has neglected much that will appear as we make our way through the mass of mental detritus that has collected about the answer to the question: "What is Crime?"

# 3. What Is Crime?

TO define crime is at once the simplest and most difficult of tasks. Everyone knows what crime is—everyone, that is, but the criminologist whose life business it is to deal with this elusive thing. Ask the baker or the butcher, and he will tell you simply and directly that crime is an act which violates a law, either by the commission of something proscribed by the law or by the omission of something required by the law. Thus it is "criminal" to pass a red traffic light, to omit making a proper income tax return, to assassinate your Congressman, to do or neglect to do a myriad of acts required or prohibited by the various laws of the land, the state, the county, the city, the township, the village. But is this what crime really means? Legally, yes. Legally, the law is the final arbiter of what crime is. If an act is not proscribed, either in commission or in omission, "on the books," it is not an offense. Of course, the law doesn't stop with this. As if to add insult to an already outraged reason which—at least to this author— balks at the absurdity of such circular thinking as eventually leads to the intellectual cul-de-sac, the law is the cause of crime, the law further requires that the criminal act be committed by a person of "competent age," who must possess a *mens rea* (a guilty mind, i.e., the act must be intentional), who must know the difference between right and wrong, and who must perform the act voluntarily and of his own choice.

But is this really all that crime is, a cold legalistic formula of prescription and proscription? If this is so, then the poisonous gutter-spoutings of our spreaders of racial and religious hatred are above and beyond the gowned majesty of this law. If this is so, then our cartelists who outfit and arm the psychopathic dupes on whose shoulders they ride to back-of-the-throne power perform no crimes as they bribe and browbeat their way to control of the state. If this is so, then the employers of child labor whose methods of operation result in the crippling, dwarfing, and ruining of a nation's treasure-trove do not belong among the criminal in certain sections of our country.

And what of the paradox which results when an act is proscribed but the proscription is not enforced? Are the offenders non-criminal? Is it only a crime when the full weight of the apprehending and juridical machinery is brought to bear on an act? If the burglar is uncaught, the murderer undetected—what then? What of the pellagra-and-hook-worm-ridden southern mob that works off its insecurities and aggressions and dammed-up frustrations against the defenseless Negro, making a perennial mockery and a laughing stock of our democratic pretensions? Lynch laws are on the books; but the authorities in such places refuse to grant the Negro the right to continued breathing on the same terms as his fellows. It is patently and painfully true that the police decide which laws shall be enforced and—quite as importantly—who shall be arrested; the prosecuting attorneys decide who among the arrested shall be prosecuted; and the courts decide what shall be done with the convicted. At each stage of the game, arbitrariness!

Which leads to the next question: who makes the laws? Who decides which acts are to be proscribed, which permitted? It has become fashionable to answer this puzzler with a respectful bow to something called public opinion. This expression, ridden to death by the uninformed as well as by people who should know better, is a pious fraud, a "walking shadow . . . signifying nothing." It is meant to refer to a set of ideas and attitudes relating to some phase of life about which the general public is informed and relating to which it gives expression. But is there such a thing? Is it not true, instead, that our sources of information are either dried up because—let us face it—we are told only what the controllers of our communications channels decide we should be told, or perverted because these same powers and dominions wish us to believe a certain way? In this country, pledged as it is to "free enterprise," "the competitive spirit," and "rugged individualism," opinion is manufactured and grafted onto a complaisant, unprotesting, unaware population by every trick and device known to science and art. This is done by special interests, by powerful individuals or groups with an axe to grind, spurred to always more intense efforts by the glitter of profits. The news is colored, facts distorted or glossed to serve special purposes. Laws are passed for the benefit of the financially powerful. In short, opinion is created of whole cloth and is rarely spontaneous as we are asked to believe. So that crime, legally, is seen to depend as well upon the shifting sands, the vagaries, and the constantly changing horizons of special interest.

The legal definition of crime is, naturally, the practical definition, but it has nothing to do with crime as such. It is merely functional, serving like the branding of cattle to mark off and identify a collection of people who have somehow acted in a way disapproved of by those who happen to be in the driver's seat as regards the direction of public affairs. It is not a definition suited to the study of crime or of criminals. We cannot be content with it because it avoids coming to grips with an age-old problem, because it does not lead naturally and effortlessly to a consideration of the causes of crime, because it does not embrace all kinds of crime, and because it has traditionally avoided involving itself with undetected crimes and unapprehended criminals.

Perhaps it will be best to arrive at our definition of crime by ridding our heads first of the mental debris, the stereotypes, biases, prejudices, and tenacious stupidities upon which we have all been fed. Foremost amongst this dross is the notion, strong in many places and with many people to this day, that crimes are sins. Such a religious definition of crime is harmful and, as we shall see, misleading. Meanwhile, since the concept of sin is embodied in religion and originates with it, we shall have to look to the relation of religion and crime.

The first crime, as has been said, was the murder and immolation of the patriarch. With the displacement of the act to a totem figure religion was born. Now, as a matter of historical fact, religion in times gone by existed solely for the preservation and welfare of the community. It consisted of a ritual of observances and avoidances that functioned to continue the group in prosperity and health, to preserve its integrity, and to safeguard its possessions. It had nothing whatever to do with the saving of souls. Gods were deities of local and circumscribed power, operating within distinct geographical boundaries; and the acts and observances performed by those people within a particular sphere of influence were designed to secure the god's favor or to avert his anger. In ancient times this belief in the geographical boundedness of a god was so strong that when in warfare one nation conquered another, it was customary to appropriate the local god and often to propitiate him immediately upon achieving victory. The conquered people understood by their vanquishment that their deity had deserted them and gone over to the enemy. The victors, however, taking no chances, either destroyed all vestiges of the local god's power, including his priests, or gave the defeated god a place in their own religious system. Indeed, somewhat later, a feature of the *Pax Romanum* was a careful removal of local images to Rome's *Via Sacra*, with appropriate and appeasing ceremonials, as well as a temporizing permit for the worship of local deities to continue as before. As a matter of fact, this custom continues to the present in the Calendar of Saints, many of whom are actually transposed tribal deities; while the object of canonization is similar to that of the inclusion for intercessionary purposes of powerful if subordinate local figures.

Hence, religious non-conformity was an offense against the community. The implied denial of a god through failure to participate in observance was, on this account, a community affair in which every member was vitally interested. Sin, in its pure and original form, was denial of the god or gods, for which the punishment was outlawry. An offender—one who by his contempt of or non-participation in appeasement rituals—was literally thrust out from the group, excommunicated, denied the protection of the god because he was put beyond the pale of that god's influence. In this condition he was highly vulnerable, a ripe prey for all men and for the multitude of inimical gods and demigods. The original religious sin, the denial, thus exposed the entire community to catastrophe; and with the rise of formalized state religions, such as Judaism in the time of Temple glory, this view was given official sanction. When the Christian power came to dominate the West, such a thesis still persisted. As clericalism waned, however, it required a law to turn a sin into a crime, because now the State rather than the Church assumed guardianship of community interest.

Defining crime as sin carries the implication of a general acceptance of sins as sins everywhere at all times; but a brief and casual thought discloses that conceptions of sins vary with the times and from place to place. As an instance, there is a powerfully phrased Biblical prohibition against using the Lord's name in vain; and yet there is today not a single nation or state which prosecutes persons for the type of vehement expression resorted to when the hammer misses aim and lights painfully on the thumb. Lest such an illustration as this be lightly regarded, we are reminded that in ancient times there was considerable weight attached to a violation of Mosaic and, later, Canon Law relating to the use of any one of the endless Names, for the very good reason that it was believed that to possess the Name was to possess the power inherent in it. So in the tradition of sin, much emphasis has been laid upon the vain use of the Name, and men have been burned for less than the explosive "For Christ's sake!" or "God damn it!" that the ordinary motorist permits himself when a tire goes flat. In digression, we should note that Man of the Middle Ages, in order to avoid the use of the Names, corrupted his cussing and came up with "Zounds!" (God's wounds) and "Bloody!" (By our Lady).

Defining crime as sin is misleading because religion is inflexible and the world is dynamic, changing. Religion is a constant, modified so infrequently in its basic practices and prohibitions as to be almost motionless, while the world moves ever onward along the evolutionary and sometimes revolutionary pathways laid down by the kaleidoscopic nature of man and the inexorable laws of his psychological, sociological, and economic progression. Religion enjoins against covetousness and greed; but it remained for a stage in the development of capitalism to create the conditions that necessitated the embodiment of Securities Laws in our legal code in order to curb wanton manipulation of the stock market to the detriment of the small investor. Birth control, practiced by primitive man to check population, practiced today for a variety of reasons, remains a sin only in the view of the Catholic Church, but is not a crime legally.

To define crime as sin is harmful, moreover, because to abide by such a definition would be to place government in the hands of the professional religionists, to encourage intensified religious strife and struggle for power, to return to the status of those lands which, under clerical dominion and exploitation, exchanged physical and spiritual freedom for the nebulous and as-yet-to-be-proved benefits advertised so appealingly by the clergy.

It may be too that to define crime as sin is unsatisfactory because sin is a relatively modern accrual. Let us, therefore, go behind the ornamented façade of religion, to the back of beyond. In short, is crime to be defined as violation of taboo? Is this what crime is?

To understand the meaning of taboo involves the kind of comprehension which, like the appreciation of a beautiful landscape, can be "felt" rather than expressed. The word has been translated variously as consecrated, sacred, dangerous, unclean, or forbidden. It has to do with negative injunctions, prohibitions regarding the sanctity of certain objects, persons, or places which vary both with time and locale. In primitive times and among primitive peoples our anthropologists have noted that these prohibitions have the effect of written law, and contrary to the layman's impression, operate to control the community in a rigid fashion, so that the incidence of violation of taboo is extremely small. But a curious feature of taboo which research has disclosed is that it was and is operative only for the great mass of people, and that on certain occasions taboo could be suspended for a time. Thus the taboo against incest applied only to the people at large, it did not apply to kings and rulers. Since kings and rulers represented the godhead, our insight into the nature of taboo is increased when we consider that these figures are representative of the original primeval patriarch to whom all things were allowable. Indeed, incest was a general custom, almost a sacred duty, of such high personages as the Egyptian Pharaohs, the Greek Ptolemies, and in later Biblical times of the kings and rulers of lands such as Rome and Judea. Furthermore, the suspension of taboo is immediately recognizable in the totem feast, an occasion during the year when it was permitted to partake of the body of the totem animal, and during which the ordinary safeguards were relaxed in an orgy of indulgence in forbidden fruits and activities. With this in mind, it becomes apparent that taboo applies to those acts which were once the sole franchise of the authoritarian patriarch; after his death this taboo continued to operate for the community-at-large as his perpetuated will, accepted and enforced by his successors and suspended only on gala occasions or as applied to his representatives.

Now the things which the patriarch forbade must have been activities strongly desired by the rest of the group, else there would have been no need either for the exemplary and severe punishments consequent upon the violation of a taboo, nor for the episodic relaxation of rules which (as we know now) accomplished the purposes of "drainage" without guilt or fear of reprisal. These acts or things were few in number and seem mainly to have revolved about the person or property of the patriarch. As strong injunctions—always negative—they were traditional, resting upon emotional rather than reasonable acceptance of precept, incorporated from an early age into the very fibre of being, hence, operating automatically and repressing behavior with forceful severity.

On the whole, the force of taboo has been dissipated over the ages, until modern Western men are relatively free from its effects. There has been an evolution of earlier taboos into certain of our laws; but there remains a core of responsiveness to taboo resident deep within ourselves. In the main, however, the diminishment of taboo has resulted from two potent features of civilization's development. Most important is the fact

that man has found ways in which to circumvent some of
the basic taboos and to perform forbidden acts symbolically
rather than in actuality. The modern world seems to provide
countless opportunities for such sublimation on a symbolic
level. But that taboo has a place in our affairs is demonstrated
by the repugnance we express when we hear of instances of
parricide, cannibalism, matricide, and incest. These acts are
today performed both actually and symbolically. The State—
as the inheritor of that immunity formerly enjoyed only by the
totem or the godhead—and such symbolic constructs as "private property," "the economic system," and other candidates
for allegiance, are attacked not only directly by acts contrary
to established law and arising from a conflict of interest between a person and any of these sacred cows, but also indirectly because such attacks symbolize, stand for, such
tabooed acts as those of which we have spoken. So that the
car thief who appropriates an automobile may, by this act,
be rejecting the authority of the father whose image remains
unchanged from the days of his infancy; the man who violates
a narcotics law may in reality be murdering his mother; or
the burglar may really be committing incest with his sister.
From the point of view of the State or of the other idols we
have erected along the thorny road of human development,
the displacement of original motives which signalized the
movement from emotion-fueled taboo to so-called reasonable
law has in these cases been incomplete and unsatisfactory.

A second feature accounting for the lessening influence of
taboo on men's lives results from the curious quality of modern
living wherein the community acts through intermediaries and
deputies. In prehistoric times, and even in the dawn of our
recorded days, violations of taboo were summarily dealt with
by the community as a whole. The offender against taboo was
himself at once and forever taboo, or subjected immediately
to the prescribed punishment of outlawry or death. This was

because in violating taboo he had done something which profoundly affected the existences of each member of the group, and the fear and awe which his act inspired awakened his fellows to the necessity of dealing with him in a definitive, conclusive manner. As communities grew, however, agents interceded on behalf of the community; and, further, as government became more distant from the masses, and as they partook in it less and less, they tended to become more sophisticated as regards the results of taboo violations, since the punishment was meted out to an offender by their deputies.

Taboo, in our day, is not woven into the web of life as it once was. Violations of basic tenets which are as old as the race do not carry with them the same intense recriminatory reaction of the great mass. We are no longer naïve, and only in the twilit depths of our beings do we hear the emotive echo of taboo. The powers of our deputies and agents have become enlarged. Only a segment of our population is so constructed as to respond to the muffled drum-beat; taboo has lost its power. Although we are herded into circumscribed areas, the psychological distance between one man and the next has become greater. Even with the rise of the socialistic state, which emphasizes the interdependency of man, we have moved toward the creation of substitutes or surrogates for the prohibitive injunctions that constrained our ancestors.

We can dispose of other "definitions" of crime without great difficulty. One fallacious and even dangerous view of crime considers it as "behavior which is against nature." It is at once evident that such a notion eventually leads to spurious and destructive views of racial superiority. Furthermore, there is no act which all men are not capable of performing, and there is no source to which we can turn for a complete account of the nature of man. It is also self-evident that the "nature" of man, as we know it, is a topic which had best be avoided, for it would seem that at least in this respect we are in no position to boast, especially at a time when the most devastating war in history has been raging, and when the bestiality, lust, and waywardness of humanity have been exposed to the shame of each one of us.

Is crime, then, behavior which is immoral? Such a definition lacks precision and clarity, apart from the fact that opinions on morals are notoriously diverse and confused. There is no moral code to which all men subscribe. Morals change with the prevailing ethical standards. There are even sets of morals for various phases of life in a single community. Business ethics are predicated on the perpetuation of the *caveat emptor* (let the buyer beware) thesis. The gullibility of the masses is endlessly traded upon. Each religion departs in numerous if minute ways from an inclusive moral code. International relations are governed by a separate ethic. What is approved in one community is damned in another. There is, finally, no stability in a definition of crime as "immoral" behavior.

Then is crime behavior which is anti-social? This cannot be either, when we consider the wholesale inclusion into law of regulations which protect the powerful interests. Is it to be considered an "anti-social" act when a Kentucky moonshiner, responsive to his culture and in accord with his community ideas, conflicts with the law by making and selling untaxed liquor, an act which is beyond the pale simply because an influential lobby supported by liquor dealers has bribed and cajoled a law through the legislature to smash competition? Similarly, in this definition the responsibility is shifted from the act of violation itself to its social consequences. Many prohibited acts which are performed each day cannot possibly be construed as anti-social; they affect no one but the perpetrator. And of some illegal acts which are anti-social to their very core, the social effects are long in making themselves felt. Again, there are acts which are nothing less than

anti-social in their effects, but which fall within the sphere
ignored by the law. The fallaciousness of defining crime as
anti-social behavior is exposed when we attempt to answer the
question, "Who shall determine what is 'social'?" We are
then forced to the admission that anti-social means conduct
that runs counter to the political complexion of the existing
regime.

The various sociological definitions of crime have had the
center of the stage for the past quarter-century. Unfortunately, these interpretations are more frequently than not
framed by men who have had little practical experience with
crime and especially with criminals. In all such sociological
definitions of crime, the matter is regarded from the viewpoint of the institutions ("society," "custom," "mores," "social
forces," etc.) which men have evolved, and they all bear
upon some *formalized* phase of man's life in groups. Some of
them tend to regard crime as a set of relationships reflecting
social disorganization; some look upon crime as a resultant
of combinations and permutations arising out of the societal
complexion; some derive crime from the sanctions imposed
by the law, which they view as an institution reflecting more
basic institutions resident in the nature and construction of
a given group. All of them, however, treat crime as some dis-
emboweled ghostly phenomenon unrelated either to the
harsh reality of the fact of crime or to the people involved.
In essence, they are lifeless, cold, academic, and unproductive.

What, then, is crime?

The only feasible way in which crime can be defined is by
considering it as a symptomatic type of behavior which is
specially and specifically motivated, and which happens, under
certain conditions, to conflict with the law. In other words,
crime is a symptom, actionally expressed, of internal maladjustment and conflict. The behavior through which it is

expressed represents, at the time and for the individual, the best (and sometimes the only) solution to the inwardly raging strife, in the same way as insanity provides a solution which makes it possible for the one so afflicted to continue his exist-ence. Crime, then, is seen as an alternate form of adjustment, responsive to basic needs and appetites, an avenue for the release of accumulated tensions and frustrations, designed to restore the integrity of the person when his security is in some manner threatened. It is merely incidental that this kind of behavior falls within the boundaries which the law tradi-tionally delimits as prohibited. What *is* important about the law is that it provides tools and instruments of punishment for those who engage in such a peculiar kind of behavior, and that it serves notice, *in advance*, of its intention to place such machinery into operation by proclaiming and publishing far and wide the boundaries of the permissible. Furthermore, society—under the terms of our definition of crime—provides the situations under which crimes are committed, since, as we shall see, its various aspects, anachronisms, paradoxes, and in-consistencies perform to precipitate criminal behavior.

Now with such a definition it is possible to call certain behavior forms "criminal," even though they are not enjoined by the law. This is because there are antecedents in the his-tory of the race from which have been derived that awareness of the special kinds of behavior included in the *popular* con-ception of crime. We have already glimpsed the time-shrouded genesis of these initial manifestations from which (so to speak) a higher, more basic and deeply-ingrained apprehension of what is prohibited and forbidden has come. Indeed, some in-vestigators have incorporated this feature into a concept of a racial superego, a common heritage of rejection of acts reminis-cent or symbolic of the original parricide. With this before us, it is possible to bring within the compass of criminality ac-tivities which even common speech identifies as criminal, but which (for political reasons) the law ignores. Thus the storm trooper whose law actually recognizes, encourages, condones, and even commends him for the murder of innocent men and women, is a criminal; while the Quaker who seeks to avoid all—even non-combat—service (and so violates the law) is merely a law-breaker. Consequently there are infractions of rules by behavior which is not truly criminal; and, on the other hand, there are acts which are truly criminal, but which are not prohibited by law. Fortunately, most of the prohibitions of the law accord with the cultural experience of what is "good for" and "bad for" the species; while the remainder reflect only the special aspects of a distinct and more than likely merely transient individual culture. But there remains a precipitate, a fundament, of common injunction, such as those against murder, theft, rape, and so on, which is universally operative if not as regards other groups (out-groups) then at least within the group itself (in-group). Laws as such are related intimately to the attitudes and customs of separate cultures or systems of government and derive from these. But crime is a matter apart from law, a way of behavior that in its working through impinges, for reasons which we shall observe, upon the law.

When crime is viewed as a symptom serving the sometimes obscure but always prevalent purposes of the organism in its attempt to maintain itself, the tiresome haggling of lawyers over the distinction between *crimes* and *torts* becomes meaningless. In legal practice, "crimes" refers to those acts which bring into operation the public instruments of the criminal law as these are initiated in the public name by representatives of the people; whereas "torts" falls within the province of private initiation of legal instruments for the purposes of obtaining satisfaction of a complaint in civil law. But the criminal, in the sense of our definition, is not alone the violator of criminal law or civil law; it is he who resorts to symptomatic criminotic behavior in order to make an adjustment of the kind which will permit him to exist.

Crime having been regarded as symptom, as behavior symptomatic of intra-individual conflict, our task is now to discover the differentials between simple law-breaking and crime, to seek an understanding of the motivants basic to such behavior, and—most difficult of all—to attempt to discover the mechanisms responsible for the translation of inward unrest and conflict into action which may violate the sanctions imposed by law.

# 4. The Kinds of Crime

IT was only natural for the ivory-tower criminologists, whose main contacts with crime and criminals are limited to a hasty tour of the local jail and an assiduous perusal (properly armed with shears for clipping items pertaining however remotely to the field) of the daily newspaper—it was only natural for them to carry over into their discussions of the kinds of crime all the detritus, the "old clo'es," and the petrified castoffs of a debilitated psychology, a directionless sociology, and a tradition-shackled jurisprudence. Consequently they made their ineffectual and unrealistic division of the kinds of crime into such infertile categories as "crimes against persons," "crimes against property," "crimes against the public morals"; and, which was worse, they trailed along in servile attachment to the apron-strings of the law in such unproductive sterilities as "felonies" and "misdemeanors." But the first crude intimation that perhaps these rubrics were misleading and untrue to the basic facts of human behavior came with the psychology-influenced division of crimes into those which were "coldly" planned, calculated, and executed, on the one hand, and those which were emotion-charged, heated, furious, intense reactions to certain situations—the so-called "crimes of passion"—on the other. This variant of the timeworn habit of separation into sheep and goats, black and white, day and night, should have indicated the direction a firmly grounded and practical classification of kinds of crime should take. But it didn't. The mind of the philosopher in crime is hidebound. He lacks the experience of actual day-to-day living with the problem; therefore the neat and arbitrary but lifeless distinctions broadcast from the lecture platform have until now sufficed for him.

These divisions, it must be admitted, followed from the definitions of crime subscribed to by the men who wrote the textbooks or who foregathered for discussions in annual conclave at professional meetings. They were abortive mainly because such people know crime only as a fact, as something already done, and because they have not lived with it or tried to treat it. So if one held to a wholly legal definition of crime, he naturally waved the flag for an unvarnished mathematical bisection of all behavior contrary to statute into felonies and misdemeanors, thereafter he precisely enumerated the laws of the land (down to those of the smallest hamlet that proclaims ordinances)—and his problem was solved. On the other hand, where a criminologist stood up for a view of crimes directed more sociology-wise, his banner was raised for the tri-partitioning of crimes into those *vs.* property, *vs.* persons, and *vs.* public morals; and thus he indicated his concern with institutions. And, finally, if he should be tarred ever so lightly with the psychological brush, he would be likely to add that each of these could be further subdivided into the "cold" and "passionate" types.

The first service our own definition of crime as symptomatic behavior renders is that of clarification of the immediate problem. If criminal behavior is to be restricted to that variant of activity which responds to certain appetites and needs in a specific direction, it becomes at once evident that there must be samples of behavior which possess the quality of criminality only by courtesy of the law. These can only be referred to as *simple law-breaking*, a performance which does not express the characteristic motivations of criminal acts, is not precipitated by the events and episodes we shall later describe, and collides with legality only because a law involving the act happens to have been written.

Simple law-breaking is a term properly restricted to areas of behavior wherein a trespass of the law is involved that is either in the nature of sheer accident, chance, and circumstance, or inherent in a situation which calls for too rapid reorientation of established modes of response. To illustrate accident as a cause for law-breaking, two cases are recalled. In the first a woman borrowed a car from a friend in order to keep a hospital appointment. The car's brakes were defective. She could not stop the car when a child chased a playmate across the road. Since the car was not her own, the negligence responsible for defective equipment cannot be charged to her, and her friend had neglected to warn her of the fault. Another case was that of a 44-year-old man who was demonstrating carp-shooting to his son. They had often engaged in such "sport" and it was a practice rather common among the summer residents of a certain district. This time, however, the bullet ricocheted along the water's surface and struck a woman shelling peas in her yard some distance down-river on the same side. In both of these the "human element" was entirely missing. They were accidents, only remotely connected with the perpetrators. But, in one, let it be observed, there was a mechanical fault or failure; in the other the unexpected operation of a law of physics. Many acts of simple law-breaking are accidental; *as a rule, these result from defective or maloperable instruments of civilization.*

Then there are those collisions with law which derive from the curious relations between an individual and the cultural setting against which his behavior is projected. Every culture, it must be remembered, coerces the individual whom it touches in a variety of ways. It dictates each facet of his life. From the cradle onward it exerts a powerful and unrelenting influence which results in the formation of habitual responses to given situations. Now when an individual, for any reason, departs from one cultural scene and ventures upon another, he carries with him more than his shirt and shoes; he is burdened even more heavily with established modes of reaction, with firmly imbedded habits. It is often the case that the habits acceptable in one culture are at variance with those of another. The Italian immigrant who was accustomed to making and using wine was therefore at a terrible disadvantage during our prohibition era; the refugees from Europe's persecutions and wars share such a predicament today. Especially if they are adults and have become rigidly organized as to habits and unpliable in their typical responses is the job of revising a life-style an immense and difficult task. Certainly a large amount of crime among Negroes who are driven by economic and social pressure from the South to the North is accounted for by this factor; while the record of the unrest and of the rather high "crime" rate among the immigrant populations of seaboard cities includes innumerable instances of the operation of this factor in law-breaking.

Law-breaking derived from *habitual practices* also includes many of the violations some writers have labelled as "white-collar crime." While no brief is held for unscrupulous manipulators of the markets, the "confidence" men and the double-dealing supersalesmen of the twenties and thirties, it is a readily verifiable fact that certain laws regulating the transfer of securities and the conduct of many phases of business and industry conflicted with the established practices and habits of persons involved. One man put it this way: "For thirty years I have been selling stocks. I had a certain approach, a way of doing business. There was nothing illegal in my methods at that time. That was the way I grew up in the business. Everything from the shine on my shoes to the porcelain jackets on my teeth was part of the pitch, the "spiel," the come-on. I had a regular method to gain the confidence of a prospect. When I talked up a stock, I blew it up like a balloon. That was how we did business; that was how we were taught to do business. Then these "cock-eyed" laws are passed. When you sell a stock now, no sales-talk, no promotion, no big-dealing. How can *I* do that? I can't. It's in me to talk big, to promote. You can't change the habits of a lifetime just by passing a law. Sure, I know that what we did—and when I say "we" I mean all of us—I know it wasn't right. But, man, that was the way things were done in our business. It's like breaking a horse to walk a certain pace. I can't do it any other way now, especially at my age."

Although there are no tears to be shed over the plight of this relic of the promotion man's holiday—it so happens that despite eighteen months in Federal custody he is "well fixed" and has returned to selling his gilt-edged apples at the same old stand—his complaint is quite justifiable so far as it touches on the psychology of habitual practices, and his predicament illuminates a phenomenon generally overlooked. It may be true that in a strictly philosophical sense the habits and customs of a people eventually become embodied in their laws (this would be entirely true if laws were solely the expression of the people's will rather than the reflection of the special interests of powerful segments); but in such cases as those under discussion, habits precede and oppose law. Change comes slowly to the human organism: its ready adaptability is a pompous fiction.

Throughout the remainder of our survey of the criminological field we shall be more or less unconcerned with simple law-breaking arising from accident or habitual reaction. This is the affair of the police and the statistician, perhaps even of social scientists who are engaged either in panoramic or punctiform appraisals of the social scene. Our concern will be with the other end of the line which can, for practical purposes, be drawn from acts of simple, uncomplicated law-breaking through the twilight zone of the type of behavior which approaches crime, to that region wherein crime in the full sense of our definition dominates the picture. This, of course, is a hypothetical line, a continuum, which cannot be interrupted at any one point, and which—like all matters psychological—allows of no sharp dividing. It is not meant to be employed legalistically in the manner of lawyers who would argue that the theft of $99.99 is an offense different in kind from the theft of $100.

The essence of our continuum concept of crime which begins with simple law-breaking and goes on to real criminal acts is that it accords with our knowledge of behavior dynamics, and permits us to formulate methods of treatment. The point, at once glaringly visible, is that as we progress along this line, *the personality of the perpetrator emerges more and more as a condition of and a requisite for the trespass.* It begins with performances in which no traces are to be found of individual and personality factors; these are the accidents due so often to mechanical failures and chance elements. From here it shades into those areas of conduct wherein habitual responses are called forth on a level where practiced reaction is the prime mover. Now our line proceeds to behavior based upon the almost automatic operation of traits of character and temperament (which we shall discuss below). From this segment it progresses into the region which—so this writer believes—is the main province of the criminologist: that place along the line where acts result from personality distortions and complications and are often expressed by behavior outside the law. Herein the wellsprings of criminal action are buried below the surface of awareness; they arise from that area, the so-called Unconscious, which is fashioned of life-experiences and which determines conduct not only in accord with the facts of environment but also, and even more significantly, in accord with the needs and appetites of the organism. As the distortions and complications of personality come more and more to occupy stage-center—until finally activity is governed solely by such inwardly-arising motivants to the extent that the world as we know it no longer exists, and the perpetrator of a criminal act is thus wholly insane—our line extends and finally terminates.

While we have left to police officers and statisticians a rather extensive portion of our linear continuum, and have resolved to have as little as possible to do with simple law-breaking, the neighboring area of acts which arise chiefly from traits of character and temperament, and which are illegal because they approach and sometimes cross the boundary lines of law, is a major concern for the criminologist. In our discussion of motivation we shall see how individual facets of personality, powerful enough to color and dominate the entire personality and so determine the life-style, have their genesis in the first years of existence. Let it suffice for the present to describe the kind of crime which may result from those permanent personality trends we know as character.

All our lives each of us is subject to description by others. Such analyses are invariably framed in terms of adjectives depicting the major impressions we communicate through a variety of channels. With most people all the separate items accomplish a fusion into a complex but unit impression. So it is that one can, and does, with a single word or at most with a phrase, categorize and brand his fellows with the inexorability —although rarely the precision—of a machine that pastes labels on tomato cans. Such an inclusive designation naturally reflects the *motif*, the theme, the characterological essence of the life-patterning of the individual in question. It is this theme, pattern, basal motif, and design of the personality which we refer to as character and which, with some, creates, generates, leads to, criminal behavior. It is not at all that the basal trend is criminal in itself, but rather that it is a motivant of such demanding force that it initiates and maintains a kind of behavior which sometimes skirts, often crosses, the thin edge of the permissible. The conflict in such cases is not internal, intra-individual; it is rather a struggle between the dominant character trend and its expression in act under particular cultural conditions. Since character trends are, on the whole, culturally derived, we shall later have to consider further the reciprocal nature of the distortion process whereby culture influences character and character exerts influence upon culture. Here it is important only to note that crimes falling in this group are frequently of the "professional" variety, the rackets, the organized frauds, and the fractional or gross but systematic looting of the public or private purse. Although the prototype of the perpetrator of such crime is to be found, on the whole, among the careerists in crime, the directors and organizers of vice, narcotics, bootlegging, conspiracy, and counterfeiting rings, there are also in this category the hordes of short-changers, the petty income-tax dodgers, the makers and sellers of defective materials, all shades and hues of speculators, and the "white-collar" peculators. In short, this kind of crime needs no elaborate and devious motivational substructure like that which predisposes to the kind of symptomatic crime which is precipitated by environmental hazards, exigencies, contradictions, or what not; it requires only a certain kind of person who behaves in a way dictated by dominating trends of character.

We find the "marginal professions" and occupations staffed by and large with such types. The stock-salesman who voiced the plaint we used to illustrate the role of habit in law-breaking was himself an example of what we are here discussing. He was a "type," a shrewd and calculating, tense, driven, anxious person who perverted each business encounter to a titanic struggle for dominance. He *had* to win, at no matter what cost. Although in the far horizon of many of his "deals" there loomed the shadow of a penitentiary gate, this fact paled to insignificance beside the immediate urge to triumph over an opponent. This pattern appeared not only in his business life; it was woven into his every act, visible from an early age in his relations with parents, teachers, school-fellows, and later in his own family constellation. When laws governing the exchange of securities became effective, he was a "natural." With him, in spite of his lament, it was more than habit that pointed the way toward difficulty; it was the inexorable working through of a special kind of character structure, undeviating in its aims and unchanging in its purposes. It made of him a swindler long before he was called one by the law.

Where the theme of character is that of ingestion and incorporation, the person so constructed that he is ever ready to take all things to himself, to bring objects within the orbit of his personal influence, we observe certain varieties of thievery. Here too may be placed the "fences," loan sharks, and unscrupulous businessmen who deflect the barb of inquiry with the pat formula "business is business" to avoid facing the prime issue that the features of character-formation and the resultant dominant character-trends literally decide the kind and quality of their business. Similarly, where the governing trend is rejection and denial we find a flouting of legality in personal life and business practices, just as when the theme is that of withholding and keeping, encounters with the law are predetermined along the lines of tax-evasion and the like.

One of the writer's most interesting cases was that of a violator whose entire existence was colored by a consuming dependency upon others. He was, as a result, easily led, almost terribly pliable. He wanted to be loved. A rejected child, he spent his miserable youth in a vain attempt to find a safe harbor where he could nourish his wish to be wanted. This led him to a nomadic style of life in which he chased frantically the mirage of his inmost urging. Unlike our salesman who *needed to dominate*, this boy *needed to be dominated*. The boldest line in his character-picture was his dependency, which led to his virtual thralldom to the whims of others, his vulnerability, his actual manipulability. So he was fated to . . . But let him tell the story:

"in January 1938 I got job with Consolidated shows. for which I was ride foreman and truck driver. We were showing in a little town of Gordonsville Virginia. I met May Evans on Friday night we started talking and she came back on Saturday night and stayed untill very late, after everyone else had left and we had started taking down to leave for the next town which was Leesburge, W.V. she ask for my name and how to write to me. Which I gave her.

"While in Leesburge I got a letter from her which I did not answer, we left there and went to Berryville to Middleburg, V.A. I got an answer there saying she would like to come there anyway, again I wrote to her and ask her not to come.

"We left Middleburge and went to Washington D.C. I got 2 letters while we were playing on Georgia ave and underwood I answered them and ask her not to study about coming to a show to get it out of her head for it was no place for her at her age then we left Washington and went to Arlington, V.A. to a place call Baileys crossroad. We stayed there for two weeks and then went back to Washington to 21th and C. St where we stayed for two weeks then I got two more letters in which she said she did not care what I said she was going to get her a job on the show, that I was not her boss. I did not answer eather letter untill we left Washington. and went to Catonsville Maryland there I was looking in the letter list in the *Billboard* and seen a letter for me, so I sent for it and it was from her. We left then and went to Jangetown N.C. where I sent her a speical delivery telling her not to come. We left Laneytown and went to Strausburge, V.A., on Wednesday I got another letter from her which I answered and told her if she come there I would never speak to her again, so we had a truck to break down on the run to Strausburge on Thursday I went to Winchester, V.A. to get some parts for the truck and when I got back it was late in the afternoon, when I left the office after turnin the bills for the parts I started to the cook house to get my dinner.

"While going down the midway there came Harriet Lebeder up

to me and said Mike I bet you cant guess who is here I could not think right then who it could be, so she said May is here, then and there I turned around and went to the office and told Mr. Hode I was quitting and he said not that he would see that she did not get a job and she would have to go back home. So that night while I was working she came up to me and ask me if I was very mad and I would not have anything much to say to her so she went on off. and just about closing time she came and told me that she had a job I told her that it would not do her any good for I was going to send her home she told me there and then she would not go home. So on Saturday I got a special delivery letter from her mother telling me to send her home I answered it back and told her she would have to come and get her for I could not do any-thing with her. She did not answer it back so we played several more small towns the following are the towns Abdgon, V.A. Wise V.A. Marion V.A. Rocky Munt. V.A. Zeblion. N.C. Silver City, N.C. Thomasville, N.C. and Martiansvill V.A. then we closed. I went to her there in Martiansville and told her that we were closing and for her to take what money she had and go home for I could not marrie her then for I only had about $85.00 and that I did not get any pay while we were in winterquarters that all we got if we wanted to stay was $3.00 for ciggretts and they give us our room and board and that I could not keep her there. We moved into winterquarters at Winston. Salem, N.C., she came on to N.C. and stayed with Mr. & Mrs. R. C. Bowen who owned the merry-go-around that was with the show, there I went to her and ask and beg her to go home so Mrs Bowen suggested that we get married then she brok and told me that she had already wrote home and told her mother that we were married. Well I did not know what to say then for it sure made me feel bad. The next day I had to go to Colombia, S.C. and get a light plant we left there when we started out the first of the year. I told her then that she just might as well come along and we would get married down there.

"So we left there on Saturday Dec 31 and went to Greenville, S.C. arrived at about 3.30 in the afternoon. We went to the court house the first place and bought a marriage licens we left there went to the Virginia Hotel and regestered as man and wife then I went and found a preacher tho he was busy write then he said for me to come back later.

"So about 7:30 we went to his home to the porch she seen several couples setting around in the room then she would not go in there she said wait till they leave then we will go. So we went back and went to a show leaving the show about 10:15 we then went back to the preacher house and the same crowed was still there so she said we would just wait untill the next day. Then we go back to the hotel she went to bed I set up alnight in the lobby the next morning she came down we went an eat. then we went to the preachers house again tho he was not at home then walk around awhile window shopping at which time she left me and went back to the hotel. about 4 o,clock I went to her room and ask her if she wanted to go back and see if the preacher had returned yet. and she said no wright quick I ask her what was the matter she jumped up and said she did not want to get married right then. We could wait till monday would be soon enough I left went down stairs to the lobby stayed about 2 hours then call her room ask if she would like to eat she came on down we had dinner together we did not have much to say to each other then. She went back to the hotel got myself a room then went to her room to get my clothes she ask me what was I going to do with my clothes I told her I was going to my room and get some sleep then she jumped up and said you are in your room Oh no not me my room is below then when she started argueing with me so I went on downstairs and went to bed. Next morning I got up went down check out left her ten dollars with the clerk then went to the Wilson Hotel and got me a room. I did not go back that day at all which was Monday that night I call the Hotel and ask for her the clerk said she was out. I went over she had done come back I beg her for 2 hours for her to make up her mind and us get married so I could go on to Columbia and get back to. N.C. to my work she would not give me no satisfactory at all said she would give me an answer Thursday are Friday, then Wednesday I meet the poter from the Hotel where she was staying he told me to come over next day he wanted to see me: Thursday I went to the hotel and was standing out front talking to him he told me May had ask him to make her some dates with some of the men around the hotel he refused her while I was standing there talking to him she came out of the hotel and left and went down the street the poter said if I would watch her I would see plenty I followed her 3 blocks and seen her get in a car with two men. She was gone about 2 hours then came back I follow her in the hotel and got permission to go to her room then when I told her to pack her clothes for she was going home well she packed her clothes I thought my worry was over but it was just begain she sent her bages to my room at the Wilson Hotel.

"She moved right in on me the clerk made me regester then as man and wife. That was another night sleep I lost for I did not go to bed next day Friday she went out about 11-clock then came back about 10 that night I seen her during the day get out and in three different cars with different men. On Saturday I made up my mind to send her home are leave her there so I had a heart to heart talk with her then when she got out on the street and started husling write I went and tryed to get her to stop tho she would not I left her on the street went got a police told him what had happen, I had made up my mind if she did not quite I would just have her locked and they would make her go home are else keep her off the streets the police went got her brought her back to where I was she told him if he would let her go she would go on and marrie me are go home just whatever I wanted her to do he let her go just as quick as he got out of sight she left went to some kind of a mission and told the preacher that I had her out on the street husling and making her give me the money so the preacher call the law they came down got me locked me up. I did not no what it was all about untill Sunday morning a police told me that they was holding me for the F.B.I. he would be there Monday. I stayed in jail Saturday night untill Tuesday before the F.B.I. came to see me when he came he wanted to know if I had a statement to make then he told me that I was charge with the mann act I did not no then what the charge was untill he explained it to me then he jumped up and raise hell because I told him that I was not guilty tho I am guilty of taking her from the states of N.C. to S.C. to marrie not for imoral purpose he said I could not plead guilty to a charge like that and left next day he came back and the girl had told him that I had her husling and I was taking the money from what he showed me and me being employed by a carnival the only thing I could do was go and plead guilty and ask for mercy of the court.

"I went before Honorable Judge _____ February 7th of this year he gave me two years 6 months Just because I was working around a carnival he would not give me a chance to talk.

So here I am. all this just because I was employed by a carnival. "This is my story just like it happen and it is the truth so help me god."

The kind of crime which is the main—and should be almost the exclusive—concern of the criminologist is that which involves the deeper, less accessible levels of the personality. It consists of behavior motivated by intra-personal strife and conflicts, deviously expressed through acts which may oppose law. It may come about because the internal harmony is disrupted by environmental demands and the organism naturally seeks a restoration of balance in order to continue living. It may arise from the failure of environment to provide adequately for the satisfaction—symbolically, actually, or substitutively— of basal needs and wishes. It may originate in an attempt to circumvent the necessity for other behavior. The list is as variegated and as endless as are the varieties of human performing itself. But herein lies the real stuff of crime and the answer to a baffling riddle. Crime as a special kind of behavior, the act itself as a symptom, may run the gamut of every conceivable offense from parking in a prohibited area to mass murder. It knows no boundaries of legality; it cuts across cultural lines. For the most part it is behavior which presents a solution to a problem, which satisfies an urgent need, which permits an adjustment to be made so that life itself can go on. It is determined behavior, an act or a series of acts performed purposefully and with serious intent in some cases, automatically and unconsciously in others. With this kind of crime we have reached the segment of our hypothetical line where the conflict engendered within the organism is expressed in performance. The exact type of crime committed is usually interrelated in a functional way with the nature or quality of the conflict. While a one-to-one correspondence is often difficult to establish, *it is a general rule that the motivants are mirrored in the act*, and that the act itself is designed thus to offer a solution to the conflict. It is imperative, therefore, to study the motivating factors which literally predispose toward criminal behavior, as well as to examine the precipitating environmental crises and influences which form not only the ignition for crime but also the medium within which crime takes place.

Our inquiry into the kinds of crime reaches the terminal point with our recognition of those bizarre and extravagant acts motivated by personality conflicts and demands and expressive of basal appetites, by persons utterly out of touch with reality and behaving in a primitive fashion dictated exclusively from within, independently of the environment. Broadly speaking, such acts are of the assaultive, murderous types; but they also comprise certain forms of theft. And here, too, belongs criminal behavior impelled physiologically by the assimilation of foreign substances such as alcohol or drugs, as well as the extra-legal expressions resulting from feeble-mindedness, epilepsy, and organic brain-damage. These are, however, transcendental causes, and the behavior is strikingly abrupt in conception and execution, often, because of this, immediately recognizable as originating from such tainted sources.

We have approached the problem of the kinds of crime by resort to the etiology, to the genetics of the criminal performance. It has appeared to us that the distinguishing feature among crimes is to be sought in the increasing degree of involvement of personality factors (comprising conflict, need, and appetite) and the consequent diminishing influence of environment. As we proceed from wholesale inclusion of the extra-personal (even non-human) to wholesale elimination of these same elements, we make our way from simple law-breaking to criminal insanity.

From this point forward we shall dwell among the haunts and specters of that special kind of behavior which we know as criminosis. Our classification of kinds has focused the glare upon the personality of the perpetrator. Any other approach to the problem of crime-kinds or varieties is likely to be merely academic and sterile. Later it will appear that the road we have chosen leads naturally to treatment and prevention.

# 5. The Motivation of Crime, I

THE fundamental truth that will emerge from our study of the motivation of criminal acts was phrased a long time ago by William Alanson White when he said that behind every criminal deed lies a secret. Crime is but the motor end of this secret which resides within the encrusted surface of the self we present to the world. What this secret is, why it lies buried and encapsulated within us, is our present problem. For an answer we direct our regard back to the fog-enshrouded days of infancy and early childhood, when were laid down the irrevocable patterns of our lives.

The quivering bundle of flesh that quits the womb has one paramount need—food. When it is fed, it becomes quiescent and remains relatively so until its internal equilibrium is again disturbed by discomfort from the mechanical pressure exerted upon its organs by the waste materials of its meal. Following elimination, quiescence is once again established, only to be disrupted by the seethings and stirrings of the gut which is physiological language for hunger. As this cycle undergoes repetition—hunger, ingestion, digestion, assimilation, elimination, and hunger again—it becomes not only an unvarying routine involving the separate organs, but also the foundation for the structure we have come to know as mind. That is, after a time, each stage of the digestive cycle is anticipated. At first the anticipation is not a real apprehension, accompanied by images and the sophisticated paraphernalia this function later employs. It is, rather, a straining forward of the total organism toward the next stage in the cycle, technically a state of somatic expectancy. The infant, then, very early comes to "concentrate" upon the satisfaction of the basic desire: the state of internal rest, harmony, integration—in a word—quiescence. Henceforward all his energies are directed toward the achievement of this happy state and his existence is supremely governed by the *pleasure principle*, the psychological equivalent of the beatific condition of internal accord. Now his life is ruled solely by an unequivocal precept, the avoidance of pain or discomfort and its corollary the search for pleasure. From this avoidance and search arises the remainder of his psychological equipment. They lead to recognition, knowing, remembering, doing and, later, to thinking.

In his blind servitude to the pleasure principle the infant becomes a virtual dictator. Not only does he exploit his environment with Hitlerian ruthlessness, but he comes soon to view himself as omnipotent. As with Eliezer, the environment springs to meet him, feeding the fires of his megalomania with the coals of care and concern. Sad to relate, however, to him, as it must to all dictators, comes the time when his power to command and coerce begins to wear thin. He meets now with frustration. Reality obtrudes itself. And, for the first time, demands are made upon *him*. The first demand our culture (and more than likely most cultures) makes is that he wait, that he put off—for varying lengths of time and for many, many reasons—the moment of satisfaction of his needs. As the days of infancy grow into months, he encounters other demands than the putting off of the moment of satisfaction: he meets with the demand that he conform to established cultural practices dictating the time and place and condition of satisfaction. Gradually he is forced to make his peace with the *reality principle*, which entails dispensing with immediate pleasure (achievement of quiescence) in order to avoid pain and perhaps to ensure pleasure at some future time. So he "learns" to adjust, to conform, to put off, to wait. Here is the most hazardous, most difficult, most important job he will ever have to do, and on his success depends much of his future.

The unequal duel between the pleasure and the reality principles, it must be understood, is fought not only in connection with the initial need for food and its manner of satisfaction. It occurs also in two other broad areas of experience. This little egocentric, selfish, unsocial being is of more complexity than a simple tube with holes at each end. Almost immediately it develops wishes and preferences about the way it is handled, the *dramatis personae* of its surroundings, the insistencies and urgings of its bodily equipage. It is of these wishes and preferences that the basal layer of personality is compounded, the so-called *id*, charged with energy (libido), and comprising the unbridled desires and appetites of the individual. In it are resident the wishes and preferences of a sexual nature, these distilled through the infant's experiences with parents or parental substitutes, its encounters with its own body, particularly the erotogenetic zones (those skin and sphincter areas which become imbued with sexual feelings either through natural design or from having been so handled as to increase their sensitivity). Finally, from the pleasure versus reality contention ensues the infant's estimate of its self and its place in the constellation of persons in which it has chanced to be born. From this arises *ego*, the complex of attitudes, wishes, and goals relating to the self. So we see that as these substrata of personality are being laid down, the infant is doing more than complacently playing with its toes; it is engorging experience, storing wishes, progressing from uncontrolled megalomania to at least surface conformity with a demanding, penalty-exacting world. With continued growth, it no longer presses for immediate gratification of its wishes, be they sexual or social. Under the impact of reality, it is forced to delay, to repress, or to transform its needs and appetites in accord with the infallible exactions of that supreme megalomane, the culture.

This culture, this collection and compendium of folkways and mores, technics and habits, affirmations and denials, is nothing more than an amorphous mass of often unverbalized traffic signals transmitted to the child by every word, act, or gesture of the persons and objects it encounters. It is communicated by the anorganic fixtures in the child's surroundings as well as by the living, moving, breathing characters inhabiting its world. Like some great press, it exerts a moulding force upon the malleable human clay, tirelessly stamping out, according to pattern, a succession of individuals shaped along similar lines. But since, in infancy, the culture is effective only through the persons and objects comprising the milieu, it becomes distorted as it passes through to the resentful child. And in this distortion, in this paradox of similarity yet difference, lies the clue to individual differences in personality. Moreover, as the culture is transmitted in such a slightly askew fashion from parent to child, more is entailed than the mere pounding and pummeling of unprotesting matter into the forms of the parent's interpretation of cultural requirements: the elements of strain and tension, love and hate, gentle persuasiveness and brutal insistence are involved until out of the dynamic interweaving the child *selects* and then *incorporates* into his self a galaxy of conduct patterns, attitudes, and techniques of conformity which constitute personality. But despite all the moulding and shaping, the fashioning and sculpting, of the sensate babe, the primary and irrepressible appetites remain. Now, however, their satisfaction can be accomplished only in relative conformity to cultural demands, which place restrictions upon and barriers in the way of gratification, and lead to evasion, repression, or sublimation.

This process of selection and incorporation of the culture eventuates not only in completion of ego but also in the formation of *superego*, that portion of self which includes those culture derivatives checking and censoring behavior—authority, precept, and prohibition. The incorporative or introjective process naturally takes place through the parents (or their delegates). Therefore, upon the manner and type of parental training—the coercive techniques resorted to and the special characteristics of the parents—will depend the way in which authority (superego) will be received and handled in later life. So parental attitudes, foibles, habits, and methods have the child at their mercy. Parents' ways of training to conformity with culture inexorably cast the die in favor of one or another personality trend. In their hands rests the chief responsibility for what kind of person the child will be. If the painful deprivations are not administered together with the balm of understanding, if the frustrations they provoke are not diluted with sympathy, if affection is denied or doled out only sparingly, if security is threatened and the emotional climate in which he is trained is a stormy one, his introjection of authority will be unsatisfactory. He will then harbor resentment, later act aggressively toward persons or objects that are instrumental in frustration and deprivation. The forbidden acts will remain repressed but surcharged with bitter feeling-tones. Conformity in relation to them will be less real than apparent. The child will perform with reservations, with a deep conflict of feelings. Toward his parents and, later, toward the authority they represent—from the school teacher to the cop on the corner—he will react with vengeful hostility. And the original wish, the forbidden act, will gnaw away at the feeble foundation of his social adjustment, producing discord and conflict. But if the regime that controls deprivation and frustration is tolerant, benevolent, exercised in an atmosphere of love, if the coercion is tempered by respect and the training given with care to provide emotional safe-guards and shock-absorbers, authority will be introjected successfully and with no conflict. Repression will be painless and relatively complete. The forbidden act will not become a source of later infection.

The ways in which a child will adjust to the stresses of later life are laid down in the very earliest years. Before the age of five the chief response-characteristics governing his relations to the world, his estimate of his own place in the culture, the role he will play in the tragi-comedy of existence—all these are already determined. To grasp fully the implications of the first formative years requires a complete reversal of our preconceived notions, fed as they have been upon the pap and nonsense of a sentimental pulpitry, art, and literature. To begin with, the infant is not a sweetly disposed object. In reality he is an exploiter whose tendencies and propensities are positively base when judged by adult standards. He is asocial and amoral. Only by depriving him, redirecting his energies, and frustrating his expression, is he brought into the community of "decent" people. By and large, it is *not* natural for him to become a stable citizen. The wonder is, as Alexander and Staub have already said, that all people do not become criminals; because at birth and after birth the infant is criminal in the traditional sense of being an individual of asocial predilections. Finally it must be recognized that even after the coercive process which bends and breaks the growing child into presenting the external signs of socialization, conformity, and adjustment, there remains a miasmic precipitate of appetite, need, wish, and desire. The control over these basic demands, these—why not use the term?—criminal impulses, the satisfactory exclusion (by any and all methods) of them from immediate awareness, is a supreme requisite. If it cannot be accomplished the culture will exact extreme penalties. The horror is that sometimes the rewards of that accomplishment are unhappiness or neurosis or insanity.

The most crucial functions toward which child training is

directed, and hence those which have a decisive and dramatic task to perform in development, are feeding, weaning, and toilet training. The personal configuration seems mainly to be determined by the way in which these elemental foci of training are handled. As a child passes through the various stages of development, the emphasis of the parents falls upon characteristic and primitive behavior modes that regularly succeed each other. These modes may be succinctly characterized as the *receptive*, the *retentive* and the *ejective*. In other words, as early life proceeds, the stages are marked by an accentuation for varying time-lengths of typical patterns of taking in, holding, releasing; later a fourth, penetrating or intrusive, is added. These characteristic, organic, dominant modes (ways) of response are liable to fixation at any level depending upon the time and place of parental emphasis in feeding, weaning, training. According to the progress of the infant through these stages, according to the fixation points achieved, will the trend of future learning and accommodation or adjustment to life's problems be patterned. The persistence of typical response modes into later life is seen thus to be a function of the way in which training is administered. Traits and tendencies of the adult mirror the stamp and quality of parental concern. We can, in a manner of speaking, read back—and so interpret a personality examined currently—by separating out his dominant trends, and in this way recapture the flavor of the nursery as well as the character of its administrators. The benignly disposed optimist who is generous, composed, even-tempered, is the product of charitable feeding, amiable weaning. But the suspicious, resentful adult who regards his fellows with sullenness and expects nothing from them is the yield from niggardly nursing and interrupted weaning. Again, the stringent toilet training methods advocated in some quarters—those which put a premium on precocity and which deal in punitive accompaniments to coercion—force the dominance of trends leading to future anxiety. Such persons tend toward retentiveness in their dealings. They are acquisitive, place too high a value on their own products, compensating in this way for the prohibitions and denials of early times.

The fixed modes of response extend moreover into behavior which makes a characteristic impress upon the culture. As a child matures he becomes acquainted with the multifarious symbols of society. He finds that there are certain areas of behavior that are surrounded and hedged about with sanctions and conditions. He absorbs the cultural stereotypes—personal sanctity and inviolability, private property and its sacredness, class prerogatives—the sacred cows, the institutions. Towards these he is forced to assume a public attitude of acceptance: but his basic attitude is predetermined by the vicissitudes of his experience and the peculiarities of parental schooling. Unfortunately it must be recorded that most of the persons who comprise Western civilization have been deprived, frustrated, thwarted, denied. Hence the subterranean feeling-tone of the mass of humanity within our culture is resentful, fearful, anxious, often outrightly aggressive and hostile. In relation to the clay-footed idols especially is the theme of revenge and retaliation observed. The working-through of such motives accounts for the ruthless drive for success, prestige, power, and leads to the hollowness of the symbols accumulated and exhibited to prove—and by so doing disprove—how they have compensated for the humiliations of babyhood. And, if the road chosen does not lead through the symbol-strewn pathway sanctioned socially, satisfaction is sought through other channels which mediate the same drives and assuage the inferiorities and the guilt through retaliation and aggression.

We have devoted some attention to personality development as it is forged in the crucible of culture; and we have also high-lighted the essential postulates of modern research as it has yielded a harvest of hitherto obscure dynamic principles relating to universal features of this development. Our discussion has emphasized the pleasure versus reality struggle, the structuralization of the individual into *id*, *ego*, and *super-ego*, the succession of developmental stages which variously emphasize the manner of environmental approach which results from the fixation of patterns at certain functional stages. Now we must return for a while to take up the question of those needs and urges which are so fundamental for an understanding of motivation, of why we behave as we do.

The normally endowed child is evolution's product as well as its servant. Within his fleshly compass resides the weary history of human-kind: resident in his very tissues are the stored experiences of his ancestors. Consequently there are certain things which he does not have to learn, activities which are, in the highest sense, natural to him. Toward the goals, the ends of such activities, he may be said to have urges or dispositions. Now all of these unlearned activities and their goals are reducible to two master trends: the *preservative* or *continuative*, and the *destructive*. Each of these can be regarded physiologically as well as psychologically. The essential fact, however, is that they each mobilize unto themselves, under varying circumstances, considerable energy. The continuative urge operates to maintain the organism, ensure its growth, and guarantee its function in the generative processes which are necessary to racial continuity. The destructive urge is the governor for all the activities and processes leading toward disintegration, death and racial annihilation. The former is a positive principle including the range of human impulses from food-seeking to love-making and house-building; the latter is a negative principle including the range from hating to aggression to homicide and suicide. For its energy the continuative urge is charged with *libido*, a hypothetical source of "power" served by the generative and anabolic (up-building) organs. As an activity of the organism becomes less and less imbued with continuative energy, it moves closer and closer to the opposite pole. Neither principle nor urge is ever found in wholly pure form. Each may be charged with elements of the other; even the passion of the love-embrace contains echoes of destructiveness and aggression. When, however, the energy-charge of each approaches equality and neither is precedent over the other, the state of *ambivalence* is achieved. The two master urges are perpetually interacting, lending to life its color, its movement. When an object or an event is *cathected* (charged with libido) it is in the service of construction. Human existence is thus polarized to some extent, and eternally in *conflict*. Such conflict becomes greater as objects and persons are cathected but cannot be enjoyed because of constitutional inadequacy or environmental limitations of the kind we have already considered in our discussion of culture.

Out of conflict, out of the contention between construction and destruction, pleasure and reality, love and hate, comes personality. Through the dynamic interaction of the components of the organism—the id, the ego, and the superego—the contentions are resolved or brought to rest in a state of tenuous equilibrium. The id, concerned with primitive satisfaction, libidinous, biologically conditioned, strives against the repressive superego; while the ego adjudicates the strife from its reservoir of self-knowledge and experiential contact.

Beyond these primary considerations of motivation, there is a psychological topography that must be taken into account, since conflict can arise within and among the three chief levels of awareness. These are to be viewed not as places or areas, but rather as convenient designatory terms to indicate the availability of psychological materials (memories, wishes, etc.) for recall and consideration. The readily available matters of experience with which the organism is not presently occupied have been designated as the stuff of the *foreconscious*. The matters which are currently of concern are stuff of the *conscious*, of which we are immediately aware. In the *unconscious* are the strivings, the desires, the id-matter, the remnants of what once was conscious; in brief, the unconscious is at once the experiential store-house and the biological granary. Conflict, however, can and does take place on all three levels, and can, moreover, be resolved on all three. This is because the components of id, ego, and superego are not strictly confined and invade all areas. Id-matters are to be found chiefly in the unconscious but on occasion may run over into the conscious as when an ungovernable impulse is given way to and behavior is unchecked. Ego-matters are resident chiefly in the conscious but may reach both into unconscious and foreconscious. Finally, superego-matter is to be found on all three levels although its region of greatest extent and import is the unconscious.

Now the resolution of conflict—among or between the components of id, ego, and superego, and staged in foreconscious, conscious, or unconscious—is always an *economical* process. That is, even though "mental" symptoms result to the extent of complete insanity, it appears that conflict-resolving invariably takes the road which entails the minimal expenditure of effort possible in the total situation. This lends a reasonableness to the most extravagant forms of activity and is of tremendous significance for the study of criminal behavior in particular. In accordance with this principle of economy, moreover, there are a number of typical mechanisms through the operations of which the integrity of the organism is maintained, problems "solved," difficulties met, and conflicts resolved. The first and chief of these is *repression*. Where ego and superego are unable to deal with a wish the consequences of which are likely to bring disaster, the wish or want is relegated to the unconscious where it may remain dormant or the conflict may continue on that level only to be dealt with by some adjustive mechanism seeking a less tentative solution. Repression is a major way in which our needs and wants are dealt with when they cannot be satisfied on the conscious level, from the primitive urgings of infancy to the special hungers of old age. It is the chief cause of unconscious conflict in that the repressed needs and wants—unless adequately handled—constitute an eternally festering wound. Next in the hierarchy of mechanisms is *conversion*, the technique through which, because of failure of complete repression, a conflict returns to the conscious in a disguised, converted form. It is to this mechanism that we must look in many cases of symptoms of bodily distress wherein no discernible organic failure or deficiency or malfunctioning occurs, and in all cases of hysteria. Then there is *regression*, through which there is an attempt to solve a present conflict by employment of avenues to solution which were found to be efficacious in earlier life, particularly in infancy. Again, there is *sublimation*, wherein a goal of value not only to the individual but also to society is substituted for the frustrated, denied urge or wish. Another mechanism is *reaction-formation*, which seeks to deny the urgent wish by performing in an opposite manner to its dictates. *Rationalization* is a mechanism which entails invention of motives acceptable to the ego and so serving to hide the basic, unacceptable wishes. *Transference* is a somewhat minor mechanism whereby libidinous energy is shifted from one object or person to another. *Identification* refers to the adoption—in order to minimize conflict—by one person of the attributes of another. Similar to the foregoing mechanism is *introjection*, whereby the characteristics of a person or event are incorporated into the personality. *Projection* is the adverse of the last and operates to attribute to other persons and objects the unacceptable conflict-generating characteristics of the self. And last among the mechanisms for dealing with conflict is *displacement*, comprehending the literal transfer of emotion from one person or object to another when the ego or superego refuses to tolerate the emotive direction which obtains. And apart from these there are others. But those sketched above, usually in combination, blend, and fusion, represent the outstanding ways in which conflict situations are manipulated. They play an important part in personality development.

It is necessary for purposes we shall later exploit that we attend now to the more detailed factors providing for personality motivation. Perhaps one of the most significant discoveries of our day has been the formulation and substantiation through research of the thesis that personality development proceeds by a forcible "weaning" (urging away from) of the child from one psychobiological stage to another. As with all else, the principle of inertia is applicable to humans. We tend to jell in the *status quo;* and it is only when we are "pushed" that we leave one setting for another. The "push" which propels the child through the developmental series which we are about to indicate has a dual nature: it is made not only of the normal maturation and growth provided for physiologically, but also by frustration and denial.

The theory of personality genesis to which we are subscribing delineates five distinctly characterized but overlapping stages—we have already outlined them broadly in describing character dynamics—through which children pass, propelled by frustration and denial, to emerge into adulthood. They derive from the interaction of the master urges, and in their manipulation by the child are subject to the dynamic mechanisms already touched upon.

The period from birth to approximately sixteen to eighteen months goes by the designation of the *oral stage*. This may be divided into the *oral sucking* and the *oral biting*, representing the chief activities of the infant and his master modes of dealing with his world. The oral sucking stage lasts from six to nine months. Motivation is primarily directed upon feeding, and the mouth is the special zone charged with libido since it is the channel through which pleasure is obtained. Little or no awareness of self as distinct from the environs exists, and undoubtedly the self and the mother (or substitute) are indistinguishable. The infant is passive, dependent, autoerotic. When, at the middle of the oral stage, weaning transpires and teeth develop, reality in the form of feeding frustration obtrudes. With a suitable weapon for aggressive behavior (teeth), with the unrolling of experiences including feeding delays and traumas (crucial episodes), and with the initiation of training in toilet habits, the destructive urges are armed and the ego begins to form. Now the separateness of self from environment is slowly achieved and id must be contained in the face of strong reality demands. At this point the child may be said to be narcissistic, with libido directed upon himself as a disparate entity. He further distinguishes the "good" (satisfying) mother from the "bad" (frustrating, rejecting) mother, and shows by his breast-biting, scratching caresses, and other behavior forms his ambivalent view of the world. He is best described at this time as an incorporative, retentive animal, and his means of aggression are strictly limited.

The *anal stage*, roughly comprising the age between six months and three years (naturally overlapping the oral stages), can be divided into *anal expulsive* and *anal retentive*. These terms place the emphasis upon the natural functions of the child, on the one hand, and the cultural attitudes as interpreted by the parents on the other. As ego develops, and the first glimmerings of superego appear, the interest of the child is naturally focused on his productions, especially since these are of such concern to his parents. While at first he lacks control over his sphincters, his bodily organization soon becomes such that he can exercise a modicum of supervision. In the early period, relief and satisfaction are brought about through the release of feces and urine. Hence the orifices functionally involved become libidinously cathected. Later the child, perceiving parental concern, becomes involved in an intense conflict: he observes that his productions are sometimes regarded as things to be got rid of because they are "dirty" and unclean; while they are to be retained under other circumstances. This provides him with another weapon for aggression, and it likewise enhances his ego. He may then, on occasion, in two ways achieve pleasure from the expulsion of products: purely from the act or from rewards and parental approbation. He may also derive aggression satisfaction from urination and defecation at times or in places inconvenient to the parents. In this expulsive stage reality and pleasure become subject to environment, and the period is used for what might be termed *reality testing,* the child experimenting with reality to see just how far he can go and, because of the consequences of his acts, repressing id urgings to ego demands when they cannot be expressed.

Anal retention is characterized by the child's exploitation of his environment, the endowment of his products with great value, and the emergence of superego. He comes to conform to the reality situation, subjugating anal expulsive behavior to ego and superego demands. He withholds his products as an alternate form of aggression and develops character traits according to parental, cultural, and personal interpretations. And he develops a "feeling" of power connected with his control over sphincter functioning.

The *phallic stage,* next in order of development, is perhaps the most crucial of all. With this period—which is again not sharply delimited but extends back into the anal stage and forward to the next stage—the aim of pleasure seeking and the mode of pleasure finding shifts from the anal regions and equipment to the genital. The child becomes interested in his genitals, manipulates them, speculates regarding them, compares them with those of his parents. He observes the large genitals of his father (brothers, etc.), the lack of visible genitals in his mother (sisters, etc.). His masturbation (which is a phenomenon dating back to early infancy) becomes charged with anxious apprehension either because of parental disapproval if he is observed, or because of the pleasure-inhibiting demands of his now developed ego and his emergent superego. Notions of sexuality develop, and the child searches the environment for a recipient of the promptings from within that are too strong to be borne alone. The choice of the male child is, naturally, the mother, and she becomes fixated with an intensely affectionate regard that is interfered with by the knowledge that she is already possessed by the father. This is the famous *Oedipus situation*. It calls for careful handling and solution. As the father (or his substitute) is conceived of as a rival, the child reacts aggressively toward him; but this aggression is accompanied by a fear of consequences arising from his bodily inferiority to the father, and so he at the same time *identifies* with the father. And since his sexuality is not clearly phallic because it still contains strong oral and anal components, the proper introjection of the father is predominantly responsible for the healthy solution to this distressing situation. Yet the period carries an additional threat, that of retaliation by the parents for the oedipal romance with the mother, as well as for the indulgence in genital manipulation. Since the child's notions are chaotic and unclear, he views the absence of visible genitalia in his mother and sisters as forceful deprivation, and apprehends that he too will be punished thus for his longings and for his aggressions. This apprehension is often reinforced by actual verbal threats, particularly resorted to in order to discourage masturbation. But perhaps more urgent is the inward warning of racial history.

For circumcision, apart from the sanitary rationalization of modern times, is the ancient symbolic rite reflecting the castrative punishment meted out by the patriarch to the sons who aimed to possess the primeval mother. That a trace of this remains is hard to deny. This *castration complex* is to be viewed as applying not only to the literal extirpation of the sexual apparatus, but to all retaliatory measures which the child can and does anticipate because of his sexual and aggressive desires. And from it and the Oedipus situation and the repression of infantile sexuality derives the completion of superego.

The libidinal cathexis is similar for male and female in the early stages. They both orient toward the mother and, because she is the direct medium in the oral and anal stages, she is the first subject of incorporation for superego formation. On the other hand, in the phallic stage the girl fixates the father. With her sexual development she perceives not only that she lacks visible genitalia, but also that the mother, similarly deprived, is her rival. To compensate for the absence of visible genitalia, she evokes a symbolic equivalent, a child. Her masturbation and accompanying phantasies are different from those of the male child only in that the father is the object and the feared consequences vary from anxiety over loss of love to perhaps failure eventually to have a child. Identification is with the mother, and introjection of the mother aids superego development. Sexuality is inhibited and repressed in the same manner as with the male.

By the end of the seventh year, infantile sexuality has in most cases been repressed, ego and superego fully formed, and the long *latency stage* entered upon. Herein sexuality, while not denied, is buried through the formation of attitudes apparently designed to protect against libidinal striving. Both male and female continue to have strong attachments to parents, teachers, and friends, but they are rarely demonstrative. This is not to say, however, that conflicts over libidinal urges do not continue in the unconscious. It is, in fact, just these conflicts which lead to reaction formations as a way to exclude them from consciousness. So the child may become critical of parental habits, join the moral crusades (signing the Sunday-school pledge), in a word, sublimate while enlarging the superego through experience.

At about the age of twelve there is a revival of libidinal strivings which includes the entire complex of repressed sexuality. This *genital stage*, which is subsumed under the genetic term puberty, is not as was once thought a dramatic resurgence of sexuality; it is rather the crystallization over a period of time of novel yet vaguely familiar ways of behavior for which the body has long been preparing. It begins with a return of oral interest, proceeds to anal, and finally becomes phallic in intent. As it repeats the successive stages of development, the same conflicts tend to arise, now, however, to be dealt with in other ways. Because castration remains a serious threat, the first interests are likely to be homosexual and the reaction toward the opposite sex antagonistic. Oral and anal behavior are evident in the first tentative experiments with cigarettes and pipes, "smutty" stories (largely anal), kissing games, and the like. Phallic behavior is noted in renewed interest in masturbation, the aim of which is autoerotic. Awakening concern with grooming and dress bespeak a repetition of early narcissism. Finally, true genitality emerges when libido is invested in one of the opposite sex and the concern is far less with receiving satisfaction than with sharing and giving love.

It is essential for our understanding that we at once realize that progress from stage to stage in this series entails the giving up of adjustments because of the frustrations which make their retention painful to the organism. But the result of each readjustment is further development and greater individualization. In the passive oral stage the dependence upon the mother is complete. As ego develops in the anal stages, the responsibility for maintaining the self and compromising with reality in order to do this becomes apparent. With phallic frustrations, the family constellation with its elements of security is threatened, and a resolution of the oedipal romance, castration anxiety, and infantile sexuality remnants is called for so that the dynamic equilibrium can be maintained. From out of this comes superego. Social responsibility arrives with adolescence as the infantile modes are reasserted and the milieu requires adjustment, while the remaining familial ties are severed. And together with all this, there are the demands that the functional modes of talking, walking, and the like be mastered; and that the educative processes be gone through in the way the culture requires.

We have sketched the phases and episodes, the stages and products, the dynamic mechanisms and concomitants of early life as if all individuals proceed smoothly through these periods, employ the mechanisms, and solve the problems. This is not the case at all. While it is "normal" for the socially unacceptable modes of infantile sexuality to be repressed, for a strong ego (capable of controlling basal id urges) to emerge, for a capable but not overly tyrannical superego to form, for aggression to be sublimated, the achievement of such a happy combination is perhaps a greater rarity than we would expect. More often the gratification of infantile wishes or their transformation into wishes amenable to gratification on an adult level is impossible; and they become encysted in the unconscious, persisting into adult life and motivating adult behavior. More often the infant or child is exposed to objects or events which have such a traumatic impact that they act to fixate behavior at a particular place or stage in development, and so determine all his future behavior. These fixation points, as has already been said, give diversity to human personality; but they are also the taking-off places for behavior which is fraught with danger both to the individual himself and to society. To handle them satisfactorily and above the level of simple repression, the individual must either sublimate them or evolve reaction formations against them. So the oral type person who was fixated in the oral sucking stage may sublimate by such typical practices as smoking or indulging appetite peculiarities; or he may develop reaction formations involving the oral cavity such as vegetarianism, teetotaling, strong smoking or kissing inhibitions. The orally aggressive (biting) type may sublimate through sarcasm, fingernail biting, and gum chewing; as reaction formations he may show a penchant for grammatical purism in speech and writing, or intense preoccupation with manners in eating to protect against cannibalistic urges. The character of those fixated on the oral sucking stage will be passive, optimistic, dependent; of those fixated on the oral biting, it will be pessimistic, aggressive, independent. Fixations in the anal expulsive period include sublimations ranging from gift-giving and philanthropy to interest in the classic arts; reaction formations contain oversensitivity to odors and emphasis on cleanliness to the point of exasperation. Anal retentive types demonstrate penuriousness or, mayhap, collector's zeal in their sublimative behavior; reaction formations may be demonstrated by behavior forms opposed to the essential drive for withholding. The anal retentive character has been described as devoted to detail, petulant, and parsimonious, showing pronounced convictions of superiority resulting from the infantile phantasy of power over his natural productions. Phallic sublimations include exhibitionistic endeavors, composing of love poetry, and the like; reaction formations vary from modesty to puritanism. The phallic character is too well known to merit description. The sublimations achieved in the genital stage, and the reaction formations, cannot be divided so readily as the others because they tend to approach each other in kind. They include work for the sake of society at large and interest in others. The genital character is the mature, well-balanced adult who has been able to achieve the adaptation of his libidinous and aggressive urges to cultural demands. Although these urges are still resident within himself and may be reactivated at any time through environmental hazards, he has achieved a balance between the components of the personality which maintain it on an adjustive level.

The motivation of criminal acts derives from the salient features and aspects of personality development we have been discussing. The "secrets" which motivate criminal behavior are here to be found. It is now our job to examine them more closely in relation to criminosis as we have defined it, and to illustrate their operationism.

# 6. The Motivation of Crime, II

ALTHOUGH, as has been stated, the answer to crime lies in those secrets which motivate every criminal action and sometimes reach into the organism's ancient history, the actual driving force behind each criminal act is a responsibility of the ego. It is the ego which performs in a criminal way, and the special characteristics of this criminal ego are the determining differentials among the handful of ways in which human organisms adjust. Once this is understood, the heretofore obscure dynamics of crime become tremendously clarified, and the mystery which has traditionally surrounded the trespasses of men is flooded with light.

Crime, together with the neuroses, the psychoses, and the resort to alcohol and drugs, is but one way of expression or outlet for the irritating, clamoring needs and intimate wants of men. It is a way of solution, but unlike the other aberrative behavior modes, *it entails the complicity and co-operation of the ego*. In this sense, we may regard the ego-structure of the criminal as tenuous and permeable, or at least malleable. The neuroses are resorted to when the ego and the id are in conflict, when id-urgings besiege the ego and, finding it indomitable, become converted into symptoms of illness so that relief is granted. In its turn the ego incorporates such symptoms and even protects them. And this it does because dealing with the symptom is far less annoying and painful than bearing the full weight of the conflict with id. So the ego of the psychoneurotic may be regarded as an obdurate one, an uncompromising one, an unchanging one. Because it is so, contact with reality is always maintained in the neuroses. With the psychoses, however, we deal with a damaged ego. The id—the elemental drives of the organism—exerts such a tremendous influence upon ego that it becomes perverted in its contacts with reality and there ensues an indifference and a negligence to reality's demands. But with crime, what confronts us is a permeated ego, a compromising ego. It appeases the insistent demands of id, arbitrates with them, negotiates suitable courses of action which will at once salve and partially satisfy the primitive desires comprising id. So crime, the criminal act, is carried out in the presence of, even with the consent of, ego. Indeed, the very fact that the individual operates so as to avoid detection is evidence of the collusion of ego in the act. And more, society should be grateful that in crime ego does exert a modifying effect upon id; for were this not the case far more vicious and wholesale crimes would crowd the pages of our court dockets. As the id-impulses catapulting the organism toward criminal performances rise to the level where they prepare for action, ego inclines them toward moderation and so modifies the forbidden tendencies.

The distinctive factor differentiating crime, neurosis, and psychosis cannot be strongly enough impressed upon the reader. Ego is the ally of criminosis, the resistor of psychoneurosis, the abject and pitiful slave of psychosis. In fine, it shares in the criminal act; it eventually assists under pressure in the formation and then the protection of the neurotic symptoms; it becomes vanquished in the insanities (psychoses). Here, too, is the explanation for the surprising observation that the psychoneurotic possesses insight into his condition and is often found to be amenable to treatment for his symptoms, while the task of treating the criminal is so arduous. In psychoneurosis ego itself remains impregnable and can exercise a critical function. In crime, ego is itself shot through with id-urgings and contaminated by id penetration to the extent that it cannot exert its proper inhibiting effect. So when treating the criminal, the only efficacious therapy must aim at locating the areas where ego has become infected, cleansing them as the physician does a dirty wound, and building a new and stronger edifice which will from that time forward be powerful enough to withstand the intrapsychic pressure.

Psychoanalysis has long held that in neurosis the neurotic *suffers out* his conflicts, while in crime the criminal *acts out* his difficulties. There is no reason to dispute such a formulation, but it should be pointed out that crime often offers—as we shall see when we examine some cases—a more permanent and sometimes a more satisfying solution to inward strife. People who come in contact with criminals in a professional or supervisory way often remark upon the fact that some of them, especially those in custody, seem to make adjustments in which they appear rather content. In cases where the crime committed actually "solved" the problem this is perfectly true. Such, for instance, was the story with a man of thirty-five who offended by impersonating an officer of the Air Corps. This fellow was apprehended when, in a night club, he was overheard by a regular Army officer explaining to his female companion the significance of the various campaign ribbons and decorations he wore. The eavesdropper knew there was something "phony" when he heard him assign the wrong theater to the wrong ribbon and non-existent decorations to other insignia. He called the M.P.s and arrest followed. On investigation it was discovered that the impersonator was also a bigamist and a forger. When, after he was sentenced, he was examined clinically and the dynamics of his case studied, it appeared that each of his crimes was a way of adjustment and solution to deep conflict and frustration. He was a bigamist purely and simply because he was incapable of sustaining a normal relationship with one woman. He needed women's affection, but as soon as it was pledged he demanded nothing more of them. Sexually he was most inadequate. What interested him primarily was that he should gain, however temporarily and by whatever unscrupulous devices, the initial evidence that he was loved. He had been a rejected child whose mother had died at his birth and whose father had been remarried to a widow with children of her own. The stepmother had no time for him, but to gain her fleeting caresses the lad would habitually amuse her by play acting. When she infrequently rewarded him with some token of affection for distracting her, he was overcome with joy. As an adult these childhood experiences motivated his entire life-style and the glamour of a uniform afforded a unique way to the hearts of the many women he pursued. Rather than develop some symptom which would awaken pity in the fairer sex or give him an excuse to withdraw from the struggle, he lived it out. In prison he was a model inmate, cheerful and complaisant. He was, he admitted, unable now to engage in his frantic search for affection and, moreover, he was free from the necessity to demonstrate his non-existent ardor toward his conquests. In this case we have a succinct demonstration of the living out, the acting out, of the gnawing basic problem.

It is evident now that when we earlier observed that there is a continuum along which, as the personality becomes more involved in the act, real crime ensues, we had reference to the ego-structure. And we can now adjust our own formulation with greater respect to the facts. Essentially, what is meant is that as we move along the line from simple law-breaking through crime, the paramount feature is that ego more and more becomes compromised by id and literally absorbs the characteristics of this primitive personality component. The true criminal, then, is he whose ego is permeated with id to the extent that it can no longer perform as an independent agent. In this respect, one may regard crime as a step on the road toward psychosis, which latter ensues when ego no longer can strike compromises with id and so withdraws. Yet it would be erroneous to regard the ego-structure of the criminal as weak. As a matter of fact, it is strong, at least strong enough to implement and execute the criminal deed. It is only that it is permeated with and has absorbed the wishes and wants, the needs and appetites that are usually resident in id. What can be regarded as weak are the mechanisms which are supposed to defend against the invasion of ego. The failure to repress, to sublimate, to convert, to displace, or otherwise to handle the rebellious urges causes the unsatisfied wants, the extravagant needs of infancy to break through. If they effect a settlement with ego, crime results; if they encounter an obstinate and unyielding ego, symptoms of neurosis result; if they triumph over ego, insanity results. The imposter whom we recently encountered was motivated chiefly by an abiding need for love or at least its initial demonstration. He neither expressed this want nor sublimated it (although in his history it was reported that he once managed dog kennels and at another time aspired to do missionary work). Instead, all mechanisms of defense failed and his ego loaned itself to his hoaxing and duplicity.

The motivation of any given criminal act is far from simple. Persons do not commit crimes merely because of one or another frustration of infancy, one or another inadequately repressed wish, or any other single drive or urge. For every instance of crime there is a sociological as well as a psychological problem present, and for the understanding of the dynamics of the act, the total situation in which it occurs and the total personality must necessarily be considered. In its effects crime is never directed away from but always towards society. It cannot take place in a vacuum; it always takes place in a social field. Such a field may be defined as the complex or configuration or constellation of influences exerted upon the doer at any given time. Its description would include not only its physical but its psychological attributes as well. Thus in depicting a social field for, let us say, a murder, we would have to survey the scene of the crime, the histories of the actors, the psychological "chemistry" of their interactionism, and the endless subtleties of the social and cultural settings against which the tragedy has been staged. For it must not be taught that the hazards and thwartings, the resentments and preferences of early life suffice independently to promote the criminal act. These are the *predisposing* conditions, the factors which incline toward criminality; but crime occurs only when these are touched off by the *precipitating* environment. And, at last, it is the environment which provides the impetus and finally makes for the actions called crime. This it does by re-awakening, revitalizing the early incidents, by placing barriers in the way of desire and wish, by arranging circumstances which conflict with the aims and goals of the organism, by denying satisfaction for needs. The environment then— or considered more broadly, the culture—engenders conflict. Such conflicts may vary from one culture to another, it is true, and the acts of individuals broadly reflect their society, but this does not mean that criminals in all societies are not comparable. The dynamic processes are common to all with but minor, and for the most part, inconsequential variations.

In the face of evidence collected from the detailed study of criminals, of day to day observation and examination of them, this writer, at least, is forced to reject the fancy and elaborate "explanations" of crime in terms of such resonant and palate-pleasing superficialities as "delinquency areas," "differential association," and like empirical constructs. Crime is simply a type of behavior predisposed by such motivational factors as we have indicated, and precipitated by the culture.

Essentially, it is an extreme form of maladaptation: because of its history the organism is unable to adapt to the culture. That this is so appears to be due to the permeability of the ego, a condition having its roots in the early experiences of the organism. The adaptation it does make is ineffective and unsuccessful, because the culture is loaded, so to speak, with opportunities for affecting the organism negatively. Its demands, codes, injunctions, standards, pressures—all of these call for moment to moment adjustment for which the organism is inadequate because of its peculiar history and because these are inimical to its basal trends. Crime is, therefore, the best adjustment it can make under the circumstances.

Now it must seem strange to the reader to be told that, for some people, crime is a "good" adjustment. And yet this statement is one of the truisms with which we deal in the study of crimes and criminals. All our activities seem to be predicated upon a need to reduce tension, to avoid suffering and pain. Each adjustment we make—no matter how bizarre or how painful it may seem to others—follows a pathway along which it will cause us less discomfort than it would had it moved in another direction. Even the Indian mystic who beds upon a nail-studded board is suffering less than he would had he not resorted to his peculiar religion to solve his conflicts. We have already shown how the neurotic symptom causes less suffering than the conflict between ego and id. With crime, it can readily be demonstrated that even with prison and sometimes death facing the performer of a criminal deed, his act is aimed to relieve tension, to give less pain to himself than some other activity would include. It is doubtful whether a real and conscious selection is involved in the criminotic's choice of crime as a way to relieve unbearable tension produced by the culture (precipitant) acting upon the personality (predisposant). It would rather seem to be a more or less automatic adjustment which follows the laws of a famous principle first announced by the physiologist, Walter B. Cannon, as *homeostasis*. This useful hypothesis is based on the observation that the body and its organs are always making readjustments so that a state of internal harmony, balance, dynamic equilibrium, is maintained. For example, when an infection threatens at any place, immediately the blood rushes antibodies to the site to give battle. So it is that criminal acts also serve as a discharge-mechanism through which tension is drained off or at least reduced. The conflict between the drives that clamor for satisfaction and the environment that either provokes the need or interferes with its satisfaction produces unbearable tension. The criminal act is an adjustment—from the observer's and victim's point of view an extremely poor one—which relieves the tension.

Briefly to review our discussion of the motivation of crime, let us now recapitulate its salient features. We first considered the psychological structuralization of the human organism in terms of its genetics through the various stages of maturation. Our attention was directed to the mode of character formation and the components of personality. We dealt briefly with the mechanisms through which problems are solved, and we saw how the early years of life are replete with hazards, especially since the passage from stage to stage entails acute and poignant frustrations. Next we reviewed the role of ego in crime and pointed out wherein crime as a way of behavior differs from other aberrative modes of adjustment. We saw the criminal ego as a participant in the criminal act because of its particular structure. The contention, long held by analysts, that the criminal acts out his difficulties whereas the neurotic suffers them out, was upheld. The complexity of motivation next engaged our attention and we spoke of the social field as a complex one acting as precipitant upon the predisposing features of personality. Crime then appeared to us as a maladaptation (from our point of view) but yet as an adjustment designed, following a principle carried over from physiology, to mitigate pain and reduce tension. Now we are prepared to review some cases and to work out the motivational factors involved in them so far as we are able and space permits.

F. V. was twenty-three years old when he was sentenced to a fifteen year prison term for the armed robbery of a post office. According to the recorded history, his mother had died when he was ten, and his father four years later. They were a compatible couple who had left their Irish homestead and traveled across the ocean to seek a better life about two years before F., their youngest, was born. They settled in a New Jersey town, and the father immediately obtained employment in the construction trade. Because of his genial, bluff, hearty exterior and a native shrewdness, he became a power in local politics, and during the time F. was passing from infancy into late childhood the family fortunes increased markedly. Six years before his death, the father was elected to the State Legislature. F. has described him as a family tyrant who domineered in the home and expected nothing less than instant and complete obedience. He was quick to punish and had a violent temper. On the other hand, F.'s mother was a subdued, somewhat withdrawn and shy woman who could never quite get over the sudden elevation of the family fortunes to such a high estate. Were it up to her the children would have been smothered with caresses and never punished for their misdeeds. She apparently lived in fear of her husband, and F. relates a childhood memory which leads one to suspect that the woman was at least once beaten by her mate.

F. had a childhood that was charged with contradictions. The home atmosphere was repressive but the streets were gay and full of adventure. He said that every time he left the house it was as if a load had been lifted from his back. He enjoyed school and progressed rapidly. The two older children, both girls, were never very close to him, and although he would quit the stifling climate of the home on the slightest excuse, he was careful always to make sure that his mother would not be left alone. Once out of the house, however, he sought compatible company in the neighborhood and engaged in all the various kinds of mischief and play most children enjoy. He recalls that he never felt right when returning from play because of the inquisition that invariably awaited him. His father and sisters believed themselves to be socially superior to their neighbors and constantly berated F. for his unwillingness to make distinctions among his playmates. Apparently they believed no one in their immediate surroundings was good enough for them, and when F. misbehaved they identified him with his playmates, using choice and descriptive epithets.

The sisters both made "good" marriages while F. was still a child and before the mother died. When the old woman succumbed to weariness and a lingering but, until her death, undiagnosed illness, the house was converted into two apartments and one sister housed the father while the other sheltered F. Although F. had been badly shaken by his mother's death, he recovered in good time and found life essentially unchanged except that home became even less attractive than previously. When, four years later, his father died, F. reports that he felt almost happy about it. This man had never been very cordial to F. and he had been a complete stranger to him after the mother's demise. When the old man's will was read and his affairs reviewed, it was discovered (much to the distress of the sisters and their husbands especially) that not even the roof over their heads was free from debt. Soon thereafter, F. quit school.

His health had always been good and in spite of his leanness and slight stature, he was wiry and strong. He became a helper on a moving van and later graduated to driving a truck. At seventeen he decided that there were no ties to bind him to his home, so he just left without even bidding his sisters farewell. For two years he lived a nomadic existence as a transient worker, roaming about the country, picking apples in New York, cotton in Alabama, harvesting wheat in the Dakotas. His life was venturesome, sometimes fraught with danger. At nineteen, arriving in California and being unable to find work, he enlisted in the Army and was sent to the Philippines. After six months he deserted, boarded an Orient-bound freighter and worked his way to China. There he immediately signed on a ship bound for the States, and after some months again found himself in New York.

He went to New Jersey and took up residence not far from where his sisters lived, but he never bothered to get in touch with them. He worked as a cab driver, associated with persons on the very fringe of society, and eventually became engaged in petty racketeering of the kind that manages to remain just within the law. One Sunday afternoon, about a year following his return, he decided to call on his sisters. They gave him anything but a warm welcome, berated him for his neglect of them; but when they saw that he had a little money they soon resigned themselves to the situation and revealed a remarkable change in attitude. They even offered him his old quarters and he felt constrained to accept.

As time went on he earned more and more from his racketeering activities and soon the cab-driving became a blind for his more profitable and less wearing endeavors. As a matter of fact, he soon became a notorious local figure and even branched out into the corrupt politics of his neighborhood. Within a few years of his return to the scenes of his childhood, he owned an equal share in the cab-fleet with his former employer, a sizable piece in the gambling and vice organization operating locally, and was a person of considerable affluence. He still resided with his sisters and they and their husbands were practically dependent upon him for support. This bubble burst suddenly, however, when he married a prostitute of local ill-fame and brought her to live in the house where his sisters resided. This girl was considerably older than F. and seemed to be very grateful and subservient to him. He withdrew much of his support from his sisters and their families and lavished his earnings on his wife. During the years that followed, not only was the house divided against itself and torn by strife and jealousy, but F. suffered one "business" setback after another. On a wintry afternoon in January he entered the post office of a sizable town on the Jersey coast and attempted a holdup. He made good his escape but was apprehended within less than six hours. Police officials were surprised at the ease with which they were able to identify F. and follow his trail. He was arrested in the living room of a sister's apartment. The whole family was assembled when they entered the house, and he made a complete confession in their presence.

The case of F. provides a fascinating instance of an individual whose life was founded and patterned upon a retributive theme, and whose activities in adulthood followed a path that had been prescribed during his formative years. In infancy and childhood F. had made two significant identifications: one of these with his domineering father, the other with his submissive mother. Toward his father he was attracted because of that man's evident success in his dealings with others. People submitted to him, tended his wants, and were in fear of him. At the same time he exuded an aura of glittering accomplishment which attracted the child even while he was being rejected and his resentment awakened. For his mother he also had two conflicting attitudes. He felt closer to her, sympathized with her and was grateful for the love and protection she lavished on him. But at the same time he despised her for her timidity and softness.

Together with these elements, F. was influenced by the obvious weight his family attached to their place in the social scheme of the community. He knew that, more than anything else, his sisters and his father prized both respectability and status.

Without pretending to do more than a superficial analysis, we can survey the dynamics behind F.'s life and his crime. The decisive nature of his identifications was a source of conflict. He was attracted to the father and thus to all males since he felt himself to have become a substitute for his mother, especially since he had played a role similar to hers all of his life in the familial constellation. He also hated himself for this attraction in the same way as he hated his mother for her yielding softness. When his mother died, he literally inherited her place; but now he also lacked anyone to provide him with affection. His world was lacking in warmth and there was no security anywhere. On the father's death the last of the ties disappeared. The sisters were more as the father had been, and deep within himself they *were* the father. But such was the nature of his innermost urges, that he transferred upon them the ambivalent identification which was as much love as hate. Their rejection of him in the days following the father's death was too painful to be borne. For example, he later stated that even though the family fortunes were in a condition of chaos, he should never have been sent to work; he liked school and had always wanted to go on to college. At any rate, he "solved" the problem by running away. His nomadism, however, was an inadequate solution, and inexorably he was driven back to the scenes of his childhood frustration. Upon his return, the immediate need became that of taking his father's place, and this he did by accumulating money, supporting the sisters, and even going into politics. But his abiding hatred and his need to humiliate the sisters (and through them his father, though dead) destroyed him. Marrying the prostitute—who to his unconscious was his mother alike for her unquestioning giving of love, her age, and her dependency upon him—was one way of revenge, yet it carried with it a strong reaction of guilt from the incest fancies which this aroused. However, even this was not enough. His robbery was for him the best solution, for this was a blow their respectability could not withstand. And it did even more: it freed him from the prostitute, laid his father's ghost, and returned him to the dependent status of his childhood. The crowning touch to the drama was his purposeful foregathering of the clan to witness his arrest. Not only was this his supreme moment of conquest, but his deepest moment of self-debasement. With this act, he punished himself and his family.

W. T. was convicted of his second mail fraud offense when he was thirty-six years old. Between the two major convictions, which were evenly spaced between his twenty-eighth and thirty-sixth years, his record includes about twelve arrests for drunkenness, speeding, and other misdemeanors.

He was a self-possessed, egocentric, highly literate man who held degrees from one very fine American university and a distinguished foreign one. With him languages were somewhat in the nature of a hobby, and he expressed himself very freely in three tongues. Here is his own accounting of his history, edited only to hide his identity and in all essentials conforming to records made available to the author:

"I was born, the fourth of four children, in a large city. My father, who comes of an old family which had contributed much to our State, was a devout Catholic, a successful businessman and almost puritanical in his outlook and way of life. My mother, on the other hand, was rather lax as a disciplinarian and of an extravagant, demonstrative nature. They were first cousins, very much in love always. I think it required a special dispensation in order for them to marry.

"My brother is almost twenty years my senior, and my sister about twelve. I never had too much to do with them because of the great difference in age, and I think also because they were a little jealous of me. I was the nuclear center of the family, especially since the third child, a boy, died when I was two. On me was lavished every attention my doting family could give. I was spoiled horribly, especially by my mother. Since father was a man of few words and a very grim, restrained sort, I never had much to do with him. It was hard to tell whether he approved or disapproved of me. I really never knew quite where I stood with him except when he let go with one of his typical jeremiads, lifted right out of the Bible and flung at me or whoever else happened to be about.

"There must have been some idea of fitting me for the priesthood, because this was dinned into my ears ever since I can remember. My mother used to dream about it, and the only time I ever recall my father getting affectionate with me was once when I was about eight and they were dreaming out loud about being in the church when I would conduct my first mass.

"I should tell you about another family member who may have exerted an even greater influence on me than my parents. This was my maternal grandfather, a venerable and distinguished Catholic layman, a great Latin and Greek scholar, whose influence in the churches of our city was tremendous. I think it was this old man who first started that business of me training for the cloth. It seems he had been frustrated in his ambition to take an order, and he put all his hopes in me. It was to him that my early education was entrusted. He had odd notions about many things, worshipped scholarship and studiousness, thought all kinds of play almost evil, and I believe he could not bear to see kids having a good time. Because of this and his sermonizing, I was kept indoors most of the time, was weak and puny, and never learned what fun was. For instance, I never learned how to throw a ball or ride a bike. I never even had a bloody nose or got a tooth knocked out. But once in a while I'd manage to sneak away for an hour or two. Such excursions only brought more unhappiness because I could never fit myself into any of the kids' groups. So I took a lot of abuse from them or stood on the side lines. Yet it didn't take long for me to discover a way in. In order to ingratiate myself with the other kids, I learned to swipe food and other things from home; and when I gave these things to them they let me take part in their games.

"I started school rather late, at about eight I think, because of my puniness. Frankly, I was considered ahead of the others and went through one class after another so rapidly that I graduated at twelve. I forgot to say that the subject of my schooling was a sore one in our house. My grandfather and father insisted on a parochial education, my mother on a public one. We compromised on a public school for the elementary years and then a Catholic high school. By the time I finished grade school, however, my grandfather had died and my folks apparently forgot about the bargain. So I just went ahead and enrolled in an ordinary high school. I finished at sixteen and then went to college.

"The college I chose was in the same city in which we lived and closely identified with our religion. My career here was quite undistinguished in most respects, although I was a superior student. But I was a lonely chap most of the time, never made any close friends until my last year, and worked rather steadily. I had decided on the legal profession. This seemed to satisfy my folks and I was interested in it in a half-hearted sort of way.

"Meanwhile, after high school and through college, I had a lot of what you might call social difficulties. I was shy, introverted, very restrained. But inside I was quite the opposite. You see, I had never learned the rudiments of social living, and in company I felt very awkward. It was hard to maintain the pretense of enjoying myself at parties and things, when in me I wanted terribly to belong but knew I didn't. I felt uncomfortable with people my own age and sought out older folk. Strangely enough, however, I soon made the discovery that this very awkwardness, even aloofness, was most attractive to women. It made them think me someone apart, even above the others, and I seemed to draw them to me in great numbers. When I learned this, I naturally traded upon it, and soon came to enjoy a Casanova-like repute. I encouraged them even more after making this discovery by a form of play acting that soon became the pattern for my whole life. I became very arty, somewhat radical in my dress and habits, and assumed the pose of a mystic. After an illustrated poem of mine was published in one of the literary magazines of the day, my status was assured. I gained in confidence, especially with women and my college mates. But as if this were not enough, I undertook to surround myself with mystery and glamour. I became a mystic, collected about me some of the college esthetes and proceeded to draw down on my head the fire of the university authorities by preaching a sort of neo-Catholicism. This was just about getting out of hand and approaching a bona fide crisis when graduation rolled around.

"My parents were going to Rome on a sort of pilgrimage, and as a graduation gift invited me along. We spent a few months traveling on the Continent, and then father had to return to his business. Somehow I managed to persuade them to leave me behind. This was the turning point of my life. The war had ended only a few short years before. Life in Europe for a young American with a little money was very exciting. I enrolled in a foreign university; it may be with the hazy notion of eventually returning to the States to teach. For a couple of years I attended the lectures and in good time received a degree after submitting a quite esoteric thesis.

"In order for me to bring all this together and make sense, I must go back and pick up a few threads.

"I have always been a very sensuous person, extremely responsive to what I think is beautiful. This has something to do with my sex life, which until I went abroad was distinguished chiefly for the fact that I had never enjoyed a woman. But ever since my sixth year, sex had been a problem with me. It was around that time that I began to masturbate; and I have continued this practice to the present moment. I have tried to account for this, because I look on any sex act without a partner as unnatural. I think, however, that as a child it expressed my love of beautiful things, and I never grew out of this even when I came to the age of twenty-one, when I had my first intercourse with a woman. But for me, beauty has always resided in things that could be handled by the senses, things that could be seen, touched, tasted, heard or smelled. Especially touched. I get a pure physical thrill, almost an orgasm, from the feel of a polished surface, a heavy brocaded material. This gives the direct clue to my interest in antiques and the profession I follow. But to return to sex, I have been most promiscuous since twenty-one. In point of fact, I seem to have collected beautiful women as I have collected other beautiful things. My interest in them, however, is characteristically short-lived in contrast to my interest in the beautiful books, pictures, chairs, tapestries, mantels, doors, figurines and what not in which I dealt. Whereas I felt little or no grief at the departure from me of some female, very often I could not bear to part with some item of value and lost much money through this quirk.

"Well, there I was in Europe, and there I remained for many years. After I had completed my schooling, I managed to work my way into the art world as a collector of rare furnishings for the very rich. To equip myself I studied hard. I gained access to the wonderful Vatican Library and to most of the famous collections all over the Continent. Before long, I had mastered the first principles of my business. My customers were all possessed of a driving urge, a compulsion, to possess things. My whole task was to estimate the depth of such an urge and its origination. This meant that such considerations as the market price of an object did not count. There literally was none. I made a lot of money, but I saved nothing. It all went into 'front.'

"In my twenty-eighth year I received a cablegram informing me of the simultaneous death of both my parents in an accident. I immediately returned to the States. When affairs were settled I found I had quite a lot of money. Rather than return to Europe, I decided to remain here. Things were slow and business methods were different from those I had known abroad. I lost a lot of money. Then I discovered that there was far less knowledge in this country regarding the items in which I dealt, that I could get away with spurious materials, fake goods. And with advertising being what it is, I was soon doing land-office business. I lost all my scruples and plunged into all sorts of underhanded activities. At the same time I began to drink rather more than I should have. And since that time, such has been the pattern of my life."

The chief factors to be reckoned with in the case of W. T. are the overprotection and indulgence granted him in his early years, and the intensive and unwholesome religious training with its attendant conflicts. It is immediately noteworthy that there was a large age-gap between the older sister and W., and that the child who came between them died while W. was an infant. He was brought up, then, in an atmosphere which hedged him about with more restrictions than were healthy. His parents undoubtedly feared to lose him, and on him they centered all their hopes and their ambitions. He became used to love which had about it something he himself has described as "somewhat overripe." In contrast, in his relations with his fellows he experienced almost the opposite reaction to his presence. Home had spoiled him for play and for mingling with other children. In order to gain admission to their circle, it became necessary for him to give, to pay. This became a source of conflict because it caused him to examine himself in a new light and to permit himself to doubt his capability to awaken love. It also perverted his values to the extent that he allowed himself to become convinced that the only love that mattered, that he wanted badly, could be had only by paying for it.

The chronic masturbation which W. claims to have begun at six is an outgrowth of the above conflict. The child sought pleasure within himself, and accompanied the act with glittering phantasies. Undoubtedly the erotic transposition from the manipulation of his genitals to the interest in objects of appeal "especially to touch," obeyed simple psychological laws. And also without doubt, his severe religious training led to horrible and overwhelming guilt over such activities.

The formulation of this case involves some elements which may and undoubtedly will strike the naïve reader as fantastic. This writer, who came to know W. T. intimately, is convinced that W. T. actually sought incarceration for its promise of security and care and even limitation of mobility—all of these matters being reminiscent of his childhood situation. In short, W. T., in a large part, committed his frauds with the hidden purpose of recapturing and re-experiencing the time when he was an over-protected child. With the loss of his money, he could no longer buy love. He even lacked the talent to maintain his "arty" pretense. The death of his parents and the economic catastrophe he experienced on his return to America renewed the old conflict. When he engaged in fraud, he was re-energizing this conflict through casting doubt upon the things in which he placed his faith—those objects of sense which were now endowed with potentialities for providing pleasurable feelings similar to those originally aroused by masturbation. The conflict was allowed to become acute. Furthermore, from an intimate knowledge of the dynamics in the case of W. T., it is known to the author that W. T. either could have avoided detection or at least left the country when his forgeries and frauds became known. As a matter of fact, there are in this country today many supposed articles of value which are really the competent forgeries of W. T. Such was his ability in his work that he was known to dealers and collectors as one of the outstanding men in the field. Only when his deepest motivations were precipitated by events beyond his control did he turn to fakery and pretense. And only then, when these produced an intolerable inward stress, did he—purposefully, but without immediate awareness—become so incompetent and lax in his work that he was led to imprisonment.

The case of C. R. provides for us a remarkable insight into those mainsprings of crime which we have been discussing.

At the age of twenty C. R. was admitted to the State penitentiary to serve a lifetime sentence for the commission of a heinous crime which shocked the quiet community where he lived with his mother and an older brother. On a certain night in the fall of the year, the police, led by C. R., discovered the body of a young woman on the floor of C. R.'s mother's bedroom. The girl had evidently been rendered unconscious by a blow on the head from a hammer which was found nearby. Following this, the girl had been stabbed sixty-nine times with an ice-pick. C. R. was apprehended immediately and charged with the crime. His admission of guilt soon followed. There was some question of his sanity, but he was declared competent by a pair of leading alienists.

C. R.'s crime has deep roots. He was born in a large Northern city, a healthy and robust youngster, the second of two children. His parents were incompatible and were held together only by their children and their religion. But their marriage was intolerable to both, and when C. was three, they separated. C.'s mother, an intensely religious woman, neurotically-inclined, opinionated, possessed of strong prejudices, and somewhat lacking in warmth, decided that she could not maintain the children at home. Therefore, when C. was four, both children were placed in an orphanage. They were destined to spend upwards of sixteen years in similar circumstances.

The experiences associated with our subject's history in the various houses to which he was sent are reflective generally of such places. He reports that his life was a miserable one, that he lived in constant fear, that the atmosphere was repressive and cold. He was beaten unmercifully, made to do extravagant penances for minor disciplinary infractions, and was exposed to the brutality, the sadism in fact, of the frustrated personnel of these monstrous institutions. The climate of the homes was outstanding for lack of warmth and affection. For the individuality of each child there was only callous disregard. Existence was regimented under conditions of pious pretense, and such a life forever marked and warped the unfortunates committed to institutional care. C. R. absorbed the philosophy of his mentors. He, too, became indifferent to the sufferings of others and came to delight in giving pain. He became shrewd and cunning in his efforts to cast blame on others, to obtain fleeting favor. His sexual life was oriented toward the abnormal by the situation in which he lived. Homosexuality was rife—there were no other outlets. He became, in short, perverted by the environment.

This history in institutions included at least three episodes when C. ran away. On these excursions he met with many sordid adventures. Each time, however, he was returned to the same environment. And during the long years his mother came only seldom to visit with him. It was an event when she did come, because she brought little gifts that for a moment enlivened the colorless limbo in which he had his existence.

Finally C. R. was "finished" with his schooling and allowed to go home. He and his brother went to live with the mother. C. found a job of a minor sort and contributed to the upkeep of the home. The mother, however, persisted in treating C. and his brother as children, although by now they had at least the physiques of men. She dictated every phase of their daily lives, maintained a tight control over the family purse, and did not allow the boys to interfere in any way with her accustomed program. C. soon became her major problem. He stole sums of money from her, once broke open her trunk and lifted and then pawned her wedding ring. She was loud in her denunciation of his behavior, threatened him with return to an orphanage, and expressed herself vociferously and unfeelingly towards him.

Meanwhile C. began experimenting with life. The sexual energies which had for so long been dammed within him were crying for outlet. He made tentative advances toward girls in his circle but these were turned aside. When he resorted to prostitutes he was impotent. Only through masturbation could he quiet his desires, and then merely temporarily and with much guilt.

On the day of the murder, which took place less than a year after he had been released from the orphanage, C. found himself to be lacking in funds. He knew that his mother kept cash and her wedding ring (which he had once stolen and pawned) in a trunk in her bedroom. He decided to break open this trunk and to do this he made his way to a neighbor who loaned him a hammer. For some reason, he decided to put off this theft until later in the day, and meanwhile to take a short walk. On his way out of the apartment building he encountered a girl who was selling some article of apparel from door-to-door in the neighborhood. She inquired whether his mother was at home. He replied that she was and offered to direct her to his apartment. She preceded him into the apartment and he indicated the general direction of the bedroom. As they passed the kitchen he lifted the borrowed hammer from a shelf and struck her. She fell to the floor. Her moans excited him; he ran to the kitchen, grabbed an ice-pick and drove it into her body many times.

In the analysis of C. R. it developed that the crime he had committed was in reality a displacement of an act he had been preparing to commit all his life. This intended act was the murder of his mother.

Now the clue to C.'s behavior resides in the oedipus situation. He had been deprived of his father at a time when this infantile conflict was coming to a head. In this case, there was no opportunity to work through the distressing complex, and he was perennially in the grip of the profound infantile attachment to the mother. Similarly, this attachment must be viewed as one which could express itself mainly aggressively, and which was insoluble because a satisfactory paternal figure was missing. C.'s mother, moreover, told the boys that their father had died, and it was only in later life that they discovered that a divorce had taken place. The father had, by the time of their discovery, accumulated another family and was residing in a nearby city.

Not only did C. have a powerful infantile love for his mother, but he also hated her for abandoning him and especially for surrendering him to the anything but tender mercies of institutional personnel. A corollary of the absorption of sadistic attitudes in such environments was the enlargement of his aggressiveness.

C.'s dreams and thoughts as well as his symbolic acts—such as breaking into his mother's trunk and stealing her wedding ring—were all indicative of his basal want. He desired to possess his mother, and according to his notions as they had been generated by brutalizing and heartless experiences, this could be done only by force. In his masturbatory fancies he imagined all types and varieties of such an incestuous act, but they all entailed gruesome and gory accompaniments such as were enacted in the murder. The homosexuality in which he had engaged found him always the aggressor, and he could be potent in heterosexuality only with mother-substitutes as the events of his life proved. But because of his rigid religious training, C. could not really assuage his intimate desires through the possession of the mother: he could not consciously conceive of committing incest. The desire had to be displaced, especially since possessing her also meant killing her. So it was that an unfortunate girl met her end, and a crime offered the solution to a situation that might have been lifted from the pages of Shakespeare.

It is impossible to exhaust this fascinating topic, and it is very likely that the human intelligence is incapable of comprehending the tortuous deviousness and multiplicity of motives behind criminal acts. Our three illustrations have but lightly touched the subject. In every instance, the personality as it has been moulded and bent through the formative years, and as it is affected by the environment, must be taken into account. Crime occurs through the operation of the precipitating environment upon the predisposing features of personality. This is the paramount message of criminology in those phases of the study which deal with the motivation of the criminal deed.

When one has become acquainted with criminals and their histories and has been permitted to observe them intimately, much that would otherwise be foreign to our knowledge becomes evident. In the field of motivation especially do we encounter unheard of influences, inexorably pointing toward prohibited actions. For instance, although it is hard to believe, it is not unusual to find men and women who, because of strong convictions of guilt for imagined or real misdeeds of early life, later commit crimes in order to be punished, literally seeking out punishment. In examples of this powerful motivant we find that the individuals have all their lives been inwardly tormented by feelings of guilt and commit crimes in order to obtain relief. Their unconscious is burdened by convictions of guilt, and when these later blossom into an offense they experience relief from the torturing phantasy. They provoke situations which will, in other words, allow them to do penance, to pay for the infringements of childhood thought or deed. Many times this reverts to the oedipus situation and reflects the guilt a child must experience because of his love for one parent and hatred of the other.

Where the body image, that is, an individual's private view of his own body, is unsatisfactory, there is a prime motivant toward criminal behavior. Paul Schilder has stressed the importance of a person's own regard of himself as a determinant of behavior. If the body-image is disappointing, if it evokes feelings of insufficiency and inadequacy, the simple mechanism of compensation may involve crime, especially where the ego has been permeated with such notions. Herein redress is sought through channels which will transgress the social sanctions. Uncounted criminologists have been misled by this feature of motivation and have instead tried to promote a spurious notion that all criminals are persons who differ measurably in a physical way from non-criminals. They have sought to spread the belief that it is the *biology* of this phenomenon rather than its *psychology* which is responsible.

Some crime is committed to protect against the commission of more serious offenses. In such cases, it is the id which clamors for full satisfaction, but the ego which urges moderation. Where this comes about, the workings of the homeostatic principle are manifest with surprising lucidity. The substituted act drains the tension created by the strivings of id. Unfortunately such a compromise rarely solves any problems. In this writer's experience, he has encountered examples of such a mechanism, but in every case there was a progressive development in the seriousness of the crimes committed, and it could have been prognosticated that nothing less than the extreme act demanded by id would suffice to call a halt to the vicious progression. It seems apparent that a respectable share of recidivism is accountable to this so often neglected phase of criminal motivation.

Beyond the features of motivation which have thus far concerned us, there is a wide range of predisposants relating to biology and psychopathology. To these we now turn our attention.

# 7. The Motivation of Crime, III

IT has already been indicated how the progressive involvement of ego is the hall mark of the criminal behavior patterning. Now it is our task to review those situations wherein the ego, either because it is debilitated through birth or disease, or becomes debilitated through the interference of an active psychotic process, performs in fashions frowned upon by the community. In this—as later when the question of alcohol and narcotic drugs arises—we shall maintain stoutly that the important thing is to remember that these processes and crime are utterly different from each other as phenomena of behavior.

Certain individuals are biologically predisposed toward criminalistic activity. It is not that they conform to criminal "types" so glibly prated of by certain physical anthropologists who follow the line first proposed by Lombroso; it is rather that they possess inherent or constitutional defects which the environment sometimes points up, which the culture highlights, to the extent that the prohibited behavior is precipitated. So far as modern research has gone, it has become apparent that to blame crime upon heredity, upon the genes, is complete nonsense. Men no more commit crimes because of their biology than they do because of the weather. Crime is a psycho-social phenomenon in which the culture, the medium of behavior, acts upon the fundamental psychological structure. As Ashley-Montague has so well stated, hereditary determinants of the nervous system do not make mind, they merely contribute the cellular elements from which mind may be organized. It is the culture, the social milieu, which then composes personality and individual psychology from the separate elements given by the genes.

And yet, in some instances, biology predisposes toward crime. This occurs when it is inadequate to cultural standards and demands.

The abnormally or subnormally endowed individual is a social misfit. In days gone by—and even in some existing societies which we egocentrically label primitive—the dwarf, the hunchback, the malformed and the deformed were accorded specialized privileges or were set aside and treated by special techniques. They had a place in the society, and they fulfilled a characteristic function. In our day they are chronically frustrated in their life-adjustment. Industry, the Services, society-at-large, have no place for them. They are unwanted. Sometimes they are shoved into the border land of the social setting and there for sheer existence are forced to engage in, to say the least, marginal activities. We regard them with a characteristic attitudinal cocktail of which the chief ingredients are disgust, guilt, shame, and a drop of fear. We are the ones who commit their crimes by refusing to grant them a secure and equally respected place in our culture. Through charity we occasionally patronize them, and some of us who feel our collective guilt more keenly than others occasionally even give them jobs or found institutions in which they can nurture their misery.

At the time when he entered prison to serve a sentence for transporting a woman interstate for immoral purposes, Y. K. was thirty-five years old. He was slightly over four feet in height; he waddled rather than walked on his bandy legs; he had defective vision and hearing.

Prison was not a new experience for Y. K. He had already been there at least twice before, both times for substantially the same offense. In his quiet voice, he would proclaim his profession to all who cared or seemed interested. He would tell you he was a pimp; and when he said this you would become aware that there was a minute overtone of pride in this declaration, as if he were saying that he was accepted by certain women, that he "belonged" some place.

Y. K. was born to an immigrant family that had settled in a northern coal-mining region. The family was very poor and continually on the mercy of the community. The father failed in practically every undertaking, even marriage. Both his marital ventures were unsuccessful. Y.'s mother was a retiring housewife, illiterate and uncomplaining. The father tried to rear the seven children (two of them half-sisters to our subject) according to old-country customs, but this was not so serious because the community was composed entirely of foreign-laborer elements.

Soon after Y.'s birth his deficiency was noticed by parents, siblings and neighbors. He was markedly stunted from his first year, dentition was delayed, he seemed apathetic, unable to learn, was late in walking and very retarded in speech. When, at about the age of four, he began to make hesitant contacts outside the home, he rapidly became the butt and target for practical jokes as well as the community scapegoat.

When he was eight his mother died and he, together with five brothers and one half-sister, was sent to an orphanage. Here he remained until the age of fifteen when he was loaned to a farmer in the neighborhood who had promised to provide a home and work for the boy. As in many such cases, he was exploited unmercifully, and any complaints were answered not only with brutality but with threats to return him to the orphanage.

It is impossible to recount the treatment to which this stunted adolescent was exposed. For the pleasure of the farmer, and later of his wife, Y. was made to perform unusual sex acts and to lend his malformed body to the perverted satisfactions of the gross appetites of his tormentors.

After three years of this Y. ran away. Unable to sustain himself he took to petty thievery. From this point forward his history is dotted with jail and workhouse sentences. Unwanted and uncared for, he finally found a "job" as a runner, messenger-boy, liaison officer, and janitor in a cheap brothel. He states the prostitutes were kind to him, frequently allowing him to approach them sexually. With all their left-hand kindnesses to him, however, he served them well by becoming the "fall-guy" for the ring which operated the houses of prostitution in that district, and twice served sentences for "operating a bawdy house."

When he was released after his second incarceration on this charge, however, he was too well known to the authorities to continue to "take the rap" for the syndicate, so they dropped him. He responded by marrying a feeble-minded prostitute, setting her up in a dingy shack near a construction project, and going into "business" on his own. For some time he was modestly successful. His final encounter with the law, and the one which brought him to the attention of the writer, came about as a result of his desire to expand his business.

In prison, Y. K. was a well-behaved inmate, although his gnome-like appearance continued to plague him and he was a very satisfactory scapegoat. On release he undoubtedly returned to his "profession," and the writer expects to see him again.

Much has been made of the role of endocrinology as a factor in crime causation. It has been held by some that the malfunctioning or dysfunctioning of certain glands produce behavior of the criminal kind. Here too, as elsewhere in the realm of biology and crime, it appears that the endocrinal state of the body may be a predisposant toward crime, but it takes the social setting to provide the precipitant for the criminal act. Glandular irregularities produce physical and psychological changes. But where society has a place for such afflicted persons, they do not resort to crime. Hyperactivity of the pituitary, the adrenals, the thyroid, and so on, lead to characteristic organic features and are apt to produce persons who cannot make an adjustment, fulfill their needs, meet their problems, or obtain even minimal satisfaction from life. If, however, these processes were reversed through medical art, or if the community permitted an adjustment through revising its attitudes or removing frustrating barriers, the sufferers would not be forced into crime as a way of adjustment.

L. G. is presently serving a modestly long sentence for participating in an insurance fraud. This is his first prison term, although he has been arrested many times for misdemeanors and on two occasions was detained for thirty days as a public nuisance. He holds a medical degree from a good school. Once, about seven years before he committed the instant offense, his license to practice was suspended when irregularities were discovered in his handling of narcotics. Yet L. G. neither smokes nor drinks nor takes drugs.

He was born to a very wealthy family in New York in 1900. Nothing in the family history is unusual. L.'s birth and delivery were normal; he was a well child and even avoided most of the diseases of childhood. His father was a surgeon of considerable repute; his mother socially active without neglecting her household or maternal duties. The parents loved the boy, but he was not over-indulged. His school career was uneventful: he made normal progress through the grades, in high school, and later in college. From college he went directly to medical school, after which he served his internship in a fashionable hospital.

L. G. married a girl whom he had known for many years soon after he set up in private practice. They had three children in five years, and were thought by neighbors and friends to be a model and happy family. But following the birth of their third child, L.'s wife "began to notice things." L. seemed suddenly to develop numerous interests he had never demonstrated before. He always seemed to be excited about something. He would engage upon a hobby, invest money in expensive equipment, and then abandon it. He appeared pallid, tense, was easily aroused to anger. Soon he was always in some difficulty or other; his practice began to fall off, his friends to disappear, his colleagues to avoid him. At last, he picked a quarrel with his wife, left their home, and lived in his office. One day his wife was accosted by him on the street. L. threatened her into suing him for divorce.

The history of this subject until he arrived in prison was a hectic one, but a little hazy. He was married and divorced three times in the following five years, changed his place of residence many times, engaged in unethical professional practices, and carried on numerous unsuccessful financial enterprises. In short, he had an exciting time and caused considerable regret to those who came into a professional, social, or family relation with him. He exhausted his inheritance, and with the disappearance of his practice was forced to abandon his profession. At the insistence of the former husband of his last wife, he became associated with a clique who were capitalizing on a somewhat obvious insurance racket. When the bubble collapsed, he went to prison.

L.'s mood was markedly and noticeably euphoric in prison. His conversation was rapid, his ideas followed each other in quick succession, he was full of plans, unable to sit still, always tense, very easily distracted. At the first presentation of his case, it appeared that he fell among the hypomanias, that he was entering upon a type of insanity characterized by excitement and overactivity. Later, however, after he had been thoroughly surveyed physically, it became apparent that he was an almost classical example of the overactivity of the thyroid gland. When this was excised, he quieted down remarkably, and at the present writing is a constrained, rather conservative person, who is ambitious only to attempt a reconciliation with his first wife and to pick up the pieces of a shattered professional and family life.

In L. G.'s case it was not the glandular condition which caused his crime. It was, rather, the glandular condition which predisposed him toward the commission of so-called wrongful acts, made him, in brief, more likely to collide with the law.


The "explanation" of crime from the side of heredity, of endowment, of given biology, is a very appealing one. It sounds plausible; but more than this, it is convenient and rather comforting. Those of us who are secure in the knowledge of non-criminal, non-insane, non-feebleminded, non-afflicted ancestry can relax in our eugenic security and allow ourselves to enjoy our and even our children's (if we make the "right" kind of marriage) manufactured immunity. But there is no more than a grain of truth in this notion. The modern biologist has been able to show that there are no born criminal or any other types, that acquired characteristics cannot be transmitted from one generation to the next. On the other hand, it becomes increasingly more evident that the endowment of an individual may be such as to predispose him toward forbidden or extravagant behavior *when the culture precipitates it*. The studies of notorious degenerate families prove nothing very significant about the inheritance of degeneracy. But they do prove that the *atmosphere* or *climate* of degeneracy in which their children are or were raised precipitated further degenerate (read delinquent or even criminal) behavior, that the social and cultural situation was of such a nature as to call forth typical forbidden responses by acting upon a possible (although remote) proneness or predisposition.

One more word needs to be said regarding biology and its role in crime. It needs to be pointed out that some individuals are more than adequately endowed biologically, and still they engage in crime. Here we must pause to realize that it is typical of our American culture that most individuals are withheld and prevented from developing their biological potentialities by the very nature of our social system. After all, a child may be given a potentiality for great invention, originality, intellect, and so on, but if he has to go to work at twelve or thirteen to support his family, if financial and social frustration— as in the case of the Negro—dogs his every effort to rise above the mass, his superlative cellular composition, his tissue and muscle excellence, are excess baggage. And his fate is to regard these as curses rather than as blessings.

Disease states not infrequently predispose toward the commission of acts called criminal. In such instances the ego is affected. As the illness ramifies and blights more and more of the organic structure which, in the final analysis, governs behavior, the ego loses its control, becomes unable to exercise a repressive or deflective function, and undergoes changes which are mirrored in overt acts. Often this is a dramatic process which family and friends view with horror and hopelessness. They watch helplessly as the person they knew so well alters his style of life and virtually loses his original identity.

Such alterations in personality are particularly pronounced where the neural structure is invaded, as in central nervous system syphilis, the encephalitides, malignant tumors of the brain and cord, and toxication of nerve and brain tissue by foreign substances such as arsenic, lead, or poisonous gases.

O. H. was the third of six children born to a New England family whose name is historic in the annals of American Protestantism. His ancestors were fighting preachers, crusaders, political, social and intellectual leaders in that period when, to paraphrase Van Wyck Brooks, New England was flowering. His parents were fiercely puritanical, morally impeccable, and the children were reared in an atmosphere of religiosity tempered by cultural refinement. The elder H. was a patriarchal, somewhat domineering pastor who attempted to raise his family to be models of deportment and faith for the community in which he preached for fifty years. The mother, although no less fervent, was inclined toward overprotection of her offspring.

O. H. was born in the second decade before the close of the last century. The birth and delivery were normal and there were no complications. He grew up in the intensely religious atmosphere already depicted. His early life was rather uneventful, primary schooling was concluded at a usual age. The records from this time show O. as a child who rarely became engaged in truant or ungentlemanly behavior. He has been described as a sensitive, shy, but sometimes argumentative child who preferred to play alone rather than with other children. Little information is available from his secondary school days, which were likewise brought to a close by graduation in good time.

At the small college he attended—one, by the way, founded by his maternal ancestors—O. was reputed to be a fair student who was more inclined toward philosophical debate than toward his studies. Consequently, his grades were only fair, sometimes poor. By dint of family influence, he was enrolled in a theological seminary of international fame, eventually achieving ordainment in the ministry of his church. When war came he was commissioned in the Chaplains' Corps and served his country well. With the demobilization following Armistice he decided to marry the girl he had been courting for many years. At the same time, he carried through an ambition for further education, and attended courses leading to the Master's Degree in social studies at a great Midwestern university. Teachers who knew him in those days have described him as "never a very brilliant student but much given to argument and dispute on relatively obscure theological and philosophical problems such as those regarding the nature of the Divinity and other rather esoteric subjects."

The young couple had three children in rapid succession, the middle child being born on the night they occupied the rectory of O.'s first ministry. O. was immediately successful, became active in religious education, and soon moved into the higher councils of his church. He achieved a modest fame as a religious pamphleteer and before long was offered a teaching post on a theological faculty.

In 1924, O. took to his bed with what was then diagnosed as influenza. He was bed-ridden for two weeks with a high fever, and, when the symptoms subsided, his physician urged a month's vacation. O., who had been working very hard, complied with this advice. He went to the mountains and after a month of idleness returned to his preaching, teaching, lecturing, and writing. He reports that he continued to feel somewhat debilitated and run down, and that a generalized weakness or fatigue plagued him for almost three years following the initial attack.

Following the illness, however, a change, at first only barely perceptible but later urgently noticeable, came over O. From a morally correct, circumspect, proper, constrained individual, he became a loose-living, profligate, promiscuous, careless person. He was no longer faithful to his wife, consorted with many women to the extent that he rapidly achieved a dubious notoriety. How he managed to continue his ministry, and even to progress to better jobs in the next few years, is a miracle this writer cannot pretend to comprehend. Nevertheless, in the early thirties he began to accumulate a criminal record. With breathtaking speed, he piled up fifteen or more verified arrests for larceny, shoplifting, stealing, acting suspiciously, being without visible means of support, and suchlike offenses. According to his family this does not complete the history in this respect, since they claim that they protected him by returning items he had stolen and interfering, by political pressure and influence, with the usual processes of the law. They could not protect him, however, when, on a train proceeding cross-country, he stole a card-case and a wallet containing cash from the pocket of a coat belonging to a Government agent. He was arrested, tried, convicted, and sentenced to four years in custody.

Soon after he arrived in the institution where he was to serve his time, O. exhibited queer behavior that brought him to the attention of officials. He engaged in petty thievery from other inmates, worked poorly, became known as an informer as well as a collector of useless items. He was referred for psychiatric examination. After lengthy investigation, the diagnosis was established as behavior disorder following encephalitis.

What had happened to O. was, briefly, this: his illness in 1924 was not influenza but encephalitis. The psychological characteristics of this disorder are such that they cause a reversal of former behavior patterns. Where the patient was once moral, he becomes immoral; where he was constrained, he becomes loose; where he was quiet, he becomes noisy. These developments do not take place at once; they follow a progressive course. Perhaps if we recall the character structure of O. before his illness and contrast it with his bizarre statements at the time this writer examined him, we shall have a clearer picture of the operationism and effects of many of the disease states in their role as predisposants toward crime. The following is abstracted from the record:

## MENTAL STATUS

*Attitude and General Behavior:* O. enters into the examination situation with considerable ease. He lolls about in his chair and seeks to set himself upon a footing of familiarity with the examiner. He is, however, somewhat restless and given to periods when he is best described as being extremely taut, although to all outward appearances he maintains an attitude of repose. He does not resent examination but rather laughingly welcomes it as a relief from his duties and begins the interview by stating that he "is prepared to abide by whatever the medical staff thinks is best." He frankly states that he is rather suspicious of all psychiatrists and psychologists, and thinks that very few of them are qualified to put into practice what they preach. He initiates the interview by stating flatly that he does not feel he should be made to suffer the "indignities" of the conditional release period and states categorically that he has no intention at this time of remaining in one place or of abiding by the other "petty and silly rules."

*Stream of Speech and Mental Activity:* The subject is very rarely capable of sticking to one topic of conversation. He exhibits a hastiness of speech with a free and rapid flow of ideas which he expresses in a well-modulated voice and with choice language. He has excellent control over his vocabulary and, were it not for a certain flabbiness of speech and a rapidity of association, one would be inclined to state that his presentation was entirely relevant and apt to the situation. He tends to answer all questions directly and in a rather superior manner, laughing a good bit, often inappropriately, and seeming very little affected by the entire situation.

*Emotional Response:* There is very little variability demonstrated by this subject. Most of the time he seems to be in a more or less euphoric mood, and even when he is dealing with subjects which would require a certain amount of constraint, especially in view of his training, he tends to be over-enthusiastic and expressive in his demonstrations. He treats his difficulties very lightly, and states that he does not feel that all that has happened to him will leave a permanent effect upon his life's plans. Most of the time he waves aside as non-essential all serious doubts upon his ability to re-establish himself in the community. On occasion he is given to making jokes about his condition and in general is unable to appreciate the significance of all that has happened to him. Rapport is always good and he does not seem to resent questioning on any topic.

*Thought Content:* No hallucinations have ever been in evidence in this case. On occasions this man states that he is "able to tune in on the spirit of the universe" and further states that he feels a psychological uplift as if a "great pressure has been released from my spirit." He has always been able to intellectualize his experiences and is not considered to be a visionary. On the other hand, close questioning reveals that he believes himself to be called to perform a philosophic task which he states the world needs and which will result in the reorientation of Christian philosophy. He claims that he has been studying the problem of philosophical justification for Christianity and Christianity as it is actually practiced, and feels that there is a "large gap between the practical aspects of this problem and the theological aspect." He believes that the Church has failed in its mission and that perhaps it will fall to him to bring about a redistribution of theological energies which will result in a better world.

So far as his history is concerned, he states that he feels no remorse regarding his delinquent activities. He claims that he stole from the railroads and large corporations simply because they plunder the poor people and make their profits by techniques which are very much related to actual thievery. He states that "What I do is really poetic justice." As pointed out by other examiners, it is quite likely that he steals first and seeks justification on moral grounds after he has committed the act. There seems to be no remorse or feeling of guilt attached to his career. He frankly admits that he had been very promiscuous with women, but seems to be unable to comprehend that such behavior should cast suspicion upon his sanity in view of his training and education. When questioned about his intimate life he states that he has "made several excursions into the realm of sin" and seems to look upon his activities as performed merely in the spirit of investigation. He demonstrates his lack of inhibition and his impulsiveness by recounting the many experiences he has had, especially with the railroads. He states that he feels that he can ride about the country freely since he has observed many individuals using the railroads in this manner. When questioned about his work, O. tells a long and circumstantial story about his trips about the country and the things he learned about the railroads. He states he has observed many people of prominence enter railroad Pullman cars and establish themselves immediately thereafter in the dining car, in which situation they ordered large meals and spent considerable money. When the conductor came around inquiring about tickets, these people merely waved him away and thus obtained free railroad fare. He thinks that he would like to travel after he is released and therefore cannot be bothered with the petty conditional release regulations. When questioned as to his means of travel, he states that it is possible that he will resort to this manner of getting around the country. Asked regarding his responsibilities to his family, he states that he feels it is impossible that he can ever again take up family life, and states furthermore that his children are now old enough to take care of themselves and therefore his responsibilities in this respect are very limited. He feels that he can never re-enter into a fair marital relationship, and claims that he can never conceive of himself as "being tied down." While there is no distinct delusional patterning in evidence, the presence of grandiose ideas cannot be denied. The mechanisms of projection are also in evidence and there are some indications of referential thinking. No retrospective falsification seems to appear in this case, although there is some doubt as to whether many of his experiences have left a mark upon him to the extent that he can recall all that has happened. So far as his present situation is concerned, he states that he wishes to place himself in the hands of the authorities for treatment since he does vaguely apprehend that there is some difference between his training and upbringing and his present status.

*Sensorium:* The subject is completely oriented and shows no signs of deterioration.

*Insight and Judgment:* There is a certain amount of superficial insight suggested in this case, but upon investigation it is disclosed that O. deals merely in terms which he has picked up through his extensive reading and applies to himself. A real appreciation of his difficulties and his motivational drives as they come into contact with the structure and laws of society is completely lacking. He engages in self-justification and explains much of his stealing activities by the fact that he did only what large corporations and groups do to individuals who have no opportunity to fight back. He doggedly clings to the rightfulness of his behavior and engages in endless rationalization of his activities. When questioned as to the type of judgment he has exercised, he refused to recognize that he has behaved in a manner which is unsuitable to an individual with pretensions to the care and teaching of other persons. Therefore, judgment is defective, as illustrated by his total personality patterning.

O.'s case is a startling affirmation of our approach to crime. The encephalitis did not cause crime; it impaired ego, perverted it so that it would compromise with and thus assuage the id-urgings which had been stifled and unsuccessfully repressed by the intense religious training and the unhealthy atmosphere of his early life.

Among other predisposants to crime is feeble-mindedness. Here we deal not only with an ego permeated and thus structurally weakened to the extent that it must incorporate and compromise with id and superego, but rather with an ego that is pliable, manipulable, plastic, and easily influenced—in short, with an immature and stunted ego, one which has not kept pace with the growth and maturation of the remainder of the organism. So it requires less of a "push," a less urgent precipitant, to involve the feeble-minded in criminal behavior. In addition, the hypothetical boundary lines between id and ego are, with the feeble-minded, far less distinct, and those mechanisms which the ego uses to divert the claims and demands of id operate with less efficiency than among the intellectually developed.

The problem which feeble-mindedness raises in relation to criminosis has two most important aspects, but feeble-mindedness as a phenomenon must be understood before the issues are made plain. Although this is no place for a digression into the psychology of intellectual inferiority, it should be recognized that there are two kinds of feeble-mindedness. There is, first, the *endogenous* type, where through accidents attending birth or deficiencies in the germ plasm, the individual is robbed of the potentiality for ever achieving normal intellectual development. Then there is the *exogenous* kind, where the development of the intellect is halted in process by hazards such as accident or disease or through severe cultural deprivation. To put the matter in another form, some unfortunate persons are not given what it takes to realize the parallel development of "mind" and body; while in others this development is brought to an abrupt cessation. So it is that feeble-mindedness produces a pitiful and often socially difficult if not dangerous anachronism. For in the feeble-minded the body continues to grow although the intellect is arrested at the specific points described by the categories moronism, imbecility, idiocy. Moreover, the insistencies of physique, the urges of their bodies, do

not lessen because they are short on intellect. If anything, because intelligence is lacking and thus cannot perform a brak-
ing, controlling, and directing task, the clamor for satisfaction
is louder.

Feeble-mindedness is a predisposant of crime because the
ego is in a sense lacking in resistance. Criminal acts by feeble-
minded individuals, however, are precipitated by the environment. The most frequent precipitant derives from a variety
of faginism. It is notorious that the moron and imbecile make
excellent dupes for unscrupulous persons who use them to
carry out their designs, who promise them cheap favors for
enacting their plans, and who of course desert them when
things get "hot." Perhaps this will explain the high incidence
of feeble-mindedness some investigators claim to have found
among prison populations; although our testing instruments
and techniques have improved so much that such promiscuous
claims are rarely made today. And, again, as with other conditions, crime may very well be the only adjustment presenting
itself to the intellectually inferior, since he cannot compete
with his more fortunate fellows.

D. C. was born in 1915 to an illiterate rural family in a Southern
state. Birth was a prolonged and difficult affair for both mother
and child. D. was the first of two living children. The parents
were sharecroppers and lived in unrelenting poverty, always
in debt to their landlord, denied every opportunity and advantage by a system founded upon special privilege for the few
and under-privilege for the many. His father was a taciturn
man who went on periodic alcoholic sprees to drown the misery
of his existence. His mother, on the other hand, took a lively
interest in the family, but because of the precarious state of her
health resulting from many miscarriages as well as their utter
poverty, there was little she could do.

D. left school after attending for four years. When he quit, he
had still not yet managed to get through the first reader. He
tells how the other children made fun of him because he was so
slow to learn, and how they bothered him with jokes and "foolish

questions." At twelve, he was regarded as hopeless by his teachers, and the family was advised to send him to work. He could neither read nor write, although he was able to spell out his name haltingly. From the odd jobs he obtained in farming, delivering packages, helping neighbors, and so on, D. was able to earn small sums which he dutifully turned over to his mother. His own wants extended to tobacco and an occasional movie. He associated with girls very little and seemed content to lead a meager existence without advantages of any kind.

At sixteen, D. was sent to an "industrial school." Behind this fancy name was the usual depressing home for the feeble-minded. How D. got there is unclear. He was accused of having stolen a horse, but according to D. this was a false charge. His story is that he had told the farmer for whom he was working at that time that he would fetch the farmer's horse. He removed the horse from the barn as he had been told to do, and thinking that there would be some time before the farmer would be returning from his dinner, he decided to go on to his own home for his midday meal. He accordingly set off down the road on the horse. Someone saw him and informed the farmer who ran immediately to D.'s shack, accused him of stealing the horse, and started the action leading to D.'s first detention experience.

D. spent six years, on and off, in the institution with that fancy name. Here he learned to weave rugs (an activity in which he would engage only if transported suddenly to the Near East) and keep himself tidy. Here, too, he learned certain homosexual practices and how to exercise animal cunning. But here he also had a chance to eat moderately decent food, sleep in a relatively clean bed, and wear shoes. Not all of the six years were spent in residence, for D. ran away many times. A report from this institution states: "This boy's residence was intermittent. We note many escapes and returns. All returns were, however, voluntary and from the compelling influence of hunger, need for rest, shelter, and comfort. We discharged him finally in 1937 when he was twenty-one."

For two years D. stayed out of trouble, working the land with his parents. One day he was sent to the nearby town to make some purchases for the landlord. He fell in with two older men who bought him some drinks, abused him sexually, then invited him to go along with them on a trip to another state. He accepted and they set off immediately in a car which apparently belonged to one of them. For two days they had a high time of it. On the third, they committed a minor violation of traffic rules, and when the policeman demanded to see some evidence of ownership, both men stated that they thought the car belonged to D. and that he had invited them on the trip. A check-up revealed the car as a stolen one. D., although he could not even drive, was convicted of the crime on the testimony of the two men, one of whom had already done time for the stealing of automobiles.

When D. was received and examined clinically, he was found to have an I.Q. of fifty-three, and the psychometrician noted a superficial overlay from D.'s having absorbed (but not assimilated) some of the stereotypes and platitudes of his past experiences. He was a youthful appearing, fairly well-nourished young man whose expression was somewhat fixed and dull and whose facial characteristics suggested some degree of mongolism. During the psychiatric examination he was loquacious and sometimes flippant, obviously trying to make an impression, and showed easy distractibility as well as ready irritability. The verbatim notes from part of the interview give a good picture of the subject and grant some insight into the problem of the feeble-minded person and crime.

*Q:* "Do you always feel so good?"
*A:* "I feel all right. I don't feel like I will go crazy in twenty-six more years."
*Q:* "Do you ever feel bad?"
*A:* "No. Nobody in my family ever got sick except my mother. She's got bad health."
*Q:* "Do you lose your temper easily?"
*A:* "I don't bother nobody. They bother me, mess me up, play tricks on me and make me do things I don't want to. My mother told me to be a good boy and I'm trying to do that."
*Q:* "Do you ever see things at night?"
*A:* "I sleep at night."
*Q:* "Do you feel like running away?"
*A:* "I figured you would ask me some fool question like that. How could I? I don't do anything wrong if someone tells me the rules but if someone tells me I know what to do. I want to get out of here and go back home to my mother."

*Q:* "How old are you?"

*A:* "Now you go asking me those hard questions again. Ask me an easy one."

*Q:* "What is today's date?"

*A:* "I don't know; I can tell the days but I can't tell the weeks. But I remember the day I came here and I will be glad to see the day I leave."

*Q:* "When was Armistice Day?"

*A:* "I never mess around with the Government none."

*Q:* "Who was General Washington?"

*A:* "You ask me too many things I don't know."

*Q:* "Who was Abraham Lincoln?"

*A:* "I can't answer such questions, I never read the Bible or things like that."

*Q:* "How many states are there in the Union?"

*A:* "I know how many there are in the world."

*Q:* "Well, how many are there in the world?"

*A:* "Thirty-eight."

*Q:* "Do you know the difference between right and wrong?"

*A:* "Yes."

*Q:* "What is the difference between right and wrong?"

A: "I don't know."

*Q:* "Was it right to steal that car?"

*A:* "I didn't take it and I didn't take the horse. They said I did. They all make up lies about me. I didn't want to do what they made me. They were going to take me for a trip. I don't know how to drive. Can I learn here?"

*Q:* "What is the difference between a dwarf and a child?"

*A:* "I don't know what you mean."

*Q:* "Where is the Mississippi River?"

*A:* "On the ground, I guess. I'm damned sure it isn't in the air!"

Before we survey the psychoneuroses and their role as predisposants of crime, a word must be said regarding two conditions which resemble the psychoneuroses but cannot be definitely included among them. Since we shall later devote a chapter to one of them—alcoholism—we pause briefly to scan drug addiction.

As a matter of fact, drug addiction in relation to crime deserves no more than passing mention. Despite the hysterical shrieking of our sensation-hungry press, despite the well-intentioned but misinformed haranguers of the public from platform and pulpit, drug addiction is of almost minimal significance as a crime predisposant and of minor importance even as a crime precipitant. The mechanics of the illness—for it does not make sense to consider either drug addiction or alcoholism as anything else—are treated more fully in the section on alcoholism and crime. The effects of drug addiction, however, are somewhat different from those of alcohol. Narcotics are mainly soothing. They function to still the cravings of id, to lull them to quiescence. The fancies produced under addiction are wish-fulfillments, and generally somewhat innocuous. Ego is narcotized and the insistencies of id are calmed by the substance. To be quite frank about it, the person under the influence of a drug is a far better risk in a dark alley than he whose ego is perverted by id (and so predisposed toward crime), and whose conflict is precipitated by a cultural anachronism. The narcotic addict is sometimes precipitated into criminal behavior when he lacks funds to purchase his drug. The social fact that we have been stupid enough to attempt to wipe out drug addiction not through a planned and basic educational campaign directed at the young, but through putting drugs on the "black market" by raising prices to fantastic levels and screaming blatant falsehoods in the press—this fact is what accounts for crime by drug addicts.

The drug marihuana has received widespread notoriety in recent years as an adjunct to crime, but scientific studies make a mockery of the publication media which spread such a fiction to increase their circulation. At a meeting of the Medical Correctional Association in New York in November, 1943, the problem was given an airing by specialists in the field. From the stenographer's transcript of the record, the following statements by experts have been extracted:

Dr. J. D. Reichard, Medical Director, U. S. Public Health Service, Medical Officer in Charge, U. S. Narcotic Farm, Lexington, Ky.: "It is possible that some of the alleged harmful effects (of marihuana) are due to auto-suggestion. It is reported that in the Near East the use of cannabis produces erotic dreams and visions. No such sensations have been reported by the users with whom we have come in contact. Since it is widely believed that the use of the drug lowers inhibitions, since the user expects to feel reckless and uninhibited, this expectation, and not pharmacological action, might explain some of the 'results' particularly among young persons."

Mrs. Florence Halpern, Psychologist, Bellevue Hospital, Member Mayor's Commission on Marihuana, New York City: "We attempted to find out what effect the substance had on intellectual functions. In some cases verbal facility was speeded up. We found that subjects were not generally willing to take larger doses than those to which they had been accustomed. When we persuaded them to take an overdose, they were slow in reading, in fact, forgot what they had read. All they wanted to do was lie in bed with soft lights and listen to the radio. When they were permitted to do as they wished, all they did was to sit around and giggle. They talked meaninglessly—adolescent philosophy. They were peaceful and quiet, not aggressive."

Dr. Lawrence Kolb, Assistant Surgeon General, U. S. Public Health Service, Chief of Mental Hygiene Division: "The use of the drug does not cause people to commit crime but may cause psychoses in some people."

We have not yet exhausted the predisposants to crime, and have now to enter a fantastic realm where both moderate and severe forms of mental illness enact a prologue to the drama of crime.

# 8. The Motivation of Crime, IV

THE psychoneuroses consist of various categories of deviation from the theoretical normal in behavior wherein the composition of the personality is balanced but for the fact that id and ego are in conflict, and the ego incorporates the symptom such conflict produces. It is the symptom which is the indicator of conflict and thus of illness, and which interferes with the wholesome adjustment of the psychoneurotic. It is also this symptom which can, and sometimes does, predispose toward crime. *The psychoneurotic symptom is not crime, nor are psychoneurotics criminals,* except accidentally in the narrow and archaic legal sense. They are tortured individuals, ill persons, who may sometimes commit crimes in the course of the inexorable working out of their problems. Of paramount importance is the realization that it is the neurosis which has to be treated in such instances, and that crime—as we must consistently maintain—is entirely incidental to such situations. Confinement or other forms of punishment directed toward the crime will never achieve the noble end of control with any of the conditions we have been discussing in the last and present chapters. With the inadequately endowed, the deficient, the biologically unsuitable, the alcoholic, the narcotic-addicted, and the disease-ridden, crime is a by-product, and management and therapy are doomed to failure unless and until the basal predisposing condition is assaulted.

Those forms which the psychoneuroses take are manifold and cannot be exhausted in our allotted space. Distinction among the various kinds and classes is achieved mainly through logical groupings of dominant symptom-trends. There are neuroses in which sufferers feel themselves driven to perform meaningless motor acts, others where they are plagued by morbid and unwelcome ideas, still others where an irrational fear is the outstanding theme, and yet others wherein fatigue and worry, anxiety over imagined ills, and organically baseless malfunctioning of organs or limbs appear. Each of these may be the predisposing foundation upon which a criminal act or even a criminal career rests.

R. E. was forty-two years old when he was sentenced to the penitentiary for a term of three years for a violation involving fraud through the mails. He was immediately recognized as an hysterical psychoneurotic whose deep-seated conflict and subsequent legal entanglement were preceded by a traumatic episode that had occurred sometime before. Here is his story:

"I was born forty-two years ago in a suburb of New York City. I was the third child in the family, another boy followed me. I attended public school in this small suburban town. I do not remember having to suffer any inconveniences in my early childhood. My folks have always been very considerate, very lovable. My father worked hard as a manager for a large plumbing concern in the city, and later owned his own business. During my public school period I took part in all sports. I was never ill outside of a cold or the grippe. I was liked socially, although most of my associates were from the working class of people. I do not remember anything of interest that I can state here that happened during my early childhood prior to entrance into high school. Even during my public school attendance, my thoughts, as my folks and all those around me know, were honest. I always ran errands for a clothing store across the street, cleaned the store, and did other work to earn Sunday church and expense money. I was very active, very nervous, always doing something. I left high school at the end of the first year, because I wanted to go to work, but I continued studying at night. After diligent study, I felt qualified to do Wall Street bookkeeping. My first job on the Street was with a firm as a board-boy, later advancing to the bookkeeping staff. One day the head bookkeeper instructed me to make an entry which I later found out was illegal. There was a big fuss about it when the matter came into the open. It came to trial and I was cleared of all guilt by this man's confessing he had taken advantage of my inexperience. He went to prison and the firm took me back to work for them. All this time my folks were lovable and faithful, and cared for me well. I paid them for my room and board, and had enough left over for additional expenses and further education. After a while I secured a better position with a Wall Street house, with which I stayed for the next few years, always advancing. I became interested in the market, which was active at the time, and started investing in it. I made a lot of money, too much in fact, and quit my job to trade on my profits. The story at this point is a short one. I was wiped out in a minor flurry, and there I was, no job, no money, but a lot of self-confidence. I was healthy, had lived a clean life and was confident in my future.

"Around this time I met an old friend who invited me to his rooms at what is now the Taft Hotel in New York. When I got there, I found a few other people from the Street gathered together, discussing a proposition. They were selling additional stock to the original holders of a certain excellent issue, but the list was so extensive that an additional salesforce was being organized. The commission was phenomenal. I got in on it and started to make real money again. One thing followed another and I went from proposition to proposition. My folks realized that business kept me away from New York a lot, although I always saw them when I was in town.

"During a business trip I met Adele, whose home was in Chicago. She was an actress, had had good parts in musicals, was well thought of by everyone. We were married and settled down in that city. I carried on my work from there. I was all business and had no other interests. It was not money that drove me on. I worked because I love it. After a couple of years, my wife and I began drifting apart. Mainly it was mother-in-law trouble; her mother had never fully approved of me and we argued continuously. I have always been the nervous type, and she knew this and would do things to get my goat. Finally I could put up with it no more, and so we decided it was quits. I made a very generous settlement on my wife, her son by a former marriage, and even her mother. Meanwhile I became interested in a very profitable mining proposition in the West, and I moved myself out there. It was a wonderful life. I bought a small ranch and continued my business by telephone with my capable secretarial staff. On a trip to the East, I met and fell in love with Ellen. This was the high point of my life. We meant everything to each other. She suited me in every way, and we planned to marry as soon as my divorce from Adele became final. When I wasn't with her, we kept in touch by telephone every night, and we exchanged letters frequently. Because we were then at the peak of my project I could not leave my ranch, and so when the time expired and the decree of divorce was finally granted, I persuaded Ellen to come West immediately. We were to be married at my ranch. Ellen took a plane from New York; I drove to the airfield to meet her and take her to the ranch where the minister was waiting. At the airfield I learned that nothing had been heard of the plane, which was reported overdue at a municipal airport two hundred miles east of us. I waited for three hours and then could stand it no longer. I put in a call and fainted dead away when I learned that the plane had crashed and all the passengers had been killed, mutilated beyond recognition.

"I don't remember clearly what happened after that. For the next few months I remained on the ranch, a very sick and hysterical person. After the initial shock I tried to revise my plans but I could do nothing, had no ambition at all. Then also a curious thing began to happen to me. For reasons which none of my doctors could fathom, I began to break out in swellings that would come and go all over my body, now here and now there. They sent me to the coast where I remained in a sanitarium for two months, leaving it in the same condition as I entered. But while I was there, other things happened to me too. I began to dread having to remain in one place and could not feel comfortable in a room unless the door was open. I knew this was claustrophobia, but knowing about it didn't do me any good, didn't clear it up. I would get terrible attacks of nervousness, my heart would pound, my ears ring, my whole body break out in cold sweat. These seemed to alternate with swellings which would one day affect my feet, another my arms, another my face, and sometimes even my throat. The latter almost drove me wild, because then they would have to insert a tube so that I could breathe.

"Since the doctors and being in hospital did me no good at all, nothing was effective, I tried another change of scene. Sometime previously a friend had told me of a new company which was forming at that time. I knew that they wanted someone to make contacts for them and represent them in foreign countries, so I undertook the job. This was a mistake; no sooner had I stepped aboard the ship than I became panicky and hysterical and they had to carry me off it. I was almost insane with the feeling that everything was of no avail. Without reporting to the firm that had hired me, I immediately set off for the East by automobile. Except for the generous travel allowance which my firm had allowed me and for the proceeds from the sale of my holdings and property in the West, I was broke. Since my own money was not very much, for the next few months I drew on the allowance my firm had given me on deposit at my bank, and went from New York to Florida where I changed my name and tried to live a new life in almost complete retirement. Meanwhile, in order to throw my firm off the trail and to stall until I could get my health back again and return their money, I resorted to a trick. I wrote them enthusiastic letters, full of promises and hinting at great business dealings; these letters I put in envelopes which I sent to an old friend of mine in Europe, and he mailed them for me from there. I even managed to get more money out of them.

"Well, the whole thing of course blew up in my face. I was indicted for fraud and here I am. I don't think I am a criminal. In all my business dealings I was scrupulously honest and that's why I had a large following and was successful until the time I became ill. It was my sickness that did it. Today I am worse off than ever. Confinement is killing me. Not only do I have those horrible fears, especially that one of these swellings will lodge in my throat and kill me, but I have fainting spells and everything else."

R. E. was diagnosed as an hysterical psychoneurotic soon after his admission. He was suffering from the symptoms he described and a severe degree of claustrophobia. Following his release he returned to his former activities. He has remarried and is moderately happy, although he has never been cured of his psychoneurosis. Like many others, R. E. has "hit the sawdust trail," going from one doctor to another. He is also a source of revenue for quack "specialists" and advertisers of patent medicines.

The case of J. McC. is illustrative of another way in which a psychoneurosis may predispose toward crime. She was a strikingly handsome woman of thirty-six who presented an unusual story which was supported in all essentials by the record, and who had been through a harrowing experience. This writer became acquainted with her case through a consultation.

J. McC. was born in a small Southern community. Her father owned considerable property which brought the family a good income. He did not have to work in the usually accepted sense, and consequently spent most of his time in a home workshop, developing minor inventions and gadgets for cheap distribution. He was a somewhat distraught and absent-minded person who had to be reminded about changing his clothing, coming to meals, and other details of everyday living. His love for J., an only child, was unbounded: he would play with her endlessly, guard her against every possible hurt, sympathize with her unrestrainedly when she suffered the incidental hurts and bruises of childhood, and would be almost mad with grief and anxiety when she was ill. J.'s mother, on the other hand, was a more practical person. She it was who gave the family what organization it had, who carried on the business such as it was, and who managed not only J. but also her husband. In her relations with J. she was straightforward and even somewhat blunt. J. today thinks her mother resented her and felt that the child came between her and her husband. Mother and daughter, at any rate, seemed to have little in common, and as the child grew they tended to drift farther and farther apart.

Little needs to be said regarding the school history of J. She was a bright child and progressed rapidly. She matured rather abruptly: her first menstruation came at the age of eleven. The dreams of this period, recovered many years later, indicated that J. regarded this event as inspired by her mother in order to punish the child for masturbation and her fancies that the mother had gone away, leaving J. and her father happily together.

At fifteen J. was within a year of graduating from high school. She was a beautiful girl with dark hair and lively eyes. An instructor at the school—a married man whom she later identified with her father especially because he was in a field which required him to be always "surrounded with gadgets"—won her affection and seduced her. She was impregnated at their first con-

tact and was thereupon thrown into panic. On the advice of the
family physician, whom she wisely consulted, she confided in
her father. Although he was shocked and angered, her father immediately took steps to extricate her. He first called on the young
instructor and informed him that his presence in the town was
no longer welcome. Then he made arrangements for an abortion under the best possible, but of course extralegal, circumstances. He decided that the mother need not be involved in the
affair, and it was carried out in great secrecy. J. was aborted of
a four-month fetus. The experience was shocking, painful, sordid,
and shameful. J. almost lost her life in the course of the operation, and in desperation her father informed the mother. This
woman acted as one might have expected. While J. was in danger
and later during her long convalescence, the mother was busily
attentive and protective. But after J. had recovered fully, she
turned from the girl and their relations were only formal until
the day the mother died.

J. returned to school, graduated, and went on to college. In
her senior year she met a young man who was attending law
school and fell in love with him. They decided to marry upon
her graduation. The match was satisfactory to both sets of
parents, the boy's family was rather wealthy, and the couple got
off to what seemed to be a good start. For their honeymoon they
chose an isolated place on the Carolina shore.

The first days and nights of the honeymoon were disappointing and embarrassing to both. Somehow the experience which
J. had gone through previously made her tense and wary in
their relations. She was frigid sexually, and although she tried
very hard to overcome her reluctances, she dreaded all physical
contact with her husband. He, on the other hand, was patient
and tender with her. At this time he knew nothing of his wife's
tragic history and attributed her attitude to natural shyness. But
this went on for three years. J. longed to enjoy her life with her
husband, but she could not. In the fourth year of their marriage,
J. became pregnant. She was horrified at the discovery of this
fact, and as her time for delivery approached she reacted with
panic, became distressed at the prospect and pleaded with her
husband to save her from it somehow. The poor man could not
understand her apprehensiveness, but he arranged for her to go
to an expensive nursing home where she could have every possible

comfort and aid. The child, a boy, was delivered. J. at first refused to have anything to do with it and could not even bear to have it around. This attitude soon waned, and J. returned from the home with her baby, determined to be a good mother and wife. For the next two months she seemed to be recovering rapidly and to be a model mother.

One night J. awoke in panic from a dream in which it appeared she had killed her baby. She got out of bed and walked to the nursery. The child was sleeping peacefully. This occurred on successive nights, and as if this were not enough, the persistent idea that she had killed her child began to invade her waking thoughts. She became driven and anxious, was afraid to keep the child near her but was even more uncomfortable when the boy was out of her sight. Her nights were almost sleepless and her days filled with one episode of panic after another. Finally, she could stand it no longer. On a day in the fall of the year, while her husband was at his office, she placed the child in a playpen in their yard, caught a train, and left town.

She arrived at her father's home late that same night, and from there telephoned her husband. Enlisting the aid of her father, she persuaded her husband she was overwrought and ill, and obtained his consent for her to remain in her childhood home for a week or two. This period passed pleasantly enough, her nightmares and obsessive thoughts left her. But the prospect of returning to her husband and child soon began to torment her. Again she ran away, this time to a large city in the North. She was without funds and soon had to attempt to find a job. She obtained one as a waitress. Then, for a reason unknown to her but crystal-clear to the student of human behavior, she began to indulge in prostitution. J. reports that her own participation as a prostitute was minimal, and that she never obtained sexual gratification under any circumstances. Be that as it may, when she was just thirty, J. met a man who was notorious as a leader of a nation-wide vice ring. He made her an attractive proposition according to the terms of which she was placed in charge of a fashionable brothel at a munificent salary. She accepted.

The denouement was inevitable. After operating successfully for a couple of years, the ring was smashed and J. along with many others went to prison. In prison her obsessive thoughts, which had been somewhat in abeyance for some years, returned.

She was treated for her psychoneurosis but was discharged un-recovered.

As a condition of the organism predisposing toward crime, the psychoneuroses are perhaps not statistically of great significance. Although all of us are prone to experience episodes when we behave neurotically—especially during crucial periods of life such as those around examination time, at graduation, upon marriage, and at other milestones marking our life-courses—there are not very many who regularly possess obsessive thoughts, experience irrational fears, perform compulsive acts, or exhibit hysterical reactions. And among those who do, it is only infrequently that these lead into criminal behavior. But at the same time, it should not be overlooked that the possibility of such an involvement is always present. Often it requires a powerful threat to the integrity of the organism to set off the latent ego-id conflict. At the time this volume is being prepared, our scientific and professional journals are loaded with illustrative cases, and this writer has had endless opportunity to observe the precipitation of crime through the disruptive and critical events of war with its horrors and threats and dangers. Of the endless cases on file, three are selected because of their bearing upon the matter at hand.

C. P., a rather asthenic appearing male of twenty-six, was received as a military prisoner with a sentence of fifteen years. He had stolen a car and driven it across state lines.

The significant features of C. P.'s background make evident not only his crime but also his entire personality patterning. He was an only child whose father had died within two years following his birth. The mother had to assume all the cares associated with maintaining herself and the child. She had always been a highly nervous type, and the care-loaded, worrisome life she began to lead upon her husband's demise served to increase her apprehension. She obtained a job as a forewoman in a laundry, a post which she held for the next fifteen years until C. was old enough to pool his earnings with her savings and thus to maintain them both. Meanwhile, C. attended school and made normal progress. After school hours, however, he had to rush right home to do the shopping, straighten the apartment, and run the necessary errands. His mother was decidedly over-protective, always seemed jealous of his friends, and through the long years lavished affection on him unsparingly. She often told him that he was her sole reason for living, that if anything happened to him she would kill herself, that he must never leave her. At times, before he left school at sixteen, she would sleep in the same bed with him, and even after that age he would not infrequently awaken of a morning to find her lying next to him.

As a consequence, C. became dependent upon his mother and showed all the signs of an attached, rather weak person who was incapable of making his own decisions, who would worry and fret over the slightest skin-bruise or headache or upset stomach. His mother would not permit him to associate with girls; he had no boy friends.

In 1942 C. was called in the draft. Until that time he had been excused from service in order to support his mother. But soon the manpower need became such that C. was asked to report. On receiving his notice at a time when he was at work, his mother destroyed it and said nothing to him. When the draft board declared him delinquent (without his knowledge), she went to them and pleaded, begged, and threatened. Apparently they saw some justice in her claims and granted him a three-month extension during which time she was supposed to arrange their affairs so that he could leave home. The end of the extension period, however, found her in hospital with a "nervous breakdown." Suspecting this was a hoax, the board chose to ignore this situation and packed C. off to the induction station. His mother rose from her bed at once, quit the hospital, accompanied her boy to the point of departure, and after a tearful parting returned home. C. continues the tale from this point:

"After they checked us in at the Reception Center, they got us ready for shipment to our assigned camps for training. It took almost a week to get everything over with and Mom called me every night. She also wrote me letters every day. It was terrible for both of us. Her letters were full of the way she felt about me being away, and she kept telling me she was going to die. It was very bad for me. I never was away from her even for a day before, and I felt awful. I was sick with dizzy spells and headaches all the time. I couldn't eat and threw up almost every meal.

"Well, they finally shipped me off to Texas. I stuck it out as long as I could. I was in the infirmary most of the time but the medical officers couldn't do nothing for me. They said that I was getting to be a real psycho, and some of them even wondered how I was accepted in the first place at all. But they also said there was no way for me to get out, and to be a man. Meantime, I kept getting those letters from Mom. She began telling me that if I didn't come home she was going to kill herself, and when she said it day after day I couldn't stand it any more. I was on a convalescent ward and had my clothes. So one night I sneaked out and walked and hitched into town. I saw a car standing at the curb. I could look in and see the keys in the ignition. All I could think of was Mom and about her killing herself and how sick I felt. I got in and drove away. Two days later they picked me up."

M. G. had always been considered unstable. As a child he was sickly and undernourished, subject to convulsions, and often got his own way by exhibiting tantrum behavior. When denied anything he would throw himself on the floor, hold his breath, beat his head against the floor, or lie down and kick his heels until plaster fell from the walls. He usually got what he wanted: his parents were indulgent with him. People of moderate means, his folks provided every convenience and comfort for M. and his younger sister. He was protected, shielded, sheltered. He developed elaborate meal-time and bed-time rituals which his parents encouraged, or at least failed to discourage. He had to eat from the same dish and use the same utensils at every meal; he had to have his food prepared a certain way, sit in a particular place, observe an involved ritual. Preparing for bed was even more complicated. An old doll had to be placed in the bed, his light had to remain aglow, a certain story had to be read to him, a ritual of kissing had to be observed in order of precedence. Night was a source of terror for M., replete with horrible dreams which would send him screaming to the parental bedroom. He feared thunder and lightning especially, fainted at the sight of blood, became nauseated at foul odors.

The history of M. between the ages of six and fourteen is lacking in significant additions to what has already been outlined. He attended school, took violin lessons, read widely, was known as a somewhat sickly, nervous, but intelligent boy. At fourteen he began to masturbate daily and this habit continued well past the time of his first sex experience at nineteen.

When our country went to war, M. was in attendance at a technical college in preparation for a career in engineering. He was drafted, inducted, trained, and sent abroad. The trip overseas was another nightmare for him. Not only was he violently ill during the crossing, but he was in a continual state of tense apprehension and anticipation. After he arrived in England, M. was stationed in London with a guard detachment. Things were rather quiet for some weeks: there were no raids and but for the sight of everyone in uniform one would hardly think it was wartime. Often there would be warnings signaling the approach of enemy planes, but they were apparently turned back by the defenses around the city, and those that did come through were beaten off before the targets came in sight. During such alarms, M. reports that he felt tense and panicky, but that he found no difficulty in performing his duty.

At last a raid occurred in which bombs fell near M.'s post. When he heard the sirens, he experienced a rush of anxiety and tension, yet he thought the incident would be similar to previous attacks. He was confident the enemy planes would be turned back. But, instead, they came on and were soon overhead. He was stationed at the mouth of a shelter, and was under command to assist civilians who were pouring in from all directions and to maintain order. The bombs fell closer and closer, and with each explosion M. felt himself growing more alarmed, more faint, more fearful. Finally a direct hit was scored on a building across the street. From here on there is no coherence to M.'s story.

Apparently M. threw away his rifle and rushed wildly from the shelter through the storm of metal and glass and dust. Miraculously unharmed, he made his way through the city. In panic he fled to a suburban district. Three days later he was picked up by the M.P.s as he wandered about the countryside in a dazed condition. He was wearing an overseas cap, regulation tunic, but civilian trousers in which were money, jewels, and objects of value. M. was tried and sentenced for desertion and theft. He still claims he knows nothing of what happened to him from the moment the bomb hit in his vicinity. He cannot account for the strange uniform or the valuables. He was diagnosed as a psychoneurotic of long standing.

E. K. was the fifth child in a family of seven children. His father was a native American from old stock, an architect employed by a prominent firm. E. had little to do with this man who had many interests which kept him away from the home until late every night. With his mother, however, E. enjoyed a close relationship. This woman, a devout Catholic, was interested in her children, possessed many ultramodern ideas as to child training, and was always experimenting with her children in the matter of training and education. If the truth were known, moreover, she seems to have been somewhat of an unstable, intellectually limited but pretentious person who followed the fads rather than her good sense. Because they could afford servants, E.'s mother had unlimited time, between pregnancies, to devote to her children. She organized her own family nursery and tried to "bring out the hidden talents in each child." Among the seven children, E. was the only boy, and as in most such cases, he was coddled and attended to beyond his requirements. It appears that E. early developed interests which were more feminine than masculine. He learned to cook, to sew, to dance, and to play the piano beautifully at an almost phenomenally early age. His male contacts were limited to his father and some cousins until he was sent to school. Outside the home he was insecure, shy, subdued, and reticent. At home, among his sisters, he was lively and the leader in play.

The most significant episode in E.'s early life occurred when he was homosexually seduced by an older boy at school when he was ten. This was the first of a series of such affairs in which E. was always the passive participant. At sixteen, when he graduated from high school, E. went to work as a bookkeeper for a woman who owned a chain of millinery shops. This employer took notice of the shy, good-looking boy, and advanced him rapidly. She also invited him to her home and there offered herself to him. This was his first heterosexual experience beyond the tentative and hasty youthful experiences in school. He did not enjoy the experience as much as he had his homosexual ones, but he entered into a liaison with his employer which lasted for almost five years. During this time he rose in the business to a managerial post and commanded an excellent salary. Nevertheless, he still had occasional sex experiences with males. Moreover, he continued to remain a subdued and retiring type.

When war came, E. was called to service. The first months were strenuous for him, but he managed to survive them. He was sent overseas and quartered in Ireland. His ability was soon noted and he was given a sergeant's rating and assigned to a headquarters group. Meanwhile he began to suffer from a variety of ailments and complaints for which no organic cause could be found. He was hospitalized frequently, seemed to be avoiding his mates, withdrew from all forms of social intercourse, and was regarded by his fellows as a mild-mannered but seclusive soldier.

One morning E. appeared at company headquarters and requested an interview with the officer in charge. To this officer E. made the confession that during the the previous night he had murdered a woman in a town about an hour's distance from camp. The following is the story as E. recalls it:

"For weeks I had been feeling bad. I know what was wrong with me now, but I didn't know then. Anyhow, I felt awful. I had crazy thoughts and I couldn't be sure of myself anytime. There were no women around, of course, except some nurses and WACs, but that wasn't what was bothering me. I just felt like I had to get away from all of it, from the soldiers and the officers, from all the men. I thought they knew about me and what I wanted. I couldn't stand their talk or the way they dressed or their voices. I was ashamed of myself and my desires. I felt I wanted a woman to be with and talk to but I really also felt I wanted some man to love me and be good to me. All around me there were men, only men. I couldn't go to the latrine unless I was sure it was empty, and it seldom was. I would wait for after 'lights out' to get undressed. I was afraid I'd get up in the middle of the night and try to crawl into bed with some fellow. I had to keep fighting it down all the time. This went on for a long time, starting right after we left the States. I don't think you know what I mean. I guess I felt like I was the only 'girl' in a bunch of men. I seemed to be all alone. And I knew what happens in the Army if you are caught doing anything sexy with other men. So I had to fight it down. But it was hard. There was a couple of guys in our outfit I thought were queer, and I constantly thought of trying to make one of them, but since I wasn't sure I was afraid to expose myself. Not that I am a queer myself, but I have always wanted to be treated kindly by men, and being among men all day every day without a really decent word was driving me mad. I thought if only I could associate with some of these fellows and leave sex out of it. Then I thought that what I needed was probably to go out with some girl and prove to myself I was a real man and then maybe I'd feel comfortable around the fellows again. So I had a pass and went into town that night and in a joint some-where I saw this gal sitting at a table by herself. She was a street gal and the set-up was plain. I bought her a few drinks and then suggested she take me to her place. She did.

"I don't know what it was, the liquor or the way I felt, but I was no good although I tried hard many times. After a while she got disgusted with me and said I was wasting her time. She wanted my money and I didn't have very much. She said I could stay if I would pay her for the trade she would have had that night. When I emptied my pockets it wasn't enough, and so I gave her a ring my mother had given me. So I stayed around but didn't do myself or her any good. She made fun of me, and all I could think of was what I really wanted and how ashamed I was. She began to laugh and I told her to shut up. She kept on laughing. I lost my head and started to choke her. Once I got started I couldn't stop."

E. was examined and subsequently diagnosed as a psycho-neurotic with episodes of acute homosexual panic. The latter is a condition that this writer's Army colleagues tell him is rather common and accounts for much of the mass of staggering sta-tistics on psychiatric casualties. As for E., prison did not do any-thing to alleviate his illness. Enforced association with males only led him into panic states time after time. These subsided, however, when he conveniently developed an hysterical paralysis.

The psychoses play a similar role in predisposing toward crime. Here we meet with the ultimate of that continuum of crime we postulated. In the psychoneuroses we observe an intact ego absorbing id-urges but not giving way before them.

The sufferer remains in contact with the world, his efficiency suffers some impairment, but he is often able to continue caring for himself and his interests. The ego remains on the scene and although it incorporates the symptom, takes it over, so to speak, it does not abandon the field to the more primitive and uncontrolled segments of the total personality. With the psychoses, however, ego is damaged, inoperative, withdrawn and completely perverted. The pleasure-bent id and the restraining superego war without benefit of mediation. The personality is unrecognizable, different from what it was. No control is exerted by the governing, directing portion of the personality. The being is swayed and bent by all the conflicts which are now neither repressed nor sublimated, buried nor deflected. The world in which the psychotic lives is not the real one inhabited by ordinary mortals. It is inaccessible to us. Sometimes, as in the schizophrenias, it is an archaic world in which even the symbols are ancient and forgotten.

The psychotic possesses no ego in the usually recognizable sense of the term. The identifications he makes are foreign to the personality his familiars had observed previous to the onset of the disorder, although they may have been lurking within him all his life. When he succumbs, he emerges as from a chrysalis a newborn personality with altered aims and goals. His ego is lost. Behavior reigns unchecked at the dictate of dark and often malign forces arising in chaos from the depths. Because of the annihilation of ego and with it its system of checks and balances, we regard the psychotic as lacking in responsibility for his acts, and he is protected somewhat by the law from having to endure the penalties ordinarily exacted for trespasses.

One would think that it is a simple matter to determine the sanity or insanity of a person who has committed an act prohibited by law. Unfortunately, this is untrue. Sometimes insanity is well-disguised and it takes the most precise and the most delicate technique to reach a decision which does justice to the accused and to society. Beyond this, so many encumbrances and barriers are placed in the way of the psychiatrists who are called upon to render an opinion in such instances that testimony before the court is counted among the most onerous tasks which anyone can be called upon to perform. Just as it is the case with lawyers, the psychiatric profession too has its prostitutes who will sell their services to the highest bidder despite social consequences. And where this occurs we witness the shameful spectacle of courtroom haggling and dispute that rebounds only to the embarrassment of the profession at large. Moreover, the legal and the medical definitions of insanity are wholly incompatible. The law is interested only in whether the offender knows the difference between right and wrong and can distinguish the nature and quality of his acts. For the psychiatrist, however, the question is different. The latter recognizes that the important role in criminal behavior is played not by the intellect but by the emotions. He understands that it is not enough to *know* the difference between right and wrong unless such a difference is *felt*. Many persons who are mad as March Hares know it is wrong to kill or to steal. The rock upon which they founder is feeling. The emotions reflect motivations through the ego. The problem in any given case for the psychiatrist is this: was or is the ego intact? does or did the offender feel his act was wrongful? was or is this feeling strong enough to implement action? was his whole personality involved in the action?

The psychoses predispose toward crime in some cases. Where this predisposition occurs, the crime is only incidental to the total picture of disorder and is precipitated by the environment. Fundamental is our understanding that the disordered individual is not a criminal; he is a psychotic. As such, his new aims, his new personality, cannot make the adjustments demanded of him; he can make only those adaptations for which he is equipped. His is not a failure to adjust, but an inability to do so.

It is needless to go into a lengthy disquisition regarding the causes, the types, and the varieties of insanity. By and large, there are those in which the condition results from organic causes such as the invasion of microorganisms during a disease process, and those for which there appears to be no direct physical origination. The latter are tentatively designated functional. Some of the psychotic states are characterized by excitement, destructiveness, maniacal behavior, others by withdrawing, depression, lassitude. Again, we find some dominated by hallucinations affecting any or all the senses, or delusions regarding the self and its destiny. In the grip of these motivations, the psychotic may incidentally perform a criminal act.

T. M. had been psychotic for many years previous to his admission to prison. The fact that he arrived finally in a penitentiary resulted from a conflict between State and Federal government. He committed a Federal offense, but he was obviously insane at the time of the act and during trial; yet the State, pleading overcrowding of its institutions, refused to acknowledge its responsibility. And in spite of the fact that the Court had a psychiatric specialist's testimony to the effect that T. M. was insane, he was still committed to prison on a charge of failing to comply with registration requirements under the Alien Registration and the Selective Service Acts.

T. was born in Italy in 1910. He was brought to this country after World War I, one of a family of mother and three other boys who followed the father who had gone ahead to prepare a home for them. Since both his parents are deceased and the whereabouts of his brothers unknown, no information regarding the early life, the schooling, and the experiences of T. is available. In his disturbed, disordered state his own statements are not to be trusted. He tells us that he went to school in Italy and quit at the age of twelve. He believes he did well in school. From the time the family arrived in the United States until he was apprehended for this offense he worked in restaurants as a dishwasher, handyman, or busboy. He states that at eleven he began to masturbate, and that at fifteen he had his first hetero-sexual experience, with a prostitute. He never married, never wanted to marry. As for living in one place, he tells us that this is against his "nature," and so he has been a rover and floater until now. Past medical history indicates that at the age of seven-teen, when working on a bread-slicing machine, he had the first three fingers of his left hand cut off at the second joint. His record shows numerous arrests for vagrancy, and on suspicion, but nothing else.

This is the man who was admitted to a penal institution for three years because he failed to comply with certain registration laws.

When examined by the psychiatrist, previous to sentencing by the court, he was dirty and untidy. Delusionary trends were present. He stated he was in communication with the spirits, that he was dead physically, that he had no religion or politics. "I am supposed to have died on the cross or in a concentration camp. I have no circulation." The psychiatrist thought T. was psychotic and should be in a mental hospital. He was sent, instead, to prison.

During the rectal examination, when directed to spread his but-tocks, he defecated. Following this, he was confined to the hos-pital where it was noted that he was unkempt and untidy. "He washes himself frequently, using the commode for this purpose rather than the sink. He stands in the bowl, washes his feet and throws water over his head. He has been noted sleeping with his feet high on the wall, and resting on the back of his neck. He has also been observed masturbating at least twice each day." Examination was conducted in his room on the ward. Appearance was wildly unkempt, hair uncombed, face covered with several days' growth of beard. He usually hugged a pillow, evidenced little emotional show except for an occasional fleeting, superior smile. There was a tendency toward flight of ideas, sentences were left uncompleted, answers were often irrelevant. He began one examination by stating that the sun was dimmer because he had just come from Mars. On hearing the toilet flushed in an adjoining room he said it was a signal which he could use at any time to make the whole place disappear. Let us continue from here with a verbatim report:

*Q:* "You were telling me the other day about having six pairs of eyes. Is that right?"

*A:* "Yeah, so what?"

*Q:* "Where did you get those six pairs of eyes?"

*A:* "I just make them myself. I just ask for them and I get them."

*Q:* "Now tell me, of what value are those six pairs of eyes?"

*A:* "Well those six pairs of eyes means that I'm the ruler of everything there is. Those that believe it they stay. I have the power over everything."

*Q:* "Where did you get this power?"

*A:* "Well, nobody has to find out how I get the power. All they have to do is just see the power."

*Q:* "How does one see this power?"

*A:* "Well, by seeing this power men disappear."

*Q:* "How do you get these people to disappear? Make me disappear right now."

*A:* "Well, that'll happen in a couple of days. I shall take over the whole heaven and earth."

*Q:* "Have you any title?"

*A:* "No, I have no title. The only thing I have is my power."

*Q:* "You told me the other day you have a title—you weren't God or Jesus Christ, but you had a title. You said you had the special title of a Supreme Being or something."

*A:* "The Supreme Being means just supreme lawyer above all —above men, skies, stars, moon, sun, woman, animals, trees, grass, air, oxygen, electricity." [On a previous occasion, he said he was the supreme bastard, that he was a devil, that he controlled everything through the circulation.]

*Q:* "Were you ever born?"

*A:* "No, I'm never born."

*Q:* "Where do you come from?"

*A:* "I always come by my spirit from the previous existence and the planet."

*Q:* "What planet?"

*A:* "The world, Mars, or whatever I give the name to."

*Q:* "What about your circulation?"

*A:* "Well, that's whenever I take the circulation of all human beings, grass, trees, man, woman, iron, matter—everything that there is. I'm the Supreme Being."

*Q:* "Why don't you grow yourself some more fingers where you have those cut off, if you're the Supreme Being?"

*A:* "Well, that's all right. I have my fingers on, but you can't see it."

*Q:* "Let me see you pick up that rubber band with those fingers that are there."

*A:* "No, why should I?"

*Q:* "I asked you to."

*A:* "Well, I don't want to."

*Q:* "Do you know what day this is?"

*A:* "Whatever day I say it is, it is. If I say it's Wednesday, it's Wednesday."

*Q:* "What month is it?"

*A:* "What difference does it make?"

*Q:* "What month do you make this?"

*A:* "What difference does it make? I didn't make it yet."

*Q:* "What about making it right now?"

*A:* "I guess Mukulos."

*Q:* "What does that mean?"

*A:* "It means the first month of the year—the first month of creation."

*Q:* "You call yourself not God, but the devil. Is that right?"

*A:* "No. I'm the lawgiver. The only law is what I created, and I create it with a voice of thunder and anybody that doesn't come under my law disappears. I make him disappear and don't give a damn. As soon as the flags of the devil disappear, which is the American flag, and all the flags of the Christians and pagans and my flag happens to be up—which is the four pointed flag bearing stars, which is not red, but is an infinite pure white. As soon as that flag happens to be there—which is the divinity of all above —has to come under my law. Those that believe, they can stay, and those that don't believe will disappear."

*Q:* "How does it happen that when you speak, everybody hears you?"

*A:* "Well, because I'm the creator of all. When I speak my voice is louder than thunder in the world below."

*Q:* "What is your big mission in this world?"

*A:* "I just save me and me alone. Everybody else can go to hell."

*Q:* "Where is hell?"

*A:* "Well, it's down below. If I want to burn you, I can put you down there and burn you."

*Q:* "How old are you?"

*A:* "Me? Well, gee, I'm so old in my other existences. But I've been here for thirty years."

*Q:* "When was your first appearance?"

*A:* "I don't know. So damn long, who cares?"

*Q:* "Do you know what season this is?"

*A:* "Well, around here it's the same season in the Garden of Eden."

*Q:* "Do you know what place this is?"

*A:* "Oh, this is comfortable for me."

*Q:* "What's my name?"

*A:* "Frank?"

*Q:* "I told you the other day."

*A:* "I don't have to remember anybody's name, because I'm connected with too many things to remember anybody's name."

This was T. M., who had evaded our laws and was sent to prison, T. M. who acknowledged only the dictates of his inner voices, and for whom the legal codes of our country did not exist.

B. E. had been sentenced to prison on a charge involving kidnapping and theft of a car. He tells a curious story of this offense: "I am charged with kidnapping. I was walking across this field trying to get away from them. They didn't say so but I knew they were after me, so I cut across the field hoping to fool them. It was about nine o'clock at night. I saw this car driving along the lane very slowly, then it stopped. I wanted to get out of town but there was no money and I didn't have no other way. I went over there and sat down in back of the car on the ground. I didn't know who was in the car or how many. I tried to think how to get the car. Then I heard them coming down the road and I figured I'd better hurry. I got up and opened the front door. There was a man and a girl in the front seat smoking cigarettes. I told him I had a gun which I didn't. I said he should get in the back seat. Then I told the girl to tie his hands with her belt. She did, but when I tried it I found it was loose. So I took off his belt and tied his hands. Then I drove off. I hadn't decided which way to go so I just thought I'd get them off my trail and drove all over the place. After a while I let the girl drive. She drove for about fifteen minutes and I decided to drive again. I asked the man if his hands were tied too tight and he said no. So then I stopped the car and tied the girl's hands with her belt. I thought I'd get to where I was going and then turn the car back to them. The man suggested I drive the girl home, so I did. Then I drove all the rest of the night and was in the next state by morning. The man slept most of the time. Once I stopped for gas and took the money out of his pocket, but I put the change back in his pocket. We didn't have any trouble and I was happy because I threw them off my trail. In the morning I left the man sleeping in the car which I parked along the road. I got into the next town by walking. It was only a mile or so. When I got there I was arrested right away."

B. E. was born to a lower middle-class family in 1907. He was the second of three boys, and his birth and formative years were without significant incident. The father was a railroad brakeman, an easy-going occasional drinker of fair habits and excellent community reputation. The mother was a typical care-worn but kind-hearted housewife. She was the disciplinarian in the family and her favorite method of punishment was sending the children supperless to bed for both major and minor infractions of the family rules.

B. was sent to school at six and remained until he was twelve. By that time he had completed the seventh grade. Teachers report him as having been a slow but steady worker, rather quiet but somewhat doggedly determined to get his work done properly. He left school to go to work. Employment history is not unusual for a person of average intelligence who lacks schooling and is somewhat ambitionless. He started as an errand boy in a shoe factory, changed to a labor gang on a railroad, became a foreman of a gang, was laid off in a slack period and reverted to a mechanical job in the same shoe factory where his career began.

When B. was twenty-two he married a girl of seventeen because she was pregnant by him and he wished to fulfill his obligations. There was no familial coercion involved; he merely felt it his duty. Until he met this girl he had never had sexual relations with anyone. Four children were born to this union but one died during a local epidemic. Trouble between B. and his wife started in their sixth year of marriage. He claimed she was a poor house-wife, neglected the children, permitted them to run about wet and naked, while she read cheap magazines or went to the movies. They argued frequently and on a few occasions the police were asked to intervene by the neighbors.

In the seventh year of their marriage, B. and his wife separated. She took the children to her parents' home, and B. moved to a hotel. He would visit the children each Sunday and habitually took Sunday dinner with his wife and her family. One Sunday he felt ill after his dinner and returned to his room sooner than usual. The next day he came down with the grippe. He states: "I sweated so bad I began to figure that my wife had given me something when I ate at her place the day before. I began to feel certain that my wife had given me something to get rid of me. I felt that the doctor was helping her to get rid of me. Then I began to think that my father was helping her too." When he recovered somewhat, B. moved to his parental home, which he never left in the ensuing weeks except to go to work. His parents tell of him as being very nervous and distraught at this time. He would spend hours adding up his price tabs for piece work he had done, and would refuse to go out. When his wife came to visit him at the invitation of his parents, B. would not let her in the house. Some time later one of his children fell ill and B. insisted that the child be cared for by his mother. When his wife came to see the child, B. refused to admit her. His father tried to persuade him to let his wife visit the sick child. B. turned on his father, shouting that he (the father) and his wife were conspiring to poison him, that no doctor could save him now. As a result of this outburst and his behavior in general, he was committed to a state hospital. Here he was uncommunicative, sometimes combative, insisting his food was being poisoned. After six months, during which his condition improved only slightly, B. was paroled from the state hospital on the insistence of his family. He remained at large, living with his parents, for some two years. During this time he was sullen, displayed a short and nasty temper, and refused to see his wife but visited his children.

On a spring morning some two years and three months after his discharge from the hospital, B. entered his father-in-law's home by way of a back window. He later said he was looking for his sister-in-law because he had been told by a "vision" upon awakening that morning that she was maltreating his children.

He planned to "get even" with her by "beating her up." "I wanted to give her a scare so I brought along a monkey wrench with me and a butcher knife. I was going to scare her good for hurting my kids." Fortunately, his father-in-law and brother-in-law were awake and heard B. climbing the stairs. They ran after him and after a struggle disarmed him. B. managed to escape. He wandered about for three days, always apprehensive and believing "they" were after him. By "they" he meant not only his family but the "visions" which impelled him to attempt his attack on his sister-in-law. When he stole the car and kidnapped the young couple he was trying to evade "them."

A. N. is the only son of hardworking parents who have always farmed for a living. Nothing is known of his life as an infant and child. His parents are uncommunicative and have refused always to give the authorities and officials who have approached them any information. They are, apparently, very much ashamed of their son, first because he has been confined in an "insane asylum," and again because he is serving a twenty-year sentence for housebreaking and assault.

A. went to school in a rural setting in Vermont. He did well except for his inclination to be somewhat of a bully in his relations with other children. He got into numerous fights and dominated the entire school because of his great size and strength. At eleven he quit to go to work in a local mill. At sixteen he got a job with a bakery and seemed to like this work very well. Presently, however, he seemed to be growing bored, became sloppy and careless in his assignments, and was fired. He then joined the Marines and served sixteen months in training and foreign service. At twenty-two he was honorably discharged. Arriving by ship in New York, he immediately obtained employment in a machine shop. He worked steadily but seemed unfriendly to his fellow workers and made extravagant claims regarding his hidden "powers" whenever he found an attentive ear. After some six months at this job, he appeared one day in the foreman's office and told him to shut off the power, that he had just received a message directing him to provide power to the machines by touching them with his bare hands. It was obvious to this foreman that something was wrong, and he called the police who removed A. to the state hospital. Here he was kept for nine months and then discharged for lack of space as "somewhat improved, no longer actively hallucinating." Upon his release, A. found employment with a delivery company, driving a truck. Late one afternoon he parked his truck outside a suburban home, attempted to force the door and, failing this, broke a window through which he entered the house. There was no one at home at the time. He smashed one radio in the living room and ran through the place apparently seeking other radios to destroy. During his search the master of the house arrived, struggled with A., but was subdued by him. However, the home owner noted the truck in which A. drove off. He communicated with the police, and A. was apprehended. In spite of his state hospital record, with which the court was presented by the lawyer it had appointed to represent A., the young man, who was now twenty-four, was sentenced and remanded to prison.

It was immediately observed that A. was psychotic. He claimed that he had to destroy all radios and television sets because from now on his body was to be used for broadcasting and receiving purposes. Questioned regarding his offense, he claimed that the house he entered contained radios which operated on his wavelength and he had been instructed to destroy them. He was concerned mainly with hallucinations and delusions relating to his body. He believed he was "a system of dials and knobs that the world must tune in on if they want the true message." He was in contact with spirits, heard or "received" voices from "the other side," had "X-ray eyes which can see all over the world and through everything." "I can transport myself in a flash through the air anywhere in the universe. My mind is television and through me the world of the spirits and this world keep in touch. I can cure all disease through touching the places with my hand. All power for machines and everything goes through me." Angels directed his actions. He feared and hated all mechanical things, was suspicious of his physician's stethoscope. Although he never married he claimed to have a wife. She was "a spirit wife. I constructed her and a child in eight hours and twenty minutes. I made this child by injecting the holy spirit into my wife by the light. It (the child) is the smartest thing in the world."

A. has never recovered, although all known forms of therapy have been used with him.

In passing fashion we have reviewed the motivation of criminal behavior. This chapter and the one preceding have discussed the ways in which certain disorders and deficiencies in personality structure act as predisposants to crime. We have argued that the primary consideration is the disorder or deficiency, not the fact of a legal trespass. We move on now to a consideration of a general personality type, the possessors of which contribute a gross share to the total arithmetic of criminosis.

# 9. Psychopathy and Crime, I

THERE is a type of behavior disorder which expresses itself particularly in the social sphere and which interferes with the ability of the person so afflicted to engage in satisfactory social relationships and activities. Numerous names have been suggested for this illness—constitutional psychopathic inferiority, moral imbecility, semantic dementia, and endless others. All these seek to describe an individual who is a chronic rebel without a cause, a disrupter, a flouter, and a social hazard of the first magnitude. He is the one whose latent aggressions are played upon and mobilized by the rabble-rouser. He is the one who commits the daring and dangerously hostile acts which make banner headlines for the press. He is the one who returns time after time to prison and for whom all the elaborate and fancy equipage of the modern institution of custody·is so much fluff. He is also the one who makes gray the hairs of wardens and keepers. We shall call him the "psychopath" or "the psychopathic personality."

Psychopathic personality is a social disorder, its various signs and symptoms acting to unsuit the individual for ordinary life among other members of the community. Such signs usually resolve to a constellation of personal qualities which reflect the opposite of the characteristics in demand by the culture. So the psychopath may show traits which would be apt and even highly desirable at another time and in another place; but in our day and given our peculiar culture, he is a veritable social abortion. There was a time when the American culture

151

could and did have a place for psychopaths where they might work out their aggressions in a manner that was not particularly harmful. This was during the days when our frontiers and boundaries were yet unfixed, when the horizons were unexplored, when each man could be convinced that the millenium awaited him beyond the next hill. But now that an agglutination of our psychological and physical setting has been accomplished, the hostility and aggression which formerly were exhausted against limitless and unbounded horizons is turned on itself and plays hob with our institutions.

Psychopaths are characterized chiefly by an inability to await the normal satisfaction of their intimate needs and desires. They obey every whim and fancy which occurs to them at any time. They are impulsive and restraint-free, allowing allegiance only to the wish of the moment, and bending every energy and talent to satisfying the overpowering urgings which arise upon the most minimal of stimulations. It seems almost that the cohesiveness of ordinary human performing, the determinative aspect of behavior, the quality which holds the "normal" person to the dull routine of daily life, which leads him to accept as necessary the progression of his affairs from point to point as he aims toward a goal or fulfills a life-plan—that all these are foreign to the psychopath. He wants satisfaction, and his extravagant, often criminal behavior is the way in which he gets it.

To aid him in his all-powerful wish for immediate satisfaction, he is provided with an intelligence of a different order than that of most of us. It is the kind which appears to a clinician or therapist as somehow more animal. It does not include comprehension of factors which enable men to live in groups, and it does not provide the foresight and understanding which serve as a brake or control on behavior. And beyond and above the peculiar intelligence which he shows, and which deflects every known psychometric device, the psychopath seems endowed by nature for a predatory social role. He is usually lithe and agile; when tapped, his great bodily systems show measurable differences between him and his fellows, which would make for hair-trigger action. He is poised and ready for aggression, because he lacks the inhibitions usually imposed upon the body by a controlling intelligence and an unstunted superego.

That the superego of the psychopath is stunted and immature is revealed by the analytical studies that have been made of this personality type. It appears invariably that, buried beneath the overlay of the years, there is a rejection of the father-image; and since it is usually the father through whom the culture is absorbed, the tenets and guidelines, the prohibitions and injunctions, are never incorporated into the personality. The personality is traumatized before the oedipal conflict has been worked through, and forever after the father (hence society) is regarded as an enemy. Moreover, since in every case the threat of castration is present, the attitude toward those who come later to assume the parental guise (the police, the courts, the prison officials) is heavy with vengefulness and perennially prepared for attack. In addition, the psychopath is burdened with guilt for the parricidal and incestuous fancies that plague him unremittingly. Because of this he seeks punishment, goes out of his way to meet it, and does so with a spirit of daring and challenge.

Psychiatrists, psychologists, and sociologists have written about the psychopath for years. Rarely does the investigator encounter agreement not alone upon the name and classification to give to this errant personality, but even upon the signs by which he betrays himself. At the moment of this writing there are on the writer's desk five bound volumes of summaries and abstracts relating to the psychopath. Most of these thousands of references deal with attempts to paint a portrait of the disorder. Let us now try to combine the essential elements of these many disparate portraits into a broad canvas which will show clearly the main features of the type with which we are concerned. It is necessary that we come to know him not alone because he is responsible for so much of crime, but as well because it is his face we see in the socially betrayed, frustrated, exploited mass that our inadequate social system has fastened upon us; and it is his face which becomes the face of the awful Leader who rides to power by awakening the latent psychopathy among the disinherited.

The male or female psychopathic personality maintains a defective relationship with the community. He is uninterested in the welfare of others and unsympathetic to the aims of peaceful communal life. From the earliest age he has rejected society and with it his obligations to it, although it is characteristic that he expects from it the instantaneous gratification of his rip-tidal wants. The goals which he pursues are not and cannot be socially acceptable, since it is a fact that satisfaction in a culture such as ours is predicated upon gradual development and proof of achievement. But the psychopath cannot wait, cannot pace the treadmill of dull routine occasionally enlivened by bright promise or accomplishment which is the lot and fate of other mortals. He rejects constituted authority since it—no matter what form it takes—harks back to and evokes poignantly the bitter hatred of the father and the triangular drama of infancy. Never having gone in his psychosexual development beyond the pre-oedipal stage, for the life that remains to him until some glandular quiescence is achieved his legacy is a chaotic sexual existence. The sex life of the psychopathic species is adventitious, non-selective, transient. Because a rapport, a communal and fellow feeling, is impossible to him, and because his drive is governed solely by a burning wish for satisfaction, the sex act is, with him, a purely biological event, lacking preliminaries or paraphernalia.

Its consummation transpires at white heat, and the object of the event is a partner not of choice but of convenience. So the partner may be male or female, it does not matter; and the act may be usual or unusual in quality, it does not matter. All that matters is satisfaction.

The psychopath does not respond appropriately so far as emotional expression is concerned. He is cool and detached: the stereotypes which in most of us evoke expressions of joy or sorrow, sympathy or disgust, fail to awaken similar responses in him. And he does not understand anything about himself, lacks insight into his motivations, or, more correctly, refuses to admit to consciousness the truth about himself. Apart from a stunted superego, he shows an ego which has never crystallized to a point where it is capable of objective self-regard: it is dwarfed and twisted, pregnant with the hates and preferences of early life, and driven by id-urgings.

Curiously, the psychopath *knows* what belongs to right and what belongs to wrong, but he cannot *feel* the difference. Whereas in most of us the conviction of right and wrong awakens a feeling-tone, with him it does not. So he verbalizes about right and he knows what is proper; but he is in the position of those of us who stand in puzzled bewilderment before an abstract work of art. It is there, and we accept it; but we do not feel and, hence, cannot understand it.

The psychopath is a wanderer, a nomad, a bird of passage, restless and rootless. No community, except perhaps the rapidly disappearing frontier type, makes an appeal to him. He forever seeks his infancy, the time when he was secure in the love of a parent. And he forever runs away from the image of himself that he finds in every place. Rejecting communal life, and because of his asocialism by it rejected, he cannot have a home and a resting place. Moreover, his egoism is strong and assertive because his development has been halted in the megalomanic stage of infancy, and like the child he demands unceasingly that he be propitiated and served. He cannot accept the responsibility for his deeds or misdeeds. He rationalizes without end, attempting to deflect censure and disapproval, projecting his faults and deficiencies upon others. Everyone is for him a candidate for exploitation, and he randomly and ruthlessly makes demands upon all who come within his compass.

There are many other signs and symptoms of psychopathic personality. The psychopath possesses unsocial habit systems. He demonstrates a persistent failure to profit from ordinary life experiences, and in this resembles the feeble-minded. Emotionally, as has been indicated, he is immature, unstable, and inappropriate. There is no permanency in his emotional ties. Stubbornness, irascibility, vengefulness, and vindictiveness are key characterological features. He is unpredictable, inconsistent, and impulsive. He is lacking in sympathy, suspicious, ungrateful, indifferent to the sufferings of others even when he is the cause of their misery. The list is truly inexhaustible. One has only to think of those characteristics and traits which make for peaceful communal living; the opposite of these is what the psychopathic personality manifests.

How does the psychopath get that way? From all evidence it would seem that psychopathy is a condition toward which an individual is predisposed biologically, but which is not realized unless set off by crucial precipitating events deriving from the life experience. Research with physiological registering apparatus indicates a fundamental functional difference between psychopaths and other persons. They show differences when their brain-wave patterns are examined, when their gross systemic responses are measured. But it must not be lost sight of that these differences may *follow* and not *precede* the appearance of the psychopathic syndrome. Moreover, the response of the psychopath, the adjustment he makes to our society, is primitive. This would suggest the mal- or dysfunctioning of those higher centers of the brain which are supposed to control the lower centers (which in turn mediate the more basic drives and motives). The neurophysiological argument is strengthened by the observation that psychopaths tend to be young in appearance in spite of their actual ages. They somehow retain the firm musculature, the trim body-build, the sprightly gait. However, this too may come from the style of the life they lead and their inability to accept responsibility, to worry over consequences. Finally, there are few old psychopaths. Somehow the gaudily-hued crazy quilt of their existence takes on a more somber coloration as they advance in years. Some are killed in brawls and accidents, but to those who survive, the years bring relative sobriety.

Analytic work with psychopaths invariably discloses a few common developmental features. Perennially there is the unresolved oedipal drama and the strange and rotten fruit of father-rejection based on intense and hateful rivalry. With this there is a failure to mount and bridle the horrendous anxiety of castration, conceived of as punishment for incest-wishes toward the mother and death desires toward the father. All of the early life is based on the rivalry theme, and this energetically interferes with the usual developmental progression through the usual stages.

The social conditions making for psychopathy are liberally provided by our culture, soaked as it is in the acid of underprivilege and wholesale exploitation. The events which traumatize the growing child and thus fix as in an antique daguerreotype his psychological development in the pre-oedipal stage, are provided liberally by a system that encourages social parasitism at both ends of the scale, that exalts the few above the many, that raises to godhead the hollow idol of "individualism," that battens upon inter-class rivalry, that maintains its hold by artificially creating minority groups and seizing upon every minute excuse to prevent social cohesion and true community.

Psychopaths commit crimes because their egos are thoroughly saturated with impulsions and attitudes of a criminal kind and because their superegos are stunted and inadequate. The standards and unverbalized contracts which we mutually create and observe for our own and others' salvation are foreign to these aberrative personalities. Not for them are our codes and precepts. They know only the crying need of id, and they are equipped to obey its insistencies without pause. Hervey Cleckley, author of the brilliant *Mask of Sanity*, argues for inclusion of psychopathy among the psychoses. As it is, he points out, we are at the mercy of the psychopaths, for neither law nor medicine conceives of the condition as of psychotic proportions. Hence, we cannot detain them in institutions for treatment and study, cannot declare them insane and so protect society from them. And yet, psychopathy, like any psychosis, constitutes an involvement of the whole personality.

When psychopaths come to prison they create additional difficulties. Although, as this writer has demonstrated in his *Rebel Without a Cause*, they can be treated individually by an analytical technique, there is available neither the time nor the personnel for such a program on the wide scale necessary. So they remain, both individually and collectively, disciplinary hazards. They are the ones whom the custodial officers most fear, who attempt escape by every wild means conceivable, who foster riots, who flout regulations, who engage in cutting scrapes, who reject every friendly advance, who practice and cause to be practiced the most vicious forms of homosexuality.

Some institutions pretend to have "solved" the problem of the psychopath by varying empirical methods. They have put their faith—following this by dubious statistics—in that old saw about "busy fingers," and have wasted fortunes of the people's money in "vocational" training for psychopaths, or have constructed imposing edifices for their safe-keeping. They have prated widely and unendingly about "treatment," meaning by this the day-to-day, trial-and-error, problem-to-problem management of recalcitrant inmates. This is so much whistling in the dark. Psychopaths can be treated, if at all, only by the systematic uncovering of the dynamic factors and events which precipitated the condition. Those in whom the attitudes have crystallized and the patterns have jelled are beyond any therapy. For these there is but one solution: recognition of the condition as a form of psychosis and subsequent removal from the community for detention purposes alone. As for the overall cure of psychopathy, this rests with the cure of our society. The crimes which psychopaths commit reflect the symptoms of their disorder. They are impulsive acts, motivated deeply, and designed to achieve instantaneous gratification of urges. As once they ran to horse stealing, so now they run to auto theft, and someday soon they will run to airplane thievery. Other acts are violent, such as bank robbery, assault, and rape. They love weapons, which give them assurance of potent sexuality and compensate for the abiding unconscious conviction of castration. Their acts are hostile—they are the cop-killers, the hirelings of groups organized for murder, the "torpedo" boys. They are also the muscle-men, the storm-troopers, the heavy-booted vanguard of the fascist horde, the truncheon-wielding sadists of the concentration camps.

The menace of this disorder should be broadcast from the roof-tops rather than neatly niched between the pages of a case-book on psychopathology or a textbook on criminology. The Leaders, whom we in our tenuous security deride as crack-pots, have found the formulae which awaken the latent psychopathy in most of us. They have uncovered the primeval symbols which arouse the resentment and the aggression beneath the skin. Armed thus, they can mobilize the million-footed golem for their aims of conquest, awaken the essential criminal who will gladly do the dirty task of shattering the temple of our security and, like Samson, pull down about our heads the pillars of our social edifice. Such is the menace of this disorder which contributes so generously to the problem of crime.

In order to understand the psychopath in his role as criminal, the following case is presented in more than usual detail. The case makes apparent, too, the deleterious effect of psychopathy upon the families of those so classified.

E. H., a twenty-two-year-old white male, made the following statement when apprehended for his crime: "I saw this car standing on the street. It had the keys in it so I got in and started driving to P. I had been drinking all Saturday night and just come out of a bar when I saw the car. I was very drunk and do not remember buying gas or the exact route I took, but I arrived in P. the same evening. Before going into P. I stopped at a tavern and bought a quart of rum. Near the tavern I bought five gallons of gas. The attendant charged me fifty cents a gallon because I had no ration coupons.

"Just as I drove into P. I remembered a friend, Al, who had been in another prison with me and whose home was in F. So I turned around and drove back to F., but when I got there I suddenly remembered that Al had been inducted into the Army a few weeks before. I then turned again and drove on to P. I went to see a friend of my sister's and her husband. I stayed only about an hour. I told them the car belonged to a friend. Then I decided to go to visit my folks in the neighboring state. I got there after driving all day and night. Two days later I was arrested by the state police for possession of a stolen automobile."

An additional postscript to the story of his crime is contained in a notation made by Federal investigators to the effect that the records of the company for which E. H. worked indicated that he had not reported since the day before the car had been stolen. It also states that during his trip to P. he had tried to sell the car to a gas station proprietor but could not produce title. However, he sold extra tires, the heater, radio and miscellaneous equipment. During this escapade he was wearing (illegally) the uniform of a soldier in the U. S. Army, and on a few occasions tried to borrow money "to get back to camp." It is also of interest to note that while he was out on bond he stole three additional autos and shot a soldier near his home town.

E. H. was born in a semi-urban southern town to rather elderly parents. As the youngest of seven children, he was raised mainly by an older sister who occasionally had to call in the father for the purpose of administering punishment when E. misbehaved. The father was a pious, hard-working, rather taciturn man of excellent community standing; his mother, a typical over-burdened housewife whose large family and home occupied all her time, was a minor factor in the family life. E. had an uneventful childhood, although his male parent writes that he seemed to get into "more scrapes and troubles than any other kid of his crowd." At an early age he showed a disinclination for schooling, was often truant, displayed tantrum behavior when he was forced by his father to attend church or Sunday School. At fourteen he left school for good, having completed the seventh grade and never having achieved more than just passing marks. His teachers report that this was not because he was dull; as a matter of fact, he was thought to be bright and clever. One of them writes: "E. could do the work, all right, but he never seemed to find anything to awaken his interest. He was my most severe disciplinary problem and really uncontrollable except when given his own way." After leaving school E. went to work in his father's store. He was not needed there, but he insisted on learning the trade and more or less bullied his parents into taking him on. Within a month the intense interest he had demonstrated in the business evaporated, and E. took to leading the unproductive chaotic life he was to follow from that time forward. At this time his major interest was in dating girls, drinking, and "going to the show." He frequented "juke joints" at all hours, did only what he wished to do, and became involved with the law almost weekly. During one of his alcoholic bouts—he soon came to consume about a pint a day—he married a fourteen-year-old girl of poor reputation whom he picked up in a "juke joint." They lived together only a few weeks.

The story of E.'s social and legal conflicts makes monotonous reading. In the wake of each, however, is his poor, bewildered family, hopeless against the overriding forces and the uncontrollable impulsions that drive their youngest son from one shameful episode to another. Rather than engage upon the weary recital, let us instead have recourse to the psychiatric summary of the case as prepared by one of this country's outstanding authorities on psychopathic personality, especially since this report (quoted with the permission of the psychiatric specialist, Dr. Hervey Cleckley) illuminates the whole problem.

"This young man's history is one of long and amazingly persistent maladjustment. It is reported that he very frequently was truant from school. No advice and no punishment seemed to influence him. During childhood he frequently stole objects for which he had no particular use. It is reported that his father was generous with him and furnished him sufficient money for his needs. Despite this he stole his father's chickens, sold them at stores and picked up just anything at hand, often swapping it for something of little or no value. For many years he had lied without compunction but with utter equanimity and often with very convincing detail, occasionally boasting of long periods in prisons where he has never been and other experiences which are entirely unreal. He often drinks and even one or two drinks, according to reports, cause him to be disagreeable and to start altercations and fights. He often wanders off and remains for several days or a week and his family only know his whereabouts when he is thrown into jail after some disorder. He began stealing automobiles at the age of fourteen. Even though his father gave him an automobile of his own, he would park his car and steal another car which he would drive away and sometimes leave in an inaccessible place. After being put on probation following the theft of a car which he drove across the state line, he promptly stole another car and took it to the same place. It was obvious that he would be caught and he was able to foresee the consequences even if perhaps not able to appreciate them in an emotional sense. He was then sent to an institution for special training and care. He was given parole there and almost at once stole another automobile. As a result of this act he was sent to prison where he stayed three years. On being pardoned there, before his term expired, he came home and went to work in a drydock. His employers report that he was remarkably irresponsible. He would quit his job at any time he chose, giving no excuse except that he did not feel like working that day or that hour. Soon after he began the work, he stole another automobile and was put in jail. He kept bemoaning his fate and begging for another chance. He spoke so convincingly and gave such excellent reasons for changing his ways, seemed to understand so deeply and fully the error of his conduct that his father paid money and got him out of jail. Two weeks later he stole another car.

"Reliable information indicates that this man has been arrested perhaps fifty or sixty times and that he would have been arrested several hundred had it not been for his father's intervening at great trouble and expense to himself to shield him from the consequences of his acts. He has forged his father's name to checks dozens of times. On one occasion he struck a man on the head with a piece of iron. Again, after a brawl in a juke joint, he was involved in a minor shooting episode in which another man was injured. On each occasion he showed what appeared to be such genuine remorse, spoke so convincingly of having learned his lesson, that he persuaded his father and other relatives he must have at last gained insight and formed real and adequate intentions of doing better. Each time, however, he returned to his old, antisocial activities without delay.

"On one recent occasion an elderly friend of his father discussed his situation with him at length. The patient promised to behave himself in an exemplary fashion and spoke as the wisest and most contrite of men might speak. He analyzed his past behavior and criticized it perhaps better than an outsider would be able to do. His advisor was very much encouraged and, despite the multitudinous failures in the subject's past, was convinced that surely now E. had learned his lesson thoroughly and would give no further trouble. E. promised to keep regular hours, notify his family of his whereabouts, to stop stealing and forging and drinking. His friend, very hopeful and optimistic, told him goodbye and left him at the front gate of his house. E. did not even go into the house and was not heard from for a week. The news then came from him in jail where he had landed after an unusually ambitious series of thefts, drunken brawling and sordid acts of folly.

"He has apparently never formed any emotional attachment to any other person. He married a girl said to be recognized as a prostitute. He promptly left her but seemed to feel no shame or chagrin about the character of the woman he married or about leaving her. He speaks fluently and sometimes eloquently about his love for his parents and of how much it hurts and distresses him to cause them the trouble and grief he causes them. Those who know him well have finally come to the conclusion, after years of observation, that, despite the excellence of his words, there is little or no actual feeling in his attitude toward those for whom he expresses affection. My own impression of him is entirely in agreement with this opinion. He has never shown any real interest in any work, any hobby or recreation. He hangs around on street corners, mopes about juke joints. When he drinks, he sometimes wanders off into the woods. Drinking does not seem to make him happy or sociable.

"During psychiatric examination E. showed himself at all times well oriented, alert and relevant. He showed no evidence of delusions or of hallucinations. He freely admitted the many thefts of automobiles but other thefts, which he didn't know I had information about, he denied with an appearance of absolute frankness. He spoke as a wise man might speak about his mistakes and expressed the utmost regret and considerable concern about the suffering he had brought on his family. In the direct examination he gave the impression of a sane and quite intelligent young man.

"The diagnosis of this case is very easy to make. He falls into the category of 'psychopathic personality.' His faulty behavior, his apparent inability to learn by experience, his many times repeated acts which get him into serious difficulties are all quite typical of cases so classified according to the official standards of the American Psychiatric Association. Unlike a mental defective, he is able to foresee the consequences of his actions at least in their outer and more objective aspects. He 'knows' that his stealing will lead to his being arrested, but he apparently isn't able to care sufficiently about the consequences, either to himself or others, to refrain. According to our official standards these cases are classified as sane and competent. I believe that to call such a person as E. sane and competent is not only incorrect but absurd. Cases of this sort, hundreds of whom I have examined and whose careers I have followed over long periods, cause more difficulty and more distress than patients with any other type of mental disorder I have encountered. Medical examiners place them in the category of psychopathic personality and do so correctly by our present standards of classification. Since this establishes them as sane and competent, they are dismissed from state psychiatric institutions, or even if they are not dismissed automatically, they are able by law to regain their freedom. On the other hand, the courts are often hesitant to deal with them as normal human beings since it is perfectly obvious even to laymen on the jury that they are by no means normal. The usual result is for such people to be brought into the courts dozens and scores of times and evade serious legal penalties through the intervention of their relatives or by virtue of their mental disorder. They are frequently sent to psychiatric institutions where they are promptly dismissed only to repeat time after time and dozens of times after dozens of times their antisocial acts and their acts which bring harm and difficulty to themselves.

"It is my opinion that these so-called psychopathic personalities, of whom E. is a classical example, should be frankly recognized as serious cases of mental disorder and called without equivocation psychotic (insane) and incompetent. This would make it possible for them to be treated adequately or, at the very least, for society to be protected from them. I have no hesitancy in stating that in my opinion E. is incompetent and psychotic. In this decision I am guided by the facts of his behavior rather than by the traditional definitions of psychosis. He does not have delusions such as a case of dementia praecox who might carry out his antisocial acts or indulge in behavior harmful to himself and offensive to the social group because he hears a voice which he believes is God's voice telling him to do so. The behavior of the patient with dementia praecox who is influenced by delusions and hallucinations which he considers to be valid seems to me more rational than the behavior of such a man as E. who behaves just as inadequately without benefit of the delusions and hallucinations which, in a sense, make the behavior of the case of dementia praecox understandable to all of us and the subject logical and proper. I believe that these cases of so-called psychopathic personality are actually suffering from a true mental disorder. The disorder does not manifest itself in delusions or hallucinations but in a loss of the ability to appreciate or evaluate the consequences of one's acts or the ordinary motives and goals which influence the normal man. They 'know' in words but they cannot feel or experience as other human beings do such human reactions as shame, love, pride, satisfaction, etc. Consequently, they are without adequate restraining or directing influences from within themselves and may carry out any act however foolish, however detrimental to themselves as social beings, however cruel or tragic, without remorse or real regret. They cannot be taught either by wise advice, by medical treatment or by punishment to find a better way of adaptation, because the motives and goals that matter to the normal person do not matter to them even though they express them glibly and sometimes quite convincingly in words. The words, however, are without meaning for them and do not refer to any real attitudes or resolutions or even serious regrets. I believe that all people of this sort should be placed in institutions and kept as long as necessary to enable them to adjust when they are released. To my knowledge, there are no public institutions at present available for them. I know of no more urgent need in the field of psychiatry and of penology than the need for proper and adequate provision for such cases as E.

"It is difficult to express an opinion on these cases under present conditions. If the subject could be committed to a psychiatric institution and held there as long as he needs to be held, I would regard this as much more appropriate than for him to be sentenced to a prison term. No matter how long he is sentenced to prison or remains in prison, he will, I am confident, continue to behave when he is released just as he has been behaving in the past. If he is sent to a psychiatric hospital, I think it probable that he will succeed in establishing himself, on the basis of our present standards, as sane and competent. If this should lead to his release, he will almost certainly continue his antisocial behavior."

# 10. Psychopathy and Crime, II

THERE is perhaps no more important problem in the whole field of criminology as it relates to the individual criminal than that of psychopathy; and it is this writer's personal opinion that there exists hardly any social problem of similar magnitude. Psychopaths have termite-like invaded the structure of our civilization, bearing with them, as an insect might bear, the germ of a social Black Death. Only recently has the condition forced itself upon the attention of planners and thinkers, and then only because there has come about an as yet dim and remote apprehension of what the disorder implies. In civilian life the psychopaths are lacking in communal spirit and radically opposed to community welfare, presenting a ready and pliable weapon for the first demagogue or Man on a White Horse. The havoc they wreak and the cost of their depredations are tremendous.

In order that they may be recognized for what they are, and that the readers of this book may obtain some familiarity with this malignancy, the following histories have been collected and are presented without comment. They were all prepared by psychopaths whom the author either knew intimately or treated. The first case is intended to serve as a warning regarding those to whom we parents entrust our growing children; the second illustrates the intractability of the psychopath in spite of all efforts to contain him and channelize his energies through the so-called sociological approach; the third is interesting for the typical history it presents and for its portrayal of the psychopath's philosophy; and the fourth is most provocative in its presentation of a somewhat sophisticated and older psychopath who employed his talents in a different manner from those in our other cases. The original manner of presentation and the spelling have been retained; only identifying data have been removed.

## MY HISTORY

"PATERNAL GRANDFATHER, sturdy Welsh manufacturer, descendant of first settlers in Virginia colony. Lived to be seventy, died throat goiter. Had 3 sons, 3 daughters.

"FATHER. Youngest son, pampered, indulgent. Univ. Grad. athlete—lady's man. Married my mother at 24. I was born when he was 26. Weak character.

"PATERNAL GRANDMOTHER. Died 1903. Tuberculosis. Scotch lady of Victorian type.

"MATERNAL GRANDFATHER. Farmer—good farm—Dutch descent. Was a Yankee in Rebel territory in War. An independent—didn't give a damn what other people thought of him as long as he felt he was doing what was right. Died 1901. Forbid marriage of my mother and father. Mother married father one month after grandfather's death.

"MOTHER. Spirited tomboy—rode binder and horses, made hay —worked in fields until 14 when she began to take on 'proportions' and grandfather felt her place was in the house. Always wanted to be a NURSE but frowned on by G. F.

"MATERNAL GRANDMOTHER. Finest of early French aristocracy. Had unlimited courage. Assumed full control of 400 acre farm on grandfather's death and ran it successfully until her death, 89½ years old. Born on same day as Thos. E. Edison. Remarkable Christian leader in community.

"MOTHER AND FATHER. Married in 1901. Father had serious abdominal operation in Sept. after I was born and began using morphine. Fighting back and forth and frequent separations due to the drug habit. Definite separation when I was six. My earliest memories father being sick and mother always nagging. Mother determined to be a *Nurse* which had been denied her by her father. Mother had had hemorrhages when I was born. Hemorrhaged from nearly midnight until nearly noon next day. Didn't know anything about sexual relations at marriage. Shocked on honeymoon, wedding night when father attempted intercourse for from her farm training only thought of intercourse with Breeding and she wasn't anxious for children immediately.

"CHILDHOOD. Went to live with Foster Parents—who were childless at six—mother kept 3rd class P. O. in small village. At 8 suddenly decided to take me and go to K., where she felt I would get better schooling and she could do practical nursing until she could enter training. Left without telling Father good-bye—that made deep impression at the time because I was fonder of father's people than Mother's and started deep-rooted hatred and get-even spirit toward my Mother.

"Had many fights in School. Put back a grade first thing because I hadn't had Music and Drawing in native Schools. Foster parents moved to K. at Christmas—they influenced my Mother to make this move. When they came North started me in Episcopal Choir and made full-fledged SISSY out of me. I rebelled but was always threatened with, 'You don't want to go back to R., do you, and grow up ignorant?' The town life and its advantages did appeal to me so I tried to make the best of it.

"Developed early habits of dishonesty. Would cheat on change from grocery store, steal bakery tickets, gyp on Sunday School collections, when given a dime would only put in a nickel. Was *forced* to attend Sunday School regularly, taken when sick for attendance record, had 10 yrs. perfect attendance record from 10 to 18, in summer often hauled 10 to 15 miles so I wouldn't miss S. S.

"Worshipped foster mother—liked her even better than own Mother but hated with intense *hate* foster father. Too strict a disciplinarian. Whipped me often with rubber syringe hose when I would run away which would be often—wander away to play without telling anyone where I was going. Developed an interest in sex early. Had complete intercourse when I was six and was quite promiscuous from 8 to 13 in K. Mother went into training at my age of 12 (age 36 for her). I often secretly wanted to have intercourse with her and would steal down steps from attic where I slept to watch her undress. Had periscope fixed up so I could watch her in NUDE. She had a marvelous figure. Often felt she and foster father had illicit sexual relations as she never was seen out with other men. I was caught at 6 having intercourse with girl 6 by father. Again at 9 with girl 8. At 10 with boy 10 —mutual sodomy. At 13 with girl 10 (threatened with State Reform School). Took active part in Liberty Loan Campaign. Designed a winning Liberty Loan poster and sold over $50,000 in Liberty Bonds in one hour. Early became *bright boy* in class, led class in marks from 5th grade on into High School.

"ADOLESCENCE. Forced to join Presbyterian Church at 12 when I wanted to join Episcopal church at 13. Told my grandparents who were Presbyterians from way back would not hear to it. Wasn't permitted to play football because it might spoil my voice for the choir. (Had Soprano Solo voice at this time). Wasn't permitted to go to Y M C A because boys didn't wear bathing suits. Sex was BAD—taboo, in slant of foster father. Saw less and less of mother since she was in training as nurse and I was left in foster mother's hands with foster father to administer punishment and see that I kept garden weeded and lawn free from dandelions.

"Only ESCAPE was frequent run away excursion to G. where I saw all the Musical Comedies,—Ziegfeld Follies, Chu-Chin-Chow, Passing Show, etc. oftentimes with other art inclined classmates from H. S.

"About this time started stealing more—sometimes $1 out of pocket of step-father, once got $5. Spent summers at (p) grandfather's where I had first a pony then a horse to ride. Started these summer trips alone when I was 10. These trips inflated my ego and were only month of year I lived for. The bars were down—did as I pleased—could always get from Grandfather all the spending money I wanted—Spent summers riding, fishing, exploring caves and sex. Used to run a Harem in a Haymow and always was able to get more girls than boys as boys seemed naturally shy. When 13 and 14 regularly had intercourse with 16 year old Irish house girl sleeping with her one or two nights a week.

"Started working in a foundry as pattern boy at 14 and made $2 a day five days and $1 for half a day Saturday. Always went to a ballgame Sat. P. M.s during summer. Was hurt at 14 when cousins were sent to Military school as Cadets and I had to go back to that *damned* Yankee H. S. Father had married when I was 14 to a Nurse in one of the Sanatoriums where he had gone for Drug Cure. I resented this *deeply*. Always wanted he and mother to make up. Felt abnormal that I couldn't have a Mother and Dad like other kids and a home and a kid brother or two.

"Became a real little REBEL from 14 on. Entered H. S. this year. Seduced Homosexually. Made good marks in everything but Algebra. Hated Algebra teacher, everything that happened in class was blamed on me—all the pranks. Rich lumberman's son who was my all time adolescent enemy, with an innocent baby face, was all the time getting me into trouble, and getting away with things himself.

"HIGH SCHOOL. Stole some 50 football season tickets at H. S. during my freshman year and sold them $1 each. (reason for stealing: Had no allowance and travelled with crowd that always had money in their pockets for drugstore treats and movies). Succeeded in sneaking them out of Principal's desk when I was sent down to his office—when sent out of algebra class. Started H. S. at 15. Had some talent in Art and Dramatics. Both of these discouraged by Foster Father. He wanted me to be a track and football star. I like track but didn't have the advantage of knowledge of basketball all the kids at H. S. had picked up at the Y M. About this time got caught with Sex with 13 year old neighbor's girl. They were all for sending me to Reform School but I brought out the fact that half the football team were *making* her.

"Was not permitted to play Football at H. S. Foster parents afraid of my getting hurt. Developed an interest in Radio, Photography, Arts and Crafts, and Dramatics. Radio in infancy then. Was able to sell some $100 worth of Hand Painted Christmas Cards, Parchment Shades (which were then coming into vogue) and enameled Bird Cages. At Easter time made $25 off of Hand Painted Easter Cards in Water Color. Summer I was 16 after finishing Soph. year went to R. Learned to drive a car, and was a *Big Shot*. Of course I was more popular than the local village boys. By this time I was an *expert* on SEX matters having devoured everything that was in the Medical Books my Mother had and having brought a volume on Obstetrics South with me that year. The summer was cut short by 'Infantile Epidemic' and I was driven back 'under cover' to be back in time for school.

"Began a regular 'racketeer' career that year. Had 500 extra football season tickets printed that were duplicates of regular tickets and were able through 2 assts. to dispose of all of them.

"This financed a social career, frequent trips and presents for my *first love*. When I found she was a Catholic shortly after Christmas I dropped her like a hot brick. By this time I was going to G. Saturdays for a regular Art Class for H. S. Students and always managed to see a Road Show or a Movie in the afternoon.

"Next summer (17) I really went to town in the little village. I had a car to drive and was out with girls every night. Would chase a girl until I had intercourse with her then drop her and start after another. Worked during day in foundry for $2.50 a day. Played baseball Saturday P. M.'s Went to T. or F. on Saturday nights. Was able to negotiate with Mil Acad. for a scholarship provided I would pay for uniforms. However before the summer was over I incurred the emnity of my uncle by buying contraceptives for his two sons (15 and 17) who were rather shy and afraid to go into the Drug Store and ask for them. When they got caught with them in their possession I of course got the blame.

"Got kicked out of M. A. for bad check in January which I had gotten in a POKER game and I being a Cadet of Honor wouldn't be a Stool Pigeon and tell *how* I came to have this check. Just wouldn't talk. As a result I was kicked out. Then I got the bright idea of going to L. some 50 miles away and wiring the kid's father for $50 to come on saying that his kid had gotten kicked out of school. Unfortunately the day I left the kid's father arrived East for a visit and I got caught in a trap and was sent to Reform School for three years.

"Here I really became a *Rebel*. I had too much education for my contemporaries. Only one other lad was in H. S. out of 400. There were no grades beyond 8. I was too soft for the hard manual labor that was demanded of me. As I was well developed and beyond schooling I was sent into woods to clear forests in winter zero weather and hoe corn in summer. Neither appealed to me. I ran away seven times, never caught, never went home, mother always knew where I was—. Was in the school only 13 out of 36 months actual time. Grandfather died leaving me out of will entirely because I had disgraced the family. All other grandchildren got $7500.

"YOUNG MANHOOD. While in the Reform School Mother finished Graduate work in Public Health Nursing and moved to enable me to start anew when I came out of the Industrial School. She had gone in debt $400 squaring my troubles in H. S. In K. and various scrapes that came to light after my arrest and being sent to Reform School.

"I came out of the Ind. School, two months before my 21st birthday. Immediately got position as Office Boy at $44 per month. In three months time was making $60 and in Sept. was getting $72 per month.

"In summer sent for credits from High and after getting their transcript filled in enough credits (forgery) to let me enter College's Evening School of Business Administration. Out of class of 80 I was elected President and had highest averages for freshman work. During year I had entered a Pub. Acctg. firm at salary of $25 a week in Dec. and kept position until end of season April 1st when firm placed me in Acctg. Dept. of Life Ins. Co. at same salary. Carried 24 hrs. credit first year at college. However, wanted to go to regular college full time and one of the Board of X. U. was an executive of the Life Ins. Co. so he helped me obtain a state scholarship and went up there in Sept.

"However, in June I had gone on a week-end camping trip with scouts from our church and on the trip had Homo Sexual relations with the Kid Brother (15) of a girl I was going with (amounted to MUTUAL MASTURBATION). We were caught by the Scout Master and reported to the Pastor of the Church (Presbyterian). He instead of reasoning with me, asked my resignation from Sunday School, Christian Endeavor Society, and asked me not to come to church unless I came with my Mother. When I left for X. U. he wrote the Supt. of that Institution and asked him if I was the type they were offering SCHOLAR–SHIPS to and of course I never entered. I was so humiliated, my ego so badly squashed that I never came back but went to Fla. where the land boom was at its height.

"Through one of the Mil. Acad. Cadets whose father owned a big development I obtained a position as Asst. Sports Director of a big Country Club. I had charge of Swimming and Sports for Juniors including Tennis and Archery. Made $200 a month at club. Was soon running around in a Chrysler roadster with fast younger set and fell hard for P. Y. She threw me over for a big-time Real Estate promoter, who was in the millionaire class.

After this, being pretty well disillusioned by the gold-diggers in Womanhood my sex interest went back to boys—Juniors at the Club. Being a hot climate youngsters fall for anything of that kind pretty easily.

"Stayed here until following fall when boom busted and I came back North with $4000 I had saved. However, during Christmas I had worked in P. O. as an extra from 4 to 12 and made about $120 a month (mail was so heavy then). Coming back to R. I stayed there during fall coaching a midget football team and taking an active part in organization and management of a Children's Theatre. My Ministerial *enemy* stopped this work in Feb. and I left town for New York City.

"First job,—bus boy in Automat, while waiting for Theatre to open March 5 where I had obtained a position as Asst. Drillmaster for the Ushers under a hard-boiled former Marine Sargent. I had the polish that he lacked and I kept this position over 2½ years, installing systems in houses in Brooklyn, Philadelphia, Detroit and St. Louis under supervision. However, I liked N Y and got started in the Stock Market in Wall Street in 1928 during daytime, continuing Theatre interests at night.

"In Wall St. went to the front as Stock Analyst and Statistician and within a year after I entered the Street was making $50 a week. Dropped Theatre and started studying the Harvard Business School's carriculum from notes and tests of one of the younger men in the Statistical Dept. had under the Supervision of the head of the firm who was an old Harvard man himself.

"Stayed with him through the crash when he sold his seat and holdings and went to Europe after placing me with another firm. In the next three years I managed to hold my own and develop a really deep love affair.

"My father died in 1929 of pneumonia sick only four days—left me $1 in his will,—explanation.

"Christmas 1931, my business associate in Wall St. died of pneumonia as suddenly as my father and I lost $40,000 through his death as well as the girl I was engaged to. She was sliding down an old fashioned stair railing and broke her neck and back and died before they got her to the hospital. I was on a Lincoln to Washington's Birthday cruise to Havana and Nassau trying to forget about Dad's and my associate's death so this just about made me feel *Life* was pretty *BITTER* and I started feeling sorry for myself.

"When I first came to N. Y. I had been confirmed in the Epis Church on Palm Sunday, and guess my Faith was all that saved me from SUICIDE. In fact on numerous occasions I set out to wreck my car but never succeeded in doing a good job.

"For the next two years I organized Prep School groups for travel tours, taking first group to Olympics in Los Angeles in 1932 (summer) 43 boys ages 14 to 17.

"Went to Hollywood and Los Angeles about Easter time and I fooled around the Movie Colony trying to make a connection with one of the big companies. Came back East again in Sept. in time for the National Tennis Matches and secured a position tutoring in a wealthy Park Ave. family two boys 11 and 8. Stayed there and on the side organized a Prep Tour to Bermuda following Spring for Easter with 65 boys going down. Had Tennis, Golf, and Swimming competitions.

"Next year I tried it on a bigger scale, went broke, and my financing agent a gambler ran out on me and took $500 in cash with him. Not being able to absorb this amount I took or grabbed $600—$700 in checks—cashed them, took my car and disappeared. Went to Florida where I bought a jockey's contract at Hileah. Took the kid to Dallas (Texas) where I was arrested and charged with moral delinquency of a minor. The charge was dropped. Went to Omaha, Nebr. and finally in August back to Suffolk Downs in Boston where I sold his contract for $2000. I had paid $500 for it. Instead of making good my bad debts when I got my hands on this amount of money I struck out for the West Coast again after lingering in New York.

"Sailed from San Francisco with the Congressional Party that were going to the Phillipines. I had bought a ticket to Hawaii but through connections on the boat managed to get on the Secretarial Staff of the Congressmen and went on to Japan and the Phillipines. Came back with party as far as Honolulu where I begged to be paid off and was—$600 and had had every expense paid while on the trip.

"While in Honolulu tried to sell automobiles near the Army post but was unsuccessful. Someone had me arrested for suspicious person as I was traveling under the name of Ben Arden and they thought I was impersonating a Dartmouth Chap by that name. Left islands on the next boat before F. B. I. had chance to check up and went on to Milwaukee. Here through a connection with a Congressman I got a position as a Statistician at $40 a week. This lasted until arrest in August on present charge.

"Was able to get a three yr. Susp. Sentence but lost job. Back to R. as a Public Acct. Junior until March 1937, when I went as Chief Accountant at $150 a month. Overwork, long hours, hot weather and failure to live up to promised raise to $200 a month made me cocky and finally bonding company in a routine checkup disclosed the Federal Charge and I was OUT like a light.

"Back in R. out of a job in August I started running out to the lake swimming and playing tennis and started having homosexual relations with a youngster. Finally caught with him in my car. Arrest—result 90 days observation after plea of guilty and was permitted to leave the state without the charge going any further.

"Back to N. Y. C. studied at School of Handicrafts for 2 months. Secured position as Occupational Therapy Worker for Men at State Hospital. Taught Weaving, Woodwork, Basketry, Porrter, Horticulture, Leather Tooling, and Carving. Worked there satisfactorily from Apr. 15th to Sept. 1st. In june met young woman patient who had had a nervous breakdown and had been sent to the hospital. Engaged to marry her August 20th. Aug. 12th Supt. informed me he had found out about me being in State Hosp. in R. as a patient and asked for my resignation on Sept. 1. Went ahead and got married in spite of this.

"Secured position as Cottage Parents in juvenile institution with wife. Stayed until Nov. 15 when we both left on account of Health and fact that they too had heard of my previous trouble with kids and I didn't want to be fired.

"Took position as Estate Manager in New York. We left there on Feb. 12 because I couldn't get along with Mr. C. who was a regular old maid who was expecting twice as much work out of my wife and myself as we were hired to do.

"We took our car and went to Florida, leaving car at my Mother's and going by train to Miami. My wife stayed down till Aug. I came back Apr. 1st and started soliciting campers for a Boy's Camp and preparations to open my own private school this fall.

"I had to leave Camp on Aug. 8 because I struck a boy who called me a dirty — — —— and also they had found out about my record. On Aug. 16 my probation period was extended two years and I was given that much more time to pay back some $600 restitution that I had not paid in the three years allotted to me.

"During Oct. Nov. and Dec. I was desperate for money. Early in Oct. I stole a wallet containing $4 in cash from a friend of a Parole Officer. Though they had no proof I finally admitted it but was arrested for Probation Violation on this charge and the record which I have recited."

## THE CASE OF P. R.

"I was born on a farm about 10 miles outside of M. My mother died about nine months after I was born from an operation of which I have no knowledge. After my mothers death, my father moved to T. where he opened a second-hand store in conjunction with a grocery store. The first recollections that I have are about this store. It seems that my father had a housekeeper that had looked after me after my mother's death. As I remember it, she seemed to be more than a housekeeper as she seemed to have quite a bit to say about things. It was she who ran the grocery store while my father took care of the second hand store. I was brought into juvenile court at the age of 3 or 4 in T. because of some difficulty that my father had with this housekeeper. It seemed that they had lived together as man and wife and that she was trying to take me away from my father and place me in a home of some sort. I remember this because it was necessary that my father take a trip to M. to get birth certificates etc. in regard to my birth and to prove that he was my real father. I remember the day that he and I both appeared before the judge. Before we went into the courtroom he cautioned me to say that I liked my father very much should the judge ask me this. I remember too, investigators coming to our house and looking over my clothes and home conditions before the trial. The court must have decided in my father's favor because I remember that he took me home and later the housekeeper whom I had looked upon as my mother until then came to see me and he told her to 'never darken his door again!' Shortly after this, he sold all the household belongings, keeping only our clothes and personal articles. He bought a truck on which he built a house and in which we travelled over the country quite a bit. We lived for a while in G. where he opened a second store but apparently business was not so good there because it was not long until we were on the road again. After looking over various towns in A., we came to R. in December of 1919 where he bought a house in a rather run down neighboorhood and in this house he started a second-hand store. At this time I was about five years old and it was time for me to start in to school which I did in the spring of 1920. My school life was uneventful except for the fact that I was often made the brunt of jibes and jokes by the other boys because I did not have as good a home as they had or I was not quite as well dressed as they were. Their mothers would caution them not to play with me because I came from a rather tough neighborhood and had no mother to look after me. This hurt me and the only way that I could strike back was to either fight with their children or do something that made them further disapprove of me. My childhood was a rather lonely one. I was not allowed to do many of the things the other children did. I had no playmates that I remember of except those whose parents let them run around at all times. I made normal progress at school and was considered to be quick at learning but somewhat of a problem because I was almost always getting into fights with the other boys. My first real trouble came when I was in the seventh grade. At this time I became aware that I was not quite as well dressed or as clean as the other boys and girls. I tried to have my father to have our laundry done by some laundry or laundress. Ever since I can remember I done the washing and ironing for the two of us. I also done most of the cooking and cleaning around the house. If I expected to have a clean shirt for school the next day it was entirely up to me. I had only 2 or 3 shirts and one pair of pants and one pair of stockings and I wore these until they wore out befor I would get another. My father absolutely refused to have the laundry done by anyone else and it was here that we had our first argument. For four or five years befor this I had been interested in electricity and radio. I was not allowed to go out of the house very much so it was necessary that I find some thing that I was interested in to keep my mind occupied. That is the reason that I have been and always will be interested in electrical and radio phenomenna.

"After the laundry incident I became more and more restless.

I wanted to stay after school and play foot-ball or base-ball with the rest of the fellows but if I were one minute late at home without a legitimate excuse I was sure to be punished in some way. I missed these boyish games and the only way that I could play with them was to stay away from home until the games were over. I would then be afraid to go home and would stay out until around 9 or sometimes 10 o'clock. I usually would go to some fellows house after the game and stay until they went to bed. When I came home I would take my punishment whatever it was and say nothing. The punishment usually consisted of a whipping going to bed without supper or a deprivation of some of my few priviliges.

"In the Fall of 1927 I started to high school. When I saw how the things were there I determined that I would do something about my home life. I got myself a job in a radio shop and worked after school and on Saturdays. With the money that I received from this job I bought myself my own clothes and was able for the first time in my life to have a complete suit. This led to constant friction between my father and myself. Naturally I stayed after school to attend various high school functions and try out for the various teams. This would be met with anger and punishment by my father. At various times I would be invited to one of the other boys home for an evening and dinner. I was able to see the difference between their home and mine and I felt this very keenly as I was not able to reciprocate because of the conditions at my home. We ate, slept and lived in one room. The rest of the house being devoted to the store. I tried time after time to explain these things to my father but he would always call it foolishness. Never once in my life was I able to go to him with my problems and receive any sympathy or understanding. He was about 55 yrs old when I was born and we were just too far apart although in his own selfish way I believed he loved me. It was while I was in my 3rd year of high school that I was determined to better my home life. I was pretty much disgusted with everything and one night 3 other fellows and myself decided to go to California if we could get a car. We had abot $35 between us. We set out to find a car and we stole one from the night school grounds. We drove this car until we ran out of money and gas and tried to steal another car so as to continue our journey. We were apprehended in L. and after spending 44 days in jail there we were returned to R. to answer the charges of Auto Theft. On the day that we were returned the other boys fathers and mothers got them out on bond right away. My father refused to help me so I was left in jail. During the investigation of our homes by the juvenile court I was found to have come from the worst. This coupled with the fact that I did not receive any help from my father caused me to be sent to the Reformatory while the other boys were probated to their fathers and mothers. I was sixteen years old when I went to the reformatory. I had never been in a place like that before and I was more or less bitter about the whole thing. I had some difficulty there with other boys on account of my age. I was young and approached by the 'wolves' of the institution. This led to many fights and with the result that I had lost in about 5 months 180 days for fighting. This helped me to get along after that as the 'wolves' did not care to engage in a fight whenever they approached me. I served 15 months in that institution. I was Paroled in June of 1931. I came home again to a different world. I could not stand the squalor of the neighborhood or the same home conditions. I was no longer a boy. I was an ex-convict and there was no place that would employ me at any kind of work. In october I left for California. I got there around the last of October. I went to a friends house out there and he got me a job with a construction co. where he worked at $4 a day. I also became interested in boxing and was managed by a man who at that time supplied the various fight clubs with their bouts. With the money that I made boxing and working for the construction co. I was able to live fairly well. I bought a second hand car and rented a furnished cottage where I lived with the other fellow that I first stayed with when I first came to california. Things were going nicely until I was layed off because of no more work by the construction co. This led to my depending entirely on the income from the boxing. At the time I was considered to be a 'comer' in the boxing world. I was getting as high as $75 and $100 a fight for my end. Of course by the time that I deducted training fees gym fees etc. I would have about $35 or $40 dollars left. From the last 3 fights I had I had not yet received my money. I was in need and I went to my manager and asked for some of my money. He told me he did not have it at that time but that he would have it soon. He kept putting me off time and time again. In the meantime I had sold the car to pay some of my debts and to live. It was in Dec. that I became disgusted and tried for the last time to get the money due me by this manager. In the meantime I had broken a bone in my hand and was unable to do any more fighting. I was almost broke. When I went to see him he told me that he had just bought a new car and that he could not give me what was coming to me until a later date. As I came down the stairs from his apartment house I saw his old car a Chrysler coach in the back yard. He owed me about $150 which was about what this car was worth. I opened the car door and climbed in and started the motor. I went to the house where I had lived for the past five months and packed all my belongings and put them in the back seat of the car and started for home. By the next morning I was in the state of Arizona. On the road I picked up a fellow that was going to his home in Denver Colo. I took him along and told him how I came to be leaving Calif. and how I had come into possession of the car. I took him to his home in Denver and after staying overnight I left early the next morning to continue my journey home. I was about 200 miles out of Denver when I discovered that he had left his suit case in the back seat of the car. I turned around and went back to Denver. I came back to his house after dark and when I took the suitcase in the house a deputy sheriff took me into custody. For this I was sent to the Penitentiary and while I was there the Reformatory Placed a holder against me for parole violation which made a parole Impossible. On May 10, 1933 I was released from the penitentiary. I came back to R. having been reinstated on parole by the Reformatory. I was unable to find a job of any kind but as beer had just been legalized a friend gave me a job as a bartender. I worked at this job until August, when I met the girl that I later married. Because of the associations in the beer garden I quit that job and went to work on the C.W.A. In January my girl and I had an argument and she went to S. for a visit. I stole a car and went to S. to bring her back but when I got there I found that she had left an hour earlier for R. As I came back to R. I was arrested in this car and taken to jail. Because of the circumstances of this car theft I was sent back to the reformatory as a parole violator to do eight months. Before I went back the girl and I were married. I had served about six months when my father died and as there was no one else to take charge of things I was sent home to attend to the funeral and adjust the estate. I was allowed thirty days leave. but because it did not seem right to me to leave my wife broke I did not return until 2 weeks later. In the meantime I was classed as an escape or rather A.W.O.L. I did return however and was eventually given my final release.

"When I came home in 1934, I tried to get a job. Things were very bad and I was unable to obtain work of any kind. My wife secured a job as a waitress in a restaurant and for a long time she was the bread earner in our family. Because of the fact that my wife was working all the time, I naturally had a lot of spare time on my hands. I began to associate with the old crowd and finally was invited to participate in some of their activities. Once in awhile I would go along with them and for my work I would get $10 or $15. These crimes usually consisted of some burgalry of some warehouse. This continued for about five or six months. It became necessary for my wife to quit her job as she was going to have a baby soon. During this time we were on relief and the only money that we had was the money that I earned in these escapades.

"After the baby was born I was fortunate to get a job as a truckdriver. I worked long hours and the work was hard, but I was happy because I was at last able to contribute something toward the support of our home. As soon as my wife was able, she returned to her work. With the both of us working we managed to get along very well. We moved to a better neighboorhood, bought new clothes and some furniture. It was about this time that I wanted an automobile. One day I came across a fellow that I had know while I was in the Reformatory. He was driving a year old Ford V–8 automobile. I liked this car very much and wanted to buy it from him. He told me that it was a 'hot' car but that if I wanted it he would sell it to me very cheap. I bought the car from him knowing at the time that I bought it that it was a stolen car. I had this car for about two months when I was stopped one night by a squad car for a minor traffic violation. In the routine checkup of the title of the car it was discovered that the car had been stolen three months previously in another state. This made it a Government case so I was turned over to them for prosecution. I was taken to await trial. In January of 1936, I went to trial and after bickering around was given a probation for two years upon my plea of 'guilty' to the charge of receiving and concealing of an automobile knowing at the time it to be stolen from another state. I rejoined my wife and we again tried to establish a home. At this time my wife was working on P.W.A. and was still the only contributor to the family. I was determined not to let things be as they were before so I again started to associate with the same gang that had gotten me into so much trouble before. While I was away they had started a new gang which by their various activities had earned for themselves the name of the 'Baby Dillinger' gang. I was invited to join this gang and I did go along withe them on two occasions but after I saw the tactics that was used in their depradations such as the beating of their victims, etc. I decided that I did not want any thing to do with this outfit. Because of the fact that I had gone with them on two occasions they would come to the house at various times to see if I wanted to join them on their forays. I always declined, but they still would come around now and then. One day the police rounded the whole lot of them up and took them to jail. There were about a dozen in the gang. Most of whom I knew or had known at some time or other. A week or so before they were apprehended, I with my brother-in-law and another fellow, burgulized a beer garden. We took some wine, cigarettes, radio, and other articles. In the course of the questioning of the 'Baby Dillinger' gang, my name had been mentioned at various times. When the police came to see me about this, they happened upon the car which had been used in the burglary of the beer garden, which was parked at my back door. A milkman had gotten the license number of the car and turned it over to the police. They arrested me at that time on the charge of burglary. They also apprehended my brother-in-law and the other fellow a short time later. When the grand jury met they not only indicted me for the Burglary but also for a robbery in which the members of the gang said I participated. I waited six months in jail before I was taken to trial. I was told that if I would plead guilty to the charge of Burglary they would annul the indictment of the robbery. I agreed to do this if they would give my brother-in-law and the other fellow a probation. They did this and March 12, 1936 I was sentenced to the State Penitentiary for a term of One to

Fifteen years, I went to the Parole Board in a year and because of the fact that I had a Federal detainer against me for probation I was given a years continunce.

"After the first year in the penitentiary my wife stopped corresponding with me except at long intervals. I went to the Parole Board again and was given a conditional release to the U. S. to answer to the charge of probation violation. In April I was taken from the State Penitentiary by the U. S. Marshall and taken to R. to have a hearing in regard to my violation of Probation. While there my wife came to see me and we agreed that we would let bygones be bygones and start all over again when I came out. When I appeared befor the Judge, he invoked the original sentence of two years and sentenced me to the Federal Pen. In November, I went before the parole board for a hearing on my application for parole. A few days later I was informed that my application for parole had been denied.

"In December, I received an official notice that my wife had filed suit for divorce against me charging me with gross neglect of duty and confinement in a penitentiary. She also asked for custody of the child."

Lewisburg, Pennsylvania<br>December

Dear Doctor Lindner:

By the time this letter is in your hands I will be well on my way to R. and what I hope will be for me a much happier and worthwhile life.

For me to leave without thanking you for the many things you have done to make my stay here more pleasant and endurable would be most ungrateful. Neither you nor I care for any display of emotion. That is the reason for this letter.

I have enjoyed every minute of our association for the past months and words cannot thank you for the opportunities you have given me to work at the things I like best and for the many other evidences of friendship you have shown me. I'm sure if I had met someone like you ten years ago my life would have been much different. However, I have quite a stretch of life before me and I intend to try to make up for all the time lost. Should I ever be a success much of the credit will be yours for showing me (in your own subtle way) the right road. I still think you are a good psychologist.

To sum up briefly how I feel, may I refer you to the cartoon of the man who has left an arm in the last handshake of a friend.

While I have never met Mrs. Lindner, I am sure she must be a fine woman. Please say good-bye to her for me.

From time to time I shall write to you and tell you how things are shaping up.

Sincerely yours,

P. R.

February

Dr. Robert M. Lindner
Lewisburg, Penna.

Dear Dr. Lindner:

It is with considerable regret that I must inform you that P. R. left R. in a stolen car sometime last Tuesday or Wednesday, and apparently headed for the south, as the police have a report that he had been in K.

On the 6th I left for California to attend a meeting and did not return until the 2nd. The morning following my return I received word from one of the interns at the hospital with whom I had made arrangements to take care of P. in case of illness that P. was in a hotel, sick. I told him to go down and investigate. This he did, and found that P. had been away from work for a week, that he had a bad sore throat and was running a slight temperature and had a head cold. He saw no reason why P. should not be out and ready for work by Monday following. On Saturday the Doctor went down to his room but he was not in. On Monday, P. did not report for work. On Tuesday afternoon I contacted P. and had him come down to the office between 4 and 5 o'clock. I had quite a satisfactory talk with him, went over the happenings during my absence and learned that he had changed his place of residence for reasons which seemed sufficient for him, that his room was cold and that he discovered bedbugs. However, this was not my opinion because he located himself in a hotel which was wholly undesirable from the standpoint of association, although it may have had better conveniences.

I had P. call up his employer before he left the office as I was afraid that he might lose his job because of a week's absence. This he did and arranged to go to work the next morning, which was Wednesday.

Before leaving for California I had arranged with P. to take Christmas dinner at my home with the family that remained and my son-in-law and his wife. This he did and apparently enjoyed a very pleasant afternoon.

He confessed to me in our last interview that after leaving my home Christmas afternoon he went to a night club, and there contacted a couple of girls; that he drank and did not go to work Thursday or Friday as he should have. In fact he did not report for work after the Christmas season.

On the morning of the 8th, about 9 o'clock, a detective came into my office with a warrant charging P. with the conversion of a Buick car which he apparently had gotten permission of the owner to take over to have the battery recharged or rechecked. The car had not been returned on time and the owner became suspicious and immediately swore out a warrant for his arrest. I immediately called his employer on the 'phone and found that he was not at work, so naturally, I came to the conclusion that P. had taken the car and left for parts unknown.

Wednesday afternoon about 3 o'clock I received a telephone call from a man who wanted to know about P. As he was a stranger to me I had him come down to the office and tell his story. He came that afternoon and this is his story.

He had recently been married, about the middle of December, and he discovered that his wife had been "stepping out." He investigated and got her to confess that P. was the man she was "stepping out" with. On Tuesday, he and his wife went to the hotel for an interview with P. but P. was not in and has not been seen since. This man's wife was a girl about 20 years old and from facts in my possession was one of the two girls that were in P's room the afternoon that the Doctor made his call.

I had a talk with Mr. M., his employer, over the telephone and it seems that when P. did not show up for work before Christmas he took it upon himself to go down to call on P. at his room and had quite a conference with him, offering to adjust his job in the factory more to his liking and to advance him money or assistance that he felt he might need under the circumstances.

The situation that exists, therefore, can in no way be laid to the lack of consideration on his employer's part or myself.

Before I left on my trip I left five dollars with my clerk to be used for P's welfare, in case he should be in distress and apparently he was for he came in during the holidays and picked up the five dollars, despite the fact that he had money coming to him from the factory. He was making about 16 dollars a week.

As soon as I learned of the warrant being issued, I contacted the probation officer by telephone and communicated the facts to him.

Well, there is the story. I thought you would like to have the facts first hand, as I know that you were personally interested in the boy's welfare.

With kindest regards and best wishes, I remain,

Very truly yours,

G. L. S.

March

Dr. Robert M. Lindner
Lewisburg, Pa.

Dear Dr. Lindner:

I thought that you would be interested in knowing that they picked up P. in Georgia, and he has been brought back to R. and is in the County Jail.

I am enclosing a copy of a letter which I received this morning and which I thought you would be interested in reading.

I have not yet had a chance to talk to the probation officer to find out just what disposition they expect to make of his case. As soon as I find out I will write you. Undoubtedly they will consider him a parole violator and return him to your institution. As to whether he will be tried on charges against him, conversion of a car, is a question.

Very truly yours,

G. L. S.

County Jail, R.
March

Dear Mr. S:

To say I'm sorry for this last escapade of mine seems hopelessly inadequate in view of all that has happened in the past. Nor is it my intention to bore you with the details leading up to it. My only wish is to thank you for the effort, time and money you have given unstintingly to help me rehabilitate myself.

Please be assured that in the future you will not be annoyed by me in any manner. You have already done more than any other person to help me. I guess I'm just no good.

In all fairness, however, I want you to know that I did try, but somehow, under the pressure of my past and the environment provided for me for the past 15 years, I failed. What's to become of me now, only God knows. I have ceased to care.

In the years to come your confidence and friendship will never be forgotten. Please believe me when I say I'm deeply sorry to have disappointed you.

Sincerely,
P.


August

Dr. Robert Lindner
Lewisburg, Pa.

Dear Dr. Lindner:

At the request of P., I am taking this opportunity of enclosing a copy of a letter recently received from him. You will note that he is in the Penitentiary and apparently making the best of his situation.

I visited P. at the County Jail two days before he left R. It seems that he was convicted of conversion of property (the automobile). Two other men were implicated with him. One, I understand, was his former brother-in-law, who by the way has a shady record in police circles here in R. P. pled guilty and thereby saved his two companions from further embarrassment.

I think he has gone up for 3½ years. P. is apparently looking forward to the time when he will be free from his obligation to society and he intimated to me that under no circumstances would he come back to R.

It might be interesting to note that before he took this last car he got mixed up with a young married woman and I understand when he was on the "lam," that he continuously corresponded with her. I had a talk with the woman's husband, who at the time of my conversation with him had only been married to her for a month or a little better.

I do not recall whether I told you that during the Christmas season P. was invited out to my apartment by my daughters and son-in-law for Christmas dinner and he seemed to enjoy the festivities of the day and later Christmas Evening my son-in-law took him to his room and left him about 9 o'clock. Subsequently I learned that later that evening he met this married woman and a companion out in a night club that doesn't have a very savory reputation. On the pretext of being ill, P. had not worked on his job for about 10 days prior to his leaving R. with the converted car.

He told me that he and these two companions went to Y. from where he mailed a postcard to the manager of the hotel where he had been rooming during this time, telling him as to the disposition of his personal belongings. As you can imagine, this was turned over to the police and P. was finally located in a place where he had secured a job washing dishes in some kind of Bar-B-Q associated with a Tourist Camp on the out-skirts of the City.

During the time he was there he was picked up by the police one night and thrown into jail on the charge of driving while intoxicated. He explained to me that he personally was not intoxicated but the man who was riding with him was. Somehow or other he was able to wiggle out of this jam and subsequently the police picked him up as a Federal Parole violator and of course he was picked up and sent back to R. His excuse for leaving R. was that he was not satisfied with his work assignment, despite the fact that Mr. M. personally visited him at his room shortly after it had been reported that he was ill. Mr. M. told me that as a result of this visit he had offered to advance P.

money for expenses during the days he was away from work and also agreed to adjust his assignment in the factory to his liking.

The day Mr. M. visited P's room he was in the process of packing his belongings preparatory to moving into the Hotel, a place where apparently he had roomed before.

All of this occurred while I was in California. He apparently took advantage of my absence to make these changes. I have every reason to believe that P. had contacted his former wife despite the advice I gave him to avoid so doing; also, apparently on his return to R. from Lewisburg, he very shortly contacted his former brother-in-law.

Well, despite all that has happened, I still have faith and hope that P. will snap out of this situation. The letter recently received from him indicates a certain amount of resignation as to his plight and he apparently is complacent in abiding by the position in which he finds himself.

He thought a great deal of you and Rev. Z. and frequently spoke to me of your kindness, inspiration and help. I trust that you may have the privilege of conducting a correspondence with him. Undoubtedly in your official capacity this could be arranged.

With kindest regards and many thanks for your kindness to P., I remain

Sincerely yours
G. L. S.

August

From P.

To: Mr. G. L. S.
Dear Mr. S:

It occurred to me that a line or two at this time informing you of my progress at this institution would not be amiss. The first thirty days are devoted to the various physical and mental examinations which have a direct bearing on the type of work you are assigned while here. It can truthfully be said every effort is made to give the individual the type of work he is best qualified for. I am happy to say that I have been fortunate enough to be assigned to the technical staff of the institutional radio system. My work is interesting and instructive and the indications are that I shall make a good adjustment here. My only regret is I couldn't make as good an adjustment on the outside. It may be that the environment provided for me for so long has rendered me unfit for any other. However, I have found that one can be far more lonely on a crowded street corner in a large city than in a prison cell. It may be hard for you to understand this, but it's true. Whether you realized it or not, I was very lonely the last time I was home. No one to care whether you are alive or well, etc. It's the price I must pay for the road I chose to travel, I guess.

My disappointment in not being able to see you again before I left was great, however, the quicker I started on my sentence, the quicker I'll be out. That's some consolation.

You remember that I completed my high school work at Lewisburg so there isn't much in the way of school work for me here. However, I have enrolled in a class of slide rule reading which will be of direct benefit to me in my work.

If you would drop a line to Dr. Lindner and Rev. Z. informing them of my progress here, I would be very grateful.

In closing may I wish you and all the rest every happiness.

Sincerely yours,

P. #00000

## THE STORY OF MY LIFE AS I SEE IT.

"I was born of american parents, in a small Ohio town, in the year of 1917 Am the youngest of two, haveing a sister 2 years older than myself and much the better of the two, I must say.

"Leaving our home in 1920 we visited numerious places, ending in Californi. Our family lived in furnished apts. & hotels for some two years, then started east arriving at Chicago where we spent 13 years.

"It was in Chicago that my schooling both started and finished.

"I compleated the 8th year of school and must say learned nothing of value, was in hot water at all times, was absent quite frequently, so gave it up and went to work at a print shop just long enough to satisfy my people for leaving school.

"At 14 I left home and rode fraight trains through Penn. & Ohio, returned and went back to school at 16 I started out & went to Texas and Californi, sence I've visited most of the states and Mexico using every means of travel.

"In 1935 I resigned a fairly good job and went to New Orleans Feb. beating my way, then to Texas, where I inlisted in the U. S. Army, but later went on to Californii, where I found work doing spray painting and car work.

"Leaving Cal. after several months I entered Mexico then returned home to stay 1½ months and going to Salt Lake City, several weeks later found me in Nav. where I was employed as a ranch hand. Returning east in the late fall I stayed in Col. and made very good at gambleng this being the trade I ply quite often, my father and uncle have follow it, since 1911.

"In the month of September I again headed south and entered the Army. I made considerable money evey mo. at cards and dice, the first pay day at the station hospital was fourtionate enough to make $197.00 at cards.

"Soon becoming bored I went A.W.O.L. and found myself in Texas incarcerated on charges of robbry with a gun which carries captal punishment there. After some 10 weeks my bond was cut to where it possible for me to make it, upon being released I immeditly returned to my post and was placed under arrest of quarters, which needless to say I duely broke and was then place in the post prison upon sobering up & returning to my post. Through the Adj. Gen. orders I was released after about 3 weeks and returned to my battery where I preceaded immeditely get into freash difficultys, being still under quarters arrest I had some sprits brought into to me, by friends, and then preceded to become high & to disregard a command given by a non. com. which seem to take a dislike to me from the start. When he endeavored to force me to do so I assulted him with a wepon which cost me a Gen. court marshal, after being returned to the brig the next A.M., that time I remained some 3 weeks and was again released by the commanding post Gen. orders. Was released in March and was hon. discharged that month. Returning north I took my time staying in Little Rock some 8 days, then St. Louis for a month. Upon arriving in Cincinnati I stayed a week, then went to Cleveland and took out seamens papers and went to all the Lake ports.

"Leaving Sandusky on July 1st I arrived in Los Angeles on the night of the fourth and immedtly made some $2,200.00 which was cut 2/3 to 1/3—.

"Being almost broke I went to Mexico, arriving at El Paso on the 29th of Sept. I gambled my way north to K. C. then east again, finding my father had gone to Chicago the last of Sept. I follow after seeing my mother for several weeks & working all the time at a dept. store where she was employed. I left for no reason other than lake of interest. Arriving in Chicago I stayed at a hotel, which is also a house of ill fame, working at my uncles place which is a smoke shope & also a gambling joint, my Dad was running the joint part time, I dealt poker four nights a week, also hustled on the side made very good. About two months after my arriving at Chicago my Dad & uncle had a disagreement, my Dad and I then rent a small Apt. togeather where I remained 3 weeks then moved down town to live with a young lady with whom I was going and contemplating marriage, but after affording her much heart ache and causing her much unplesantnes, we came to the parting of the ways, as was inevetable. She was highly educated and had caracture and was the presonification of class, that was to be expected. Our parting came late in the fall, with my going on a drug and whiskey spree, that was to last until my mother had me incarcerated in a institution. In the mean time I had contracted syphills and went to Hot Springs Ark.

"It is even yet, after 3 years of separation, hard for me to think of her without regret She was everything that was good and fine, why she even spent a moment & time with me is still beyond my comprehension. She lost her friends and social standing, which was of the highest, over me. There was 5 years diff. in our ages, her being the oldest & have two fine children, home payed for and two Beauty Shopes. She wished to seel her home it being very large & buying one smaller for her children & I. Also she wish me to start a place of business with her furnishing the required funes. It was only after lossing my happy home, 'and I was happy' that I fully realized my sad mistake. Often she enters my thoughts, and am afraid she will continue to do so. Sence then Ive had several women with which I've live, also taking eveything in return of little if anything. During my resent 80 days freedom I stayed in a hotel with a woman much my Sr. I drifted away from her through lacke of interest needless to say she also had my best interest at health, all to come to nought. Then there was one, my com. law wife in Fla. with whom I stayed some 5 months the last time and went to a chain gang over. We got along fair, haveing quite a little in common. I was confined to the hospital on two different occasions for D. T., Then came back to Chicago where my people have me placed in the Gen. Hospital for drugs, after being released from the workhouse for disorderly conduct and deadly assult with a razor. On August 8th in 39 I went to New Orleans and fooled with drugs again on a small scale, getting involved on my last charge of any consequence. Received 15 months for Moter Vehical Act. being released in 1941 and then broke C.R.V. and committed the present offense.

"In view of my past, I sometimes wonder if when all's said & done the gain was worth the effort. The road which has been travelled is so rocky that at times it would seem well to give up, then in the space of several hours something happens to change the whole outlook of everything. This does not come as a depressive thought, rather as a contemplative one, in other words one wonders. I like to live my life day by day & like everything as an adventure, rather than tie my self down I've always been (in a sence) satisfyed to ramble. Although at times there is no point to anything, even life it seems. My own conception of my self and it seems the above and following will bear me out, is that I'm headstrong & willfull, selfish, and want my way at all times and go to most any length to attain it. Am invearabley in hot water due to this. It seems for some reson I hold everything most people respect in contempt, why is beyond me, but this is true, I seem to get a kick out of doing just what is considered unconventional, such as drinking, gambling, running with lued women, and living high. I arrived at this conclusion some time ago but am unable to curb these dissieses.

"There seems to be something that's lacking, but am unable to name it. Am always seeking something, what, I can't say. I do things to people & things that I clame to care for and know at the time that it will hurt them, but go right ahead anyway. After am sorry, but turn right around and do the same thing or worse. In this one respect my sister is similar, although she tends to be a introvert where I am a discided extrovert.

"Although of the same parants, she is vastly different. She is honest as the day is long, a trate of my mothers, and very candid at all times regardless. She's refined and showes her breeding conducts herself as a lady. I take after my dad, drink, gamble, and like the excitement of life. Must say that regardless of his preffession, he's word is good, he's liked and respected anywhere he has ever been and can return and enjoy the goodwill of eveyone.

"It seems I've acquired the faults of eveyone of my people & none of there good points.

"To compensate for this I've study and tryed to advance myself & have tryed to cultivate a pleasing personality but seem unable to do so. I let my true feelings show to easily it seems, I say just what I think and devle take the hindmost, regardless of who or what he is, or his position. This has cause me much unpleasantness, but little if any regret. At time I can make myself most obnoxious, and delight in doing so, why again am unable to say. You can lead me, but never drive me. If a person does not appeal to me he can get me to do nothing, where if I like a person, and he goes about it right I'll go out of my way to please. Have always enjoyed independence and hope to continue to do so. I wish to state now that I've come in contact with life very closely and find it as a general rule very unpleasant with very little happyness, so there fore I take what I can where it's to be found and ask no questions. Can say that I have no great longing to change the places I've been anythings that's transpired, People I've come in close contact with for anything, although I sincerely wish that some of my ways where different. I say this because there is little I've not tried, & some of the people that I've met are priceless. Have been in most every walk of life and must say as a whole my life has been full. Then again it has been useless in one sence of the word. As you may have already came to the conclusion am very unsettled and unstable in thought & action. One time I'll react one way & to the same thing a day later I react just opposite, half the time I dont know myself which way I'll jump till I've landed. This may sound vague but it is the way I am as near as I can express it & define things, the sad part it's too true. There seems to be no way that I can help myself, because I've tryed, but at the moment that things happen they seem to take there own course, after there is many things

that I should have done, but didn't. A long time ago my people
gave me up for hopeless, It seems that I can trace some of my
trates through my people as my Dad & uncles have all one time
travelled, have one uncle that was around the world from 1902
till 1913. I think my rambling came from haveing travelled with
my people when I was young, as I can vaguely remember some
of the places we live. One reason I've never worked is because
wages will not maintain the life that I've been use to leading
prior to this; therefore have never been able to make much at
honest work. Am of a very restless nature & that one reason for
my always being in some trouble, am highstrung, and when in
a mood nothing seems to matter, so thats one reasons for my
getting high and having a fling, then things seem somewhat
better for a while. This seems to come at intervilles of a month
or two sometimes longer, but it comes infallabley.

"Am aware that this brief resume seemingly tends to con-
tridict itself but it is as true as I am able to rationally & clearly
explain it. This brings to mined a verse that came to my attention at one time which has left me with the impression that
it applys to one of my make up:

> 'The thing that I am seeking,
>     Should not be hard to seek.
> I hear its haunting echo
>     through every word I speak.
> Though I must always wander,
>     I do not find it sweet
> There is no distent visin
>     to draw my restless feet
> my road is seldon easy,
>     and I do not find it gay,
> For there seems to be no loved ones
>     to help me on my way.'

"Then the last verse sums it up adequately.

> 'The thing that I am seeking
>     should not be far to seek,
> but I shall always seek it
>     down all the roads I go,
> but I know I shall not find it,
>     for my heart has told me so.'

"Am sorry but this is as much as I am able to remember, and at that had to suplement several lines. I think it fits my case to a extent, have always been seeking something that is still vague, and yet at times, it seems almost clear, yet I could not have it.

"My present incarceration is for forguery, which was done for no reason other than financial gain. Finding myself in Chicago with lack of funds and in possession of the checque in question, I delibertly cashed it using my own name and identification. I gave the matter long and serious contemplation and still am unable to give any rational reason for not using subterfuge. I could easly have did so. My concept is that at the time I was absolutely disgusted with every thing in general. Immeditly after finding that I had no worries at the moment the full realization of my deed was brought home to me and after contemplating and introspection I walk in to the F.B.I. office and inquired if they were looking for me, finding they were I readly admitted my part but refused to name anyone. My only plea was for consideration, due to the fact I felt that it was time a definite step was made to make something of myself. This was to be of no use whatsoever. When younger I was prone to imitate my Father by wearing his hat and shoes. To an extent I still imitate my Father. At the age of 8 I was caught on two different occasions with girls of my own age behind the church by my sister & again once in the haystack by the girls sister, my people heard from this both times. At thirteen we has a maid which had an affaire with me. She had been out late with her boy friend and came in, using her keys, but going out again she left her key and was lock out. She came in through my bedroon window, and descied to sleep there for the remainder of the night, that was the beginning of an affaire which lasted till my Father found out through my sister telling my mother. The maid was immedily discharg.

"When we had first came to Chicago & I was about 6 my family had difficulty through an affaire my Dad was having with a lady that live in the apt over us. If I am not mistaken she had an abnormal passion for men, but can not remember her ever have molested me. Have at times had abnormal relation with wemen myself, only at times, in a different sence then that of my father. Thats the only time there was ever trouble of that nature in my family. My great failing when young, was my Dad pen knife, was taking it all the time, much to his anger. Also took his gun on several occasions.

"While on my uncles farm, there was a girl, 16 months my senior, we were very close for some two years, and corresponded for some 4 years, it was while in the Army that I stop writing her, although, even yet I send a card occasionaly, and on Xmas. Have not so much as ever kiss this girl as she is very shy, although her letters are more a prayer. It was she that prompted me go to church the little I did attend. My age was at 15½ when we first started going togeather, my people hoped for a match of some sort, feeling I would strighten up. Had contemplated this myself.

"While living in California, and at the age of 3 or there abouts, the boy living next door & I stold a hen from the chicken yard of some people who lived near, this was my idea intierly. The lad in question was of my age, maybe a year older. Yet again at the same address, I took a twenty dollar bill from the kitchen table and placed it under the rear wheel of an auto in the back yard. Upon being asked about the money, I steadfastly refused to acknowledge any hand in its disappearance. Later in Cal., my mother having taken me into a store, I came out with a teddy bear, which she immeditly made me return.

"In Chicago, shortly after our arrival there, and much to the lady downstair's anger, I drowned her five kittens & killed her cat with a club. I have always found cats in any form obnoxious animals.

"I shall write down a verse that you'll find runs true to life.

'Life is just a game of poker,
  and happyness is the pot.
Fate deals you five cards in the cradle, and you play whether
  you like it or not.
And sometimes the frame doesn't seem on the square, when you
  pick up your hand and discover you were born without even a
  pair.
But there ain't no use kicking and squacking, you pick up your
  cards and begin to figure, plan and puzzle,
While fate looks on with a gun.
  Now some of us bet all we got
On a dinky little four flush, and sometimes it wins the pot.

While other break up openers and try for a middle straight,
They know the chance they're taking and find their mistake to
late.
Some can't help cheating against all good advice,
But in the long run they always pay the price.
Now most of us play straight poker and I'll tell you boys its
hard,
When you're there with bought ends open and can't draw the
winning card.
I've always been a loser and it seems I never could win.
I'm just a dreamer who's waiting for his ship
That never comes in.'

"This I find is a resume of life as a whole. I often have the
following dream. That I have in my possession a gun which will
not fire, It seems that inverably that my father is in need of
assistance, and upon my apperance on the scene with a gun that
it will not fire, or if it does nothing happens. I have the dream
frequently. Also I dream of the use of a knife and cut about the
face. I've been cut myself on several occasions, once on the face
and again on the leg, consequently I am deathly afraid of a
knife, I know numerous fellows that carry knifes for the sole
reason of use and protection.

"My earliest remembrances start from about the age of 5. It was
at that time my parents moved from my Brith place to Fla. I
remember that at that time Florida was in a tremendous boom &
we lived in a tent with apple box for flooring and were glad to
get it. I started going to public school at the age of 7 & did very
well in school and was always very well liked by my teacher's.
I was always deathly afraid of my father as he has a very violet
temper & has given me several very bad beatings but I have always loved my mother very Dearly. At the age of 9 another
boy & myself ran away from home & went to S. C. where he left
me and returned home. I was picked up & my mother came to
S. C. after me. Had a very good time on the trip & deceided to
try it again & so about 6 mo. later I left home again & traveled to
Arizona where I got into some very serious trouble by stealing
about $400 from a fellow for whom I worked. I soon returned
home & started to mixing with a gang of boys older than myself.
And as these boys has a great deal to do with the next 7 year's

of my life I will give them names 'Mutt' the leader of the gang, 'Six toes' another member 'Ray' & Myself. My job was to steal cars for the gang to pull jobs with for which I received $100 each time I got one. I always liked these boys because they treated me as if I was as old as they, and always give me smokes & money.

"One evening Mutt came to me & told me to get a car & I asked him what kind of car he wanted & he told me to get something that would run. And so at about 8 o'clock I got the car & picked up the rest of the gang. Mutt said he would take me with him that night & so away we went to a town about 45 miles away & drove in front of the place where I parked with the motor running & Mutt & Ray went into the place & Six toes stood outside with a sawed off shot gun. In a few minutes they came running out & jumped into the car & Mutt yelled 'lets go', & so away we went. As we were coming back on the highway I was driving about 40 miles per hour and all of a sudden I heard a report like a fire cracker and the windshield shattered. Well we got away from them and got to out hidout & Mutt opened the sack & counted the money there was about $850 of which I got $150 as my share. It was so exciting that I made Mutt promise to take me on the next job. Well we pulled a few more jobs and then things got hot & the fellows had to leave town. They did not suspect me because I was too young. & so after a while I went to work for the C. Co. It was there I met a man who had a great deal to to with the Co. & I wish to say that I have always been big for my age which enabled me to get the job. Well as I said before I met this man whom I shall call Mr. July, He immediatly made friends with me & invited me to his home it was thene I started to become 'wise' as that is the term that is used. He was queer & as I had never before had anything to do with a woman I enjoyed it very much. It was through his pull that I got a job at the office there. & it was there that I met the woman with whom I had my first intercourse. Well it is sufficient to say that it was intensely pleasant to me & I could not seem to want to leave her. And it was through my going around with her that Mr. July became jealous & caused me to lose my job & then she moved away & there I was out of a job and that was that. I would like to tell something which I have never told before. I have 3 sisters & have never relly cared for but one of them. of course I dont mean that I dont like them but I never felt the atraction for either one of them as I did for Joan. It has always seemed to me that my father never cared much for Joan & so me Being afraid of my father & Joan Being afraid of him we stuck together. One evening a friend of my dad's a fellow whom I shall call John came over to our house and asked if Joan & I would like to go for a ride & as I was reading & told Joan to go ahead if she wanted too which she did. In about an hour the car stopped in front of the house & Joan ran into the house crying & I asked her what was the matter & she refuwed to answer until I threatened to hit her & then she said 'John made me do things I didn't want to do.' I immediatly ran into my dads room & got his service pistol which is a 45 I ran over to this fellows house which was about 4 blocks away & the only thing that saved me from being a killer that night was the safty on the pistol & I did not know how to work it. I am still looking for that man.

"A few years passed during which I worked at several odd jobs & then I got a job with a tailor with a chance to advance myself but I soon tired of being tied down & decided to leave home again. This time I went to P—— & when I arrived there I could not get a job & so I turned to the easiest way of making a living, which was running around with queer's & I made a great deal of money which I spent as fast as I made it. I stayed in P—— about 8 mo. & then I made the aquantice of a girl whom I shall call Peg & she introduced me to a girl named Dot. I ran around with these two girls for quite a while and then one day they asked me to take them to Chicago & being very much in love with Peg I agreed & away we went.

"We got as far as Cleveland & we were picked up by the police & the girls were sent back home & in about a week I was released and went back to P——. There I met a fellow & he & I started to pull jobs & we got along all right for a while one day I noticed that my penis was very swollen & sore but there was no discharge & very soon the glands in my abdomen began to swell. It was on account of this that we went out one night to try & steal enough money to get a doctor fore me & I got caught breaking into a parked car because I couldn't run. I was given 3 mo. in the city prison & I found our I had syphliss. It was there & then I swore not to go with any more women & got out of there & went home but did not stay long because I was afraid that some of the family would get the disease & so I left and joined the Army. How they missed finding out I had the disease I do not know but about 6 mo. later I deserted and was gone for 7 mos during which time I roamed about the United States. I finally went home where my parents convinced me it would be best to go back & so I went back & got 6 mo. & a dishonorable Discharge. Which I did.

"When I got out of the Army stockade I went back home for a short period of time & then went to New York. After arriving in New York I met a man who runs what is called a peg house my job was to hang around all night & if a queer called up I was to go to his room. I could mention a few names of Big people who are that way both male & female but I will not do so as I dont feel it is necessary. I met one fellow whom I shall call Bill. who is a Multi Millonaire in Y. I lived with him for about 6 mo & then I took all I could get from him & left. When I got to Z. it was the same old story until the fatful night myself & 3 other boys went out and robbed a filling station & got caught. I have often heard of poetic justice but here it was at last the boy that put the finger on all of us got 5 to life in the pen & the rest of us got 1 year & 5 years probation. I found out when I got in the county jail that I had the clap, which all resulted in my not keeping my word about women. And so for a period of about 4 months I stayed in the county jail. And I was taking treatment for the syphliss at the same time.

"After I was in the county jail for a short period of time I was pronounced cured of both diseases & was sent to a road camp & from there I escaped and went back to new York. A very funny incident happened after I escaped I was in a town & trying to catch a ride when a car pulled up and stopped & I got in well the swell part of it was & I have laughed at it many a time was that this man was a Federal Agent & as I found out later a very good one his name I will not reveal but he gave me a long ride & he gave me $1.50 & he told me to be careful & not to get in trouble. Boy was I glad to get out of his car I thought for a while that he was going to take me down and fingerprint me but he didn't. When I got to New York I started playing the queer's again & finally 2 other boys & myself stole a car & started for Miami. We were arrested in M. & was tried & was sentenced to

3 years in a federal Reformatory & was sent to Chillicothe Ohio & there I got into a great deal of trouble & was transferred to here & so from there on you know my record here.

"I am afraid you will find this a rather rambling account of myself & very uninteresting but it is the best I could do. It is not very much given to details but it is a rough outline of myself & I hope it will suffice as I hate to write. That is why I made this as brief as Possible."

## AUTOBIOGRAPHY OF A CONVICT

"My earliest recollections are of a small neat, two storied frame house with an enormous backyard where grew a number of trees. This was 'home.' Our family consisted of my father, mother, an elderly great aunt, and myself. There was also my beloved companion and protector, 'Queen', an aged daschund. Our neighborhood was what is commonly called 'middle-class', and among our neighbors were doctors, merchants, politicians etc. Their children were my earliest playmates.

"I have a rather misty memory of my third birthday party but then there is a lapse until that period when I was 'four goin' on five.' At that age, I played soldiers and often spent hours hunting tigers and bears in the vastness of our yard, accompanied always by faithful and patient 'Queen.' All too often she was forced to play the part of tiger and I am led to believe that my wild yells must have proven too much for her, because one morning good old Queen lay dead in her basket. I cried for days, my heart filled with remorse for the many indignities I had heaped on her understanding old head. To this day, I use Queen as a standard when comparing the qualities of dogs and sometimes people!

"About this time, I became acutely concious of my father. Up to then he had been a vague somebody who lived in our house. Now, seeking a new companion I turned to 'Pop.' But, Pop never wanted to go hunting or to play soldiers. And if I made too much noise, Pop would see to it that I quieted down. He never whipped me, but for some reason his very presence in a room was enough to send me scurrying to the farthest corner of the room.

"My mother was swell. She was Irish and possessed all the

good qualities of the Irish. She laughed sang and joked—except when father was around—and she was the one who told me bed-time tales and bound up the wounds a tiny boy acquires in the course of his busy day. It was Mommy who took me to my first movie, and it was Mommy who even taught me how to fight back when other children attacked me. Though she has grown old and fat with the years, I still see her as she was then: slim; rosy-cheeked; with long raven black hair and a musical laugh. My life has been a terrible disappointment to her and I'd give anything if I could do just one thing which might make her feel a little proud of me.

"My father was an atheist, but mother was a Catholic. There-fore, when the time came for me to attend kindergarten, I was husteled off to St. —— Parochial School, where I learned my A.B.C's. When I was about seven years of age, I became quite ill. The doctor prescribed fresh country air, good food etc. Fortunately my people owned a large farm which was rented to a German family who agreed to take care of me. This family—let's call them the Schultz family—were probably the meanest, lowest people I have ever known. The ill treatment I received at their hands has left an indelible mark on my memory.

"When ever my parents visited me on week-ends, they found me decked out in my best clothes and literally living off the fat of the land. But, just as soon as they returned to the city I was shorn of my fine garments and thrust into a pair of ugly 'Cut-downs.' I was forced to work in the fields and was fed very little because 'it was bad for boys to eat too much'! I was whipped and scolded for even the slightest mistake and on one occasion forced to go to school wearing girls shoes because I had soiled my own. That day I played 'hookey,' and, since my absence was noted on my monthly report card, I lived in terror of the day when they would note that one day absent.

"By dint of much lying I was able to outwit everyone for several months, but one day my teacher dropped in to find out why I never returned a signed report card. I ran away and hid in a nearby patch of woods, but late at night, scared, tired and very, very hungry, I crept back only to receive a God-awful 'shellacking.' Now, I could probably have gotten much better treatment had I complained to my parents, but frankly, my father's gruffness frightened me quite as much as did the threats of my caretakers. But, furthermore, I know that neither of my parents would have believed my tale. The Schultz' were 'fine people.' (They paid their debts; attended church; worked hard and kept their home in good shape. Therefore, they were 'good' people.)

"At the age of ten, I was again able to live with my parents. I attended my old school and progressed nicely with my studies, but I began to rebel against the discipline of the Catholic Church. I had begun to read a great deal and an independence of spirit began to manifest itself. I often played truant from Sunday Mass, but was awfully careful to remember the seasons of the church so that I would know what color vestments the priest wore. Every Monday, Father —— would visit the classroom asking whether we had all attended Mass. On one occasion my reckonings were a bit off, and when he asked what color vestments had been worn, I blithely answered "purple." That was the wrong answer and without another word I was hauled off to the boiler-room and given a fine whipping by the outraged priest. Had I told him the truth in the beginning I would have been punished anyhow, so feeling extremely peeved I rushed from the building. For the first time in my life, I ran to my father for help. After listening to my story he took me back to school, called out the priest and promised him a thrashing if he ever dared lay hands on me again. I guess dad did this more because he hated priests than because of any concern for my sore bottom! At any rate, in the hearing of the priest he told me I needn't go to church again unless I really wanted to. That was simply fine from my point of view. Mother didn't dare object, because she was too afraid of Pop.

"Transferring to Junior High School, I made the acquaintance of a number of 'down town' boys and since they seemed to be getting a lot of fun from life, I readily joined in their escapades. Despite the fact that I was twice brought before the Juvenile Court on truancy charges, I managed to graduate with high honors at the age of twelve. A year of High School followed during which I found myself getting into more and more scrapes. I walked a chalk-line at home when in Dad's sight, but when away from home I was a hellion. Finally the patience of the school authorities was exhausted and I was expelled. After loafing around for almost a year, I was given a job as office boy in the office of a large motion picture company. I was now a working man!

"By this time the war had wiped out my father's business, and every dollar counted. I felt independent as hell as I was helping to support our home. Following a scolding over some trivial incident, I took my pay one Friday and went on a trip to B. Naturally twelve dollars didn't last very long, and on Monday I was back on the job but getting kind of hungry. I managed to patch things up at home, but from then on Dad used to meet me on paynights. This close surveillance irked me considerably, so a few weeks later I left the building by a rear entrance while Dad waited out front! I do not think he ever forgave me for that. At any rate he set his face sternly against me and I was really on my own. My life was mighty difficult for a few years. I worked at odd jobs when I could get them and quickly spent whatever I earned. At the age of sixteen I even engaged in several boxing bouts with fair success. However, I became somewhat girl conscious and needing money for show-off purposes I committed a series of petty robberies. Many of my former schoolmates were enterprising bootleggers during the prohibition era and some of them had earned quite a reputation for toughness. One fellow in particular though only a few years older than I, had already become a 'Big-shot.' I thought it would be grand to have other folks think I too was a 'big shot,' so I laid a plan for robbing a certain building in a nearby city where a collection of coins were on exhibition. I had already arranged for the sale of these coins, and the job went off rather well. I paid my mother a visit, flourishing a big roll of money. Now, my mother had worried herself sick over me, and knowing full well that I must have done something wrong in order to acquire so much money, she asked a family friend who was also a police lieutenant to speak to me. In the language of the criminal, she 'put the finger on me.' Mother did this because she felt it would be better for me to go to prison than to continue along the paths I had been treading. To make a long story short, it was a comparitively simple matter for the authorities to convict me and I was subsequently sentenced to an indeterminate sentence in the Reformatory.

"An amazing transformation now took place. I shied away from old associates and spent a great deal of time reading instead of getting into trouble. My deportment throughout my entire stay in the institution was exemplary. I studied hard, worked hard, and even prayed a little. By the time I was released on parole after serving nineteen months, I had lost all zest for adventures of a criminal nature. I have never quite understood what brought about this change in temperament. Perhaps some talks with officers known as 'square shooters' did the trick? One man in particular (his name doesn't matter) had more to do with my reformation than any other factor. He reasoned with me like a father and never failed to praise me for any little worthwhile act. That man brought to light—then cultivated—every decent impulse which had so long lain dormant in my makeup. He taught me to see how common, low and dirty were the 'Wise guys' I had previously admired. He taught me how to stand; How to speak; what to read; and gave me hundreds of little tips on behaviour which were of use to me in later years.

"After my release I remained on my good behaviours for about two years. I had a 'steady' girl friend and the future looked rosy. I was all set to become a 'solid citizen.' Then came the day when my girl friend, upon learning of my 'past' decided that we were'nt meant for each other. I blew up, so to speak, and quitting my job I left town and, in the course of a couple of years I visited almost every state in the Union plus a few foreign countries. I earned my way as a seaman, boxer, dishwasher, carnival roustabout and whatever offered itself. But no matter how badly I fared, I never again resorted to thievery.

"One night in ——, I became acquainted with Dr. —— an itinerant evangelist who appeared to take a fancy to me. He needed a secretary and somehow, I seemed to fit in. I never made much money, but I was quite happy doing this work. Through the tireless coaching of the good Doctor and under his sponsorship, I was able to pass the entrance requirements at the Bible School of the University of ——. During my two years at school, I supported myself by occasional preaching chores, and by odd jobs. During this time I continued to live well within the law, though I frequently found myself sympathizing with those outside the law.

"After receiving an offer to edit the monthly organ of a religious sect having offices in the city of ——, I quit my studies. The publication lasted little more than a year, and I was forced to do a little preaching in order that I might live. Still, it made me sick to preach a lot of mush to old men, silly women and stupid children. By a great stroke of luck, I made a contact with a prominent publisher who installed me as religious editor of the ——. In quick succession, I jumped to a number of small town dailies, barely earing a living, but having a lot of fun out of life.

"Early in 1930, I organized a corporation for the purpose of publishing weekly community papers known to the trade as 'shoppers.' (These are usually tabloids supported entirely by advertising and are distributed gratis in large quantities in certain sections of a city.) At the beginning, I floated five such papers in as many different cities. Except for advertising, the contents were alike and all were printed in the same centrally located plant. Production costs and overhead were low and my rates more than satisfactory to advertisers so I enjoyed a brief success. I began to think of myself as quite an important personage. I took part in a bitter election and when the smoke of battle had cleared away, my man had lost. From that time on I fought a losing fight. The cities in which I was operating passed so many ordinances which affected my papers adversely that I was forced to quit. I did manage to save a few dollars from the wreckage, because at the time of the bankruptcy proceedings I had already disposed of the greater part of my holdings. While this was not exactly illegal, it was however, morally wrong. Still, it was a matter of me or the other fellow and it is perfectly normal to adopt that line of reasoning, isn't it?

"Early in 1933 I found myself peniless in New York and being in that predicament offers a great many problems for testing the wit of a man. I even went so low as to rob the wallett of a man with whom I had been engaged in a drinking bout. I reasoned thus: This fellow has a home, job and income. I have nothing. Therefore, the loss of a few dollars will be only a temporary inconvenience for him. But to me, those few dollars represented the necessary capital for a 'comeback' effort. Unfortunately, I couldnt seem to make the grade and for a whole summer I had to sleep in the park. However, a daily trip to the bath house and a frequent change of linen served to keep me looking fairly presentable so that when I first met the girl to whom I am now married, I was able to indulge in a little bluffing.

"My wife is still a most attractive woman despite the difficult life she has led with me. When we first met she was a very lovely girl of seventeen and I a somewhat bedraggled thirty. At first I was intent on merely a brief amorous adventure, but in course of time I found myself actually wanting to make good for her sake alone. (She believed in me then, and I have every reason to think that she still does.) We set up housekeeping, using her money to begin with. She quickly became pregnant, and I became frantic with worry. Money went like water and there were many days during which we ate little or nothing. We were forced to move to cheaper and dingier quarters while my bad luck persisted. I secured a few temporary jobs but the going was pretty rough. Often enough I felt the urge to go out and holdup someone or to resort to burglary, but the fear of causing her more trouble held me in check. Finally, through the intercession of a friend I was placed on the sales force of a large corporation. In a short while I was promoted to the office of service manager. We had now begun to climb again, but not fast enough to suit me.

"When an aquaintance offered me a half share in a bookmaking enterprise I eagerly fell in with the idea. Because of my position, I was able to control considerable 'play' and our profits on good days frequently went over the hundred dollar mark. With this added income, I was now able to 'keep up with the Jones!' I bought a home and furnished it throughout. My wife had every convenience including maid service and our infant son was given every advantage. Unfortunately, I failed to look to the future and therefore never saved a dollar. I thought my job would last forever and since people are always gambling, I was certain my whole future was assured.

"Suddenly our venture began to strike snags. Our small reserve fund rapidly melted away. Worried but having every confidence in the old adage that 'bookies' never lose, I concocted a plan for raising cash in a hurry. As service manager all complaints; all requests for servicing, and all reports passed through my office. I was in complete charge and there was no one to question me. Without going into details, my plan was to substitute new machines (I had access to stock) for those requiring service. Our customers were flattered at such service and went their happy way, leaving me in possession of a machine whose serial number was 'cold.' It was a simple matter to do a little book 'juggling' in connection with this activity and since I was always asked to double check the stock inventory, it was easy for me to insert the serial numbers of the machines I had palmed off. (Naturally I kept a record of them.)

"At the time I was doing this, I was 'kidding' my conscience along by telling myself that I would make restitution when my streak of bad luck came to an end as I was sure it must. Perhaps I might even have done so, but the bad luck, instead of ending, became worse. Losing my head a little I gambled myself and that was the absolute height of stupidity. Despite the fact that I was disposing of at least one hundred machines a month to an export firm, my funds continued to melt away. My extra marital adventures too, were costing me a great deal of money. Our sales-manager was a rather attractive woman who appealed to me strongly. She was probably the only person other than the auditors who might have discovered my peculations. Therefore it behooved me to pay her a great deal of attention in order that she remain blind to my activities. Naturally, I was unable to lead a normal home life and frequently stayed in the city for days at a time. Yet, in my heart I was genuinely sorry for my wife who I loved dearly. But enmeshed as I was there was nothing else to do. To 'reform' now meant discovery and disaster.

"One night a friend in the auditors office informed me that there was to be a special audit of my accounts. Instead of standing my ground I became panicky and resigned the following day. Luckily my books were in fool-proof condition and all that could ever be discovered was the loss from stock. I had no jurisdiction over the stock department and—theoretically—no access to stock, so how could anyone blame me for the shortages? When company officials visited me a few months later and asked for help in straightening out the records I stood 'pat' on all inventories I had O.K'd and on the fact that my own departmental records were perfect. There was little they could do and the blame was partially shifted. It was most unfortunate that others had to lose their position, but after all, self preservation is the first law of nature. I am normally a most generous soul but there are times when a man must toss his ideals overboard.

"I was again jobless and head over heels in debt to people who could not be 'stalled.' It was 'Pay up—or else!' I had no wish to die just yet, so I sold my house, furniture, insurance and even my wife's jewelry. We were back in a dinghy apartment. My wife took these reverses like the really swell person that she is. My vague excuses and generalities satisfied her and she continued to believe me the victim of circumstances.

"In order that we might live I was now forced to tackle all manner of jobs, eventually winding up on W.P.A. rolls. In the meantime however, by dint of much cajoling, flattery and plain 'bull' I had wheedled enough money from a group of friends and relatives and had floated a new neighborhood paper in time to catch a lot of Christmas advertising. Following the holidays there was the usual business let-down and within three months I was broke again. Except for some political work I was unemployed until I landed on W.P.A. My political connections were good enough to have me made a foreman within three weeks of the time I first entered W.P.A. ranks. After almost a year of patient waiting I was set to land the position as supervisor of labor for the entire area. Then came another bad break. All W.P.A. employees were ordered fingerprinted and my old reformatory record showed up, plus the record of two other arrests which were of no great importance. Informed that I was to be demoted to the ranks I resigned hoping to protect my rating in the event of a subsequent reinstatement. The economic condition of my family now became grave. Somehow, I couldn't land anything, and even home relief was denied me because of having voluntarily resigned my W.P.A. post. Rather than let my wife, who was now pregnant again, and my son, go hungry I feigned a desertion so that authorities were forced to tender them relief immediately. My wife understood the necessity for this and we remained on the very best of terms. I came home almost every night after the neighborhood had gone to bed.

"No one can even exist on the pittance doled out by the home relief bureau, therefore I found it necessary to supplement my wife's income. I also had to live myself. Fortunately I was able to participate in a bitter election campaign which netted me a neat sum but this soon dwindled to nothingness. My wife was now in the advanced stages of pregnancy and money had to be gotten somehow. I now began the series of stupid frauds for which I am now serving time. By assuming various aliases and by providing false credit information I was able to purchase considerable merchandise, which I then sold. My orders were 'staggered' so that each week's deal provided just enough money for my own living expenses plus a margin for the family. In other words, I committed a new crime each week. Had I found suitable employment, I would have ceased my fraudulent activities, but unfortunately like the proverbial pitcher that went to the well once too often, I went a little too far and wound up serving time.

"I feel no animosity towards the sentencing judge or towards any official with whom I came in contact. Naturally I am saddened by the knowledge that I am to be separated from my family for so long a period of time, but I will not cry over spilt milk. I merely feel that I lost in a sort of game, and being the loser, I must now pay off.

"There is no way in which I can honestly justify my criminal 'career.' Perhaps I lack moral stamina.

"At this point I think it advisable to list in their proper order the arrests which make my record appear blacker than it really is. Each arrest will be truthfully explained and the disposition of the case given.

"In early boyhood on two or three occasions I was brought before the juvenile court on truancy and allied charges. In each case I was merely reprimanded and returned to the custody of my parents. The last time however, I was held in the Parental Home for six weeks. In 1920, I was arrested and charged with unlawful entry, grand larceny and possession of deadly weapons. The charges were justified and I was subsequently sentenced to the State Reformatory for an indeterminate period. At the time I was seventeen years of age. After twenty months I was paroled. After that nothing appears on my record until 1930 or 1931, when I was picked up on suspicion. Was never even arraigned, was released a day later. There was no reasons for this arrest, and it might have happened to any stranger in a strange city.

"In 1935 I was charged with perjury in the first degree. The grand jury refused to indict, and I was dismissed. In this case, I had sought a position with an agency, and on the application appeared the question: 'Were you ever arrested, etc.?' To have answered in the affirmative would have lost the job. Quite naturally, I answered 'no.' Later this application was notarized without my knowledge. This was proven by competent witnesses before the Grand Jury, hence their refusal to indict. Immediately following my dismissal on the perjury charges, I was re-arrested charged with the violation of an obscure law which reads as follows: 'Any person who obtains a position or place of trust by means of any false or fraudulent statement shall be guilty of a misdemeanor.' On this charge I was found guilty and given a suspended sentence.

"The last arrest was the one leading up to my present plight. Upon my arrest, I co-operated with authorities in every way. By my cooperation, they were able to clear a number of cases off their records. I pleaded guilty to ten counts."

From psychopathy, which is a predisposant to crime, we turn now to another much confused and erroneously regarded problem in criminology. Alcoholism occupies a unique place in our view of crime. It is both a predisposant and precipitant, and as such forms a fitting transitional topic between our discussions of the predisposing factors in crime—which have really been our chief concern thus far—and the precipitating factors, which accrue from the world about and the special terms of the current social organization.

# 11. Alcoholism and Crime

ONE of the most persistent fictions of our time is that which tends to equate crime and alcoholism. Both the press and, unfortunately, a large segment of otherwise well-informed and even professional opinion show a strong bias in this respect. Blue-noses, of course, tend to capitalize on the apparent but completely unreal identification between these widely separate phenomena. But in point of fact, alcoholism does not necessarily lead to crime and cannot be regarded as an underlying cause of criminality. Each is a special form of behavior, originating independently and from markedly different causes, although one may and often does accompany the other. Yet so long as the fiction of concomitance is maintained, just so long will it be futile to expect adequate solutions to either.

Crime is a symptom of underlying intra-personal conflict which is precipitated environmentally and provides a solution through action involving the incidental societal sanctions of the culture in which it transpires. Alcoholism is also a symptom of inner discord and similarly aimed toward a solution of persistent problems, but expressing itself mainly personally in its effects. Put another way, the *direct* effects of crime are observable in the sphere of community interest; while the *direct* effects of alcohol are visible in the alcoholic himself. Thus the two phenomena are worlds apart.

Yet this facile and convenient differential, as unavoidable as Cyrano's nose, is only one of many features of distinguishment between alcoholism and crime. Others relate to fundamental dynamisms.

It has been observed and widely commented upon that men drink to excess for a variety of reasons, but all formulations can be reduced to the proposition that alcohol serves to withdraw the ego from participation in the conflict situation. The narcotization of the ego or its literal excision through alcohol so that it can no longer serve as a censoring, criticizing, rejecting agency allows free play to those solutions to conflict offered by the unconscious in the form of basal impulses and urgings. In this respect alone, alcoholism and crime are manifestly of a different order, since with crime the ego is permeated with compromise formations and with modifications of forbidden tendencies but is ever-present and, in fact, provides the behavior with somewhat of an individual stamp and characteristic. Furthermore, clinical observation serves to support this important distinction and even leads to the belief that the ego-structure of the alcoholic is different from and weaker than the ego-structure of the criminal and the neurotic, hence predisposed or prepared for narcotization and excision. All evidence points toward the fixation of the alcoholic in the oral incorporative or sucking stage. Herein the elemental goal is the pleasurable quiescence following oral gratification, and reality is something to be reckoned with only because of accidental but poignantly acute frustrations such as too early withdrawal of bottle or breast and feeding delays. Indeed, the character structure of the alcoholic allows of no other interpretation at the present stage of our knowledge. Investigators have tirelessly commented upon, and Charles Jackson in his *The Lost Weekend* has immortalized, those pre-ego oral traits of the alcoholic: his desire for immediate satisfaction of wants, his unreasoning expectation of unending well-being, his chaotic and unchannelized urge for self expression, his circuitous techniques for avoidance of responsibility, and finally his intensive, strainful, continual craving for purely emotive experience. These are tendencies laid down and fixed at a time when the ego is in formation, when the demands of physiological growth and cultural requisites have not yet enforced reality acceptance. And they persist as prime motivants. Moreover, they eventuate in the special features of the alcoholic, which universally seem to include profound maternal attachment and identification leading to latent or overt homosexuality, typical dependency and lack of ambition, and what appears to be an urge toward self-destruction in expiation of trespasses phantasied by the superego and aided by the essentially deficient ego-preservative trends. In summary, then, the alcoholic drinks to immobilize, narcotize, excise, his already so predisposed ego since it stands in the way of the expression of his fundamental urgings; and in this way he "solves" the intimate conflict between desire and ego prohibition.

Apart from its function in excising ego, alcohol further serves to enable mobilization of conflicting tendencies within the personality in a more pure form than is possible in a sober state. The evasive mechanisms which, after all, are tools of ego, are not utilized, and the raw, naked, brutal contention that may reach far back into the dim history of the drunkard is exposed without benefit of compromise. Intolerable reality either disappears as ego participation in it lessens, or it is superseded by the megalomanic conceptions and program of the autocrat of the cradle—which the drinker has now become.

The situation with regard to crime is quite different. In the first place, the true criminal act is performed in the presence of ego and almost always with its complicity. The ego consents to the activity and even implements it from its warehouse of mechanisms. And beyond participating in the crime, it often even protects the act by employing its talents to avoid detection. In the second place, the criminal act can be motivated variously from all stages and phases of personality development. It can and does stem from fixations in any period and does not necessarily relate exclusively to the oral episode.

And yet it would be erroneous to dismiss alcohol from the serious study of crime and criminals. Crimes *are* performed by people in a state of complete or near drunkenness; and it has happened innumerable times that alcoholic indulgence *has* been a precondition for the commission of a crime where the likelihood of its performance in the absence of such indulgence would possibly have been minimal. Moreover, the *indirect* effects of alcohol bear an intimate relationship to the problems involved in crime.

Those effects of alcoholism which we may label indirect are perhaps the truly nefarious and malignant by-products of the illness. They ramify to touch the lives of others, and such is their infectiousness that they influence even succeeding generations. The problem of the criminologist especially would be a far more simple one if excessive drinking reflected on the drunkard alone. But such is the nature of this "flight from ego" that the drunkard prepares by his excesses the soil in which the criminogenic virus finds a lushness and a promise of nourishment elsewhere unrivaled. All those hazards which modern dynamic psychology finds indispensable for both the predisposing toward and precipitation of the criminal act can be found in the distortion which the alcoholic wreaks upon the environment. This writer can produce instance after instance of criminal acts wherein the remote responsible factor was the deterioration of family life and the perversion of the wholesome family constellation. As family members "solved" their personal conflicts and surmounted their intimate frustrations through alcohol, they created the optimal circumstances that permitted the occurrence of crucial episodes which in turn dramatically affected the careers and life-styles of growing children. At the risk of laboring an obvious point there comes to mind a handful of examples. There was the assaulter of an Army officer who resented all authority and whose military career was spotted with summary courts-martial for insolence, refusals to obey orders, and like offenses. Festering among his earliest memories was the shameful image of a drunken father clad ingloriously in stained drawers and administering a terribly severe whipping to a four-year-old for some minor breach of family discipline. How introject that kind of parent, and through him the many other authority figures up to and including his military superiors? Then there was the car-thief who evoked the heart-rending description of a sluttish, sodden mother who periodically offered herself to the male population of the neighborhood in full sight of her children, in at least one of whose ears forever after echoed the dissonant symphony of laughter, creaking spring, and ribald shouting. And, finally, there was the bank robber who vividly recaptured the dread loneliness and fear of the empty house, the bare larder, the wild foraging through back-alleys, the vengeful quarrels and hate between alcoholic father and a mother on whom the burden of support fell. These are endlessly variable themes from the same score, reflecting the secondary and derivative effects of alcoholism upon persons who are not themselves alcoholic but who suffer for the sins of their forebears.

A feature of more distinctly sociological import in the relationship of alcohol and crime relates to the undesirable contacts with the law made through arrests for simple drunkenness. Our police blotters are crowded with such entries, which reflect more than anything else our confused thinking on the subject and the inadequacy of our techniques for handling the problem. Arrests for drunkenness and misdemeanors complicated by drunkenness such as "disturbing the peace" comprise the greatest single statistic of "crime." Where the need is for treatment, for inquiry into causes, for care and understanding, we provide the filthy lockup and the foul stockade, replete with the stench of vomit and the tender ministrations of minor politicos. And more, we provide a "record" of the misdeed, marking the misdemeanant with the ineradicable brand of social disapproval, toying with his destiny and so adding fuel to the fires which are consuming him.

As to the crimes which are committed by intoxicated persons, they are, for the most part, behavior manifestations which have been checked until that time by an inhibiting ego armed with the many tools and instruments for repression or deflection of primitive, elemental urges. That this is so is borne out by the mathematical fact that the offenses fall mainly within the categories of sexual crimes or crimes directed against the person of another individual. It is a noteworthy and clinically substantiated fact that even where the precipitating factor in a criminal act by an intoxicated individual is of an environmental (socio-economic) kind, it is rare that the act is directed against the social trappings or framework; rather, it is almost always directed against a person. And even in those cases where an offense goes by the name of larceny or fraud or what not, it is possible with but little effort to discover behind it the personalized reference. So it is that the intrinsic value of the act is far different and far more profound than it superficially appears to be. This was beautifully illustrated by the recent case wherein sabotage was charged to an alcoholic whose manifest (surface) discontent was with a meager pay envelope, but whose latent vexation harked back to a stinging humiliation of childhood. The real intention of the act was directed against an agent who was, on the surface, independent of the State and only connected with it by an involved symbolism.

This same case illustrates yet another generally overlooked subsidiary problem in excessive indulgence in alcohol. Only when drunk could this man have behaved criminally, for his

ego contained energetic remnants from former military service, and when sober he could no more have conceived of himself as capable of performing such an unpatriotic act than he
could of living under the sea. Indeed, in daily contact with
criminals the observer is struck by this convenient amnesia
for criminal events, an amnesia which recurs so monotonously
as to be almost boring. The man who trespasses under alcohol
will rarely "remember" his offenses: his "excuse" being, "I
was drunk." But if the whole story is known it appears that in
sobriety the ego is unwilling to admit the facts, and shame-
facedly—but thankful for a skirt behind which to hide—allows
of its own dereliction of duty. This it will do so readily because it truly cannot conceive of the self in terms so base, so
unflattering, so unlike its customary view of itself, as a recognition of the act would entail.

Alcohol may be viewed as one of the foremost precipitants
of crime because of its peculiar catalytic action. Just getting
drunk may not lead to crime, but getting drunk does serve to
mobilize the internal contradictions and conflicts, to point up
and make urgent the appetites and needs which are smoldering
below the limen of awareness, and so to ignite the fuse. Nowhere is this better exemplified than in those instances where
latent psychopathy is brought out under intoxication. Those
checks and safeguards which a vigilant ego usually maintains
are rendered non-operative, and the bitter contention between
superego and id which is at the crux of the disorder resolves
itself in the compromise formation of behavior we recognize as
psychopathic. As a matter of fact, this mechanism and function of alcohol as a mobilizer for the latent trends and tendencies of the personality is perhaps the core of the alcohol
problem, lending a pointedness to the popular notion that
under intoxication the "real person" is disclosed.

It should not be overlooked that alcohol, like other narcotics, is in a manner of speaking also a protector from the

criminal act. That is to say, the function of alcoholic over-indulgence on some individuals and in many instances is not disruptive, not evocative of socially or personally disapproved behavior. It is rather salutary and solicitous. In the manner of a famous academician who is reputed to have said, "Whenever I feel like exercising I lie down until the feeling leaves me," resort to alcohol is not infrequently had to give the quietus to disturbing phantasies of criminal action and even to strong impulses toward such behavior. In such cases the repressed has risen to the surface either through environmental happenstance or through a failure of ego properly to deflect by the usual techniques, and has there been recognized for what it is. Where this occurs, however, it is usually a sure sign of absolute superego dominion. One lucid and provocative example of this so frequently ignored aspect of our problem was presented by the ministerial student who during a summer vacation at a resort with his wife was tormented by adulterous fancies and lascivious impulses toward all the women who disported themselves in relaxed attitudes within his sight. To quell the rising storm within him, he resorted to drink. Dynamically, one could say that he placed his faith in superego to prevent what would have been a drastic episode in his life—one caused by an act even more ruinous than drunkenness. It was almost as if—to be less precise and technical about our terminology—he knew that when his permeable and impressionable ego was out of the way, his despotic superego would smother the fiery inward turmoil. This tortured divine was and is not alone in his successful experimentation with alcohol to safeguard against behavior manifestations which border upon or literally entail crime. And it is well never to lose sight of the cogent fact that there is a reverse and possibly brighter side to this coin we are examining.

In connection with this selfsame dynamic, it should not be overlooked that this (shall we say) sublimative feature is in a sense evident in the resort to alcohol as one way of achieving synthetically an internal balance, of relieving accumulated tensions, of promoting intra-organic physical and chemical equilibrium, which literally protects, in some instances, against crime. The present writer is a vociferous if only minor champion of Cannon's monumental conception of *homeostasis,* that physiological, automatic, self-preservative insurance against disintegration. He believes thoroughly in the notion that there is a design behind all symptom, and that the body labors ceaselessly for the everlasting maintenance of a dynamic balance. This has been observed especially in those disorders that are characterized by episodic demonstrations. In psychopathic personality, for instance, the outward signs and manifestations of the disorder in terms of *overt* hostility, aggression, and tantrum behavior are not continuous and always on-going; but they show a characteristic rhythmicity much as do the convulsive displays of the epileptic. Such periodicity of symptom functions to relieve tensions, to restore internal harmony, to re-achieve quiescence—the display, while personally or socially harmful, has an aim. In a similar way, the alcoholic bout as observed in the periodic drunkard is the handmaiden of homeostasis. And if we are to be grateful for small favors, we are duty-bound to express appreciation to those who "drain" through alcohol, thus substituting an innocuous enterprise for a perhaps far more serious infringement or trespass.

A discussion of alcohol and crime would indeed be inadequate were it to overlook two special features which your author likes to refer to as "the alcoholic phantasy" and "the romance of alcohol." The mechanics of the phantasy are extremely simple and have already been sketched. As the fluid exerts its effect, as ego is narcotized and the higher senses toxified, reality fades and the drinker regresses to that life-stage when from the lofty throne of the high-chair and the limitless domain of the cradle he pontificated like some Renaissance duke. Inadequacies, insecurities, anxieties—these are all replaced by roseate illusions of ambition achieved, honor won, talent recognized, worlds conquered. Such fancies characteristically are not sick nor moribund, but they follow an uncomplicated infantile pattern wherein the basal needs and appetites of the alcoholic are acted out in all their futile glory. For the interpretation of the alcoholic phantasy no special insight is wanted; indeed its transparency is almost painful. It is undeviating in its aim and, except for inconsequential shifts in scenes and players, standard in plot. Moreover—and for the criminologist this is the crux of the matter—it is accompanied by a motor discharge. Herein it is seen to differ from the day-dreams and the nocturnal dramas.

No more poignant or expert accounting of the alcoholic phantasy exists in all literature, scientific or lay, than in the relating of the incidents so trenchantly etched by the author of *The Lost Weekend*. This writer recalls especially the sequence wherein the protagonist, deep in alcohol, fantasies himself as the concert pianist whose rendition of a classical concerto is such a marvel of technique and talent, and, also, that masterly episode in which he so cunningly, so deftly, lifts a purse.

For the alcoholic the phantasy is wish-fulfilling, of course. But unlike the dreams of day or night, it tends toward discharge and immediate acting out. It transforms reality and is a fertile source for action transgressing law. In fine, it is regressive to the stage of uninhibited megalomania and autocracy, of dictatorship and—so to speak—"natural" criminalism.

The tendency of the alcoholic phantasy is to be repetitious in theme if not in content. In one of the writer's cases, which incidentally exhibits all the dynamics and relationships already covered in our discussion of alcohol and crime, the phantasy was a beautiful saga of triumph. This patient is a man of forty-three years who was convicted of a theft from an inter-state shipment and sentenced to three years in Federal custody. Prior to this arrest he had clashed with the law five times, on each occasion having been charged with intoxication, and serving from one to three months in a local lock-up, from the description of which we are now gratefully spared. Born in a Midwestern farming community and into a congenial if some-what strait-laced family, he was the second of four children. He took the commercial course of a good high school and upon graduation entered the school of business administra-tion of a large Eastern university. Before receiving his bachelor's degree, however, he quit to engage in a small in-dependent commercial enterprise. In this he was modestly successful, and at the age of thirty was offered the editorship of a trade journal. He held this post for five years, losing it when his excessive drinking caused his work to deteriorate. Meanwhile he had married and become the father of two children. Marital life was superficially happy until he joined the unemployed. After a quarrel with his wife three months following his dismissal, he merely walked off and set out upon a nomadic career, finding work where he could and when he was not too incapacitated through drink. Some of the jobs he managed to get were quite good ones, but his employers soon learned of his habits and dismissal followed. One night he was awaiting the train that was to take him away from the scene of one of his failures. It was very late and he was the only occupant of the station. He was drunk, as usual. The door to the baggage room was ajar; he entered and at-tempted to make off with a package. In this he was observed by a telegrapher in the ticket booth. In jail the following morning he denied the theft, vigorously protesting that he could not have committed such an act even while drunk. On initial psychiatric examination he admitted two previous hospitalizations for chronic alcoholism and delirium tremens.

He was frank, anxious, somewhat manneristic, remorseful. Intelligence was superior, insight superficial, and judgment was found to be fair. During treatment by hypnoanalysis he recovered the essentials of the theft and it was revealed that it was a part of the persistent phantasy which was a component of the illness. In this phantasy he was usually a playwright, acclaimed and applauded by the world. Often he would view himself, properly attired and beribboned as for some diplomatic or academic function, in a box at the opening at one of his great plays. As the curtain falls and the cries of "Author! Author!" resound throughout the immense auditorium, he rises and holds up his hand for silence. Then, wittily but with condescension, he utters a few well-chosen sentences of appreciation to the audience. A variant to this so satisfying fiction has him, the same famous playwright, seeking a lost manuscript, the only one extant, of a satire so biting that to keep it from reaching the public and thus causing a governmental upheaval, the henchmen of the political figures involved have conspired to filch it from him. It is perhaps anti-climactical to report that the package this patient removed from the station baggage-room represented for him the missing master-work.

When we review the relationship of alcoholism and crime, we cannot help but be impressed with the potency of the romance of alcohol. By this is meant the legend and the glamour attributed to the fluid, the appeal which has grown up about it, the beliefs and attitudes associated with it, in brief, the psychological complex and halo effect which accrues to drinking. In this writer's opinion it is the romance of alcohol which is responsible for more crimes than the alcohol itself. It seems not unlikely that much of over-indulgence is engaged upon with the full expectation—and hence the preparation or "set"—for particular effects, and that these effects then come about independently of the exertions of the beverage. Certainly this has been found to hold true in the endless and disheartening procession of cases observed clinically in the recent war years. Army prisoner after Army prisoner gives the same history. There was the rural or semi-urban environment, the sober and sympathetic yet firm parents, the modestly successful school career, the subtle discipline of the neighborhood, the quietly adventuresome life. Then there was the hectic time of induction—the severing of the psychological umbilicus. And then came the freedom of Army life— for with all the regimentation and discipline of the Services it cannot be denied that for most boys and men the bonds that really matter, the ties that truly bind, are almost completely loosed when they set out upon this greatest of all adventures. At this point there is brought to bear upon them a myriad of influences ranging from loneliness, insecurity, and fear to the newspaper and radio fabrication that one must get drunk to be socially acceptable. And over and above there play the myth and legend of alcohol which have somehow become woven into the fabric of our culture. Embodied in this romance are some of the following canards: drinking makes for courage, drinking enhances sexual attractiveness and prowess, drinking increases skillfulness, drinking makes one happy, etc. So these boys are "set" for drunkenness almost before the cork is pulled. For most of them there has been no previous alcoholic experience. Besides the low tolerance for alcohol which they must have, we should reckon with the romance involved.

A twenty year-old Army prisoner typifies the situation. He is serving a sentence of almost twice his years for having assaulted his Sergeant. The home from which he originated was regarded highly in the community; his father was a church-warden and land-owner; his mother was a former school teacher. He is the fourth of five male children, all of whom are serving their country, and one of whom was made prisoner by the Japanese on Bataan Peninsula. Our subject's school and community record contains not a single blemish. He lived at home with his parents in a Virginia mill town, graduated from high school at eighteen, and immediately went to work for his father. He was interested in sports, the movies, and fiction-reading. In 1941, just before entering the Army, he married a childhood sweetheart. In the Army he made a good record, was considered satisfactory soldier material, and received his Pfc. rating very soon. One night he and a friend entered the Sergeant's tent and proceeded to attack the sleeping man with the butt ends of their rifles. The verbatim notes from one of the clinical interviews are most interesting:

*Q:* "You say you had been drinking?"
*A:* "Yes."
*Q:* "Would you say you were drunk?"
*A:* "Boy, and how!"
*Q:* "Had you ever got drunk before going into the Army?"
*A:* "No. I never even drank at all before I joined up."
*Q:* "Then why did you start drinking after you joined?"
*A:* "Well, all the boys drank. It gave us something to do. We used to have a lot of fun. A guy can't be a stinker. We all went together."
*Q:* "Why?"
*A:* "Well we had good times that way. Didn't give a damn about anything."
*Q:* "What do you know about alcohol?"
*A:* "I don't get you."
*Q:* "I mean, before you began to drink did you know what the effects of alcohol would be on you?"
*A:* "Oh, sure."
*Q:* "Well, what did you think?"
*A:* "Oh, that you got drunk, forgot yourself, raised a little hell maybe, had some fun, played around a little."
*Q:* "Does it take a lot to make you drunk?"
*A:* "Hell no! I get drunk on the smell of the stuff."
*Q:* "What did your folks think about drinking?"
*A:* "Well, they never drank."
*Q:* "Never?"

*A:* "Well, weddings and such. Maybe a glass of beer or wine once in a long time."

*Q:* "Why did you fellows attack the Sergeant?"

*A:* "Well, he'd been riding us a long time. Acted like he was General Marshall or your old man all the time."

*Q:* "Do you think you would have attacked him if you hadn't been drinking?"

*A:* "No, I don't think so."

The purpose of this review has been to highlight the major considerations involved in any discussion of alcoholism and crime. It has been held that, as behavior modes, they are distinct from each other, that while there are areas of correspondence, in reality they are disparate psychological entities. Of all the statements and propositions we have advanced, this is undoubtedly the most pertinent, since it points a way to treatment. The techniques which have been evolved for the alcoholic *and* for the criminal have been those of management alone. It would be folly for us to refuse to grant recognition to this fact—folly because it is nothing less than a betrayal of trust to cry treatment when all we have been doing is to fashion crutches to carry the alcoholic and the criminal over from one episode to another.

The treatment of alcoholics, just like the treatment of criminals, must start from the premise that these are ill persons whose symptoms are of a peculiar order, although they reflect fundamental disturbances of function. It must then proceed to dissect out and expose root-causes for these illnesses and, in the light of modern knowledge, must subject these causes to the dynamic re-orientation and re-integration which constitute the mainsprings for the true therapy of those psychogenetic vexations which plague and crucify men.

# 12. Crime in the Prevailing Economy

MUCH nonsense has been perpetrated upon an unaware public, including uncounted generations of students, by both the champions of and the opponents to the view of economics as a factor of importance in crime. So-called and self-styled "economic scientists" have frequently lost their heads over this topic, the press has been divided, the virgin pages of numerous journals in the fields of sociology, criminology, and economics have been the bloodless sites of fierce custard-pie battles which were interrupted from time to time to allow participants to make obeisance to the hollow gods of scientific objectivity and dispassion.

Writers of textbooks on criminology have presented the most amusing spectacle of all. With a nod toward Marxism, they have decried the current economic chaos; while, with a cautious eye to their jobs and an ear cocked for the sometimes not so distant tramp of the vigilantes, they have hastened to add enough "buts" and "ifs" and "howevers" to temper their polemics to the irritative quality of warm milk. To render the confusion even more confounding, they have borrowed enough statistics from the Marxist-Leninist camp on the one side and the National Association of Manufacturers on the other to assure the kind of double-talk that encourages students to consign them and their books to that limbo where they cannot interfere either with the students' preconceived notions or with their plans for the next week-end house-party. In short, these writers have used a perfect technique for the prevention of thinking and the preservation of the status quo.

In this work, however, we are pledged solely to the search for truth about crime and criminals as it emerges from the study of human behavior. We shall not, therefore, refrain from toppling an idol or two if it stands in the way of our vision; and neither shall we employ the perversion of statistics which seeks to "prove" a case about which we have been collectively prejudiced by every organ and mode of propaganda imaginable.

What are the facts?

The facts are these: The prevailing economy that obtains over most of the world is *the* important precipitant of crime; the prevailing economy is also a powerful predisposant toward crime.

Before we attempt to support the two facts just stated, it will be well to orient ourselves in the economic climate. To do this, it is necessary at least to state some of the contentions of the opposing schools.

Those who wave the banner for the economic causation of crime as all-important start from the proposition that, like all other phenomena in life and history, crime is economically determined. They seek to show capitalism as a kind of practice which by and large creates a laboring class upon whose toil society is founded, and which operates unceasingly to increase the volume of misery among the working, laboring masses. They argue that, under capitalism, real wages are forced lower and lower, and this decline in real wages in turn forces the living standard to a lower level. They point out that it is to the advantage of those who benefit from this feature of the economy (the capitalists) to hold and to keep the great mass at this level; that thereby they insure greater profits to themselves and create a situation of insecurity which operates to their benefit. They also refer to class stratification, the breaking up of humankind into groups which cohere out of self-interest and for mutual support, and which are naturally antagonistic toward each other. This is the class struggle, in which everyone takes part. Society is thus seen as in a perpetual state of internal warfare. As a product of capitalism, a number of psychological attitudes are supposed to accrue to the individual, depending upon his class and his "conditioning." If he is a member of a controlling capitalistic group, he is a champion of private property, a natural despoiler and exploiter of his fellow man, an adherent to the thesis that individual effort can achieve the miracle either of status or of monetary success—perhaps of both. If he belongs to the middle class, he seeks to emulate the attitudes of the class above and to support it chiefly because he is blinded by the staggering possibility that the system provides a means whereby he, too, may become one of the chosen. And if he is one of the huge working or laboring mass, he is motivated (unless he has been perverted by propaganda from above) by a natural revolutionary zeal for collectivism, for progress, for freedom from bondage. Moreover, these same spokesmen for economic determinism play a pitiless searchlight upon the products of capitalism. They point the accusing finger at the by-products of this economic tyranny: the miserable slum with its crowding, its dearth of hygienic facilities and plethora of occupants; the lack of education and the positive denial of opportunity for higher culture to the masses of men; the improper care for growing children which results under such circumstances; the emphasis upon individualism and selfishness that saps the ethical and moral roots of a culture with high pretensions; the social parasitism among both the very rich and the dole-grubbing poor; the relentless conduct of industry for personal profit at the expense of the health and sanity of those who operate and attend the machines; the strangling of all noble, high-purposed, beneficent, altruistic attitudes, and the substitution for them of egoistic, vain, and self-seeking impulses. And then they indict certain natural elements within the capitalist economy, and to these directly attribute criminal behavior: unemployment, and its psychic effects of depression, doubt, and disgust; centralization of dependent groups into slum areas, where attitudinal contagion is more than likely and where energy-diverting techniques are limited; great economic crises, cycles, seasonal swings, making for insecurity and forever projecting the image of misery and want; wars and imperialistic ventures for trade outlets and access to raw materials; the instability of the individual budget and the attendant anxiety over accident, disease, and old age; the rapidity of price rises as contrasted with the slowness of wage increases. Of such a nature is the argument of this group.

On the other side of this ideological fence are those who argue that the role which economics plays in crime is a minimal one, that it is simply one factor among many. Such persons are usually defenders of the capitalist system of economy. They argue, first of all, that their opponents are piling all their social eggs in a single basket; and they object to this practice, claiming it is a betrayal of reason and scientific method to explain everything by a single rule of thumb. The accusations they answer by pointing out that the bulk of the poverty-stricken do not commit crimes, and that if the decriers of capitalism are anywhere near correct, this should not be so. Hence, they think that other factors, too, enter into causation. Moreover, they quote chapter and verse to testify that capitalism has operated everywhere to improve the living standards, to increase wages steadily. And they think to clinch this point by showing that during the twenties, a period of rampant prosperity, in spite of near total employment, the crime rate reached new and fabulous levels. So far as the system in itself is concerned, they are inclined to be aggressively apologetic. They admit that some employers are "bad," unsympathetic, egotistical, and selfish; but they point with pride at the many evidences of paternal concern of such "noble figures" as the Fords, Hersheys, Rockefellers, to name but a few. They also claim that without the profit drive, men would be lacking in initiative; that bold and adventuresome spirits would not arise; that progress would be stifled if a man could not work for personal gain. They even admit a certain amount of necessary evil as inherent in the system of capital economy, but they deny that the evils are important enough to condemn the entire system. Another argument of which the debaters on this side are fond is the one in which they reveal that even comfortably fixed, sometimes very wealthy, people become involved in criminal activity, proving thereby that there is more behind crime than economic want and privation.

Now one of the most curious features of this debate between the accusers and defenders of capitalism as it relates to crime is that both discount—when they do not entirely reject —the only available source of information regarding its role. The incliners toward socialism denounce the high crime rate in capitalistic countries; the defenders of the capitalistic system hotly counter that the economics of capitalism are not solely responsible for this. Then the champions of individualism fixate the Russian experiment and with pardonable delight seize upon the fact that under Soviet rule the crime rate, especially among juveniles, has soared—and this under conditions which presumably avoid the hazards of capitalism. To this the socialists answer (1) that the Soviet Union has not yet achieved socialism, (2) has had to expend most of her energy in planning and preparing for the great war and therefore could not attack the problem in full force.

While the debaters are locked in a struggle which has in actuality been taken from their hands and entrusted to mortar fire, 16-inch naval guns, diplomatic intrigue, picket lines, policemen's clubs, and ballot boxes, certain relationships between economics and crime (and law-breaking) have been worked out by investigators. A few are here presented as indicative of the way much objective research into the problem has proceeded. The methods of research rather than the conclusions (which are subject to considerable variation depending on the time, place, sampling used, and even upon the individual characteristics of the investigators themselves) are of the greatest interest to the student of criminology.

There are about four chief ways or methods by which it has been hoped to measure the relationship between selected economic factors and crime.

(1) *By the study of trade cycles and convictions.* A general correlative trend has been worked out which would seem to indicate that when commodity prices increase, crime increases; that in periods of depression, by and large, crime increases; that in periods of prosperity the types of crime that increase are those classed as violent or against persons, and those popularly attributable to (or somehow involved with) alcoholic excess. Such data as result from these studies are obviously inadequate. They constitute more than anything else an indictment of the hypotheses from which the studies proceed. They do not distinguish between law-breaking and crime; they reveal nothing about the kinds of people who commit the offenses; and they lump into a single heap all offenses under a blanket rubric (like crimes *vs.* property), ignoring the differences between offenses which may be as disparate as filching a postage stamp and embezzling a sum equal to the national debt of, say, Finland. Moreover, such research leaves out of account the economic and social status of the participants in the prohibited activities. The seriousness of this omission cannot be overrated, for it is a commonplace of our society that the likelihood of arrest, conviction, and detention is far greater for a destitute offender than for one with

ready cash (or connections) to buy his way out of trouble or hire someone to do it for him. And, again, it must be considered that the economically powerful make the laws, which are intended to support and protect them and their interests. Therefore, apart from the restrictions on sheer robber barony which have been imposed on the economically (and hence every other way) powerful only recently, the laws of our land are directed toward the maintenance of the powerful in power. Finally, many laws by their very own definitions immediately exclude the probability of offenders against them originating from any other than the lower economic group, as witness the regulations governing employee conduct during the heyday of the W. P. A.; while others, on the other hand, confine offenses to the upper economic classes as, for instance, do the Securities Exchange Commission regulations. So that any "proof", for or against the economic factor as a causal agent in crime, must be most carefully weighed when it results from this way of investigation.

(2) *By the comparison of seasonal fluctuations with crime rates.* Handling data in this manner shows that there is a lessening of crimes *vs.* property in warmer months with a parallel perceptible rise in crimes *vs.* persons as the weather grows hot. At the same time it is characteristic of our economy that, as the weather grows colder, layoffs and unemployment due to the abandonment of outdoor projects and trades increase. The anachronism in this economic by-product is that this occurs at a time when economic need in terms of basal realities grows more urgent and pressing, and that prices tend to rise as the temperature falls. Again we find the same research fallacies in such propositions: the personalities of the offenders are left out of account; the laws applying to property are discriminatory; law-breaking and crime are used interchangeably.

(3) *By the study of the occupations of convicted persons.*

The approach by such a method as this tries to classify typical offenses as more likely to be committed by individuals in certain trades or specialized units of the economic structure. Thus it has been shown that agricultural workers, seamen, and miners are more often *convicted* of property damage, sexual offenses, and arson, than of any other "crimes"; sailors and soldiers swell the ranks of those convicted of rape and personal violence; skilled workers and commercial employees indulge heavily in acquisitive trespasses. Investigations along these lines bend over backwards to "prove" that it is not the occupation itself which is an influence on crime, but that opportunities for committing certain types of crimes are more likely to be present in some occupations than in others. A pretense of reason is loaned to arguments of this type by the circular redundancy of such propositions as, "bank embezzlers are usually employed in banks." At any rate, it is a rare study which even pretends to investigate the kinds of people who enter certain occupations, their adjustments to such assignments, and the motivations which encourage them to engage upon specific "crimes."

Slicing the same cake a somewhat different way are the researches which indicate that the unskilled laborers are represented in the figure for total offenses by a higher mathematical symbol than other "classes"; that certain commercial types contribute more heavily than others; and that because both of these are found more frequently in populous areas, the crime rate of cities is thereby considerably greater than that of rural, or at least less densely inhabited, regions. To stop at this—which is what almost all such projects do—is to contribute nothing to knowledge of the kind we are seeking.

(4) *By investigations of the economic status of convicted persons.* Efforts along these lines come up with such august and revelatory announcements as, for example, that lower economic groups contribute, in proportion to the population,

a greater number of *convictions* than other segments. In addition to the variables we have already indicated, such as personality, law-breaking as distinguished from crime, and others —all of which must be taken into account no matter what phase of the crime *vis-a-vis* the economic order relationship is to be studied—the glaring realities of our social and cultural setting must also be given a prominent share, statistically or otherwise, in reaching conclusions. It must be recognized that the indigent and even the marginal groups toward the lower end of the middle classes cannot afford adequate legal talent, lack political pull, have no comeback, and are unable to pay fines. Moreover, they even present themselves (by the appearance of poverty and the psychological overlay of fear, insecurity, even excessive humility) in a manner suited only to evoke hostile reactions in a courtroom, where the assorted personnel from the mighty judge to the political footballs infesting any court of law as flunkies and hangers-on are imbued with fierce and irrational prejudices against the poor and with a haunting sense of guilt which hides under vindictive bias.

The futility of such research is apparent to those who approach the problem as observers of human behavior. But there is another way of viewing crime in the prevailing economy, a way which takes into account not only the harsh actualities of the time and place in which the activities transpire, but also the humanity behind them.

As a psychologist your author is incompetent to pass judgment on an economic system as such. But as a scientist whose concern is with the effects of economics and other aspects of life upon behavior, he is qualified to express the opinion that no form of economy yet evolved satisfactorily meets the needs of the people it touches to the extent that it does not directly precipitate crime (among other things) or predispose toward criminal behavior. This is as true of capitalism as it is of state socialism, communism, technocracy, the Townsend Plan, or what not. All of them are founded upon a poor psychology, or fail entirely to take psychology into account. One would almost think each had been formulated in a different universe, inhabited by nightmarish creatures who only remotely resemble men and women and children. The socialistic (or the communistic) form disregards, as an example, some of the basic motivational considerations such as competition, the need for accumulating the symbolic trappings and displayable evidence of whatever form of success is fashionable, and is untrue to some facts which can be observed in almost any nursery. It also makes the fundamental mistake of emphasizing (in the words of Philip Wylie) "goods instead of good"; and while it condemns the materialism of capitalist culture, it itself is based upon what it considers inexorable laws embracing dynamics of materials which leave basic human qualities out of account. It de-emphasizes and emasculates the role of emotion and life-history in individual human affairs. The psychology upon which it is based arose in the dusty laboratories of Europe where philosophers, recently turned psychologists, painstakingly plotted the effects of numberless units of physical experience upon the skin and its contents. A rebirth and resurrection came when from Russia went forth the celebrated notions of Pavlov and his "conditioned reflex" thesis, and the supreme climax was capped with the behaviorism of John Watson in the United States. These ideas and their implications soared and flamed for a time like Roman candles, eventually to fall to earth to occupy a less impressive and more modest niche in psychological science. Yet, for a time, they loaned experimental backing to the economic theories of socialism. Their repudiation in part is good evidence of our statement that despite the claims of ardent devotees of Marx, Lenin, and Stalin, the psychology of human behavior does not wholly substantiate their views. This, however, is not to say that socialism and psychology are completely incompatible; only that certain tenets of socialism are not in accord with the more basic facts of behavior.

Capitalism, too, especially the form of it which is practised in the United States, is ill-founded psychologically; and to its inadequacies we shall devote more space than we have assigned to its only serious challenger among economic forms. This we must do because it is the prevailing economy in this country, and as such deserves the closest attention in any survey of crime.

Crime as we have defined it is "natural" to an economy of the kind we in this country encounter, chiefly because the system is so constituted as to make higher and greater demands upon the organisms, the individuals, who compose the nation than they are capable of meeting. The economy, in other words, is of such a nature as to present, at every turn and almost daily, such precipitating circumstances as are capable of touching off behaviorial responses falling in the class of crimes. This it does, while at the same time neglecting to provide adequate moral or attitudinal safeguards which could be incorporated into the personality in sufficient numbers or strength to preclude criminal action. More explicitly, the economics of capitalism is inadequate to the basal needs and impulsions of the bulk of humans it affects either directly or indirectly. The capitalist economy is one of frustrations, hungers, wants, dissatisfactions, and in this psychological sense it is in monstrous opposition to the kind of creature man is. The fact of criminal behavior (among other kinds of behavior) can in part be accounted for by certain marked and unavoidable particulars of capitalism in the United States. The prevailing economy is so constituted as to create desires which can be fulfilled or satisfied in only a minority of individuals, leaving a residue of unrewarded striving and frustration among the many. For the creation of such desires, capitalism depends mainly upon the awakening of aims and longings completely foreign to psychological adultism, and hence it is to its advantage to contain the great masses in virtual infancy, which is to say dependency and ignorance. Its single criterion of successful living is the amassing of goods, all of which have only limited use, and most of which are especially designed to give but transitory pleasure. Hence, even in the accumulation of materials, there is no security and no permanence. Desires are falsely created, but made to adhere to the personality by welding them as firmly as possible to basal impulsions and needs. So, for instance, most advertising has as its end the ignition of sexual impulsions or, more properly, the awakening of sexual responses. In order to create a market for it, the product is linked with a sexual need. The infantile wish for recognition and prestige and elevation above one's fellows is similarly treated. Now this would not—except in a larger sense—be so bad if most people could still the artificially created appetite, or could satisfy the need. But by the very nature of the system only a certain percentage of the population can ever reach such a happy state, and such is our knowledge of how to play upon the myriad-keyed motivational instrument that no matter how great an amount of wealth collects under the hand of any person, all his needs cannot be satisfied. In any case, there has never yet been invented a lipstick or girdle, a necktie or undershirt, a perfume or perambulator, which would turn a drone into a queen. Yet hand in hand with the system's whole-cloth creation of wants, and even considering the hollowness and emptiness of the material forms invented to still such wants, goes the miserable companion-piece of desire—frustration. Most persons in whom the needs are awakened cannot satisfy them because they lack the material wherewithal to effect a purchase. They have, at this stage, been aroused in the very deeps of their beings: id has been awakened and clamorously besieges ego, which in turn has recourse to its deflective devices. Outward evidence of the involvement of ego sometimes is recognizable as the "sour grapes" reaction, as the uninformed and chaotic kind of radicalism, as compulsive behavior with the end in view of driving forward to the amassing of wealth, or as one of numerous other forms of reaction. When this occurs under conditions where ego is unsuccessful, frustration mounts and turns to aggression. A conflict is then precipitated between id and superego, with the primitive personality component doggedly determined upon satisfaction and superego either implementing id's demands upon ego or opposing them. If superego has been properly nurtured and proportioned, and if ego is obdurate, a conflict which is worked out *within* the personality ensues. If, however, superego is ill-formed and ego is permeable, the result is often crime, since id exercises a decisive effect upon ego, and as we have already pointed out, it is ego which commits crime.

For most people the efforts of ego to obtain satisfaction for the wants which a capitalist economy creates are doomed to failure. It requires money to satisfy such wants. Money is most difficult to obtain, and there are only a handful of very undependable ways in which a lot of money can be obtained without prolonged effort. So we are in the presence of an economic system which, because of its nature, acts as a precipitant toward crime, neurosis, and psychosis by holding out temptations with one hand and denying satisfaction with the other. In short it precipitates an internal struggle which, depending upon the life-history of the organism and its predisposition, may result in crime. For most people, the capitalistic economy, whether they realize it or not, is an almost continuously frustrating one.

Even if much of what has already been said were an exaggeration, the prevailing economy is open to criticism by a psychologist—and is viewed as a decided precipitant of crime by a criminologist—for the reason that its competitive nature makes impossible demands upon those who possess inadequate equipment or ability. The goals which are set before each child, often while it is still in the cradle, are fantastic and completely beyond the reach of the majority of the people. Yet these children are imbued with an undue fervor of ambition by our schools and by our press.

The most difficult fact for man in a capitalist society to realize is that he, like millions upon millions of his fellows, is a rather ordinary and prosaic person. Dynamically regarded, what occurs is that all our ideals under capitalism are directed upon the maintenance of cradle megalomania. The ego only rarely has a chance for real insight, for the setting up of an ideal which will include—and will be relatively content with—a knowledge of mediocrity. So it comes as a shock to most people to have to merge with the mass and to be buried beneath the protective obscurity of the majority. But the haunting prospect of individuality gnaws at the vitals of almost all of us, and contentment with the cipherdom that is our universal fate is rare. Herein lies a reason for crime. And, for those whose limitations are even more serious, a conflict so generated makes them a ready prey of those unscrupulous intelligences in whom the drive for prestige is unchecked by even a rudimentary sympathy for the common cause. They cannot adjust in any other manner than crime, for the promptings of id are unbarred by an ego that contains as its ideal a mirror-image of these selfsame id wants. The sheer wastefulness of such an economic order is pointed up by the inability of the system to provide a place for the superendowed. Even he of high ability, unless chance singles him out, is foredoomed to waste his talents, to be denied the flowering and fulfillment of his abilities, in the endless struggle to keep his body supplied with the requirements for life. Yet, as if in bold advertisement of its guilt, the system rewards the clown, the baseball hero, and the movie queen far beyond the mathematical comprehension of most of us. In truth, we have turned into a nation of parents whose highest hope of salvation lies in producing all-American ends so that they and we can realize private utopias through the endorsement of cigarettes and breakfast foods.

The prevailing economy, which is an integral element of our culture, further is of such a nature that it contains conditions which lead to marginal activities that lie on the borderland of the prohibited. Thus only the minutest environmental push, the merest hazard or temptation, is required to thrust the individual over the edge. In times of stress, the surrender to the primitive need is, needless to say, implemented from the environment; and it is perhaps at this point that some of the more "fancy" theories of criminality by association and imitation are fruitful explicatory concepts. The economy of capitalism demands a sort of "Sunday-only" morality wherein by mutual agreement the *whole* moral code is in abeyance and "anything goes" for six days of each week. In our country the by now thoroughly discredited and regretted Prohibition era abetted such an attitude. But this sad period in our history serves as a continual reminder that there exists a broad expanse of service and supply which flourishes under the individualistic, only moderately controlled and contained economy. This is the socio-economic fringe which by centrifugal action has been thrust out from the community but nevertheless battens upon it by providing shoddy substitutes for wanted goods and services which the economic system denies wholesale to the participants. By now some of these marginal occupations have become veritable institutions, viz. pawnshops, night clubs, road houses, bars, tourist cabins, gambling joints, brothels. Like Solomon Grundy, they are born anew each Monday. But for our purposes it is important only to point out that they are but one brief step removed from what is at least legally beyond the pale. This hinterland has a Tiffany glitter but only a

Woolworth value. It attracts the frustrated and the needful who throng to it in the happy expectation of surcease or of realization of secret wishes. Its proven inadequacy, except for the mentally enfeebled, is a contributory precipitant to crime. And as for those who cater to the trumped-up wants and the ballooned needs, they are perhaps even more vulnerable than others. Moreover, lest the reader forget, this wide band of service and supply is but one of the artificial creations of a capitalist economy. The list of other enterprises, "professions," and employments which have no really solid and secure base in the economy is almost endless. These include the middle-men, the in-betweeners, and the fashion-born artisans and dealers. These people are of necessity insecure in their occupations and consequently are at the mercy of every economic breeze. They live always on the thin edge of disaster. Popular pressure and sometimes legislative whim make them law-breakers, as we have seen; sometimes they are precipitated into crime by the failure of an ego to resist invasion by the acute wants which the environment presents.

The capitalist economy is one which naturally produces a glaringly unequal distribution of wealth and foments inter-class strife. It is bolstered by an understandable imperative to contain each segment of society independently of all others, and its aim is to discourage the principle of "in unity there is strength" from obtaining an ideological foothold among the broad masses. With realism and purpose it therefore seeks to maintain itself by a type of education designed to discourage a true community spirit. It is questionable—and a most pro-vocative speculation—whether the system could survive for a generation if it did not foster its preachments and propositions in the schools and in the churches. It has crowded people into slums and industrial suburbs; it has held the means of produc-tion to be of more value than human life; it has permitted the almost unimpeded growth of economic rackets—such as borrowing and installment plans—which lend a transitory coloration to existence and bring within impermanent proximity the mirage but not the reality of satisfaction.

The indictments that we have made thus far are not intended to do more than highlight the inadequacies of the prevailing economy from a purely psychological point of view in order to help us understand the persons and problems which are of immediate concern in this book. Regarded from the viewpoint of the specialist in human behavior, the system leaves much to be desired. That this is perhaps dimly perceived by people who are not students of behavior is indicated by the steadily declining birthrate (except in wartime) in capitalist countries such as England and the United States. This bespeaks an over-all response to frustration among parents and a general unwillingness to expose offspring to the same insecurities, anxieties, and fears that they have experienced. It further indicates a need for new values—a topic that will engage us presently. And, finally, it must be admitted that full personality development, especially among women, is denied all but a handful in our society. So we are, owing in part to the economy under which we live, a civilization of as yet untapped and unrealized potentialities.

The prevailing economy acts to precipitate crime by confronting individuals with problems which are evocative of dormant infantile situations of denial, anxiousness, fear, insecurity, and frustration. In infancy and childhood these problems were met by typical behavior adjustments involving retreat, aggression, appropriation, and other modes of behavior; and such adjustments may become the themes of later life as well if the proper circumstantial constellation is present. Situationally defined, the economy is both deprivative and punitive, while the persons whom it affects are striving for satisfaction and reward. Crime, then, can be and very often is precipitated by the economy. In these instances, as the following case illustrates, it is a patterned response touched off by a feature of the economic circumstances which prevail.

The facts about E. U. that appear on the record do not shed much light on him as an individual; nor do they explain why he committed the act for which he served a very long sentence. These facts show him to be the second son of a family of eight children born to parents who had emigrated from Holland in the eighties of the last century. E. U. was born in 1895 and grew up in what appeared to outsiders at least to be a stable home. His father was a pattern maker, a highly skilled artisan who was regularly employed. The old man was a rather philosophical type: he was content to leave the practical matters of the household to his energetic wife, and to spend his time after working hours with his pipe, a mug of ale, and a chat with other habitues of the corner saloon. E.'s mother, on the contrary, was a buxom and vigorous person who had never quite got used to her husband's slovenly ways and who was never without a scrub brush, a broom, a pot, or a needle in her hands.

E. attended the city schools where he was noted as an alert, rather eager, and very curious boy. His teachers thought his appetite for knowledge most unusual and remarked on the way he would seize upon each new bit of information. After completing the grades, he enrolled in one of the early vocational schools. Here he maintained the same high scholastic standards and was graduated at sixteen with many prizes and honors. He immediately secured a job with a manufacturer of engineering equipment and enrolled in evening classes in an engineering college. In 1915, when he was twenty, he managed to enlist in the French Army; when our country entered the war he was transferred to his own flag with a lieutenant's commission. E. served with a distinction that won him two decorations and a promotion on the field. He was superficially wounded twice, the last time shortly before the Armistice. Rather than return to the States upon his release from the hospital, E. secured a discharge abroad and an assignment by an American manufacturer of agricultural equipment to sell machinery in Europe. The next few years he spent travelling about the continent. In Italy he met an American Red Cross worker whom he married after a brief courtship.

E. and his wife returned to their native land in 1924. E. had made considerable money and wanted to strike out for himself. Accordingly, he resigned his position and with his brother as a partner organized a firm to compete with his old employers. He had a number of happy inspirations so far as designs and improvements in efficiency were concerned, and his firm started making money right away. Like most men at that time E. invested a large share of his funds in the stock market and for a while enjoyed, on paper, a millionaire's state. With the great crash of 1929, E. was wiped out. In an effort to redeem his pledges, and in other manipulations, his business and personal interests and property all went down the chute. The year 1930 found him a broken-spirited draughtsman working for a low salary in a small concern. Late in 1931 this outfit went out of business.

In the spring of 1932, E. attempted to hold up a moving picture theater box office in broad daylight on the streets of a Midwestern city. There was some gunplay but no one was hurt. For this attempt at armed robbery, E. was given a long sentence.

Such is the outline of the tale. Behind it rests a world of psychological data that the observer would never have suspected.

E. and his older brother had always been rivals. The eldest child resented E. and strove to dominate him in every situation. They were always engaged in competition at home for parental, especially maternal, favor. Apparently the brother was not only the stronger but also the more physically attractive of the two, and it was he who won out every time. E. could gain sympathy or comfort or attention only when he was hurt, or when he had scored a major triumph. He loved school because he had no rivals and could "feel free"; also because he could identify with his teachers and with historical characters. Intellectually he was superior to his brother, and the curiosity of which his teachers spoke was only a means whereby he could fashion a weapon with which to vanquish his brother.

This theme of sibling rivalry—to use the apt phrase of David Levy—was the prime motivant in E.'s life. An entire volume would be required to treat it adequately in this one case alone. Suffice for us to know that it was this ancient conflict which was touched off and mobilized by the economic reverses which E. met. Not included in the official record is the fact that even in their business relations the brothers continued their rivalry (or at least E. considered their relationship one of rivalry). E. was determined to outdo his brother and, indeed, had patronizingly offered him a partnership in the business. He even claims he "cut him in on the royalties from some of my patents." Of the two, E. was the one who had plunged the more heavily on the market. At the risk of making the case appear fantastic, one could almost say that there was something purposeful in the ruin which E.'s speculation brought to the partnership. But the brother survived. As a matter of fact, he returned to his old position with an advertising firm and suffered not greatly from the economic debacle.

A postscript to this hasty review of a case which illustrates the precipitating role of the prevailing economy is added by the notation that E. had been persuaded by his wife to ask his brother to obtain a job for him. This request was made over the telephone on the evening before the attempted holdup. The brother invited E. and his wife to dinner the next night so that the matter could be discussed. E. recalls that his wife remarked "what a shame it was" that E. had to wear the same shabby suit each time his brother saw him. . . .

It is most important that, especially where the economy plays a role in extralegal behavior, crime be distinguished sharply from simple law-breaking. This can readily be accomplished by bearing in mind that in instances of the latter, *the personality of the offender generally does not participate in the action, is in fact foreign to it.*

The prevailing economy very often is also a predisposant toward crime in that it makes directly for those conditions under which it is impossible for a developing individual to achieve wholesome personality maturation and integration. The teeming slum resulting from the haphazard crowding of economically dependent groups into circumscribed areas, the consequent lack of privacy, the harassment of daily life, the dreary enslavement to a narrow task—these affect the parents, color the atmosphere of the home, make for endless opportunities for traumatization of the young, and in all provide a mentally unhygienic climate for the growing child. And this is the harvest he carries with him into later life, and thus the pattern of frustration and dissatisfaction is perpetuated. In cases such as the one below the economy has predisposed toward crime; but it does not stop there: it has also laid the groundwork for personality aberration to the *nth* generation.

N. T. was a slum product. When he was three his family migrated from Poland and established themselves in a large eastern city in a community of their compatriots who had preceded them. This was in an industrial area, crowded, begrimed, odoriferous, and sprawling. There were no playgrounds, no places of amusement other than saloons, cheap dives, gambling joints, a couple of burlesque houses, and many poolrooms. The section was dominated by the political wardheeler who worked hand-in-glove with the gangs that sprang up on every street corner. The community was further torn by racial strife in one direction, religious intolerance in another, and divided again cross-sectionally by social cliques within each group.

N.'s parents were illiterate in English, confused by the life around them and bewildered by having their preemigration dreams vanish in the stink and rubble of the reality that urged itself upon their senses daily. They were at the mercy of every economic ill-wind, and existence was for them a succession of heart-rending struggles. The family of six children and the two adults were crowded into a three-room tenement. There was no privacy, no peace, no chance for aloneness or relaxation. The children were forced into the streets for play, which became a more unwholesome than healthful occupation. N. attended school in the neighborhood and made fair progress; but there too he and all his fellows were regarded snobbishly by their teachers. N. reports that he was sent home on one occasion because the teacher "could not stand my smell."

N.'s initiation into sex came early. He not only observed his parents while they were occupied with it, especially on those occasions when his father was drunk and would force his attentions on the mother regardless of the presence of the children, but, in addition, watched a woman in an adjoining apartment who carried on a brisk trade to eke out her family income. It was customary for most of the children of the neighborhood to view these proceedings from a vantage point across the alley. Moreover, N. was intimate with at least one of his sisters in childhood.

All of these things acted to traumatize the personality of N., to preclude for him the possibility of satisfactory personality integration. Ego development was poor and inadequate: he could not formulate the kind of Ego Ideal that would give his life the direction and the aims he needed to live in any community but the one into which he was born; he could never introject a proper societal image for superego maturation. What he did absorb were attitudes and patterned responses that were, if anything, guarantees of a life in crime.

N. drifted from one gang to another. He was arrested almost once each year from his ninth to his fourteenth birthday. Each time he was probated to his parents or given a suspended sentence. These offenses were usually gang affairs and N. was apprehended mainly because he was unable to run as fast as his fellows. Soon after his fourteenth birthday, N. was implicated in a theft from a warehouse. He was sent to a reform school, where he remained until he was eighteen. Upon release, he returned to the home of his parents. His father secured him a job in a local mill; but N. was soon fired from this when it was discovered that he was stealing and selling company-owned equipment. N. then joined the "poolroom and street-corner brigade." He was inadequately developed, psychologically unresourceful, malintegrated, predisposed toward crime by the conditions of his birth and rearing. So N.'s story from here on out is a common tale to be encountered behind any barred window. It ended—for a time at least—with his arrest for a theft from the mails. It will, without doubt, be taken up again when his six-year sentence has expired.

We have surveyed the part the prevailing economy plays in crime. To us it does not appear as a "cause" of crime or as the source of "causes." In our view it acts rather to precipitate criminal behavior or to predispose toward such activity. We have found that the basis for our indictment of the capitalist economy is that it is psychologically unsuited to the kind of creature man is and that it is an inadequate and hence a punishing, depriving, frustrating one. This is not unique with capitalism, however, since it appears that no economy yet offered to man has been satisfactory from the psychological point of view.

To look upon the prevailing economy with its products and by-products as both a precipitant (in some cases) and a predisposant (in others) is to take the first step in explaining why all persons who are adversely affected by the economy do not commit crime, and why some who are adversely affected attempt adjustments through other behavior forms. In the majority of instances, the hazards and contradictions of the economy evoke patterns of behavior dating back to a time when the actional course involved performance-modes of aggression and appropriation. The state of the ego, then, is the determining factor in the decision whether the individual will behave criminally. But it is the economy which has precipitated the conflict or predisposed toward it. We shall find that a similar formulation obtains also when we review our topic in the reference-frame of the prevailing culture.

# 13. Crime in the Prevailing Culture

$T$HE word *culture* is one of those tyrannical collections of letters for which all manner of definitions abound. For us it will mean the grand total of the attitudes, governing ideas, group motivations, and common goals of all the elements contained in a society. It will include its institutions, its traditions, its wants, its dynamisms, its prejudices, and even its superstitions and fears. We have already described it as a coercive force in molding and shaping personality, and have intimated how it, in turn, is altered and influenced by individuals or groups. Now we must regard it as a crime producer and precipitant.

Any discussion of economy should lead naturally to an examination of the culture it produces, for the economic techniques, purposes, and values rule the guidelines for those social patterns and principles which the word culture seeks to express. So it is that the prevailing culture directly reflects the prevailing economy. In a very basic sense one may say that the economy produces the culture, which it then uses as a tool for the creation and maintenance of a medium in which it can best operate. Hence, the behavior patterns peculiar to a given culture revert to its fundamental economy. Here, as everywhere, the relativity of phenomena is impressively apparent, and this makes it further obvious that crime is not and cannot be a product of law.

If it is true that the prevailing economy is ill-suited to the nature of man and therefore foredoomed to precipitate crime or predispose toward it, then it remains correspondingly true that the culture which stems from such an economy is similarly inadequate, frustrative, and deprivative. And unless one is hopelessly naïve, intellectually perverted, or blissfully blinded to reality, he can observe daily and with all his senses the truth of this proposition. The attitudes and goals screaming from every newspaper headline, the unctuous or strident incitement from every broadcast announcement, the window displays, the advertisements, the political pronouncements, the theater and the motion pictures—all of these cry social havoc. As students of a way of human behavior we cannot be content with the usual sociological techniques of describing the institutions, social structures, and other elements of the culture in terms as esoteric and precisely sterile as black marks on an areal map or linear scratchings on an ecological graph.

It is impossible either within the scope of this volume or even of an average-sized library to hold up the prevailing culture for an examination of all its countless aspects. But we can fixate certain of the more obvious and perhaps significant components for purposes illustrative of our chief concern with crime and criminals.

An outstanding and unavoidable feature of the culture important for criminological inquiry is the moral climate of the times. Herein we are faced with an inconsistency which is a genuine pesthouse, breeding conflict and making for those maladjustments to life that are so frequently expressed in the symptom we recognize as crime. In our churches and schools we preach a so-called Judeo-Christian ethic, which on examination and in practice proves to be a morality painfully unsuited to modern life as it is prescribed by a capitalist economy. We elevate as conduct rules the utopian ethics of the Sermon on the Mount and the Ten Commandments almost from the moment of birth; yet if an individual should take them seriously, and try to live his life according to them, he would not only be a complete failure in the eyes of the community, but he would, more than likely, be sequestered summarily in the nearest hospital for the insane. This dichotomy between preachment and practice has come to be an almost accepted part of our cultural code. Parents unwittingly and perhaps out of a "sense" of tradition breed a species of creature whose paramount accomplishment is the failure of one hand to know what the other is doing. Committed to the disapproval of falsifying, we consciously encourage lying and exaggeration. The child on leaving the birthday party where he ate too much ice-cream and got sick, fell from his chair and bloodied his nose, had his eye almost gouged out by the elbow of his neighbor, is whipped soundly if he fails to thank his hostess "for a lovely time." The business man boasts to his family about the deals he has "pulled off," schemes to evade declaring his true income, and retains attorneys for the sole function of finding loopholes in the law. The much-vaunted free enterprise that is so reverenced is often merely freedom to cheat and to lie. The "ethics" of business is in truth sometimes a set of conduct norms which are opposed to the best interest of the buyer. And as if this were not sufficient, it is the churches which occasionally spread a velvet cloak to hide and nourish such admitted evils. Within recent and painful memory we have witnessed the blessing of imperialistic campaigns, the sanctioning of rebellion against a popularly elected government, the protection of intolerance, and even the condonement of murder and brutality. Many of our public and private institutions are façades behind which lurks the crassest materialism imaginable. We boast of national chastity and circumspection, but certain surveys in the field of sex morality are so damning in their implications that they have been withheld from the press. Monogamy is our belief, but polygamy is almost our practice. Sobriety is our boast, but inebriation is almost our habit. Tolerance is our brag, but discrimination our common practice. There is little consistency between preachment and practice.

There is no question but that the moral values, the ethics, of contemporary society are "good." The difficulty is that they are impossible in practice. Were we suddenly to give them more than lip service, governments would fall and the economy would collapse. They are hollow pretenses which are tragic and productive of much aberration from crime through frank insanity. Unless a child is completely feeble-minded, he must recognize the anachronisms, usually while he is still in the home, or at the latest at the moment he leaves it. Dynamically, this would indicate that the image of society which is introjected during infancy through the parents must of necessity be of such a nature as to form a superego forever fated to be without substance, and in futile opposition not only to basic trends, but also to reality. We need seek no further for the elements of conflict. It is probably very nearly true to observe that many of those who do not become criminals (or neurotic or psychotic) would do well to reflect that they have retained their "purity" by coming to terms with duplicity, deceit, and hypocrisy. These are the qualities chiefly in demand for successful living; they are the qualities our culture rewards with power and prestige.

But we should pause to consider the fact that, bad as it is, the moral climate is slowly changing as the economy undergoes its dialectically changing course; that, for instance, our sex morality is not so flagrantly hypocritical as it was in Victorian times; that business ethics have improved over those of the feudal economy and even over those of the flagrant robber barony of post Civil War times. Yet although hope abounds for the evolution of a culture that will not predispose toward crime nor present situations precipitating criminosis, it remains a fact that these are just what our culture does now.

Ogburn has happily named a phenomenon that relates distinctly to the moral climate and indeed to all aspects of culture. He calls the time-gap elapsing between the development of material culture and unmaterial culture the *cultural lag:* that is, the ideas, attitudes, behavior modes and patterns tend to persist although the tangible realities outrun them. Certainly this is psychologically true and of importance in our study. Immigrants, for example, retain the abstract and behavioral patterns familiar to them although they have crossed the frontiers and oceans to new scenes. Children bring with them to adulthood the attitudes of infancy and the sediment of parental example and injunction. The super-ego, indeed, is for the most part archaic and outmoded when compared with reality. Invention in communication and transportation especially tends to increase this lagging attribute of culture. And nowhere is the phenomenon so vividly demonstrable as it appears when one surveys modern material culture and balances it against the essential psychology of man. Throughout its early history the organism is the nucleus of the universe, the center of activity in its world. It becomes habituated to this satisfying state; but as it ages it makes the uncomfortable discovery—often by way of harsh experience—that it is expected to surrender its autocratic controls over the environment, and to obey a very different code. And this latter mode is engulfed as superego, introjected through the parents. But as it ages still more, it discovers how ruinous it would be on a practical level to act in accord with this superego. So the organism is met with serious conflict, often acted out in crime. This is the simple explanation for many acts which are committed in a search for punishment, in that frantic and curious impulsion towards self-abasement and castigation which comes to some because they have violated the code of superego and cannot be free until they have received the full measure of chastisement as they once did.

Apart from the moral climate of the prevailing culture and the lagging tendency of its abstract attributes, there are other matters a criminologist cannot ignore. Among these are its complexity and its structuralization. In a country such as ours it is impossible to make out a case for a single, over-all culture. Not only is there a vertical division into economic classes, each showing peculiar qualities, but there is within each a horizontal segmentation cohering with respect to any one of many features such as color, religion, nativity, and occupation. Every environment through which an individual moves in a single day (and society is, after all, the blanket name for all the environments which compose it) has its special culture. One kind of behavior is apt for the office, schoolroom, or factory bench, another for the home, and a third and fourth for those other settings through which a person progresses. Each requires a specific set of adjustments to be made under penalty of exclusion from the group. Formerly it was possible to live an entire life within the overall culture of the times, the perhaps specialized culture of the community, and that of the home. Now, and particularly with the high mobility potential provided by rapid transportation and communication, only the most isolated do not have to be prepared for manifold and rapid reorientations and readjustments within brief periods of time. This, by the way, is one great factor in the description of our times as hectic and harassed. Who would survive must be equipped as the chameleon for rapid changing. He who is not so equipped, who possesses a rigid personality organization, must suffer. In the attempt at such adjustments, crime appears, and nowhere is this seen with more tragic overtones than, for instance, in the sudden thrust from civilian to military life, or in the shift from rural to urban settings.

The structuralization by color, religion, and nativity has broader implications than those of a particular individual's adjustment to the groups with which he is identified. It cannot be ignored that our prevailing culture, although it pretends otherwise, invokes penalties from—or at the very least excludes from its benefits—minority groups. These frustrates, in a manner of speaking orphaned by the culture, "solve" the problem for themselves by crime. The predisposing effects of this cultural fact are illustrated in the case which follows. In this instance the prevailing culture acted to prepare for a life-long criminotic career.

G. J. was the fourth of five children born to a Negro couple who came North during the Reconstruction period. The father was an itinerant preacher who devoted his entire life to aiding and furthering the social and economic equality of the Negro. In this work he was helped by his wife, a former slave girl who had received a modicum of education because she had been assigned as a sort of attendant to the mistress of the house where she served.

The family lived a gypsy-like existence, moving from place to place in the years between 1875 and 1887, and depending on the hospitality of fellow Negroes in the various places they visited. G. was born in their wagon during a sleetstorm on a bitterly cold night in 1883.

From his earliest childhood, G. was influenced by the vision of his father who looked forward to the day when his people and the white folk could live side by side in love and peace. The religion his father preached, although it would have been—and still would be—disowned south of the Pennsylvania line, was a beautiful and simple one of brotherly love, reward for virtue, and hell-fire for sinfulness. It was one for Negroes and whites alike, and G.'s father attempted to attract to it persons from both sides of the color line. Since he was a sort of Stone Age Father Divine, he collected about him a few disciples, some of them white. Soon his single wagon became a minor caravan, and G.

recalls the fervent singing of psalms around the campfire at night, the sense of sanctity and reverence for his white-haired, black-skinned father, and his childish dreams of the time when all men would be brothers and his father would rule over all.

These dreams received their first setback on the night, some four years following G.'s birth, when his mother was again in labor. It was a prolonged affair and the midwives were able to perform their function only after many terrible hours had elapsed. G.'s mother hemorrhaged badly. The caravan was parked on the edge of a small Maryland town. That night also some Klan heroes determined to "send the niggers packin'." They attacked the caravan and although its members defended themselves with prayers and pitchforks, started them on the road. G.'s mother died toward morning.

Caravan life continued for G. until his father died in 1888 after a lingering illness. The disciples took the J. children. It was G.'s lot to be taken, at the age of five, to the home of one of his father's white disciples. So long as his foster parents were alive, G. was well situated. When he was six, both of them were carried off by pneumonia, and their eldest daughter and her husband took over the small family of two white children and G. He was immediately made to feel inferior, was not permitted to sleep in the house but was quartered in a barn loft. He was beaten and abused, both in deed and word. At the age of 10 he ran away to a Connecticut community of Negroes where he was taken in by a charitable family.

G. attended the local schools and was a better than average student; starting with a handicap, he soon caught up with his age level. When he was not studying or preparing his lessons he ran errands, worked as a bootblack, delivered papers. Spare time he spent in a local library reading everything he could on racial problems, the Civil War, and the Negroes. He hated white people, blaming them for his mother's death, his father's failure, and his own cheerless existence. He resented his color, burned with indignation at the slights and insults he received, determined someday to strike back. When he left school he apprenticed himself to a local barber and quitted the family with whom he had been living. He managed to steal small sums from his employer. The money he got in this way he conscientiously saved in a box which he hid in his quarters. When he had accumulated a sum he felt sufficient for his needs, he left the town and went to New York. On arriving there he purchased a fine wardrobe and with this, a glib tongue, and a frail body full of hate as his stock in trade, he began a series of crimes motivated chiefly by a burning wish for revenge.

G. first obtained employment as a general assistant in a barber shop in a fashionable Broadway hotel. He learned rapidly the art of lifting a wallet as he brushed imaginary dust from coats, adjusted clothing, or attended to a customer's wants. When he slipped on one occasion he was discharged. His next job was as a waiter in an exclusive restaurant. He did very well at this until he again became (as he says) "overconfident." This time he was turned over to the police, and although it was his first arrest, he was given a jail sentence. Prison put the finishing touches to his personality. When he emerged, he was a man with a mission.

G.'s first act was to obtain some money by a bold deed which does not call for detailing here. Then he set about organizing a new "religion." It was a protestant faith in the original sense of being motivated by protest toward the social and economic discrimination against the Negro. He was high priest and prophet of this new faith; and he oriented it according to his profoundly intimate knowledge of what the Negro lacked most in his daily life, his hurts and the indignities he was made to suffer. It was exclusively negroid, had an elaborate and secret ritual, held as its tenet the supremacy of the Negro, preached a Negro gospel that believed Christ and all the Disciples to have been Negroes, promised a Negro heaven. This venture was very successful financially and had G. not become involved with a woman in his congregation, he could possibly have become the organizing genius of a popular cult. His indiscretion with this lady, however, unmasked him and he was again evading the police because he had paid out of congregational funds for the expensive favors he received.

After another, and a longer, vacation in a barred, state supported institution, G. was released. He managed to get together another "stake" and then began an even more fantastic series of exploits than any he had yet engaged upon.

Assuming the title of a doctor of medicine and a high-sounding alias, G. set himself up as a representative of a fictitious foundation whose purpose was to erect a medical center where Negroes could receive the care and attention they needed. This center was to include an all-Negro medical school and to be a teaching and training nucleus for Negro nurses and physicians. G. confined his collecting activities to whites only. He managed to make his way into the homes of the great and affluent whites of the land, and from them he usually received generous contributions. This he attributed cynically (and perhaps justifiably) to their abiding guilt and also to their fear that unless some such project were supported, their own institutions would be forced to handle the matter. At any rate, he did well for many years. He lived in luxury, salving his conscience now and then by supporting various Negro educational projects. Often he was arrested for obtaining money under false pretense, and he spent some years on and off in county and state prisons. Upon each release he would move to another state. The racket he worked was good for at least forty-eight variations, and he managed to get away with his act for long periods by cultivating a professional, servile, unctuous manner. His boast was that he never stole a cent from a fellow Negro. Before he died of old age in a prison hospital he made the brag that the whites had supported him since his sixth birthday.

The role of the prevailing culture may be summarized by pointing out (1) the broad cultural atmosphere which orients parental attitudes and conditions under which children are reared and superego is molded, (2) the paradoxical nature of the culture which elevates a set of ideals diametrically opposed to reality and impossible of realization, and (3) its complexity and heterogeneous structuralization which demand rapidity of adjustment and frustrate by denial and exclusion. These features are the wide and general implications for our study. They enact the part of predisposants, sharing in the sculpting of personalities who are prepared thus for exhibiting their effects through the symptom of crime. Again, they operate to precipitate such symptomatic behavior by presenting situations which for some organisms are insoluble upon any other level of adjustment.

Now with such an orientation as our discussion has so far provided us, it becomes possible to view special aspects and derivatives of the prevailing culture in their dynamic function in crime without resort to the kind of slide-rule automaticity which ignores the vital human material basic to all our deliberations. From the wide mass of cultural side-effects at our disposal, we shall select some to exemplify and enlarge the approach to which we subscribe.

Among the environments which deserve special attention is the home. It does not take extraordinary insight to regard it as perhaps the most significant setting for the determination of everything that goes into the patterning of behavior. It reflects the habits, attitudes, customs, beliefs, and social status of the parents; and it exerts a profound effect upon the child not alone in terms of the atmosphere of rearing, but as well in the impact of its physical appointments. It would appear that every home is operative upon its members along the principle of what can be called a *domestic theme*, which is best described as the fundamental feature of relationships among the members, the home's economic status, and its cultural level. Where the theme is one of integration, affection, and mutual interest, a healthy medium for growth and maturation is assured. But where the theme is of a disruptive kind, and the home one in which drastic events obtrude with such frequency as to become almost habitual, the groundwork for eventual aberration is laid. With the child who is in its formative stage, there will be reflected in both ego and superego this domestic theme, and so predisposition toward criminal behavior (or other forms) will result. The precipitation of crime, in other cases, comes about when, for any reason, an alteration in the theme eventuates, and adjustments to new circumstances are required. These alterations operate to awaken old and lingering non-resistant areas in the psychological constellation. So it is seen that the culture, as reflected in the most primary of all environments, the home, can be both a precipitant and a predisposant toward criminosis.

A domestic theme of particular significance in crime is that of culture conflict. In the period from the final decade of the last century to the years immediately preceeding the first World War, our immigration doors were left wide open for purposes of obtaining cheap labor. The hordes who entered brought with them their own abstract cultures, and in establishing homes on these shores tended, from habit, to perpetuate sometimes the forms but more often the content of the cultures from which they originated. In infancy, their children were impregnated with this alien culture content. Once somewhat free of the home and exposed to the streets and the schools and to other children, they were forced to lead a double life, or at least to strike cultural compromises. Every study of delinquency and crime known to this writer has pointed to their high rate among native-born children of foreign-born parents. Exactly what the critical item consists of is not known, but it is suspected that the superego and the Ego Ideal patterned in infancy by immigrant parents, contain goals which are projections of the parent's disappointments and frustrations. These are, by and large, in conflict with the culture patterns outside the home, and necessitate delicate readjustments almost continuously. In order to still the demands of the Ego Ideal and the superego, the adjustment seized upon may be criminal. Certainly this was the chief predisposant in one of the writer's cases where it appeared that the son of an Italian immigrant who had come to this country with a vision of gold-paved streets dancing before him, but who had settled into the bitter drudgery of day-laboring for pitiful wages, was imbued with the image of power and glittering success from the cradle on. He achieved such power and such success through gangsterism during the prohibition era.

Law-breaking from cultural reasons is very common and reverts to the patterned responses and attitudes of the home. This fact accounts for the cultural offenses such as whiskey-making among mountaineers who have a long and, in the sense of their own community mores, even honorable tradition. The same applies to immigrants from Mediterranean countries. Hallowell notes a case of communally-sanctioned murder of a woman in the Canadian Northwest who was reputed to be a *windigo* (cannibal). This, like the disposal by murder of the aged among some primitive peoples, is similar to law-breaking from cultural pressures continuously applied in the home.

An instance which neatly illustrates the conflict in the immigrant home and gives it a particular emphasis because it is so extravagant and has such an unusual twist, is the case of R. D.

R. D. never knew the exact date of his birth nor where it occurred. He recalls only that he spoke Italian, except for a choice collection of swear words, until shortly before he went to school. He remembers living in a squalid tenement—he and his brother and an elderly couple whom they called "ma and pa." These old folks were kind to them, but exercised little control over either of the children. When he was six, "a man comes to our tenement and I am told that he is my father. A short while later he comes back and takes me to a woman and tells me she is my mother. She was a beautiful woman in a stocky, European sort of way. I didn't take to her, and the longer I knew her the less I thought of her, until there came a time that if I didn't hate her then I disliked her to a point that I'd do anything than be near her."

This woman who was R.'s mother had a curious history. She had been the daughter of a socially prominent Sicilian family and had become a sort of underworld queen in her own land until a particularly obnoxious scandal forced her to quit her native soil. When she came to this country, she set about employing her dangerous beauty and talents in carrying on the same type of projects at which she had proved herself so adept. Patterning her activities along the culture-within-the-culture lines of terrorist societies in her home land, she built around her an atmosphere reminiscent of the bloody tales of certain Mediterranean secret societies. Her children were undoubtedly illegitimate. But, perhaps because of the lingering feeling of guilt regarding them, she had them brought to her and, in her own way, made an effort to arrange some sort of home-setting for them. She was unsuccessful in this, of course, because her own culture included different standards and aims than the environments the children encountered away from her home. She could not alter her own habits since these had become deeply ingrained with time. Her ways were alien to the ways of other mothers and R., in telling his story, emphasizes his perpetual wish to have had a "real American mother." R.'s mother was a Latin virago, a sort of evil matriarch who ruled with an iron hand a collection of assorted Italian males who in our own day would be called gangsters and racketeers. Yet while she lived a lawless, reckless, high-handed existence, she also professed and practiced piety. R. states that he was early struck by this paradox. "In her room was an altar-like affair with candles burning under a figure of the Virgin. She prayed continually, even while we knew she was planning and carrying out some of the most unimaginable schemes. She tried to make us as religious as she was; but we both always wondered how she could whale the tar out of us for sleeping too late to make the early Mass yet do the things we saw her do. She was the organizer of every kind of vice in the Italian section of the city and there are even some cases where as I look back on it she must have been behind some of the stabbings and other things that happened pretty often in her territory. Yet she was sure completely sold on the Church."

R. could not get along in his mother's home. "In the school it was one thing and at home it was another. Her ways weren't ours and I think that she felt it too. She tried to bring us up in her way and maybe if my brother hadn't got run over by a truck before he was thirteen, she might have done it with him. But I couldn't see things her way so I got to hate her."

Some of the incidents from R.'s experience are informative and illustrate not alone the cultural gap between mother and child but also the fateful history of a neglected child; for when his mother found she could not shape R. to her design, she rejected him outright.

"Mother then opened a roadhouse within a year after father's death. It was an expensively built place that she didn't bother to pay much for. It got so that I would hate to mention my name to anyone for fear they would be some of her creditors and I be made to feel that I should say something in her behalf when actually I didn't feel that I could excuse even the smallest of her acts.

"I think that I was almost seven when I went to live at the roadhouse; it goes without saying that I got very little schooling when I lived with her. At first my teacher would send notes home with me to mother about me not being properly dressed but nothing happened, then she took to sending me home which didn't help either.

"Mother's youngest brother with his family came to our town to live, and it was arranged that I should live with them and only come to Mother's place for lunch on school days. It was at this time that I felt hurt most. It happened that in school that our teacher had us make valentines. I made one too and the teacher thought it was nice. She sat in my seat with me and asked to whom I'd send it. I didn't know anyone I wanted to give it to so I thought I would give it to the teacher, but she persuaded me to send it to Mother, which was no easy job. At lunch time I dropped it in Mother's mail box. A cousin, older than myself that we'll call John, would go to the roadhouse every morning to run errands if there were any, because it was always good for a quarter or a half-dollar. Anyway, he'd get the mail and take it to Mother. At first Mother thought the valentine was from my brother, and started to make a fuss over it, till she learned the truth, which she did before opening it. She threw it away without saying anything. That wasn't so bad in itself because I had expected nothing better, but my cousin John had to bring it home to show it to the family, and spared no details either. If I could have cried I'd have felt better, I believe, but I didn't. Of course my aunt had to put the thing away. I later stole it and tore it up. If I didn't tear it in a million pieces it wasn't because I didn't try.

"Christmas morning was another one. Everyone at aunt's house was getting ready to go visiting that morning. That is everyone but me. Aunt insisted that I go too because of Mother. Mother was still in bed when we got there, so the seven of us went up to her bedroom, my brother had come home from a private boarding school and was already in her bedroom when we got there. After wishing her a Merry Christmas she gave my brother either a five or a ten dollar goldpiece and the rest a dollar bill with the exception of me. I can still see that bedroom and how quiet everything got. If there was ever an urge to kill I had it that day. How long the silence lasted I don't know, it seems ages, till my brother spoke up. He insisted that she give me a dollar too, which she refused. After some argument she gave me a quarter which I didn't even thank her for, even though I was prompted to by my cousin. When we came out the back door to go home I threw it over the roof. My cousin told my uncle about this and he gave me a beating.

"Sometime in the following summer, mother and her brother had a difference so I went back to live with her again. That fall she was arrested on a liquor charge. She was released on bail, after which she decided to go to New York to raise money to fight her case. When she left she asked a family across the street to take care of my brother and left me to take care of myself. I slept out at the roadhouse and got my meals whenever and however I could. While she was away an accident occurred. One of the boys where my brother was living was burned about the legs by some kerosene I had been put up to steal. Even though I wasn't there when he was burned I got the blame for it. When Mother got home a little before Christmas I avoided her because I was told that she was looking to catch me. But I would have known that even if I hadn't been told. Even then I was a fast runner. Being small I had to be or resort to throwing rocks. On Christmas eve, though, I let two of my cousins talk me into taking me home with them. They took me home all right but to Mother's home instead of their house, for which they got a dollar apiece and I got a beating and had all my clothes taken from me and was locked in the bedroom with a threat of another beating if I got blood on her pillows or sheets. As soon as the door was locked I opened the window and climbed out on the porch roof. Then down a pillar I went and around to the side of the house and in the coal shute to look for something to wear. I found a shirt and a pair of pants of my brother's in the dirty clothes hamper, and a sweater hanging on the cellar door, but no shoes. I left the same way I came in. It wasn't until two days later that a neighbor tried to call me in to give me a pair of her son's shoes, but I wouldn't fall for that trick twice, so she left the shoes in a field behind her house, and I watched the shoes for a long time before venturing out to get them. After getting the shoes I went back to school, and when the teacher asked where I had been I told her I had been sick. I kept going to school but not going home. The school was far enough from home that I didn't feel any danger. Everything went all right until the end of January and it was then that my brother found out that I was going to school. He knew he could catch me so he came to my classroom and asked my teacher to keep me after school so that he might take me home as I hadn't been home in over a month. Of course the teacher thought all this very strange and when I refused to answer her question for her she went to see the principal. He in turn called me up and still I refused to answer questions. I was then taken back to my class. During recess I wasn't allowed to go out but the teacher sent out for some milk and graham crackers. After recess I was again taken to the principal's office and this time there was a detective there. He and the principal tried to question me again without success, and then I was taken to a detention home. On the way to this detention home I thought, Oh well, it can't be as bad as it was at home. But I was wrong. The house itself was an old Dutch colonial place and to me it had an evil air about it from the first moment I looked at it. I was searched and put in a high-ceilinged room which was very gloomy because the lower part of the window was painted a light green. There were three of these windows and a heavy wire grating for a door. Other than a table and two benches there was nothing else in the room. There was a railroad below us although I never saw it from this house. I would spend the time counting between trains and listening for them. I afterwards thought of this in relation to Christianity. How could any Christian permit such a thing to happen to children!"

R.'s history is continued at this point with the object of presenting his interpretation of a segment of his life after he quitted his mother's immediate orbit. His story from this point forward illustrates the end-product of the broken home which is discussed further below and provides insights as to the reasons why such miserable situations predispose orphanage products to crime.

"I must have been in this detention home about a month and a half, but I can never be sure of that because time seemed so long. I know that for three days I was completely alone, me and that damned railroad. I slept in the attic. There were some twenty or twenty-five bunks with slate instead of springs and a straw tick. No pillow or sheets. Just two blankets that smelled of creoline as did everything else. In all the time I was there I only changed clothes twice and also had two baths, and that was on the last two Fridays and because I went to court. We could always tell who was going to court by the baths. We had no toilet in either of the rooms.

"The first time I went to court nothing happened. There were about eight or ten of us and we were put in a little room, and after a while I was taken to an office where I sat all morning and most of the afternoon. It was a little after noon that a woman and a girl came in to talk to a man at the other desk. This woman was trying to get her son out of a jam. When her son was brought in and the man stepped out for a few minutes she started talking Italian, telling her son to say that he was sorry and that he wouldn't do it again. Of course this all made me think of how nice it would be to have a mother and one that would fight for you instead of trying to brain me most of the time.

"I have often thought about this thing called chance and how funny it works out at times. If there hadn't been so many of us the second time I went to court and if I hadn't been last I would not have been sitting in the doorway when a woman walked in the outer office and saw me. She had a little girl in her arms. She went up to the counter and set the girl down and started to fill out some papers. Once in a while she'd turn around and look at me. After she got through she came over and asked me my name, which I told her. Then she went back to the counter and talked to an office girl and filled out more papers. When she got through she picked up the baby and told me to come with her.

I went without even asking a question. I was so glad. I was taken to a receiving home, and what a difference! I was given some going over too. All my clothes were taken and burnt, given a bath, had my hair washed and got clean clothes. It was supper time by the time I was through. We sat at the table with the two women that ran the place for the social agency. And when after supper I helped one of the older girls with the dishes, both the women thanked me and told me how nice it was of me to help. I had never been thanked before or even told that I had done anything well or even nice. I have never received that much attention in my whole life as I did in that first half day. I never did mind as I did with so many other people, doing anything for those two women. In all the four or five months I spent at this place I was only scolded once and that was for cutting my hair to make paint brushes for several of the kids who wanted to do water colors. In later years we laughed over it, but it was a little embarrassing to remember the only scolding that they ever gave me.

"Sometime during my stay at the receiving home I was taken back to court. This time it was to find out if this woman I ran away from was my mother. She was to be there and said that she would come to court to swear, prove or what have you. The only catch in this was that she didn't show up.

"It was in the late Summer or early Fall that I left the receiving home and was taken to an orphan's home. There was three of us that went together. While this orphan's home wasn't bad it wasn't good either; it was a Catholic home and emphasized religion. I think I spent more time on my knees for not knowing my catechism than I did for prayers. Bible history! I never knew the first lesson, didn't even try to learn it. All that I did learn was to parrot a string of prayers that never did make sense to me. Then came the question of baptism, no one knew if I had been baptized, and so with no time lost I was baptized. It was explained that all babies not baptized would go to Limbo, and this was pictured as a place if not hell, then the nearest thing to it. What a lot of sadism man creates in his God and religion—or is this a form of masochism?

"I wasn't there very long before I found that minding your own business wasn't enough. You had to fight, and often, to be left alone. And there was always an older boy to egg on fights. I sported a lot of shiners and I gave a few too. I learned that even if you had to take a bad beating but could hurt the other guy just once, only once, then he would be apt to leave you alone in the future. Those that were too big to fight, well I still had rocks and that was an old game with me. Yet it took me better than two years to teach them that I wasn't going to be fooled with, and I mean sexually too.

"I didn't get along well with my teacher primarily because of my indifference to religion. To me she seemed overbearing and I think I delighted in getting her goat, even though I'd get a worse beating by not crying. I think now that was my only way of fighting back. This same Sister had my detail in bed-making and cleaning out of a morning. There was something wrong with my work all the time and I'd have to give up some of my play-time because of this. What was the use of even trying. We would get to see two or three shows a year and had a couple of picnics a year. 'Treats' of course were the big thing in our lives. We'd get six to ten of them a year, when someone happened to think of it. What kid doesn't like candy, just a nickel's worth? As you no doubt have guessed by now, I'd lost most of these privileges, almost all of them. Now I'll have to introduce you to the cause of most of my misery, 'Snot-nose Louie.' This is the name he was always known by and a very apt name too. He always had a running nose which he'd wipe with a rolling and upward thrust of his fist. In the course of some time he'd added some quarter to a half inch to his nose. My friend, Sister Schoolteacher, saw to it that he became my charge. Louie was about my age and if the truth were known he might have been the stronger. I've had many a tussle trying to get him washed when tricking wouldn't work. Even though he was a dumbbell, a moron, and wasn't all there upstairs, he was cunning. He soon exhausted my limited bag of tricks. I had to eat with him, sleep next to him, and then catch hell when he was dirty, which was all the time. I expected to see the picture 'Captain Blood' but I hadn't taken Louie into account. I was so darned mad at losing that show that when the nun wasn't looking I grabbed Louie by the hair and dragged him up to the bathroom. I never let go either until I was through washing him. This time I used brown soap and a scrub brush, a nice stiff one too. I got the snot off Louie's nose with a few layers of skin too, and I never had trouble with Louie again.

"I liked swimming so much that I'd sneak off the campus with four or five boys and go down to a dirty little place that wasn't more than a dozen feet wide and a couple or three feet deep. We made it deeper with potato sacks that we stole from the storeroom. Just to be caught with a sack was worth the worst or best beating you'd ever get. It got so bad that the 'good Sisters' would have roll call at random to see who was missing, and heaven help you if you didn't have a good excuse for not showing up at a roll call. At roll call you'd use your locker number. I was there most of the time when it came to roll call, but I missed up one day. I waited too long behind a shed on the edge of the campus for my hair to dry. I and nine others got caught between the supper bell and Sister's patrol. As soon as she left the yard we tried to sneak into supper unseen but with no luck. All but two of us got caught. Tony and me decided that as long as we were missed already and would get a beating for it, we would run away. We tried to sleep in the stacked corn but the insects wouldn't let us. That was a long night. The next morning some of the boys brought us something to eat and two of them decided to stay with us and a little later three more joined, making it seven in all. Being Fall, we didn't have much trouble finding something to eat. We had to be on our guard all the time, not from the police but from the 'good' citizens of the small towns we went through. These citizens would form posses and chase us all over God's little acre. It seemed to be a game with them. I know now how the fox feels when he is ganged up on. First we lost one and then two, only to have the remaining four get holed up in a swamp for three weeks by a posse so large that I thought half the world was after us. One dark night we tried to give them the slip by going across the tracks and into the river and floating down it. I was the first over and was already in the water before we were discovered. The other three made it back to the swamps. I tried but was cut off. I ran down the tracks a way toward the road, which happened to be the only highway in the burg. I guess they must have thought I'd left the guys behind me chase me right into the arms of the party waiting out at the highway. Just a little above the road there was an abuttment of a bridge from which I took a running high-dive. I managed to lose them in the dark. I swam down river for what seemed ages but I guess it was about an hour. I came ashore on what I thought would be a safe spot. I hadn't taken into account lovers though. We were all surprised, but I moved first and fast for the water. The water was deep inshore and the man dove in after me. I was too tired to make a race of it so I used a little cunning instead. He made the mistake of coming up near me from his dive and I had played at ducking too often not to take advantage of that so I grabbed his hair and held him under. He couldn't have been a very good swimmer or else he lost his head because he could have taken me under with him long enough for me to let go. Anyway, I think I meant to drown him and if it hadn't been for his girl who came in also I maybe would have. But I didn't know it until she started to beat a tattoo on my head with a shoe. She like to beat me half to death with that darn shoe. I was never so glad to get away from anyone so much as I was from her. She made a nice job of closing one eye on me. I was a sorry looking mess when I got back to the home that morning. And I was a sorrier mess after the 'good' Sisters got through with me. First they gave me a dose of oil and then put me in a nice, clean, old-fashioned nightshirt, and then went to work with leather belts. And who should be on the welcoming party but my friend 'Sister Schoolteacher.' 'Ha,' she said. 'We'll make you cry this time.' But she gave up in disgust. Then I was thrown into the shoe room in the basement. I had company though so it wasn't so bad. There was a sink in the shoe room but no toilet and when the oil starts working on me we pried a floor board under the sink and used this hole for a toilet. We stayed locked up until the day before the whole of the institution was to move to a new place which was about seventy-five miles away. I don't remember just how long I spent in the room. It must have been a month but it seemed a lot longer. About this time I started to hate 'little people' in 'little jobs,' people that get drunk with very little authority and love to crack the whip. Anyway I had more than enough time to hate and damn everyone that I had known and also ones that I didn't know, like my parents for bringing me into this damnable world."

The home in which the domestic theme is poverty provides a favorable climate for predisposing toward crime by deprivation and frustration. Just as important are the concomitant attributes of such situations. Usually this is an overcrowded home in which there is little chance for child training and no privacy. The opportunities for traumatization of the personality are beyond counting. The parents reflect in their attitudes toward children the bitterness of their own lives. There is a proportional disrespect for other family members and an overemphasis (justifiably) upon the material culture which is denied. Existence is directed upon animal satisfactions, since these are all the environment has to offer. Parental supervision is necessarily limited. Socially satisfactory goals are not aimed toward, and the society which is introjected is a hostile and denying one.

Related to the poverty-stricken home is the one that is characterized by the degenerate behavior of its members. It were space wasted to elaborate upon this variety except to note that individuals reared under such situations containing brutality, drunkenness, immorality, law-breaking, crime, and vice become habituated to an environment of degradation and low ideals. They become, like some this writer has seen and as is illustrated by our next case, creatures of id whose egos are rotted through.

It would require the specialized literary talents of an Erskine Caldwell to do full justice to the case of Z. J., who was born on a farm in an Eastern state and into a family known throughout the region as "a bad lot." The house which still stands and shelters both the farm animals and the family was set into the woods about three miles from the state highway and on the outskirts of a small village. There was only one rail connection to this village, and the daily train delivered necessary foodstuffs and mail. So the two hundred people who comprised the village were somewhat isolated from the rest of the world, and as a result they tended to intermarry and live their lives somewhat along the lines of a specialized community cultural pattern. Z. never knew who was his mother. He states, and the record shows, that twelve people inhabited the house during his childhood, but it is not clear what relationship each bore to the other since they were all, so it would seem, connected. The identity of the woman or women who nursed Z. offers no clue, because someone was always lactating.

The author once attempted to work out Z.'s genealogy with him but soon had to quit this interesting project when it appeared that one of the women fell into the following possible categories of relationship: sister, aunt, mother, sister-in-law, niece, mother-in-law.

The matings among family members were open secrets during Z.'s childhood and continued to remain so at the time of this writing according to the available correspondence. So also were drunkenness and brutality. Within the community tradition was the sort of perverted code of honor that would be incomprehensible to an outsider but that was always self-evident to Z. This code was beyond the law and superior to it.

Z. somehow managed to survive the first fateful years. He slept in a corner of the shack with three or four relatives of his own age, ran wildly through the woods and fields, was at an incredibly early age introduced to sex, and instructed far beyond his years in every form of vice and perversion. Meals were at unpredictable hours and there was no attempt to discipline the children. No one exercised any authority in the household; everyone was without prestige in the eyes of the young ones. He who had the most cunning, the sharpest bite, the deepest scratch, won out.

At eight, Z. was sent to a rural school. A bus called for the children at the highway and delivered them at the same place after hours. Z.'s first delinquent act was connected with this vehicle. He confesses now that it was he who set fire to it while demonstrating the use of matches to the other children. At the time it was impossible to prove it and he was not punished. The school years were unprofitable to the other children as well as to Z. One bitterly harassed teacher attempted to struggle with thirty children in six grades, the stove in winter, and insects in summer. Z. was often truant, and when at thirteen he quit to go to work he could just about write his name, read simple stories, and perform primary arithmetical operations. He obtained work as a hired hand on a farm near a neighboring town. For six months he appeared to be doing well, but in the seventh it was discovered by the farmer that Z. was stealing eggs and chickens as well as home-canned goods and selling them in town. He was arrested and confined, while awaiting trial, in the local lockup. That night he escaped and made his way to the family shack. In the morning a posse of outraged farmers beseiged his place. Z. and his presumptive father (or grandfather, or uncle) tried to fight them off with shotguns and in the fracas one farmer was wounded. Finally Z. surrendered. He was taken for safe-keeping to the county seat, and soon thereafter sent to the reformatory.

In the reformatory Z. was a constant source of trouble. He was assigned to work on the farm but was removed when it was found that he was introducing some younger boys to certain perverted practices involving the livestock, and also to homosexuality. Within the institution he was uncontrollable. A psychiatrist who spent some time with the boy concluded that he was a cultural product, had average intelligence, could not adequately be described as a psychopath, demonstrated no signs of mental disease, but was really "a creature of vicious habit-systems." When he was sixteen, Z. was released. On arriving in the place he called home, Z. was greeted warmly by the family who had prepared for his home-coming according to their custom. There was a big party and everyone got roaring drunk. In the morning it was discovered that the old man (presumptive parent) was dead, and when the evidence was collected, it appeared that Z. had contributed to this sad event by shattering a chair over the departed's head in a quarrel pertaining to the proprietary rights to one of the household women. Within a month Z. was serving a ten-year sentence for the manslaughter charge.

After six years, at the age of twenty-two, Z. was paroled. Again he returned to the eyesore in the woods, and seems to have been determined to lead a "better life." He cleared some land and began to work it. Within a year he accumulated a "wife" from among his relatives. She has described him as "no different from any other man. He hit me some and he drank a lot of whiskey." The authorities, however, discovered that in addition to drinking whiskey he was also making it. Convicted, he received a two-year sentence. When he finished this service he was twenty-six. Meanwhile his wife, whom he had left with a set of twin boys and a daughter, had presented him with another child. Z. suspected one of his brothers, but never felt the matter of sufficient moment to make any complaint.

The pattern herein indicated continued for some years until Z. was taken into custody on a rape charge. He is still serving time for this in the State penitentiary.

Much has been written of the broken home, the situation in which the usual integrity of the family has been destroyed through the death of one or both parents, the introduction of step- or foster-parents, divorce, separation, illegitimacy, home-placement, etc. The dynamic effects of these features along lines dealt with in this volume are self-evident. What needs to be emphasized, however, is that the domestic theme of the broken home can be carried out under an exterior of domiciliary accord. The integrity of the home, for example, is just as much disrupted by factors which are not displayed in an open rupture. The homes where a parent is alcoholic or sexually promiscuous, or where the interests of the children are secondary, where the child is neglected, or where the parents are incompatible yet remain together out of regard for social or religious convention—these too are broken homes. Perhaps an illustration including a number of such features will serve to highlight this point. This is a tale of progressive family deterioration.

O. E.'s father was a physician and his mother a leading church-woman and a civic organizer in a suburban town in Pennsylvania. There was one other child, a girl, who was always somewhat sickly. On the whole, from the time of O.'s birth in 1919 to his seventh birthday, the family unit seems to have been an intact and stable one, its internal relationships being close and affection-ate. O. was a bright youngster who, to that time, had had every material benefit his parents' financial and community status could provide. He was carefully nurtured and, according to all avail-able reports, he matured rapidly. O. himself believes his early childhood to have been a happy one. A change in the situation came about when the home picture underwent significant altera-tion.

"My father being a tall man around six feet two inches, and possessing a rather deep voice, held my attention more than anyone else in the family. As I can fairly well remember when I was around five or six years old, I enjoyed sitting on his lap. He would, as a rule, nearly every day bring me home a piece of candy from his office. But it seems that he suddenly changed his attitude towards me and the whole family by the time I was seven or eight. I remember his sudden lack of interest toward me. He would tell me to go out and play or to go up to bed when I would come to him to talk or ask him questions. I noticed this mostly because of the sudden stopping of his bringing me candy. He began drinking and coming home drunk nearly twice every week. My mother, and also my sister, would quarrel something fierce with him whenever he came in drunk. Finally he even quit practicing and began laying around the house part of the time and in a pool room or gambling room the other. His love for me transformed into negligence, and resulted in a series of reprimands and not too infrequently a whipping by the use of his razor strap. At the age of seven I became extremely curious and for some unknown reason cherished playing around the railroad siding platform next to a lumber yard where they loaded in lumber. I enjoyed more than anything else to watch the switch engine travel back and forth pushing cars in place. But this enjoyable episode soon came to an end. My father gave strict orders to me and to my mother that I was not to leave the back yard of our home other than to go to a movie on Saturday afternoons or to school. For this reason, in particular, I began to resent my father in silence but my resentment was complicated. I feared him and hated him for punishing me, and yet, I admired him because he was big and for the authority he held. I wanted more than anything else to be grown up and as tall as he. I would day-dream about being as tall as he was, and would ponder happily to myself on what he would do with me if I would do something wrong then. I was convinced that I would someday be bigger and stronger than he, and would make him fear me. My great dream was to become a railroad engineer. That desire stayed with me for nearly seven years. I don't remember exactly how I lost interest in it.

"After being told to remain in the back yard of my home, I began to devise methods by which I could elude my father's eye. Since he was away during the day only my mother and sister were left at home besides me. In the winter, of course, I went to school. During the summer, while he was away, I would either ask my mother's permission to go somewhere, generally to the store, or I wouldn't bother, just sneak out the back gate. Whenever I sneaked out I would feel like an adventurer and in a strong sense imagine myself as being a grown-up on my own. But on the other hand I constantly had a gnawing feeling when I sneaked out that my father might find out. Whenever my mother detected me in doing something wrong she would always threaten me by saying that she was going to tell my father when he came home. But she never did. She, I soon discovered, would only say things to frighten me and therefore I proceeded to take more liberty in her presence.

"I got a lot of beatings, however, but I remember one in particular. I got involved in some childhood escapade, and my father proceeded to whip me. My mother then intervened, shouting, 'Leave him alone, if you behaved as well as he does everything would be all right.' My father replied, 'What the hell do you want to do, spoil him?' This was a phrase which I heard quite often from him. Then he became very angry with my mother, threw the strap on the table and left the room. My mother took her handkerchief and wiped the tears from my eyes and sympathized with me. From that day on, I became completely devoted to her, although I had always thought much more of her than I did of my father.

"It was about this time that he began drinking even more heavily. My sister would also get whippings from him for going out on parties and dances against his will. She being ten years older than me, she would argue with him and loudly denounce him as a no-good, lazy drunkard, and brute. And would always threaten to leave home. A few years later she did. She got married to a fellow who lived in our neighborhood, and applied for a divorce a month later. She returned home completely miserable.

"From then on until I was nearly eighteen years old my family would have terrible quarrels—mostly over my father's drinking. Once he came home and became so mean with my mother (this was when I was around thirteen years old) that I went and got the police to quiet him down. In the years that followed (that is from my seventh to my eighteenth) my father drank habitually. The family quarrels were abundant. His old attention towards me and my sister was transformed into almost total negligence.

"When I was about fifteen years of age, I was out on the streets nearly every night until midnight just to get away from my father and the awful atmosphere of that house. And this was the beginning of the end for me."

Apart from the deterioration of home living which the case of O. E. reveals, some additional light is thrown on a significant by-product of our culture by his further remarks concerning the moving pictures and their effect on him.

"At thirteen years of age motion pictures became my favorite pastime. Upon entering a theater I would always feel awkward and very small; upon leaving it I would feel like a big shot and would strut with an air of authority and knowledge.

"The moment I entered the theater I would, by hook or crook, maneuver myself into a front row seat. I can distinctly recollect my reason for this act. I was under the impression that it was a privilege to occupy a front row seat and that the nearer that I was to the players on the screen the better I could understand and see it. I would sometimes make believe that I was one of the actors in the film. For some reasons, which I cannot define, I would always envy and admire the cowboy outlaw, especially the leader of a gang of rough looking characters. I suppose I was a victim of cowboy fever, for about three years. Then my attention suddenly moved from the cowboy to the gangster. I enjoyed immensely those films which depicted 'Two-gun mobsters, and sallow-faced racketeers.' I would thrill at the scenes showing a gunman shooting a police officer. I thought it quite fair and necessary for a gunman to shoot a police officer, and brave, because the poor gunman as I could see it, was always being hounded by the police. I had accumulated the story of Robin Hood somewhere and decided that he was a great and brave man, and the same of Jesse James, because both of them robbed from the rich and gave to the poor. And my family was poor, very, very poor in fact. There were times when I was around ten or eleven years old that we did well to have two meals a day. We went on relief from the city for several years as my father was too old to practice—and too drunk. We had to move and my mother had to go to work nights on her hands and knees in some office building scrubbing floors for seven dollars a week. My sister worked, when she could get a job in factories, restaurants, and department stores. When I was eleven, I began selling newspapers and magazines, and even at that age clearly realized my profits as being very meager. I wanted to help my mother and sister and I had thought of becoming the man of the house. I actually used to wish that my father would leave the home as he would always threaten when he was drunk and arguing. I conceived of myself as being looked up to some day by my mother and sister as a smart and big man. I would sneer at other kids in the neighborhood whose people had neat appearing homes and whose fathers had good jobs. There were a number of things of which I was very jealous which the other children around me possessed.

"Therefore, it became an honorable thing to me for a man to be a gangster, robber or big shot. It soon came about that the big shot and the swindler on the screen developed into very smart men as far as I was concerned. I would burn with envy and dream for hours after I would see a film showing a swindler taking some foolish rich man or company for a huge fortune, and the big shot gangster with his bullet-proof limosine, big luxurious apartment house, big offices and immediate attention. I would watch how prompt and precise the big shot's henchmen would obey his commands. I liked authority, this was what I dreamed of becoming, a big shot. I would absorb the way the big shots and gangsters would dress. I followed suit. When I was thirteen I was trying to dress and make myself appear as a man, would walk around and stand on street corners with my coat collar up around my face, a hat over my eyes, and a cigarette dangling from my mouth. I adopted as best I could their slow, calm way of speech, twitching eyes, and was disappointed because I could not grow a small black mustache. I would even get a newspaper, fold it, and carry it around in my coat pockets so it would show. I wanted to be looked upon as a brave character."

O. E. is serving an extended time for the daring act of impersonation which climaxes a long career in crime. In this offense, he assumed the role of a father-authority figure and behaved much as the movie heroes he worshipped. His present offense reveals the motivations behind it poignantly: father-hatred, compensatory reactions for the inferior and shameful social status his father's alcoholism brought upon the family, the need to supersede the father-figure, the urge to achieve through dramatics similar to those presented on the screen the symbols and trappings of his secret ambitions.

Another environment which exerts itself forcefully upon the organism is the community. As with the home, it is possible in every instance to make out a *community theme*. Our economy being what it is, it has arranged such themes along rather clear-cut lines, and one can fixate any given locale with a phrase which indicates the dominant role. It is almost possible to make out a community "personality" (as sociologists have discovered) and such personalities can be described adjectivally much as can their human counterparts. There are unstable and immature communities such as trailer camp sites, boom areas, and development regions; whereas some present a fixed, mature, even rigid organization. The unstable ones are rather characteristic of our American culture and seem to provide conditions which both precipitate crime and predispose toward criminal behavior. The precipitating features may result from factors certain investigators have made primary causes of crime, factors such as differential association with criminal elements and imitation of criminal behavior modes. The predisposants, however, result from conditions which form the background for later conflict. The "crime-gradients" set up by some research studies indicate a core of crime in industrial slum areas with diminishment as one proceeds toward the edges of cities and toward rural settings. While these would indicate a falling away of precipitants as one leaves the city, at the same time other studies have shown that the crimes performed in the places distant from the core tend to be more serious, and involve greater violence, although they occur chronologically less frequently.

In surveying the situation alluded to, it is possible to have recourse to the centrifugal theory of community action. To this writer it appears that all communities behave like a giant centrifuge in their early days, throwing off behavior which does not suit the idealistic purposes of each settlement. Thus criminal behavior and the foci of vice are to be found on the outskirts and borders. The phenomenon of frontier behavior is well known. And in this connection it is to be observed how roadhouses, shady inns, places of rendezvous and assignation today crowd the approaches to cities and towns. But after the settlement has grown, it tends to engulf such places along with their mores, and they become islands of underprivilege and frustration. Yet the remainder of the settlement continues such centrifugal activity. Finally each community possesses more than one infectious area; but lawbreaking tends to concentrate in the older areas, while crime appears in the newer, for these are frequented to a higher degree by frontier personality types.

Coincident with such a consideration it must be taken into account that the types of frontiers where compulsive criminotic behavior can be worked off have been disappearing. Our economy has nurtured a culture that, for the broad masses, has abruptly limited horizons. The abstract horizons it has substituted for the physical open spaces are denied to the many since they can be attained only through long and arduous educational preparation. Persons are therefore constrained within psychological and physical space. A dull monotony has come upon us with capitalist imperialism. Timbuctoo and Toledo both are tending to look alike. Moreover, the energy that was once expended in the uninhibited exercise of both imagination and physique is now limited and formalized into the drab patterns of the artificial playground and such-like. Viewing them, one little wonders at the attractiveness of vicious amusement centers, dance halls, barrooms, alleys, street corners, and abandoned tenements.

We need not devote too much time to the schools which

transmit the culture to their charges. Suffice it to note that our educational system is pledged to the propagation of the myth that even if this is not the best of all possible worlds, there will be "pie in the sky when you die." Our teachers are ill-paid, although theirs is admittedly the most important function in our society. They are insufficiently motivated because they labor under a social inferiority which is best reflected in the size of their monthly checks. In the social hierarchy they are perhaps a notch or two above the garbage collector, but our American tradition is far more likely to award the apple to the latter, especially if he manages by a coup to obtain the town monopoly. The teacher has little status and less prestige. He is expected only to foster the American myth, and this must not be allowed to be interfered with by truth, as certain authors of history texts and teachers of biological and social sciences have learned. From a psychological point of view it is evident that the schools operate to implement and emphatically to nourish the kind of superego formation which we have already noted as being utterly and hopelessly at odds with reality *as the ego must daily encounter it,* and which will conflict with the fundamental urgings of id. It is in this sense that we can regard the educational system as an important predisposing factor in criminosis.

Were space available, one could continue this discussion of crime and the prevailing culture almost indefinitely. The essence of all the verbiage would be that, like the economy which sires it, our culture is of a nature to produce unbearable tensions which act upon the personality and initiate the adjustment modes recognized as crime; and, further, that the culture predisposes by arranging the conditions which nurture personality types of the kind that can be readily precipitated into criminosis. The cultural areas we have not covered include many and important ones, but we have tried to make evident the similarity, for each area, of the dynamic principles upon which this survey of the crime problem is based.

In our next chapter we shall deal with some outstanding by-products of the generalized discontent with the cultural and economic setting as we have reviewed it, by-products expressed in conflicting ideologies, and themselves playing a numerically minor but psychologically decisive role in criminal behavior.

# 14. Crime and Ideological Conflict

THERE is one characteristic of our time that makes it unique in the history of the race. It has suddenly become a matter of great importance what the average man or woman thinks. At the moment of this writing, great forces are locked in struggle, not over markets, nor land, nor possessions, but over moral and ethical abstractions. Alternate ways of life for common men and their children are at stake. National boundaries and allegiances become unimportant, and men die for the triumph of one set of ideas over another. The conflict is not limited to a single decade or even to a single century. It has been in germination for a millennium and will probably last for generations to come, although it may well be taken again from the battlefields to the regions of mind, where it is less accessible to the atomic bomb and the strafing plane.

Because thought transcends accustomed boundaries and narrow national loyalties, it is possible today to speak of confraternities spreading over the face of the earth, united only by similar ways of thinking. Such a situation creates particular problems for the student of criminology, for it often happens that in following out lines of conduct dictated by ideas, behavior contrasts with the prescribed codes of the several national states. Individuals make their appeal to higher and less tangible authority than written law; they look to these imponderables for the sanction for their actions; and they hold as unimportant the transitory benefits to be derived from acquiescence to legality. At the same time, the popular conception attaches the label of wrongfulness to those who do not hold with the shifting majority. So the ordinary concepts of right and wrong, good and bad, and all those other convenient judgments are meaningless. We despise the way of life of the fascist and look with horror and disgust upon his activities. In his turn, he believes he is acting from highest motives and in the service of a lofty ideal. The fifth columnist in Madrid, who by treachery, murder, and stealth paved the dictator's way, was convinced of his rectitude, just as the Japanese at Pearl Harbor were perhaps acting according to their own highest principles even when they prepared the way for their bombers to the infamous "stab-in-the-back."

Beyond the flagrant examples provided by saboteurs, spies, fifth columnists, and the like, more ordinary and no less significant are the instances, daily reported, which are provided by violators of the Selective Service Act, Conscientious Objectors, political assassins, polygamists, followers of religious faiths who refuse to salute the flag or to send their children to school, lynchers, anti-Semites, and those who commit the many legal trespasses which may arise from affiliation with outlawed political groups, from labor strife, and from the fight against certain political forms or philosophies. What impresses one immediately is that there has been a rounding out of the historical circle. The fact is that today men and women, in every land, are being sent to prison for what they think and believe. Law, again as in the heyday of the Church, has extended its effective area to the inner life of man.

For us, the entire problem into which the observations we have recorded resolve themselves is a serious one. Are individuals who engage in extra-legal conduct in the service of unpopular ideas and attitudes criminal? Or are they merely law-breakers? In the light of what we shall have to say later about treatment, it is of tremendous concern that these questions be decided.

The problem we have posed can be answered only by reference to motivation. We need to know why certain people join certain movements, what intimate needs are met by their loyalties to specific ideas, what lies behind evasion of requirements set by various laws. The fascination of such a study lies in the observer's knowledge that such groups are joined, such faiths are professed, and such laws are ignored, in full view of the fact that punishment at the most, and social outlawry at the least, are assured the perpetrators.

The passage of the Selective Service Act by the Congress served to do more than set up the machinery for the eventual induction into the Services of millions of fighting men. It created a new kind of violator by providing penalties for refusal or neglect to abide by its provisions. Men between the ages of eighteen and sixty-five were required to report for registration purposes, to hold themselves in readiness for possible military service, and above all to maintain permanent contact with local Selective Service boards. One would think that such simple responsibilities were easily met; but it transpired that even these minimal regulations were evaded or ignored by thousands. The manifest reasons given by Selective Service violators to account for their offenses differ widely. Some were "afraid" and sought to escape participation; some simply "forgot" about the regulations; some "didn't know" what was required of them; some "neglected" to maintain contact; some were anxious to keep their whereabouts from becoming known to their families (especially deserted and support-seeking wives), the police, or creditors. Then there was the group—whom we shall set apart to consider later— who objected to the provisions of the act, on either conscientious or religious grounds. Finally, there were a few who were downright disloyal to this country and owed allegiance abroad.

It has seemed to this writer, whose experience with Selective Service violators has been extensive, that the overwhelming bulk of these (exclusive of the Conscientious Objector and the religious objector) have been immature, irresponsible, floating types. A composite picture of the typical violator of this act would show him to be an individual of slightly below average intelligence, in his early thirties, of somewhat alcoholic tendency, with no specific emotional or family ties (although a deserted or divorced wife may be hovering somewhere in the background), with a very poor work history of the common laborer or restaurant worker variety, and a nomadic career behind him. He has been arrested a few times for vagrancy, loitering, trespassing, or disturbing the peace. When he was apprehended he pleaded that he had been neglectful, and he offered to serve immediately. Personally, he is mild-mannered and apologetic about himself. He lives from day to day, satisfied with only enough to smoke, any place to sleep, a diet consisting mainly of "coffee and . . .," and an occasional drink. Since he is already somewhat of a social pariah, he is disinclined to value very highly the benefits of social acceptability. His immaturity is patent, and his knowledge of events is limited. The newspaper is, for him, something to put between the blankets for warmth's sake; the cafeteria and bar-and-grill juke-box are his cultural fountainhead. He has always been content to move with the sun and the harvest. He is not overly concerned about his present plight, and he often regards prison as a place where a kind providence has miraculously provided him with three meals a day and frequent changes of laundry. His personality rarely contains elements of aggression or hostility, and he is best described as unconcerned. When he is released he will take up again his wandering and aimless style of life. If, by chance, he manages to get into the Service, he will make an uncomplaining soldier, and after the war his address will be either a Veteran's Hospital or in care of some local Public Assistance office. If his war experiences prove traumatic, or if he encounters severe problems, he may be found some day in an institution for the mentally ill, where his diagnosis will very likely be "simple schizophrenia."

The alternate type of Selective Service violator is a dependent, neurotically inclined person who either consciously or unconsciously seeks evasion because (1) he is fearful of his latent homosexuality, which he dimly perceives as bound to lead him into difficulties when he embarks upon the hypermasculine type life of the Services; (2) he is aware of his intense fear of being hurt or killed; (3) he cannot abide the thought of being severed from his usual family attachments (especially his mother or, if she is deceased, her substitute in the form of sisters, brothers, or other collaterals), or removed to unfamiliar places; (4) he possesses strong inferiorities which he is unwilling to expose, as he knows he must, in the fish-tank existence in Army camps; or (5) he is afraid of the hidden and secret sadism which may be brought to flower by military training.

To sum up, the Selective Service violator is rarely more than a simple law-breaker who possesses a personality type that has led to his violation. Technically, he has been found to be either of the schizoid or psychoneurotic personality variety, although exceptions are occasionally met in practice. He possesses an intact ego, in either case, which is free from criminotic tendencies, although in the schizoid type it is evident in some that the ego is giving way before a psychotic process. The Selective Service offender, then, is not to be regarded as a criminal.

N. W.'s father was a Lithuanian peasant who immigrated to the United States in 1890. Like his compatriots, he moved to a mining town in an Eastern state and soon found himself a coal miner, equipped with a wife from the Old Country, a shack in shantytown, a skyrocketing bill at the company store, a litter of children, and eventually a union card. Of the six children, N. was the third. He was born in 1908, spent a childhood wandering over slag heaps, exploring abandoned mines, and attending a parochial school under the strict discipline of the Sisters. At nine he was permitted to transfer to the public school. Here he made a satisfactory record, showed a normal scholastic and physical development, and was considered "an ordinary but slightly more quiet child." Among his friends he was never the leader. His oldest sister has reported that he was always even-tempered and "everyone used to take advantage of him."

N. seemed determined not to follow his father into the mines. He finished the grades when he was fifteen and entered a high school in a nearby city. He cannot explain now why he left after two years. In any case, he quit schol and began roaming about the country. There was no design in his traveling, he merely went from place to place, obtaining various laboring jobs, living alone except for those occasions when he could find some congenial female to share his boarding house bedroom with him. His occupational range was considerable from 1923 to 1940. He has been, at various times and in many places, a short-order cook, dishwasher, waiter, busboy, truck driver, road worker, canvasser, handyman, harvester, usher, janitor, mill hand, factory worker, and many other things. His "criminal" history includes arrests for vagabondage, peddling without a license, drunkenness, disturbing the peace, hitch hiking, trespassing, being a suspicious character, and loitering. N. served sentences ranging from thirty days to six months in stockades, workhouses, county jails, and on chain gangs in twenty-three of the states.

In 1938, at the age of thirty, N. was turned in to a state hospital for observation for mental disease after an arrest for drunkenness. He was detained for three months. Admission diagnosis was "chronic alcoholism." During his stay, this was changed to "simple schizophrenia," and he was discharged with a final diagnosis of "no psychosis, schizoid type personality."

Following his discharge from the State Hospital, N. went to live with his youngest sister and her husband on their farm. He earned his keep by helping as a handyman, and remained with them until the summer of 1941. He had registered in the draft with the local board at the proper time, but as he later put it, he "hadn't given it much thought." That summer he experienced a sort of resurgence of his restlessness, and one day simply bade his adopted family farewell and "took off." N. was not present when his Presidential Greetings arrived. About six months thereafter he was arrested for vagrancy in another state. When the records were checked, it was found that he was wanted for evasion of the Selective Service Act.

N. was sentenced to three years in Federal custody; however, under the terms of an executive order (No. 8641), he was released to the Army after he had served about fourteen months. In spite of his obvious schizoid make-up and his history he was inducted and is now, so far as this chronicler knows, a soldier in the service of his country.

Individuals who profess a conscientious objection to war present an interesting study. They may generally be divided into two groups: those who base their protest on religious arguments, and those whose refusal to participate arises from philosophical (moral and ethical) considerations. Most curious is the fact that the manifest (surface) objections of the members of each group are similar—although each will vehemently deny this fact. What separates them is the secret motivation behind their protest.

In considering the group which we can conveniently designate "religious," another division must be made. Many Jehovah's Witnesses, all Mennonites, and a large number of other people have been born into the faiths they profess. Hence, their functioning may be regarded as being on a habit level entirely. The behavioral patterns they demonstrate spring chiefly from habitual responses, from deeply fixed systems of reaction. Theirs is not a reasoned rejection, but a blind obedience to settled and predictable response modes. In following the habitual line, they are naturally taking the path that offers least pain, the one that is most free from anxiety and tension. It is the deviating individual who suffers. The born Witness or Mennonite finds it far more comfortable to spend a year or two in prison than he would the same time in the Army. The scion of an orthodox Jewish family is tormented by doubts and severe guilt feelings when he breaks the dietary laws; just as the strayed Catholic retains forever the gnawing, inward bite of conscience when he trespasses prescribed regulations or ignores his duties. So it is that many who object to military service and oppose war on religious grounds are not—as has been romantically supposed in some places—suffering martyrs. On the contrary, they are followers of habit, who are quite comfortable in their protest, and often rather smugly self-confident in their righteousness. And in the places of detention where an obliging government has confined them, one observes how nicely they conform, how they draw about them the armor of their faith, and how it shapes a comforting shield for them. They are "good" prisoners, of course.

The other kind of religious objector is the one who has recently joined any given group. The smaller and less popular sects overflow with these people. They are those who join a movement out of deep and often devious psychological motives. Many join out of sheer loneliness and the need to identify with something bigger than themselves. Man is so unutterably lonely, encased as he is within the confines of his skin, cut off from real contact with his fellows, feeling by himself his own pains, his own sorrows, and really unable to "share" his experiences. So he continually seeks and reaches out for the basic community he desires, and he therefore sometimes attaches himself to a group which promises to provide a sense of community and offers him the happy but deluding prospect of merger with others.

Protest against one's lot in life, the role one has to play, and the station one must assume, is another motive for joining. Indeed, to this observer, this is the most important and frequent of all motives. Numerous sects and branches of religion have their beginnings in this, and they thrive on the exploitation of such a principle. Protestant in the original sense of the word—protesting against the social or political or economic situation—they gather within their folds the disinherited, the disavowed. To them they bring a comfort nowhere else to be found. The Witnesses, with their blessed and angelic horde of exactly 144,000, promise to all who believe the visitation of Armageddon upon earth and an undreamed-of bliss to follow. Meanwhile, the true believer experiences endless satisfaction. His narcissism is bolstered by the ministry he performs, the prophetic extra sense which his faith provides, the conviction of special choice which he has. That ego which was dragged through the hopeless bog of deprivation and want is, so to speak, lifted from the mire and laved with a cleansing fluid. Life becomes meaningful as the intimate wants for love, for identification with others, for security, for status, are satisfied, and, at last, the powerful father-image, great, just, punishing, and rewarding, bolsters the faltering superego. In this latter respect Lenin's dictum that "religion is the opiate of the people" applies directly; for as meagerly rewarded toil, privation, and insecurity exact their toll and point toward the highroad of rebellion, the intense protestant sects aid in deadening the irritations caused by these things and strengthen the tottering superego.

All of this is confirmed by a rapid survey of the branch-and-twig sects. There are those which meet the need of the Negro for status, positing a heaven where whites will ride in the rear sections of Jim Crow cars, have their talents restricted to bus-boying, elevator car operating, stevedoring, cooking, cleaning, and other menial occupations; where God will be a "person of the darker expression," and all "will be of one glorified flesh." There are those, too, which by wild revivalism channel the emotional dammed-up aggression and confine to a canvas tent what could spill over in blood and pain. And, in the north, where the corset of puritanism imprisons biology, the Shakers and Rollers and whatnots find an orgiastic release in their devotions which an otherwise chill community cannot disapprove.

It cannot be doubted that the extravagant sects we have described meet needs which are basic and powerful. And the people who comprise them find there the satisfaction for such wants. Therefore it appears, again, that these personality types are, likewise, non-criminotic. If, for the profession of their faith, they must come to prison, within the walls they are usually happy, for they are still seeking for (and often finding) the satisfaction they crave.

The case of A. J. presents an interesting study of a personality type which becomes attached to a protest faith in satisfaction of some of the motives we have so hastily reviewed. Perhaps he is a poor illustration because he went on to a psychosis and finally to suicide, but his tale is, if anything, a slight exaggeration which serves to highlight and confirm our conclusions.

A. J. was born in Poland in 1902. His birth was entirely normal and his early history—of which there is no information other than scattered reminiscences of the subject and his siblings—was uneventful. He grew up in a farming community near the old Russian border. When A. was five, his father emigrated to the United States, intending to send for his family of seven children—of whom A. was the fourth—when he had earned enough for their passage. His mother A. describes as a kindly, indulgent, illiterate, and sympathetic woman. As for his father, A. recalls him as an unstable, overbearing, suspicious, and quarrelsome person who was quick with blows when his slightest wish was not immediately obeyed.

When A. was ten he accompanied his mother and the other children to America. Here he attended school in the great industrial city where his father was employed as a machinist in an automobile factory. In school A. had a difficult adjustment to make. He was handicapped by unfamiliarity with the language and consequently was placed in a lower grade than his age or intelligence justified. Because of this and the strict, restrained, and often punitive atmosphere in his home, A. became sensitive, withdrawn, and shy. At sixteen he quit school, having gone only as far as the fourth grade, and went to work in the same plant as his father.

The family situation, which at its best was never very good, worsened after A. went to work. He was required to turn over all his earnings to his father, and in spite of his age was subjected to strict discipline. Quarrels were frequent because of his father's low threshold of irritability, and he was exposed to continual nagging from his brothers and sisters for whom he was the perfect foil. At twenty-one, therefore, he joined the Army. During adolescence he had become interested in a musical instrument and he wisely reasoned that he could become adept at it in Service.

During the following six years, A. served in the Army. He was a good soldier, was assigned to the Band, and rose rapidly to a sergeantcy. He made very few friends, attended church regularly, had two heterosexual experiences, and became proficient in his music. In the middle of the fifth year of his enlistment A. began to experience nostalgia and depression. He started to use alcohol excessively and to go off by himself to brood. Although he longed for human contact, he was unable to make friends with the other men because of his shyness, and he maintained only an occasional interest in women. Because of this he asked for and received an honorable discharge.

After quitting the Army A. returned to the town where he had lived with his family. He secured employment as a house painter and lived a quiet and secluded life which was highly routinized and without relief. He worked during the day, cooked his own meals, practised his music, went to church. In 1935, as he was leaving his job for the day, someone handed him a leaflet prepared for proselytizing by the Jehovah's Witnesses. He became interested, attended meetings, read the literature faithfully, and found in the movement "the meaning of my life." Within a year he was the most active member in the community. He gave up his job to devote his full time to preaching. His personality underwent a remarkable change. No longer was he withdrawn and friendless. Now he was full of plans, important to himself and others, and in the midst of a community of other devoted Witnesses. Life became exciting for him. He had a mission. When ordered to report for induction in 1942, A. refused on the ground that he was a minister of the faith, that the order was contrary to his religious beliefs, and an infringement of his constitutional rights. He was taken into custody and sentenced to three years of confinement.

A.'s early institutional history was the usual one for members of his group. He was observed to be engrossed in Bible study most of the time, or to be reading the various tracts and pamphlets which guide the sect.

After he had been in confinement some ten months, A. one day approached an official with the statement that he was "willing to confess everything." He stated that on the previous evening he had heard Walter Winchell "tell the whole world about my shame." Because he was obviously disturbed, A. was removed to the psychiatric ward. Here he was noted as being morose, self-accusatory, sometimes tearful, restless, and agitated. The following is pieced together from the notes of various examinations:

"I ruined myself when young, I masturbated. I think that's what caused it. I was twenty or twenty-five and I went to a prostitute. I was no good. What's the use. Nothing can be done. I live until I die. Walter Winchell. The Government knows. Something shocking happened. My father died ten days after I was arrested. It's my fault. My mother dropped dead on the street. He died over her. I don't know what's going to happen. I wanted to live up to the commandments before I sinned. I became a J. W. They don't want me. No one can forgive me for what I did. I was ruined. I'm a disgrace to the J. W.'s. I touched my sister. She was twenty-one. My mother exposed me. She told the draft board. They told the government. They're going to kill me. It was blindness of mind when I touched her. She pushed me away. I touched her in 1934. In 1935 I became a J. W. This is the only truth. . . . He (Walter Winchell) said over the radio that I raped someone at home. He said this last Sunday. It's propaganda. They have it in the newspapers. The draft board told everybody. They called me a rat. I should be killed. Kicked around like a football. It must be me they mean. It's on my conscience. . . .

The government knows about it. They'll keep me here. They'll charge me with rape. The judge knew about it. He made an awful face when he read my sentence. He knew I had masturbated too much. We shall all be destroyed."

Sometime during his confinement on the psychiatric ward, A. wrote the following letter to his examiner. "In my confession I did not state the true facts, being greatly shamed by them. I first started to act Ungodly to my sister in 1929, when she was fourteen years old. Feeling and touching her from the back three times. I recall also touching her from the front. This I kept up for about three years and she told this to her mother. I never intended to do any greater harm to her. The rest of the story I know government officials know. I can tell from the *Watch Tower* articles and from the newspapers I know my mother has exposed me to the draft board. This is the act of Jehovah God and I know I am a condemned man. There is no hope for me, cast away from this organization and to be destroyed by him in due time."

Soon after this note was received, A. J. committed suicide by slicing his wrists and completely exsanguinating himself.

E. L. possesses a name to conjure with in social circles. His father was a promoter and speculator who gambled with his inheritance and made and lost several fortunes. He died of general paresis when E. was twenty. As for his mother, she is a socially prominent and capable woman of puritanical habits and a strong sense of family honor. Both parents were of old Southern stock and college educated. Their marriage resulted in the birth of three boys, of whom E. is the eldest. At the moment of this writing, the other two sons are officers in the Army. The following account is pieced together from a recent examination of E.:

E. L. was born in 1910. Delivery was normal, no instruments. He was a delicate child to at least seven years of age. Had the usual childhood diseases. Described as very sensitive and given to moody behavior. No tantrums, but preferred playing by himself. Because of delicate health he was kept at home and did not attend school until age eleven. First school was a Quaker Institute. At sixteen he was sent to T——. His grades were only passable; he was not considered a disciplinary problem, but was regarded by teachers and students as an individualist and somewhat "queer" in the sense of being different from his fellows. Active in athletics.

E. left school at the age of seventeen and through the influence of his family got a job as a runner with a Wall Street firm. After losing part of his inheritance in speculating on the market, he drifted from one job to another in the field of advertising. Believing he could write, and desiring especially to do choreography for the ballet, he attempted to devote himself to art but now admits his productivity was low in quantity and poor in quality.

In 1932 he went West and worked on a ranch, herding wild horses and living an active, adventuresome life. He had earlier showed athletic inclinations and was especially fond of riding, at which he attained proficiency as a member of a State cavalry unit. In 1933 a paternal uncle took him on a cruise through the South Seas, visiting many romantic places. He was quite impressed by this experience and became "convinced of the essential oneness of the human family." He was also fascinated by primitive religion, and from that time forward read and studied "the mysteries of the jungle and the East." On his return to the States, he successively became an enthusiast for the Silver Shirt movement and the Isadora Duncan group. He became a disciple and co-worker of a famous team of dancers, mingling with an arty crowd, and attempting to do choreography. At this time he obtained employment selling vacuum cleaners. He also studied and practiced occult phenomena under the guidance of a Japanese Shên-Buddhist.

At the suggestion of a friend, he visited the Harlem headquarters of the Father Divine movement, experienced conversion, professed his belief in the Divinity of the leader of that movement, and from that time forward devoted himself to it. He took up quarters in Harlem at the bachelor apartments of the organization and worked in the Peace Restaurants. Later he moved to a Divine Hope Farm and worked there until his arrest and incarceration. He completely severed all connections with his family and his former friends, and remained adamant in his refusal to acknowledge them.

*Past History:* The subject has had a clear record to the present. He was indicted in 1943 for failing to report for assignment for work of national importance in violation of the Selective Service and Training Act. Although he registered with the local board and appeared for his physical examination, he refused to be present for induction.

*Present History:* Sentenced to three years in Federal custody, E. entered on his term in apparently high spirits, accepting his fate and professing his conviction of Father Divine's influence on him and the rest of the world. He was predisposed to mingling with the colored population, protested frequently against racial segregation, took every opportunity to "give testimony" to the "Living God Father Divine." His institutional record, however, was satisfactory. His behavior on the job and in quarters was good, and he was described as a willing and cheerful worker. He refused any contact with his family and stubbornly resisted all attempts to bring them in accord with him through correspondence and visits.

*Physical Examination:* No evidence of organic disease. History of tonsillectomy, otitis media, childhood exanthemas. No deformities or abnormalities. Musculature firm, nutrition good, habitus erect. Anal skin tabs present, dentition poor. Neurologically he was essentially negative in all respects. Blood serology was negative.

*Attitude and General Behavior:* Subject greets the examiner with "Peace," and composes himself comfortably in the chair. He is courteous, except when any doubt is cast on his statements, or when his beliefs are questioned. At such times he shows considerable stubbornness and tends to be sharp in his answers. There is some posturing and much restlessness.

*Stream of Speech and Mental Activity:* He is voluble, sticking with a sort of urgent perseveration to any topic. His voice is loud and rises to an intense pitch as he continues talking. At times he is really preaching. Vocabulary is better than average, but there is some repetitiveness and a hint of echolalia. He is not distractable but gazes steadfastly and with burning intensity at the examiner. He resorts to many typical phrases such as "Thank Father," "persons of lighter or darker expression," "the alleged mother (or father, or brothers, etc.)."

*Emotional Responses:* He displays an almost euphoric mood most of the time, claiming he has a sense of peace and an "inward radiance of joy." However, facies are only minimally responsive to emotional stimuli, and generally emotional expressiveness is somewhat shallow and superficial.

*Content of Thought:* The subject is wholly concerned with the movement whose leader is Father Divine. He is convinced of the divinity of this man and professes his belief in strong, unequivocal language. He states he has heard the voice of Father Divine many times and he describes an ecstatic conversion experience during which he hallucinated a "great white light and heard ethereal singing." He claims entire devotion to Father Divine, believing that his behavior is directed and controlled by him. He rationalizes his history as one long process of "coming into truth," and his attitude on this subject is one of worship. He indulges in phantasy regarding his past history, refuses to acknowledge his mother and father as parents, and rejects his family with bitterness, claiming he "will not be bound" by any ties except those which "bind me to my divine Father." He believes his family should have followed him now that "I have found the way." Reality sense is dulled, and he seems to have constructed a separate world from his beliefs. He has stated that on occasion, when he is talking or singing, he is actually talking or singing with the voice of Father Divine.

*Sensorium:* Subject is well oriented and the sensorium is fully intact, giving no evidence of deterioration. However, much of his history as given verbally by him consists of fantastic enlargements of facts designed to justify his position and religious notions.

*Insight and Judgment:* Insight is present but of questionable depth. The subject is wholly under the influence of his religious convictions and has constructed a self-satisfying view of the world. He is unshakeably fanatic in his beliefs, mystical in his inclinations, crediting what appear to be auditory and visual hallucinations with reality, and deluded as to his entire system of belief. Judgment, since it is under the influence of his delusional constructs, is likewise impaired.

*Additional Features:* There is an aberrative sexual element present, observable in his chaste celibate past, his inability to form any satisfying heterosexual adjustment, his penchant for his manhood, his rejection with vehemence of his mother, his preference for wholly male society, his inversion of biological interests to the extent of preferring the company of "persons of darker expression" beyond the normal.

The motivation in E. L.'s subscription to the faith he professes is obvious.

The Conscientious Objector who does not draw upon any specific religious form as a rationalization for his objection is also to be regarded from two angles. A very few are the products of habit training in the same sense as has already been described, and with these we are concerned only to remove from them the stigma of criminalism. The others, it would seem, are similarly non-criminal, but present a series of highly interesting psychological motivants.

At the outset, it must be realized that here is a topic on which most of us are prone to level highly biased and prejudicial judgments. It is the belief of this writer that very, very few Conscientious Objectors are cowards. Indeed, many of them are brave men. *Why* they are brave is a different matter.

There are Conscientious Objectors who resist service from the most noble of convictions. They recognize the moral wrongfulness of war, perceive the skeleton beneath the uniform, reject the sonorous talk of our leaders, and armed with history and statistics seek to convince the rest of us. Yet they would willingly take up arms for causes in which they believe and, indeed, undergo considerable torment in the course of their resistance. Such individuals are mature and balanced. They are usually vindicated by events, just as Debs and others who in World War I preferred a prison cell to participation have been vindicated by the disclosure through Congressional investigation and otherwise that that war *was* a war of imperialism. In such characters we observe a highly developed superego and a consequent successful introjection of Society which is all-embracing in scope. This group is characteristically free from psychoneurotics, psychopaths, criminaloids, or psychotics. They show no deviating psychological symptoms. Among them are the true humanitarians.

The parents of S. H. are well-to-do Negroes. His father is a practicing physician of excellent professional and community standing, and his mother is a sincere and charitable person who is interested in civic affairs, especially as they touch members of her race. The H.s are the only Negro family residing in that small northern community. Their home is in the better residential section of the town and is reported to be a sort of cultural oasis where the more intelligent and enlighted people of the area foregather. Dr. H. is a specialist whose services are in great demand, and he is economically secure. Both parents are college graduates. Their three children, of whom S. is the youngest and the only boy, have been given every advantage.

S. was born in 1916. He enjoyed a normal and healthy childhood which was given a special flavor by the congenial atmosphere of his home. Very early in his career, although he was the only Negro boy in town, he demonstrated qualities of leadership. Other boys followed him eagerly in their play, and looked to him for guidance with their problems. In school, S. was an outstanding scholar. He achieved consistently high grades without much effort, was the school's outstanding athlete as well as a social and intellectual pride. On graduation from the grades he won highest honors. This happy career did not vary in high school; as a matter of fact, S. was president of his graduating class, valedictorian, and prize-winner.

At eighteen, S. went to college. Where there had been not even the trace of discrimination in his home community, he now found the situation somewhat different. The social climate was less friendly. Although the college he attended had liberal pretensions, S. could "feel" the resentment he aroused by his presence. At this time he was a handsome, bright-eyed, casual youth. By dint of great effort, he managed to maintain his high scholastic and athletic record, even to surpass his former accomplishments. In his junior year, he was elected to the presidency of the student government organization, the presidency of the debating society, the presidency of the student Christian body, and other campus groups. Together with a handful of Negro boys and girls at the college, he founded a liberal eating club which eventually developed into a non-fraternity movement. At the same time he dropped his former affiliation with the Baptist Church and became a Quaker. His ambition, as he formulated his future at this time, was to train himself for leadership among Negroes, to devote himself to social service with them, to work toward equality of economic opportunity for them, and to dedicate his life to the cause of world peace, since he believed that only under such a condition could the problems of his race approach solution.

S. graduated with the B. A. degree in 1930. He immediately affiliated himself with the American Friends' Association and was assigned to a social service unit to work in the slums of a large city. He remained at this assignment one year. At the end of this period, he became secretary and executive administrator of a welfare organization. At the same time he continued his efforts with democratic groups and peace organizations.

When he registered for the draft, S. filed a conscientious objector's claim. At the time he was called, this claim was honored, and it was decided to send him to a Public Service camp. S. refused to obey this order. He was declared delinquent and sentenced to a term of four years in Federal custody.

In prison S. was immediately recognized as a leader among Negroes. He joined with recalcitrant groups in protest work strikes aimed at eliminating local evils, consistently maintained and spread his philosophy, was regarded with respect and admiration even by prison officials to whom his activities caused considerable annoyance. He refused a number of opportunities for release to work camps or to the armed services. His position is logically maintained, and he is completely devoted to the high ideals which have guided his conduct all his life.

But there is another kind of Conscientious Objector, a kind whose protest arises from urgencies of nature and serves to meet needs about which he lacks insight. In this accounting it is impossible to detail all the categories into which such persons fall, and only the main varieties will be considered.

Conscientious objection is quite frequently a form of re-action formation. A line of behavior is embarked upon which follows a special design of withdrawal from the self-acknowl-edgment of powerful homosexual or (sometimes) sadistic trends. The protest is usually overdetermined—as most symp-toms are—and that is why the most extravagant protestors fall within this group. The present writer has ample evidence from his experience of this type. The consistent picture of the latent homosexual, as he presents himself in the guise of objector, is one of a somewhat effeminate, well-mannered, college-bred, artistically inclined, highly-intelligenced, un-married youth who has ambitions either in the arts or in social service as a sublimation. He has had no heterosexual experiences but has maintained "platonic" relationships with girls. While he does not "know" of his homosexuality as a fact, he shows a distinct fear of it. He recognizes that he enjoys male company, has perhaps even been a college athlete, patronizes progressive youth group organizations, was a Boy Scout and maintains an interest in movements such as the Y. M. C. A., The Oxford Group, and such like. He originates from the upper middle-classes, and his father is likely to have been a professional. He is frequently an only child, although it is more often that he is the only male child in the family where there are two or more female siblings. In accord with the reaction formation, he is in a special sense too masculine, with his hearty good-fellowship, his insistence on muscle culture, and his over-joining of male groups.

There is much about L. N. that is Byronesque. There is also a little of Browning in him, and something of Jeremiah, Savonarola, St. Francis, Oscar Wilde, and Walt Whitman. There are very few things that he cannot do, and do well. He is a poet, an athlete, a scholar, a painter, an aesthete, and much more. Today, at twenty-nine, he is a handsome youth of athletic build who speaks persuasively for his beliefs.

L. N. was born in 1916. His parents were the social arbiters and intellectual leaders of the sedate university community in which they lived. The father was a professor who had authored a number of books in his field; his mother was a college graduate who occupied her considerable spare time by managing a book-store and antique shop. Both parents had inherited large sums and consequently regarded their occupations more as avocations. The home reflected this; it had about it an aura of charm flavored discreetly with a touch of Bohemianism. N. was the middle of three children, the only boy. His birth and early rearing were in the hands of experts. His French nurse was a capable woman who subjected him to a mild type of discipline. In all, his childhood was happy and sheltered.

At an early age L. showed signs of a bright and quick intelligence, as well as an unusual sensitivity. At six, it is recorded, he wrote a play in verse for his Sunday School class to perform, and at ten he began to take a lively interest in political economy under the proud guidance of his father. Meanwhile, in the classroom, he surpassed the expectations of his teachers. Bilingual because of his nurse's teaching, he had a distinct advantage over his fellows which was in no wise lessened by his having had a year in Europe with his parents during his father's Sabbatical. But not only was he proficient in his studies; he was also active in athletics and social affairs in the grades and in the private high school he attended.

At sixteen N. went to a famous university on a combined athletic and scholastic scholarship. He became the outstanding athlete of his school, achieved national recognition in football and swimming, and was elected to Phi Beta Kappa. On graduation he went abroad to study political economy. His year in a foreign land between his twentieth and twenty-first birthdays was exciting. He participated in an international sporting contest, traveled the continent on foot in the company of some friends, became an organizing spirit behind the Oxford Movement, wrote some exquisite verses, and got to know many literary and political figures in the countries he visited. When he returned to the United States he joined a colony of divinity students and dilettante social workers. Among this group he found a girl with whom he fell in love. After a highly poetic courtship, they were married.

The marriage was doomed to failure before it started. L. had never had any sexual experiences beyond the flirtations which his good looks and rugged masculinity had inspired. His wife was—as one would expect—somewhat of a masculine type. They could not adjust on any but a "platonic" level, and after a year of inconclusive experimentation they decided to devote their energies to the causes in which they were interested and to continue their relationship on a plane of "pure friendship, brotherly love, and mutual respect." Accordingly, they threw themselves into their studies, their social work, and their spirited championship of a variety of peace and religious movements.

When L. was called in the draft he refused to report for examination. He had been classified as a Conscientious Objector, but when his refusal was received he was declared delinquent. He objected to service of any type, claiming that he could not conscientiously participate in any phase of the Selective Service program. He chose, instead, to go to prison.

It is apparent that the clue to L.'s pattern of life is provided by his marital failure. He does not recognize his latent homosexuality as a prime motivant in everything he does.

The unconscious sadist is also a member of this fraternity, and in his scrupulous reaction he embraces the code of the Conscientious Objector to war, again overdetermining his actions. He joins any sort of movement which will help him contain his essential aggression and his buried wish to destroy. He would vehemently deny his sadism, but it becomes apparent in his too obvious verbal disavowal of aggressivity.

Reaction formations against homosexuality and sadism are not the whole of this tale. Perhaps an even greater role is played by the mechanism of sublimation for these two trends. It is to be noted that the artistic pretensions and the overt profession of love for all of humanity are common to this group. It can, furthermore, be taken as an almost general rule that few Objectors come from the laboring masses. These two facts in combination mean that the symptom—for such is Conscientious Objection from these motives—is based upon the availability of tools in terms of origin, opportunity, and education. The sublimating Objector, then, satisfies his needs by engaging in behavior on a higher and more socially approvable level. For actual homosexual behavior he substitutes a generalized love for all men and reserves his sadism for whatever system he is attacking by brush or pen or chisel.

There are, too, Conscientious Objectors who find in this

mode of behavior an involved and curious way to express a psychoneurosis. Those in this category are sometimes seekers after punishment, and Objection offers them a highroad to their need which dates into their early history. Often one finds in their background a deep hatred of the father and an inadequate resolution of the Oedipus conflict. In making their protest they directly subvert and reject Society as they did once the father, and since they expect and want punishment, they find the rejection satisfying. Added to these are, of course, the obsessional types with fixed ideas arising from experience and the compulsion toward objection, the fearful and anxious and insecure neurotics, the dependent characters, and the other variants on the Conscientious Objector theme of which we cannot here treat.

As we approach the topic of the agitator, subverter, and enemy-within-the-gates, we must tread with care. We have seen that such persons often perform their deeds at the behest of high motives and convictions, and that they can be sincerely devoted to a cause. Certainly the boys who slipped across the border from France into Spain to join the anti-fascist forces of the Republic fall into this class. Although with this writer's prejudice—and with the reader's, no doubt —it is hard to credit fifth columnists with the same commendable principles, it cannot be otherwise in many cases. At the same time, the field of political agitation, subversion, and extra-legality offers a unique opportunity for frustrated and thwarted personalities, as well as for true criminal types. The fascist philosophy and way of life, with its glorification of aggressivity, seems to make a special appeal to the latter. The psychopath in particular is eminently responsive to creeds of dominance such as Nazism, and indeed the whole design of fascism is pointed at the awakening of the latent psychopathy within the broad masses. From them, when the proper formula is announced by the Leader, spring the brutal character types who swagger and crack heads with a sadistic joy in the doing that rivals if not surpasses that of all other acts. Toward the Leader, they display an adoration based upon the identification of their own egos with his. It is a process of merging, since he is the realization of their own perverted Ego Ideal. As for the broad mass, they show a form of moral masochism natural to authoritarian rule. As Alexander has stated so well, they become like serfs in a feudal state, "secure and protected even though less favorably placed in a fixed archaic structure," and hence less hostile toward their superiors. Moreover, the psychological climate of fascism is aided, and the production of psychopathically-oriented leaders hastened, by the fact that the social displacement characteristic of the pre-fascist era leads to resentment and aggression, thus mobilizing the latent psychopathy by serving as a touchstone.

For those who subscribe to the philosophy and practice of fascism a special word must be said. Apart from a very few, those known to this writer have been vicious psychopathic types or twisted and tormented souls who have failed to displace their essential criminality in other directions. They are typified by the pock-marked pimp who composed the Nazi hymn of hate, and they are poetically recalled by the plaques —characteristically fixed to taverns and dens—celebrating their dubious heroics. The whole crew in the magnificent gallery which, for example, John Roy Carlson in his *Undercover* exposed, and who have cavorted to our national shame in halls of Federal justice, is made of fundamentally criminalistic psychopaths who screen their aggression, their hostility, and their enduring guilt behind social double-talk. All the classical symptoms of psychopathy are illustrated in each of them. Their hatred of progressive governmental forms is, really, an index to their pre-oedipal fixation. Their guilt they attempt to saddle upon a scapegoat—the most readily accessible minority.

This writer will undoubtedly be accused of communistic sympathies for this; but it is the psychological truth that the same rarely applies to left-wing radicals, even the labor agitators, despite the opinion of many writers who have declared otherwise, mainly because such writers are so comfortably fixed in the *status quo*. On the other hand, it is similarly true that, among this latter group, are found a larger percentage of psychoneurotics.

The cases which follow are each typical of the essential criminals who profess fascism. One is that of an individual of native American birth who responded to the siren-call of Nazism, which awakened familiar echoes within him. The other epitomizes the storm-trooper, with his special psychopathic mentality.

F. W. possesses a classical psychopathic history. As a matter of fact, his story is a model for our thesis that the social and political implications of psychopathy are far more serious than the individual and familial. F. went on, in his development, to the logical end-stages of the psychopathic patterning, and in this sense his case can be regarded as a prototype.

F. was born in Prussia in 1902. His family boasted membership in the petty nobility, but they had lost their landholdings as a result of the gambling of F.'s grandfather. His father, however, was a professor at the university, and the W.'s were comfortably fixed since he had developed and organized a medium-sized business around some chemical patents. His mother was a woman of good family, but sickly after the birth of F., and unable to exert any influence on his life, especially since she died when he was six.

The early years of F.'s life are unrecorded, and he is somewhat reticent about supplying details. He does tell, however, of the portentous house into which he was born, of the strict discipline to which he was subjected, of the gloomy and repressive atmosphere in the huge stone mansion. He recalls little of his only sibling, a brother about four years his senior, and remembers only their jealous competition for the joy of climbing into their mother's bed each morning. One detail which emerges in his memory with startling clarity is a recollection of falling asleep one evening when he was about four in his mother's bed, safe and secure in her warm presence, and then the hypnagogic perception of himself being lifted from the bed, and finally the cold fear of awakening in his darkened room, alone and friendless.

Within a year after his mother's death, F.'s father remarried. From that time forward F.'s life was miserable. Although his stepmother never maltreated him, he felt unwanted and alien. His father never devoted any time to him, except when it was necessary to administer punishment, and the stepmother concerned herself mainly with raising a child she had by a former marriage and the begetting of other children with her new husband. At ten F. ran away. He got as far as a large town in Bavaria, where he was apprehended by the local police and placed in an orphanage. Of his life here, he refuses to tell. At fourteen, however, he ran away from the orphanage and wandered to a Baltic port where he was picked up by the military authorities and, in spite of his age, impressed into naval service aboard a cargo vessel. At the outbreak of war with the United States, the ship on which F. was serving was detained in an American port, and the crew confined on board until they could be removed to a military prison. One night, however, F. lowered himself over the side and swam ashore. Since he could speak some English, he managed to make his way overland through to Mexico and from there to South America. He will not tell what he did to obtain funds on the way, but his half-smile when he persists in his refusal to talk about this trip is evidence enough of the kinds of acts in which he engaged.

F. remained in South America until 1923, at which time he shipped aboard a fruit-carrying vessel that was bound for the States. At a quarantine station he eluded the authorities, and six months later was at work in a factory in Detroit. He soon found that there was service for a man like himself, and for the next few years was a muscle-man and strong-arm expert for a terrorist organization, a forerunner of the notorious Black Legion. His talents soon were appreciatively regarded by certain men charged with the responsibility for preventing the organization of workers into unions, and F. was well on the way to a fortune. At this point, F. again draws the curtain.

In 1933 F. went to Germany. Actually, he was sent for by Nazi Party officials. He was enrolled in a school where the curriculum was much to his taste, and after two years, armed with false papers, a new name, and even a few identifying scars, he was sent to the United States in the vanguard of the fifth column invasion. Here he set up a sort of school within the framework of the Bund. He remained five years. In 1940 he went back to the Reich for a sort of refresher course and further instructions. Six months later he was in the United States again. He was, unfortunately for him, apprehended when on making an application for a seaman's certificate, it was fortuitously discovered that he had perjured himself.

During the term of his confinement, F. was an unruly agitator and conspirator. Psychiatric examination disclosed, beyond doubt, his essential psychopathy, tinged with sadism and homosexuality.

B. B. is one of the prizes in this writer's collection. At the time of this writing he is serving a sentence for "conspiring and committing seditious acts." His behavior is that of a martyr to a good cause, but beneath his unctuousness lies the unregenerate psychopathic character, the hater and destroyer, the harbinger of the apocalypse. The acts which brought B. B. to the attention of the authorities read like a more sedate transcription from Sinclair Lewis' *It Can't Happen Here*, or Lewis Browne's *See What I Mean?* B. B. held meetings and distributed subversive literature both before and after our country's declaration of war on the Axis powers. In these meetings, B. B. upheld the Japanese for their attack on Pearl Harbor, championed the Axis policies, derogated our President and our military leaders, was, in fact, a fascist supporter and subverter of the first order. All of this, of course, B. B. denies, vehemently and with a piety to be found only in Fourteenth Century Spanish depictions of the Crucifixion. He contends that the "little group" of which he was the führer was "one hundred per cent American, opposed to no creed or color or race . . . a force for Americanism," in fact; that he was "given the Judas treatment by false witnesses, disgruntled politicians, and ward heelers whom I consistently exposed for the public." B. B. is indeed a character worth our attention.

B. B. was born around the turn of the century. His father was an unstable man of good education and background who held some rather responsible government posts until he contracted a disease which forced him to quit the usual scene of his activities. Since his marital affairs were likewise in disorder, the father separated from his wife at the same time. Eventually the separation was legalized through divorce. Shortly after this, the father entered the ministry and settled into a somewhat less hectic middle age with his second wife. B. B. remained with his mother. Of her we have little information, except the knowledge that she cared for B. B. and her other children until he was about five. Then she turned the children over to various relatives, assigning B. B. to her maiden sister. Beyond the fact that B. B. claims to have seen her only once again in her lifetime, nothing more can be established about her. She died under rather mysterious circumstances—murdered, it was rumored—shortly after she remarried.

B. B. is the third of eight children. One of his sisters has been confined to an institution for the mentally disordered for the past fifteen years. Of the others, two are deceased, one is an Army officer, the rest are scattered about the country in civilian occupations.

His maiden aunt was very strict with B. B. She was a religious woman who tolerated no nonsense, and his emotional instability which exhibited itself in tantrums, convulsions, enuresis, and destructiveness were, to her, devil-inspired and amenable only to the birch and daily prayers. She placed him in a denominational school where the discipline accorded with her notions, and received him at her home only on holidays. On his sixteenth birthday his aunt fell ill, and B. B. returned to her home to aid in caring for her. During the year which followed he became much attached to the old lady, and on her death he was "so overwhelmed with grief and responsibility" that he suffered a "nervous breakdown," for which he was treated as an out-patient by a local physician. After six months, he enlisted in the Army. Before his outfit was to sail overseas, he decided that he "had no reason to take up arms against another country," and went A.W.O.L. It was at this time that he again saw his mother. His visit, however, was interrupted by the military police, who returned him to the Army to face charges of desertion. At the hearing it became obvious that his mental condition was somewhat chaotic, and psychiatric examination followed. Apart from the disclosure that he was completely deluded—he believed he was Jesus Christ —the doctors discovered a penile lesion and he was placed under treatment for syphilis. One year following, he was dishonorably discharged after court-martial.

Released from the military, B. B. became (as he phrases it) "an itinerant merchant." He canvassed house to house, selling patent medicines, wash boards, magazines, and other salable items. On one of his tours he met and married an attractive schoolteacher. Shortly after the marriage he was arrested on a charge of burglarizing a store and given a probation sentence of two years. His wife was outraged and shamed by this. She threatened to leave him if he ever became involved with the law again. B. B. won her sympathy, however, by declaring his suicidal intentions should she ever entertain such a thought. He settled into a selling job after this escapade, and life moved smoothly for three years. But the happy state was short-lived: B. B. became interested in another and wealthy woman. The marriage culminated in divorce, and in court his first love disclosed his sadistic sexual inclinations, his lust for money and fame, and what she called "his crazy ideas."

For the next five years B. B. devoted his talents to sales promotion, bond selling, and public speaking. He was a suave and persuasive talker who enjoyed his own voice and his obvious ability to "put things over." He toured the country as guest speaker for service clubs and eventually landed in a State which is noted for harboring the most extravagant characters and giving them an audience, if nothing more. He was particularly successful with women. His second marriage was contracted with a wealthy dowager who believed him to be a misunderstood genius and who was willing to put up the cash for his numerous ventures in return for an occasional word of endearment.

B. B. next ventured into politics. He claims he did this only to obtain a hearing for his "social theories," and, indeed, his success was meager. But the depression years in the early thirties offered him a perfect chance to capture the allegiance of the displaced and disgruntled few who were looking for a place whereon to project their frustrations. By speaking and writing, B. B. pointed the way for them. It was a highroad to totalitarianism, but of this they could not know. Armed now with an audience, B. B. proceeded to make of his organization a miniature fatherland. He had his goon squad, his troopers, his furtive underlings. And he had, what is more important, a palpable image of himself as Leader.

The whole dream was shattered when an alert F. B. I. pounced on B. B. and the other gutter führers. Perhaps the final blow to B. B.'s pride came when he was recognized as a psychopathic character who gave strong indication that he was suffering from paranoid schizophrenia, and that the possibility of neurosyphilis was also to be considered in achieving a proper diagnosis.

In this chapter we have attempted to penetrate a field that is overgrown with prejudice and even hate. It has been our aim to discover whether individuals who perform extralegally in response to ideas and beliefs can be considered criminals. We have seen that, among these, there are true criminotics only in rare instances, except for the cases where the philosophy they profess provides actional outlets for secret motives in themselves criminal. It is obvious from all we have said how inadequate is our law, how it fails to distinguish among offenders, how it often punishes non-criminals.

# 15. The Forms of Crime

THE peculiar direction of the symptom we have called crime is not a haphazard thing at all. It has its roots in the needs of the personality and is determined by a concatenation of influences which include the biology of the criminal as well as the environment. It should be obvious that a short, excessively fat individual with heart disease would make a rather poor type for second-story work, no matter how imperative the underlying need for such a variety of adjustment may be; while opportunities for the commission of various proscribed acts are limited in certain communities. But apart from the restrictions to the acting out and fulfillment of the basal impulses imposed by environment and biology, it is, in the final analysis, the nature of the strivings and wants which ordain the form of the crime committed.

How this particular problem has been mishandled by writers in the field of criminology will be evident from the barest inspection of textbooks, or the perusal of primary sources in library stacks. With but a passing and usually somewhat forced bow to the intimate psychology of the offender, the discussion is diverted from the really important and significant determinants of an act to a laborious setting forth of the *manifest* purposes of the trespass. Thus we learn that X. "wanted a big car to drive, one like he saw in the movies," or "he robbed the F. residence in order to get enough money to take his current sweetheart to Cleveland for a weekend." If this is not the approach utilized, then we are led through the dreary parade of statistics, in which hieroglyphs are pompously arranged to "show" why certain offenses are perpetrated; and thus attention is effectively diverted from the *latent* meaning of the act. Such procedures are terribly inadequate. They not only present a false picture of the crime situation, but they impede progress toward the treatment of criminosis. We need to know what we are treating, and how to differentiate the treatment of one kind of criminal from that of another.

The writer has elsewhere and at considerable length discussed the case of "Harold." He was able to show the complex and devious motivation underlying his activities in crime, and to work out the latent and intimate meaning of his individual offenses. To illustrate our thesis in this chapter, one incident is herewith extracted from the total record.

Harold committed many offenses. The list of his crimes is a long one and ranges from petty thievery to near murder. During the course of the hypnoanalysis which he underwent a curious fact emerged. It appeared that Harold was not averse to company in the commission of a crime, unless it was the crime of burglary of a house. When a store was to be robbed, a warehouse looted, a car stolen, or a stick-up performed, Harold had no objection to sharing the job with a companion, or even to participating in it with a gang. Yet, when he was to enter a house to rob, he insisted on doing it alone. In the following extracts from the book, *Rebel Without a Cause*,* it becomes clear why Harold robbed, what intimate want his behavior was designed to allay, why he *had* to enter houses alone.

L: *Now, Harold, I want to get back to the problem of why you stole?*

Why did I steal?

* Lindner, Robert M. *Rebel Without a Cause*. (Second printing.) New York: Grune & Stratton, 1944.

Well; I can't tell you the reasons. I don't know. When I was twelve, when I used to hang out with that gang of kids, we stole everything that wasn't nailed down. I went to school, to St. A—— School, and several of these fellows were in the same class with me and they lived in the same neighborhood. So I got into this gang. We were all the same age, most of us the same size too. I wasn't smart; but when it came to seeing things about stealing, to planning things out and so on, I could do better than they could. We used to divide ourselves into three groups and we'd separate, here one section and there one section, and so forth, and we'd steal everything that wasn't nailed down. Then we'd bring the stuff to the clubhouse and if it was anything good we'd split it up. I guess I thought I was a pretty smart kid, not afraid of anything or anybody. I didn't have very many companions before I started going with this gang. They all seemed like swell, very swell fellows to me. There was another fellow named Billie—I don't know whether he or I was the leader—and most of the other kids looked up to us. When they'd steal something they'd show it to him or to me and we'd get together and decide what to do with it . . . batteries and car tires and everything like that. I guess I took a delight in having all these kids come to me and treat me like I was a father. . . .

L: *What does that suggest to you, Harold?*

It would suggest—that because of my—relations at home with —my father and my mother, I would naturally look for something like that—to balance off my feelings.

L: *You're beginning to see why you stole. Now carry your line of reasoning a little further.*

Well, I used to feel that I wanted to be with the gang because I wasn't wanted at home by my father and mother.

L: *Why should you feel that you weren't wanted by your mother?*

Well because she was paying too much attention to my father. My father would work hard so when he came home he would be angry. He'd say his back hurt and he'd tell my mother about it, and my mother, right away she would treat him like *I* wanted to be treated. I wanted her to pat me on the head too. Like the fellow was telling me last night; I wanted somebody to see that I do the things I ought to do . . . wash myself, comb my hair and things like that. I began to look into that yesterday after he said it to me. I tried to reason it out. It's true, I always wanted my mother to. . . . Maybe that's the reason I like Perry. That's a good one! He makes me wash myself more than two or three times a day. He sees that I keep clean, that I don't sit around in dust and dirt and things like that. My mother used to see that I kept clean but sometimes she used to—well—she—when she'd tell me to do something she didn't mean to tell *me* that because she wanted me to do it. For instance, sometimes she'd tell me to brush my teeth for the reason they were dirty. I guess she saw my teeth were dirty and she'd make me brush them; but she'd make anybody brush their teeth when they were dirty; not just like they were *my* teeth. She would treat my sisters and myself about the same when it came to something like that, keeping clean. When she said something to me like that it wasn't emphasized for me as a particular individual.

L: *And you, of course, wanted to be treated individually and specially.*

I find that's true, very true.

L: *So that now Perry is, for all practical purposes, playing the role that your mother played. And he is very well suited to that role, isn't he?*

I guess he is. If my hair isn't combed. . . . He notices every-thing and he tells me about it and keeps on telling me and telling me about it until I correct it. These other fellows, Carlson and Dobriski, they seem to me. . . . If something is wrong with me, my hair all mussed up or my face dirty, they wouldn't tell me about it. When I find out about it I get sore for their not telling me. Maybe they want me to become a bum like they are?

L: *So Perry is, in reality, a substitute for your mother?*

Yes. . . .

L: *Then that is the real reason why you feel the way you do and that you don't want relations with him?*

Yes! That's it! That's it!

L: *Are you sure you understand it?*

I do. I get along with Perry. I like him a lot. Some of my friends don't like him. I tell them I can take care of myself; I know what I'm doing; but when I tell them that they only get madder. I guess I feel sorry for Perry. He hasn't any friends, only me. Now, after what we just said, I know it's more than just feeling sorry for him. At first I didn't talk to him, but I did like him. Sometimes when my hair isn't combed he tells me it looks like a mop. "If you had a wooden leg they could use you for a mop." When I don't shave for two or three days he won't talk to me. "If you don't shave you look like a bum."

I guess Carlson is right. I want somebody to run after me, brush my hair and tell me what to do. Well, he said I was easily led. If I see him I'm going to ask him what he means by that. I guess he means that anybody could be friends with me easy. But he's wrong: I really dislike to talk to people. When I'm talking with Perry or Carlson or Dobriski and they start talking about me I don't like to talk about myself so I switch it away. I don't like to talk about myself even with Dobriski. . . .

L: *Do you recognize the fact that you actually dislike Dobriski? Has it ever occurred to you?*

O—I—I don't. . . . He's o.k. He's—a good kid. He's supposed to be my—best friend, but I dislike him because he hangs around with people I dislike. . . .

L: *Is that the only reason?*

I used to like him a lot. I used to like him very much. He used to be just like a brother to me. I guess when he went away from the cell-block where we were living and started to hang around with somebody else I started to dislike him then. I talk to him but when I do I get mad right away and I want to fight him. I threatened him a lot of times already but it finally winds up that it doesn't do any good. I never had a friend like he was to me at first. In the sunlight when I look at him his eyes are in a funny position. That's a reason why I dislike him. He's got a chin like my father too. Inside the building he's got nice soft eyes but outside in the sunlight they look hard to me, cruel. I used to like him a lot, more than anybody else; but he is different from me. He picks on a lot of different people, the wrong kind of people, for friends. I know he dislikes Perry.

L: *Do you think perhaps you dislike him for that?*

Well, sometimes he appears to me just like my father. That's the real reason, I guess. Sometimes he acts to me like my father. He curses Perry out when he is with me, calls him all kinds of names. He never does it in front of Perry though, and one thing I will say: he talks very nicely about Perry in front of anybody else. He wants me to do everything he enjoys doing. He has real wide shoulders, big arms and hands, big bones in his arms. Sometimes when he picks up his pants and sticks his chest way out he reminds me of my father. Every time I talk to him we get in an argument. Dobriski reminds me of my father in his attitude on people that have a knowledge on some subjects too. He rationalizes his own lack of knowledge and he says they probably don't have any idea of real life. It used to make me laugh. I know it just serves his inferiority feelings. I don't like those friends of his. Sometimes he talks to me in Polish too, just like my father.

Just last Sunday—you know—when the sun's rays were coming in and moving and jumping around, I was sitting at the table and I didn't know what happened. I didn't talk with anybody. I felt like throwing my plate straight up in the air. Then, in here, when we talked about it—my memory—what I was trying to hide— you know. . . . I didn't speak to Perry for three days and even when he wanted to talk to me I wanted to walk away. That's the same way I treated my mother at home sometimes. My mother would call me and call me, and I used to turn away and run. I used to treat my mother like that. Then when I came home she'd give me a beating. When I came home maybe a week later she'd feel sorry and I'd feel rested and better.

Carlson, he doesn't dislike Perry very much: he likes Perry but he don't like the idea of my associating with him. But I don't care what people think. I don't worry about it. I don't have to report to anyone, especially any inmate. They're all small-minded. They probably think—if they have the choice between the good and the bad—they all probably think the worst. Dobriski and I used to live in the same cell-block for years. We hung around together and were closer than brothers. O, we'd argue and we'd almost come to blows, but we'd always get back again and be friends.

L: *But as Perry has more and more played the role of mother to you, so Dobriski has more and more taken on the role of your father. Is that right?*

Yes; I'm sure that's right. A long, long time ago we were playing down at the end of the yard and another friend of Dobriski's said something. We were rolling those balls and it was in the winter. Well, this fellow said something about my eyes. "What the hell is the matter with you? You're not too damned blind to see that, are you?" I got sore. I felt like hitting him with the ball but I threw it on the ground and walked away. Dobriski said he didn't hear it but I know he's a liar. And that reminded me of my father too, because one time I got into a fight with somebody about my eyes and my father hit me. I told Dobriski to get rid of him but for three months he kept hanging around with the fellow. He used to eat at the same table with us next to Dobriski. So I told Dobriski to get him off our table, to do anything to get rid of him, and it lasted like that for a few months. That was the first time I realized that there was something about him that I disliked. I avoid' him sometimes like I avoided my father. My father hit me one time when I was going to fight with somebody. I was only about sixteen and this guy was a man around forty-five. He was drunk and he said something about me in Polish. I started cursing him out and I was going to hit him. My father was there and he hit me from the back, hit me in the right ear. Then everything really started going bad with my father. I didn't want to talk to him at all. I always remember that and this incident with Dobriski reminded me of it again. They both seem to be about the same, Dobriski and my father.

You know . . . ripping up that matchbox, now I know why. You see, I went outside and wanted to take a rest and I saw Dobriski with two other guys I dislike. These two fellows called him over and talked to him. So I called him a stooge and he got sore and I walked away. I was thinking about my father all the time. So I guess I was ripping the matchbox just to take out on something how bad I was feeling. . . .

From what I am trying to understand about myself, why I've committed a lot of crimes, I think I was trying to prove to myself that I was more—superior than I was; that I was trying to prove my superiority. It's like myself are really two people and I try to prove to the other person that I'm more superior than he is. I would take a lot of risks and unnecessary chances, even when I went swimming or stealing, to prove myself superior to what I really was.

L: *Let's return to the question of your stealing activities, Harold. Why did you take articles that didn't belong to you?*

Perhaps because I wanted to possess it. . . .

L: *And why did you want to possess it?*

Well—I—I—ever since I can remember—because—these things —my mother. . . . Well, because ever since I can remember I wanted to possess—my—mother—more than anything else. . . .

L: *Way back in your childhood you became definitely con-*
*vinced that you could never surpass your father and possess your*
*mother. How, then, did you possess things after that? By stealing,*
*by taking, as substitutes, things forbidden to you. Does this ex-*
*plain to you why you went alone when you broke into a house?*
*Can you understand the symbolism?*

It symbolizes—walking through a door—having an intercourse.
Now I see. . . . I—I couldn't have anyone else go with me. That
was one way to—possess—my mother. . . . Now I see. I can see
—all these things—what they mean. And it is right.

L: *Obviously you couldn't get things merely by asking for*
*them. There was only one way for you to possess your mother,*
*which is in many respects a perfectly normal childhood desire.*
*In that stage of a child's life, the child is jealous of the father, so*
*jealous that he actually wants to get him out of the way, even to*
*kill him. We call that the "Oedipus fixation." Have you ever heard*
*of that before?*

Every criminal act, as we have shown, contains the seed
of its occurrence. There is behind each deed a secret history.
It is not accidental that burglary satisfies the essential wants
of one criminotic person, murder another, car theft another.
The deed itself is both symptom and symbol. Perhaps nowhere has this been more clearly established and verified than
in the work of the psychoanalysts and analytically oriented
criminologists. The pioneering formulations of Alexander
and Staub, for example, in their brilliantly executed *The*
*Criminal, the Judge and the Public*, detail three carefully
worked through cases which show beyond doubt that the
intricate and personal mechanics of the acts discussed could
have resulted in no other trespasses than the thefts in the case
of Bruno, the near murder in the case of Karl, and the killing
in the case of the infamous Madame Lefebvre.

For the most part, criminotic behavior is highly individualistic and, indeed, bears a sort of personal stamp, as it were,
a trademark, which results specifically from the matters we
have been discussing. It is well-known that the police and

other agents of apprehension have been able to capitalize upon this proposition by studying intimately the peculiar preferences of criminals and utilizing the knowledge thus gained for the purpose of fixing offenses upon known offenders.

To achieve an inclusive classification of the form of crime based upon the multitudinous combinatory possibilities of motivants is, of course, out of the question here. Yet we have hinted at the general direction in which certain hungers, inadequacies, unfulfillments, and accidents of rearing and weaning point. This we did in an earlier chapter where we discussed the effects upon character formation of events within the developmental course, as well as in other sections dealing with motivation. At the same time, to work out a one-to-one correspondence is well-nigh impossible. It is true, however, that some psychoanalysts have traced a handful of crime-forms to their motivational wellsprings: the latent sources of such phenomena as compulsive stealing (kleptomania), compulsive fire-setting (pyromania), and a handful of other offenses are understood. Moreover, others have taken a slightly different direction, concentrating on the developmental stages of early life and the possible fixations at such levels. Arthur Foxe, for example, derives larceny of a car, unlawful entry, and vagrancy from fixations in the early oral (oral incorporative) period; disorderly conduct, forgery, embezzlement, pickpocketing, burglary, assault and murder from the late oral (oral aggressive) stage; such proscribed acts as extortion, intermediate forms of burglary and robbery from the late oral-early anal -late anal phases; armed robbery and swindling from the late anal; and arson, rape, and bigamy from the urethral and phallic stages.

It would seem, however, that another approach from those already mentioned is wanted. This should be directed upon the primary and compelling need, the urge and source of conflict which finally determines the form of the criminotic symptom. Actually, such a method for designating the form of crime calls for arduous and careful research. It must be based upon intimate and prolonged study of true criminotics in order to separate out from the total organism, in each case, the predominating—or better—the *prepotent motivant*. Then this understanding must be evaluated in the light of other knowledge regarding him, knowledge about his physiology and the type of homeostatic readjustment it encourages, the limitations or special burdens placed upon him by the accidents of heredity, and finally the nature of the precipitating environmental constellation of factors which set in motion the activity. That this *can* be done and will be rewarding is beyond doubt. It offers the only possible hope for a real therapy in crime. Moreover, it will eventually lead to a classification of crime-forms based upon prepotent motivants which, with the application of learning and experience, will permit utilizing the form of the crime itself to provide the first hint of the function it has served, the need it has met. However, this reading backward from the crime-form to the prepotent motivant cannot ever be a completely faithful technique, since so much overlapping occurs and it is possible that the same form can be the result of a complex of motivants.

It seems clear from the hesitant attempts this writer has made toward achieving such a classification of prime motivants that several deserve consideration. Among them are those which satisfy basic needs for the relief of *guilt*, assuaging an impelling search for *punishment*, others which depend upon the satisfaction of *masochistic* and *sadistic* urges, still others which are definite *reaction-formations* whose designs are defensive. Then there seems to be a range of forms such as those legally labelled "impersonation," "fraud," etc., which have to do with wants for status and recognition, those which depend upon *identification* as the essential psychological element. Yet another group betrays *regressive* yearnings and signalizes the utilization of prohibited ways to find solutions, ways which might have been suitable in an earlier time of life.

The foregoing is meant to be suggestive and does not pretend even to scratch the potentialities of this method of prepotent motivants. Yet it must be emphasized that every criminal act has a function: to sate a desire, relieve a want, still a conflict. It is, as we have said so many times, a symptom. The form of the crime is a general index to the prepotent motivant; this, in its turn, is indicative of the psychodynamics of the act and the personality of the offender; and this last is a guiding arrow, pointing the road to treatment.

The crime-form, functioning as it does, is a unique thing for a particular personality. It always has a job to do, as we have said; and it further appears that there exist instances where, because it is an incomplete thing, an inadequate act, the design of it somehow fails to meet the need. As we shall see when we come to discuss the development of criminal careers, the endless roll of offenses characterizing some criminotics (exclusive of the psychopathic personalities, the simple lawbreakers, and those who are essentially neurotics and psychotics rather than criminotics) is due to nothing more than a constant seeking for the proper form of crime which will meet the crying need of the personality. The fact that a career in crime suddenly halts is due, not to the obscure operation of an *etwas* which pulls the individual up sharply, makes him contritely acknowledge his previous misbehavior, and converts him to decent citizenship: instead it is due to the natural fact that, at long last, his act has satisfied the prepotent motivant(s) which provided the basic dynamics for his past performances. More than this, close study of the problem will reveal also that many acts not only fail to allay the anxiety, decrease the tension, resolve the conflict, or do whatever they are supposed to do—they, in fact, increase the tension, heighten the anxiety, point up the conflict, and, in fine, forcefully *demand* a prolongation of the disordered, chaotic, criminotic patterning. As we shall show in the next chapter, where this strange and exciting phenomenon occurs we can note a regular progression in the seriousness of the crimes committed, until the pot boils over, and the career in crime culminates in a disastrous episode. Here we meet with the case where, as it was phrased in the sixth chapter, "nothing less than the extreme act demanded by id would suffice to call a halt to the vicious progression." And, curiously, not only does this fundamental psychological fact account for both recidivism and the mystifying feature of development in a crime-career from minor transgressions to major trespasses, but it frequently applies to the kind of behavior adjustment inmates make within prison walls. The docile and adjusted inmate is more than likely he whose criminotic act has more or less satisfactorily fulfilled its function. More of this later—but in passing it should be remarked again how useful the concept of prepotent motivants can be, for it leads, among other things, to a scientifically derived and plausible as well as objective basis for prognostication, both for intramural *and* post-release adjustment.

A discussion of the forms of crime must include some consideration of its manifestation not as an individual performance but as an enterprise sometimes shared in by more than one person, by groups, gangs, even whole societies. Numerous attempts have been made to describe and explain the construction and rise of criminally motivated mutual or organized enterprises. Classifications have been achieved by sociologists, and there has been worked out a variety of convenient ways of separation into a handful of categories. Such categorical arrangements do little more than serve the questionably useful purpose of distinguishing among criminal actions engaged in by more than one person either in numerical terms, or in

respect of their organizational construction, or with reference
to the kind of bond which encourages the cohesion of members. So, in the literature on the subject, we find talk of com-
panionate crime, professional partnerships, gangs, associations,
confederacies, traditional, predatory, fraternal, and ritualistic
societies—the so-called criminal tribes. The usual procedure
followed is to trace the progression from the single-handed
violation of rules through the lower and higher organizational
forms in which laws are broken in concert. The reading of
such material is fascinating and instructive. We learn of the
lore of organized crime and its tradition, of its emphasis
on professional skills, the culture-within-a-culture attitudes
which its members possess, and of its own code of mutual
aid, exchange, and protection. One becomes impressed especially by the way in which "organized" crime has carved
out for itself a special place in our total social organism, how
its tentacles reach into areas which should remain free of
criminotic taint and suspicion; how it forms affiliations; indeed, how it depends upon the complicity of corrupt police,
shyster lawyers, and prostitute politicians who betray a public
trust. More than this, certain forms of crime are shown to be
particular objects of organized crime, since they are the most
lucrative. Among these are to be placed especially those with
ancient and historical traditions; crimes such as commercialized
vice, piracy, fencing, burglary, banditry, kidnapping, gambling, blackmailing, bootlegging and smuggling, counterfeiting, trafficking in drugs, and the like. We learn further of those
marginal professions with caste or class traditions which rest
on or within the borders of concerted criminal enterprise: the
pawnbrokers, usurers, loan-sharks, quacks, fakers. Particularly
interesting are the vivid accounts of bandit gangs and outlaw
groups, of organizations in opposition to regnant political
authority, of guerrilla formations and revolutionary combinations which dispute with the existing government. The parade

of exotic characters and exciting structures is endless, and volumes could be and are filled with resounding names and highly colored tales. Across the pages troop Chinese bandits, the James brothers, Pancho Villa, Filipino bandaleros, Puerto Rican nationalists, German communists, the thieving devotees of the Indian Goddess Bhawani, the Sicilian Mafia and its American importation as the Black Hand, the Italian Camorra, and finally the rackets in the United States, the Capone gang, and Murder, Inc.

The formation of criminotic organizations, whether they include two persons in association or more, follows the same principles as those which govern the genesis and continuation of other kinds of groups, except for details which are specific to the nature of the goals and special for the types of personalities involved. By far the most adequate approach to group psychology, an approach which uncovers the root principles of group formation, was made by Freud in his *Group Psychology and the Analysis of the Ego*. He was able to show that two basic propositions are the chief determinants. The first of these is that the members, the individuals, all share a common libidinal element, have an embracing interest, that is, which is founded upon similarity of life experience, hence upon equivalent dynamic needs and wishes. In the second place, there is required of the individuals a positive relationship toward the leader, with whom they *identify*, and whose attractive qualities they incorporate within their own egos as Ego Ideal. It is this leader figure who stands central in the group, and who represents for each member the realization and fulfillment of his most intimate and, in a sense, atavistic urges. So the dynamics of group formation is akin to that of love, founded as it is on shared interest (libido) and incorporation of the loved one's qualities (identification) for self-realization. From this it results that the personality of the leader is the paramount feature and comprises the chief clue to the psycho-genetics of group formation.

In the group that is oriented crime-wise, it is the leader who is chiefly responsible for the acts committed. His followers are bound to him by strong ties which receive their energy from his libidinal attractiveness and his representative psychological value, since for each individual component he is the substitute for yearned-after figures of infancy. The qualities and attributes his minions lack, he supplies. The special need they cherish, he satisfies. For each one he plays a particular and special role, the power of which is enhanced by the completeness of the incorporative process.

There are no associations, confederacies, gangs, or other organizational varieties which are free from leaders, no matter how spontaneous the foregathering may seem. There is always a unidirectional vector toward one figure in the group, although his peculiar role differs from follower to follower.

These considerations go far toward explaining why some criminotics operate only under the aegis of a leader and in the relative anonymity of a gang. Like Harold, who could not burglarize in company, their need is for existence within a framework which satisfies their peculiar want. And apart from the libidinal and identification conditions which are met, criminotic endeavor in a group offers other possibilities. Exclusive of the leader himself, the guilt for an act need not be borne alone, on the one hand, while on the other, the residual superego can be more readily overwhelmed by the acting out in concert. Moreover, it is also possible to understand from this how readily the impulse toward criminotic behavior is communicated to persons who would, under ordinary circumstances, restrain its exhibition. On the basis of powerful satisfactions offered by the libidinal and identifying possibilities, and predisposed by an ego so constructed as to be permeable, the leader and his group present a precipitating circumstance of great weight in determining behavior. In this lies also the reason why certain motion pictures, radio programs, newspaper stories, and syndicated comic strips contain potent germinal prerequisites for delinquency.

One rather startling observation that clearly emerges from our consideration of group criminotic behavior is that it offers the final proof for our earlier intimation (Chapter VI) that crime is a station on the road to psychosis. The criminotic lives in another world, a special community with interests and ambitions different from those of the rest of us. He even has a unique argot. In a very basic sense, he is not living in the real world—a common enough notion, it is true, and one signalized by the words "underworld" and "demi-monde." This indicates a withdrawal from reality, not so severe or definite as that shown by the psychotic, but none the less demonstrable. His allegiances and loyalties are different; as with the psychotic, a special element pervades his thinking; his world contains nightmare creatures who to most of us are simple policemen, servants of the state, and custodians of our welfare, but to him are dreaded prosecutors and enemies regarded paranoiacally.

The case which follows serves to highlight some of the points made with regard to group criminosis. It is the best one available to the writer, but is somewhat inadequate for the total purposes of this discussion since not all of the accomplices of this truly criminotic leader are in places where they are accessible to investigation.

This concerns V. G., whose real name was at one time an "open sesame" into a virtual twilight kingdom of commercialized vice, crooked politics, and corrupt government.

V. G. was born many decades ago in a quiet Midwestern town. His parents were well-to-do, very religious in their inclinations, and beyond reproach in their visible conduct. The father was a minor official in the local government; he took his responsibilities seriously and made steady progress toward his goal, which was to occupy the state gubernatorial chair. So far as is known, he was uncorruptible and honest, and V. states that these qualities were really what kept him from realizing his ambition. V.'s mother was sickly after the birth of her only other child, a daughter five years V.'s junior. It was her illness which, in the main, led to friction within the home and made of it a psychological shambles. Although the real story is unobtainable, from the hints V. G. has dropped in conversation it seems highly probable that the father, his religiosity and honesty notwithstanding, was thwarted in his erotic relationships with his wife following her illness. He believed she was shamming pain and fatigue in order to avoid sexual contact with him, and violent scenes, touched off by the most insignificant of daily events, soon became a commonplace. Because the mother was ill (and showed it), and because they were in her company most of the day, she was able to obtain their allegiance and "turn" them against their father. Outwardly, of course, the family remained intact.

From the age of five onward V. G. and his sister were in allegiance against the father. As he grew older his mother and sister made V. more and more the organic center of the family, relegating the "old man" to a subordinate position, tolerating him and, in later years, conspiring against him in ways which even now V. G. refuses to recognise as petty. But the end result of this situation was that V. G. became accustomed to leadership. Indeed, he possessed qualities of leadership quite apart from those grafted on to his personality by his adoring sister and mother. He grew into a tall and handsome youth of high intelligence. His school career was eminently successful, and his social success knew no bounds.

After leaving high school, from which he graduated near the top of his class, V. received a scholarship in engineering from a college in a nearby city. There he founded a branch of a national fraternity in his field. On graduation, such was his pre-eminence in fraternity affairs that he was offered a job with the national organization. He accordingly moved to the city in which headquarters were maintained. Within a year he had met and married the daughter of a local political figure. It was 1918 and V. was offered an Army commission. By this time his father had died and he had brought his mother to live in the home he had made for himself and his wife. Because of his acknowledged and evident leadership qualities, however, V. was assigned to special duties such as those connected with recruitment, bond-selling, and the like. He was thus able to remain at home, or near it, throughout hostilities. After the Armistice and following his honorable discharge, V. became actively interested in politics. His wife died of flu in 1919 and his mother took over the management of his household.

With the advent of prohibition, admirably suited as he was by reason of personal qualities, location, and his position as a minor politico, V. organized a rum-running gang. He attracted to his banner all the backwash of the war, some returned servicemen who were unable to readjust, a couple of trigger-happy ex-soldiers, and the flotsam of the dislocated war workers who had been left stranded by the closing of munitions and supplies industries. The criminal tone of the organization became more and more pronounced. Constructed along business lines and protected by V.'s growing political stature, it invaded many phases of community life and provided numerous opportunities for the exercise of the special talents of its members. It "took over" brothels, gambling houses, and speakeasies, exacted tribute from restaurants, laundries, and landlords, and collected licensing fees for a wide variety of enterprises. Under V. G.'s guiding hand it became more than a local power: it soon reached out and spread its influence into the sedate halls of the state legislature. Here it literally "bought" representatives and through them obtained concessions and special privileges. Its subsidiaries, road-building companies, construction corporations, etc., became wealthy. To clear an operational field for itself and to discourage competition it maintained a "pay roll" of "muscle-men" and "torpedoes." Because of his political stature and his "connections" with the great and powerful of the land, V. G. was able for many years to avoid prosecution, although he was known to be behind almost all the vice and crime in his state. His underlings were apprehended from time to time, but so great was their fear of reprisals from V. G. and, in some, so firm their personal loyalty to him, that he was never directly implicated by them, although they were indicted and sentenced on every statute from larceny through murder. At last, however, an irregularity was found in V. G.'s tax returns and it was on this charge that he was finally sentenced to a prison term.

V. G.'s outfit was held firmly together by a number of elements, the strongest being a powerful positive identification with him that, on the surface, expressed itself as loyalty. Each of his henchmen found in him the ideal to fill the need in their own personalities. For one he was a father-substitute, sternly portioning out punishment and reward; for another he represented the providing mother. This writer knew two of V. G.'s followers. Both of them were orphans, and each had suffered deprivation through neglect. They often protested that he took them "out of the gutter," "made men" of them, and gave them "a real chance." Neither recognized the role he had played in their lives, the crying needs he filled for them. Beyond this, the members of V. G.'s far-flung empire were bound by ties which held them in strong association, ties resulting from a basic community of aims arising in the very recesses of their personalities.

In our examination of the forms of crime we have revealed how the final manifestation of a criminotic behavior patterning depends upon the prepotent motivant, and we have discussed the importance of this concept for the study of criminology, pointing out its widespread implications. We have also undertaken to survey the dynamics of criminosis as it occurs in cases where acts are consummated in concert. Both of these broad topics imply the unsoundness of the usual approaches and the inadequacy—except perhaps for statistical purposes—of the literary distinctions hitherto utilized. Our attention is now directed upon the absorbing theme of careers in crime.

# 16. Criminal Careers

THE idea of the "professional criminal" and that of the "habitual criminal" have been twin millstones about the hypothetical neck of criminology for decades. There are otherwise sober-minded students who would have us believe that some individuals make a relatively conscious and purposeful decision to enter crime as a life's work, schooling themselves in its techniques, developing precise skills, and collecting a philosophy consistent with their practices—all in a determined and deliberate fashion. Or if development toward professional or habitual status takes place not by self-conscious progression, then it is supposed to occur through a "processing" procedure in which society, by way of providing experiences and associations in crime, acts as a monstrous assembly line, shaping the subject and making of him, in the end, a different order of being. Careful attention has been given to this matter, and there have resulted some scholarly studies which indicate a maturational element in the developmental course of criminotics. It has even been shown that the "processed" offender (as one writer calls him) possesses special characteristics by which he can be identified; that he is a *specialist* with limited but potent skills; that he possesses *status* accruing to him by the cultivation of connections in the proper legal places and his standing among his fellows, as well as through certain outward evidences of his success in manners and dress; that he shows *consensus*, or an *esprit de corps* with his fraternity; that he prefers *differential association*, consisting of instrumental contacts with politicians, police, and court officials; and that he maintains *organization*, or assistive or reciprocal arrangements within his "profession." Sutherland (who derived the foregoing) believes further that schooling in technique after selection by recognized "professionals" is necessary for the neophyte in his passage toward "professional" status. Walter Reckless, another writer on the subject, points toward the progressive development of criminal careers through the life history of such individuals, and remarks the evolution of such careers in terms of major and minor accomplishments, comparing them in this way to other professional careers. And for the sources of infection that initiate this apparently inexorable process and keep it on course, most authorities level an accusatory forefinger at the usual sociogenic factors: association with other "criminals," progression from one branch of criminally disposed organization to the next higher with developing skill and maturity, the "agencies of mass impression," including books, movies, and the radio, contacts in penal institutions, and residence in crime-productive areas.

All of this may be true. It is undoubtedly correct to view the recidivist, the ofttimes "loser," as a product of an on-going process which irrevocably stamps him with recognizable characteristics. But to offer this as explicatory for the disappointing spectacle of the same faces returning to custody again and again, and for the inescapable conclusion that there appears a deliberateness to all of this, a "drivenness," so to speak, which holds the spectator helpless as one delinquent after another begins upon this virtual descent into hell, is to counterpoise another merely academically derived, sterile formula against the experience of everyone who has observed true criminotics.

The explanation for careers in crime, and thus for recidivism and recidivists, is to be found in the pitiless dynamics of the unconscious, against which nothing avails but the satisfaction of elementary wants, real therapy, or organic debilitation. No matter how glibly we may speak of the characteristics objectively attributable to the "confirmed" criminotic, or with what pulverizing condemnation we view the precipitants of criminal behavior, in the ultimate accounting these are but secondary features. The continued commission of criminotic acts is indicative solely of a compulsion toward the execution of the single ultimate performance which will satisfy the absolute minimum of the demands imposed upon the organism psychologically. As with a clock that is wound, the impetus is continuous until the mechanism is spent with time or shattered by interference. The psychodynamics are very simply phrased and have already been repeatedly stressed. From the id there emerges the propulsive, predisposing gamut of need which occupies the malleable ego and impels its actional complicity. The prepotent motivant determines the specific act, as we have said, but conditions arising both from within and from without are decisive for the amount and quality alike of the surfeit afforded. The role of the superego depends, of course, upon its specific structuralization for a given personality.

We can make out two chief varieties of recidivism or, better, *repetitive criminosis*. There is the one kind where a progression from delinquency to major transgression is noted; there is the other where a set proscribed act is monotonously reiterated. In the case of the former, it seems that the essence of the matter rests in the inability of the ego to engage in the kind of behavior which will quench the fiery appetites of id. What the primitive layer of the personality demands is either unavailable or, more frequently, denied and figuratively held at a distance by a superego which is yet capable of exerting a reining effect. The manifestations which spot the intervening record from the first overt evidence of criminosis until the final episode are designed as compromises, meant for momentary quiescence. Often they even contain the seed of that act which will finally restore balance to the organism and grant surcease from the terrible inward compulsion. In any case, they are mere stopgaps, corking for an instant the volatile, clamoring, basal wishes.

C. W. was born in 1920 on a farm near the Canadian border. His mother reports that she had a very difficult time throughout her entire period of pregnancy, and that in her seventh month she was advised by her attending physician to remain abed until delivery. C. was her third child, but with neither of the others, both girls, had she had any trouble. She writes, "I almost lost C. while I was carrying him, then I almost lost him right after he was born." On the third day following delivery, C. contracted pneumonia, and only by the devoted efforts of the hospital staff was he saved from death. All of this, however, seemed to increase C.'s value in the eyes of his family. From the moment he was brought home from the hospital until he finally left the family fold, he was petted and pampered. An older sister has written of his early years: "C. was the only one in the whole family who ever mattered especially to our mother. She was crazy about him and I guess she still is. It is hard to tell you about this because my memory isn't so clear, but we always felt that it wasn't right. I know mother was glad C. was a boy and after the difficult time she had with him while she was pregnant and later on she always said it was worth it. You see, she came from a large family of girls and her father died when she was an infant, also she was very much in love with our father and thought that his running around at that time was because he had only women in the family and wanted a son. . . . Mother always gave C. the best of everything and really let him run wild." Apparently Mrs. W. made every effort to stress the masculinity of C., and there is every reason to believe that she emphasized his maleness beyond the point for which his normal growth would permit. C. once told this writer that his mother seemed to look forward to the time when he would be sexually mature, and later on in life took great interest in his reports of sexual activity and conquest. As a matter of fact, she insisted on being kept informed about his sex life and questioned him at great length following each en-counter. There is no doubt that she identified herself closely with the girls and women who submitted to C.'s advances, and that the incest motif was the strongest in her relations with her son. There are even details, supplied by C., which lead to the suspicion that she did her utmost to entice C. into intercourse with her. One of his memories is of her "peculiar" manner of fondling him and her absorbed interest in his genitals.

So far as C.'s father was concerned there is little to be re-corded. Mr. W. was enthusiastic about his son but very un-demonstrative. A railroad engineer and later an official of the company which employed him, he was a taciturn fellow whose hobby, coin collecting, occupied all his hours off duty. Yet, C.'s father was the only restraining influence in the boy's life. He deplored the techniques of training his wife followed, and dourly predicted from time to time that someone would have to take the boy in hand. Whatever punishment was meted out to C., Mr. W. administered. He and his wife often quarreled with each other over C., but the woman's will always prevailed. It is true, how-ever, that following C.'s birth, Mr. W. no longer sought outside company, and it would seem that he realized at once that C. was replacing him in the affections of his wife. The same sister who has already been quoted writes further that, ". . . she (mother) would sometimes take C. from his bed and sleep with him in her arms on a wide couch in the living room. Not only that but they (father and mother) used to quarrel a lot about C.'s deportment in school, and she would encourage C. to act tough and get a big kick out of it."

The school history is unimportant in this case. C. was an average student but a disciplinary problem. One teacher claims: "The problem with C. was that we could get no cooperation from his family."

When C. was eight years and eleven months of age, he was arrested for *petty stealing*. He entered a store and remained as if to make a purchase. A woman shopper placed her change purse on the counter while she moved away, and C. took it. He stood innocently by while she searched for it, even helped with the search. Another woman, however, had viewed the little drama and exposed him on the spot. A policeman was called and C. taken into custody. He was held until his father arrived and then turned over to the strenuous ministrations of his parent and the case dismissed.

In the same year C. was again arrested for participating with other boys in the neighborhood in a *thieving* raid on their school's athletic equipment. C. was placed on probation for one year and his father requested to pay his share of the damage to school property. At nine years and six months C. was turned over to the police by an irate mother who charged C. with the *sexual abuse* of her six year old daughter. The Court extended the probationary period and recommended to C.'s father that the boy be examined. This examination failed to disclose anything of importance, although the doctor recommended that the boy be subjected to more firm handling in the home. His mother, however, remarked that "boys will be boys," and boasted in her neighborhood that: "My C. is more of a man at ten than most are at twenty."

The next recorded arrest occurred when C. was 10 years and five months old. This time it was for *shoplifting*, and he was sent to a home for wayward boys. Here he was in continual "hot water" but was released after five months. At that time he was examined by a physician with some psychiatric training and described as ". . . rather impulsive but pleasant and intelligent." Less than two months following his release C. was once more apprehended for *shoplifting*. This time a heavy fine was imposed on the parents and C. received a firm warning—which availed nothing because he was back in a month for the *theft* of equipment from a garage. By way of interest, and in connection with this series of offenses, the letter from C.'s sister states: "This is something none of us can understand. C. broke into a garage with a gang of kids. The police came while they were there and they all ran but C. He just stood there and went along with the policeman with a smile on his face." The Court was once more inclined to be lenient and released C. to the custody of his parents. Again the following month he was arrested for *stealing* but was dismissed. Within two months he was charged with *burglary* of a home. This time C. was sentenced to a long term in a "reformatory." The attending psychiatrist at this place failed to achieve a diagnosis and affirmed that ". . . he is a pleasant lad who shows no signs of mental disorder. There is a deep attachment to his mother. He is not aggressive although he likes to talk tough. Sexually precocious."

The years at the reformatory had little visible effect on C. When he left at sixteen he still had a "baby-face." His manner was somewhat hardened and he had picked up a lot of information. The family picture had been altered by the death of his father, and although the pair had never been particularly friendly, C. seemed to regret this more than would have been expected. In fact, Mr. W. had died a year before C.'s release, and it appears that the occurrence had an effect on C.'s conduct. Previous to receiving the sad news C. had been a relatively "good" inmate, but the week after he learned of it he was caught in an attempt to escape and was punished severely. When questioned regarding this attempt, C. said that "he felt his mother needed him badly now, and he also took considerable onus for Mr. W.'s death."

About five months following release from the reformatory, five months during which he worked in an apprentice capacity with a printing firm (a trade at which he had become proficient during his incarceration), C. *stole* a car that had been parked across the street from a police station. He merely drove it to another part of the city and left it there. Significantly, he also left his wallet on the seat. When apprehended he stated that he had stopped to buy gas on his way across town, and that he had paid for the purchase with bills removed from his wallet!

C. served two years in the state reformatory for this transgression. By now he was regarded as an "incorrigible" and "habitual" criminal. His institutional behavior was, however, model. During a riot in the reformatory he refused to take part in the general disorder, and it is reported that he spent most of his time in study. He was eighteen when he was released. "On the street" for six months, he lived with his mother and an unmarried sister. They were both shocked when one night F.B.I. officers called for him and charged him with having participated in the *looting* of a warehouse and the *theft* of furs. Since the property belonged to the United States Government, he was tried in Federal Court and sentenced to two years and six months.

It was during this time that the writer made C.'s acquaintance. C. was, at this time, a handsome youth with a bright smile which illuminated his face and loaned it an innocent cast that was hardly in keeping with his deliberate attempt to act tough. He showed no definite psychopathic signs, did not seem resentful or hostile, or even aggressively inclined. On one occasion he expressed interest in "getting to the bottom of all this," but apart from a number of lengthy conversations with the writer, no formal attempt was ever made to work out with him the psychodynamics of his repetitive criminosis. He was discharged on conditional release and once more took up residence with his mother. His sister had married and his mother had prepared a small apartment for herself and her son. It was money wasted, however, because C. was back in the penitentiary in six months, this time to serve three years for violation of the *National Motor Vehicle Theft Act*. There was about this offense something curiously reminiscent of the other time he had stolen an automobile. He abandoned the car about one mile on the other side of the line which separated his home state from another, then he called the probation officer and informed him of his whereabouts, requesting permission to leave the district. The probation officer asked him how he had got there and C. replied that he had "driven over." C. remained in that state three days, then returned to his place of residence. When the theft became known and had been reported, C.'s probation officer recalled the telephone conversation. C. admitted the offense. The intramural history of C. after his return to the Federal institution is relatively clear. He was involved in one fracas because another inmate had made an uncomplimentary remark about his ancestry. In due time, he was released.

About four months after C. was released the writer came upon a newspaper article detailing the story of a robbery and its sequel. Three men had taken part in the holdup, which was perpetrated during the noon hour. They made their escape and went into a moving picture theater. In the men's room they began to divide up the "take." An argument broke out. There was some gunplay. Two of them were killed outright and one was seriously wounded. C. was one of those killed.

The sophisticated reader has undoubtedly worked through the dynamics of the case of C. W. His offenses represented a progressive series of attempts to expiate guilt and to seek punishment for the incestuous desires, encouraged it would appear by his mother, which plagued him from infancy through early adulthood. Confinement did two things for him: it prevented him from committing incest and it gave him a little of the punishment he undoubtedly sought for his underlying desire as well as for those occasions when he had engaged in behavior of incest-symbolic significance. None of the penalties and punishments sufficed, although he spent a brief lifetime of search for the proper and satisfying way to expiation. All of his "slips" in behavior—his overlooking of the wallet, his telephone call to the probation officer—were designed to place himself in the way of retribution. When he attempted to escape because his mother "needed" him he was undoubtedly (although unconsciously) seeking punishment for the success of his most cherished ambition, the riddance of his father. In readily assuming the guilt for his father's death he was only assuming what to his innermost being was already a fact. If C. had not been killed when he was, there is no doubt that he would have gone on to murder and the gallows. As it was, it is more than likely that C. actually killed one of his comrades in the last crime, and so, at last, paid the full accounting for his ultimate wish.

Repetitive criminosis of the variety where an individual rehearses the same act comes closer to the sociologist's formulation of "professional criminality." As successive instances occur, the perpetrator naturally acquires certain proficiences and characteristics peculiar to his specialty, forms spontaneously or by design—or by the curious fact that society at present requires that a "criminal" *live down* to what is expected of him—those associations helpful to him. He may even develop a rationalizing philosophy for rather obvious and self-protective reasons. There are, however, two paramount causes for repetitive, *reiterative* criminosis. In some of these criminotics the superego fixes the limits of transgression and, like a road barrier, blocks further and more disastrous kinds of behavior from reaching the level of action; in the remainder, the act, incomplete as it may be, provides sufficient drainage for id-urgings to be acceptable. In other words, as pertains to the latter, it offers a solution: it is a successful adjustment, and as such is immediately engaged upon again when the pressure from within demands release.

N. S.'s history bears more than a faint resemblance to what takes place when a phonograph needle becomes stuck in one groove. All of his offenses are but variations on the same theme.

This man of thirty-six is an orphanage product. Records indicate that he is illegitimate and was placed in the children's protectorate in a large western city after he had been abandoned. Nothing much is known about his early history, nor does he recall anything beyond the drab monotony of the daily round, the rows of cots in a long dormitory, and the shabby clothing all the children wore. He remembers fleeting occasions when he was singled out, groomed carefully, and marched off to a pleasant room where he had the feeling of "being in a fish bowl. . . . I remember once somebody there, some lady, asked me to recite a poem. I'll never forget the poem, either—

'I saw a ship a-sailing,
A-sailing on the sea,
And, O, it was all laden
With pretty things for me.' "

N. attended school for the first three years in a building across the road from the orphanage. He thinks, but cannot recall exactly, that this was a denominational school, and he remembers vaguely that the teachers were all women who wore a uniform similar to the garb of nuns. "Anyhow," he tells, "they were rough, whoever or whatever they were, and treated us like dogs, not children." In his tenth year N. was "farmed out on trial" to an aged couple in the same city. He was back in the orphanage in six months. It seems, according to N., that the elderly couple found him "too rambunctious, too dreamy, and too independent." Schooling was continued, but this time in an elementary school about a mile from the orphanage. N. was a good scholar with "just a tendency toward day dreaming." He made rapid progress and graduated at fourteen. During all these years, N. remembers, he spent "a lot of time just dreaming. I read a lot and used to put myself to sleep by constructing beautiful stories. I dreamed I was a prince in disguise in order to get away from a wicked uncle who wanted to kill me so that he would inherit the throne when my father died. I would make believe that my mother knew of this evil plot and had had my father put me in the orphanage. This was a good game and I would go to sleep each night with the feeling that it really *was* true, and that someday the other kids and the officials would find it out. The other children didn't like me, I'm sure. I never played with them too much, and I guess I treated them like I was their superior in every way. I think I also acted superior to the officials too." Upon graduation from the elementary grades N. was sent to a technical high school and permitted to board at the orphanage. He had ambitions in architecture and a facility with the drawing pencil. For two years he did very well in his studies. He read widely and wisely, and he participated in one or two athletic contests. Yet, in everything he did, he showed an inclination to dramatize his role and romanticize his behavior. Thus he continually identified himself with the protagonists in his reading, and to compensate for his failure to distinguish himself athletically, fabricated grandiose fictions.

When N. was a little more than sixteen, and in his third year in high school, the orphanage was bequeathed a more elaborate home outside the city. Rather than move with them, N. chose to obtain a job as a store clerk and to continue his studies in the evenings. Soon, however, his enthusiasm abated and his energies gave out—or else the pull of other and more satisfying pursuits was stronger—and N. quit school. At seventeen N. was arrested. A woman charged him with—as far as this writer can make out—the following:

She claimed to have come into the store to make a purchase of a piece of luggage. N. waited on her and, noting that she seemed dissatisfied with what he had to offer, agreed with her that the choice was unfortunately limited, but claimed that he could obtain the precise article she was seeking at his "father's department store," mentioning here the name of a famous establishment. She foolishly gave him some money on the strength of this promise and told him she would return in two days. When she came again, N. pretended that he had never made such a promise and, indeed, challenged her to produce proof of her accusation. The matter was presented to the manager, who called the police. N. finally confessed, was brought to court, and given a suspended sentence after he had made restitution. In addition, he was fired.

N.'s next job was as a copyist with an engineering firm. His wages were somewhat higher than those on the previous job, and he spent most of his income on clothing and books. He worked for this outfit for almost two years until he was arrested and sentenced to a reformatory on the charge of obtaining money under false pretenses. It seems he had bought himself a suit of evening clothes and wore them frequently when he went to dine by himself in a certain restaurant. Here he became familiar with the waiters and the manager, to whom he introduced himself with a name borrowed from the society columns of local papers. He always tipped lavishly and disported himself as a perfect gentleman of exceptional breeding. One night, in the middle of his meal which, as usual, he had ordered with great care, he suddenly called the waiter and, in an embarrassed and apologetic manner, told him he had left his wallet at home and could not pay for his dinner. He asked to see the manager. The manager appreciated the situation and told N. it was of no great moment: he could pay for his meal some other time. N., however, explained that this was not the sum of his difficulties, but that he had a date in a few minutes —and here he mentioned the name of a well-known heiress-to-be —and would be terribly put out by the annoyance of having to go all the way home for his wallet. The manager was obliging—to the tune of a loan of one hundred dollars. N. thanked him with his usual graciousness and departed. After three weeks had elapsed the manager investigated, learned that he had been deceived, and N. was soon on his way to the reformatory. Within the institution he behaved excellently, and when the time came for him to be released, he left with the sincere good wishes of the personnel. He was then almost twenty-one. Through the offices of an official at his place of confinement, N. obtained a job similar to the one he had held before his incarceration. He worked hard and steadily, progressing eventually to a post of considerable responsibility. Meanwhile, he courted the only daughter of an upper middle-class family. The romance culminated in marriage, and here N.'s career struck another snag. Apparently he had represented himself to be what he was not—although both N. and the girl, who divorced him after less than a year, refuse to discuss the matter further— and the beautiful idyll went up in smoke. Soon after the final papers were granted N. found himself once more behind bars. This time the matter was more serious in point of the amount of funds involved.

It was 1934, and the parade of refugees from Nazi persecution had begun. One night, while standing in a Manhattan hotel bar,

N. began a conversation with a well-dressed citizen. N. spoke with an assumed accent, and with great care to his choice of words. As the evening wore on, and as N. noted the increasing mellowness of his companion who was now particularly attentive and absorbed by the fictional anecdotes with which N. was regaling him, N. made the casual disclosure of his "true" identity. Swearing his friend to secrecy, N. revealed that he really was the son of a distinguished middle-European nobleman, a prince in fact, who had been sent ahead by his family to make certain financial and social as well as political arrangements against their flight from the outstretched arms of the Gestapo. He hinted at connections in high places and at a fortune in jewels and gold waiting to be smuggled across the German border. His friend was intensely interested, pledged secrecy again, and invited N. to dine at his house the following evening. N. did so and won over his friend's wife and everyone else he met in the course of the next months. Then there came a day when N. finally worked up to the grand finale. He was now an intimate of the family and at dinner on a certain evening he gave them the "pitch." He explained that the time had come for him to return to his father's house and complete his mission, but he feared that unless he received some aid, not only would his aged father, the Prince, and his mother, the Princess, fall into the none-too-tender hands of the Gestapo, but the family treasures would be lost as well. What he needed was cash, lots of it, enough for his return trip (which a connection in the State Department in Washington would take care of so far as permits, visas, etc., were concerned) and for bribing border guards, Party people, and others, as well as money for the passage westward of his parents and their incidental expenses not only abroad but in the United States until they could get settled (for, of course, it would take time to dispose of the precious goods and to convert the other treasure into dollars). His friends fell—only to awaken some months later to the terrible fact that they had been fleeced.

N. was thirty when he came out this time. He immediately obtained another job, again on the recommendation of an institutional staff member. Soon after, he married, but this time there was no uncomfortable fiasco. His bride knew all about him and he concealed nothing from her. His high intelligence, good manners, and other personality assets helped him toward advancement. When war came he was only thirty-two, but because of his record he was classified as undesirable and excused from service.

In the fall of 1943 a young pilot registered in a hotel in New York. He wore wings and captain's bars. The name he used had a "Jr." affixed to the name of a ranking officer in the Army. A respectful clerk, observing this, approached the captain and made a discreet comment. "Yes," said the captain, "he's my father." Whether the clerk gossiped or himself became suspicious is not known. But N. was soon serving another sentence for impersonating a Federal officer. He is a model inmate.

As in the previous case, the dynamics in N.'s history are painfully obvious. In each instance, be it noted, N. was the son of somebody, somebody important, whereas in reality he was the son of no one. The childish dream of belonging, of being secure, of being somebody, was juxtaposed to his real history of being a stranger, of being tolerated, of being always in doubt, of being nobody. These protests were episodic. They gathered over a long period, creating more and more anxiety, until they would break out into the commission of an offense, the nature of which brazenly proclaimed its antecedents. Moreover, in each case they were precipitated by environmental crises—interference with his planned career, marital troubles, war, and the disappointment of being declared unworthy to serve his country. And behind all of this is the child in his bed in the orphanage, spinning a dream of security so that he can sleep.

Within the compass of the present topic of repetitive criminosis (criminal careers and recidivism) fall some of the most interesting manifestations to be observed in the entire field of criminology, for herein are to be found the purest cases of criminosis. The simple law-breaker is naturally excluded, as well as the criminotic who so fortunately, by a single spasm of the personality, alleviates for all time his need and never again is compelled toward an outward demonstration of criminosis. With regard to this lucky fellow it should be stated in passing that most cases of this type arise from a predisposing need for punishment which is satiated by the unit performance; while the remainder, a minority, must have been born under favorable auspices, because they never again encounter the kind of precipitant which will stir the smoldering embers.

It was stated earlier that the course of careers in crime—whether of the progressive or reiterative types—may be terminated by one of three influences. The most important of these is, of course, the satisfaction of the persisting needs through deeds performed or punishment received. The second deals with therapy.

While this is not the place to speak of treatment, it should by now be obvious to the reader that the reference here is to penetrative techniques which will seek out and discover the pathogenic sources of the criminosis and accomplish a dynamic reorientation of the entire personality. Salvage work of this kind is limited by a variety of factors among which the most significant are the crudeness of our therapeutic tools and the inadequacy of our knowledge. But it must be forcefully impressed that all the elaborate and expressive paraphernalia of our present judicial and punitive equipment are foredoomed to miserable failure, that the solution for repetitive criminosis rests not within the massive architectural abortions which blot otherwise pleasant landscapes, but in deep psychotherapy.

A third way in which an end is put to repetitive criminosis is through the eventual achievement of quiescence over a period of time until the moment comes when the acts no longer receive the support of the organism, since it has become debilitated with age or disease and unequal to the tasks set for it. In instances where this occurs, it is likely that the predominating motivational factors were of the variety to require either motor expression of sexual drives—in which case the natural thing transpires—or of a sort calling for rather strenuous physical activity now limited through disease, accident, or the aging process. Here, if the motivants retain their original force, there may be observed a sudden shift into a new and more suitable crime-form (which is rarely satisfactory and goes far toward accounting for persistent criminosis among the aged); or else there ensues a psychosis (more common among aging prison inmates); or, again, the drive may be expressed by symptomatic minor transgressions, excursions into perverse sexuality of the pedophilic variety, vagrancy, and resort to alcohol and drugs for their narcotic potentialities.

In what has been treated in this chapter lies the essence of the problem which faces the criminologist, especially one who is concerned directly with treatment and prevention. The general approach we have utilized throughout this volume has borne fruit in cutting through the mass of data on the subject and arriving at the fundamental propositions basic to any truly effective approach to this area of knowledge. Through the application of consistent dynamic principles, as they appear in the behavior of repetitive criminotics, it has been possible to relegate the derived and secondarily related features proposed by academicians and sociologically biased investigators to the importance they deserve, and to view the implacable, relentless processes which drive the criminotic organism toward its fateful destiny when the fuse is once lit by the precipitating circumstances.

# 17. Juvenile Delinquency

ALTHOUGH our newspapers have only within recent years discovered juvenile delinquency, the commission of legal trespasses by boys and girls under sixteen has perplexed criminologists and practical penologists for centuries. The problems involved have been completely baffling, not only because there has grown up around this phase of the field a most confusing literature—a literature in which abundant "evidence" is presented to support now one and now another and contradictory feature of causation or of treatment —but also because the barriers to understanding the youthful offender are so doggedly effective. In the main, investigators have suffered from the same psychological hazard that is common to research workers in animal experimentation; everything must be inferred, since the pontifical worker is not himself the dog or cat or child under observation. Moreover, our specious and anachronistic morality interferes. It is hard, even painful, to regard the fresh-faced kid as a full-blown criminotic, possessing a fundamental predisposition toward criminal behavior; hard and uncomfortable to believe he is not basically "good" and in need only of the sympathetic attentions of a scoutmaster, a big brother chosen from among the more stable citizenry, or just a quiet talk with one of the local ministers. Perhaps here more than anywhere else has the fatal spore of sentimentalism been bred with disastrous effect. And yet, as is well recognized by everyone, here is a major site for an assault upon the crime problem.

What needs to be understood first of all is that the bulk of delinquency among youths and children is adventitious and stems directly from the myriad deplorable conditions which sociologists and social planners have decried. But these feeble voices in the wilderness have been drowned, for the most part, by the clatter and clang of machinery for profit, and the miserable slum. The inadequacy of recreational facilities, and the other countless abominations of current society, continue to exert their evil influence. The acts committed by most children and youths—acts which are legally prohibited—do not arise from the dark motivations common to those of criminotics, but from spontaneous situational reactions for which the community itself can take the blame. The author recalls, for instance, his own childhood when, on one occasion, a group of boys was eager to play ball but could find no place in the neighborhood to carry on this activity. It was in the city, traffic was heavy, and we were all cognizant of an ordinance prohibiting ball-playing in the streets. The only vacant space with room sufficient to permit using a bat was the school yard. This was surrounded by a high wire fence with barbs set at intervals along the top and curving downward on its inner aspect. It was a Saturday afternoon and the grounds were padlocked, as they were every afternoon after four and throughout the weekend. One of the boys, however, obtained a pair of wire clippers, and we all participated in fashioning an opening in the fence through which we crept. The yard was spacious, and there followed an hour or so of uninterrupted sport and fun. But a patrolman came by, and soon we were on our way to the police station. Parents were called and, after receiving a severe reprimand and a fine, we were dismissed with a horrible warning. It was no use trying to explain that there was absolutely no other place to play.

Adventitious delinquency, however, has an implication which is of special significance for the development of criminosis, an implication that results from two of its by-products. One of these involves the "halo"—or in this case, the "horned" —effect. When a child has once committed a trespass, although it came about either mischievously or through a fault in the community, he receives a neighborhood notoriety that sometimes cuts him off from fellowship, forces him in on himself, and encourages the development of unwholesome attitudes. He is identified socially, poor behavior is expected of him, and he finds himself a pariah with whom it is forbidden to associate. Again, it is possible that the single haphazard performance may, indeed, provide an acute satisfaction for dormant needs so that, in the future, such acts are resorted to when the particular need or tension becomes manifest. The response thus may become habitual, even automatic, and a criminosis highly probable. Where this transpires we are faced with the alternate possibilities that the organism of the child is predisposed toward criminosis and needed only the slight push from the environment to activate the behavior patterning and fatefully thus to determine the course of his life; or that the superego development has been such as to make it rigid, and it has not until that time permitted the possession of the ego by id-urgings. Once superego becomes relaxed, there is a rapid redistribution of personality elements, and it can never again exert its accustomed influence. It is now forced to play a subordinate role, usually one confined to the evocation of guilt.

Both of the by-products discussed are, unhappily, retroactive. Not alone does the halo or horned effect operate to identify and stigmatize the child or youth, but the adventitious delinquent himself is subject to the adoption of derogatory attitudes toward the community and its agents. He nourishes grievances, identifies those who have brought him to his present pass, projects upon them all the bitterness and resentment and hostility he has stored for having been humiliated and having suffered. Depending upon the way he has been treated by emissaries and deputies of society, his style of life changes. Particularly is this true when he is removed to an institution. In these places, because of their very nature, any underlying criminosis is brought into relief. If no basic criminosis is present, however, there ensues a pattern of response which may resemble that evidenced by the true criminotic. This last is a highly interesting phenomenon, and because of the way in which it works, produces a sort of mid-zonal class wherein it is possible for an individual to show character defects and trends resembling those demonstrated by real criminotics. While in numbers this group is very small, it is, nonetheless, to be taken seriously. Boys and girls who are placed in institutions, reformatories, or detention houses of one kind or another are therein exposed to endless opportunities for character molding at an age when this is more possible than at any other time in their lives. When we consider the utter maliciousness of the influences which are brought to bear upon them—no matter how "modern" the institution—we should be surprised that any once-incarcerated delinquent ever evolves into decent citizenship at all. In point of fact, it is a tribute to the many children who have passed through these places without ill-effect that they have escaped one of two things, the flowering of a criminosis or the development of pernicious character traits.

The account below concerns one of the most "modern" institutions for boys in this country. It has been advertised in the press as a "model" place. Its representatives have made public pronouncements of its glories, textbooks have cited it to advantage. While it is true that the report refers to 1939, it is doubtful that conditions have changed.

"It was in 1939 that I was sentenced to one year at K. school. I was fifteen. Almost immediately after the sentence I was hand-cuffed and transported by automobile to the institution. En route to the school I was informed by the officer who was taking me that if I co-operated and behaved myself there I would have no trouble.

"This institution is on the top of a sort of small hill and when one views it as a visitor I imagine it appears like a respectable school. Immediately on my arrival there I was taken inside the main building, given a number, and asked innumerable questions. I was then ushered across an avenue. As soon as I got inside the building I was ordered to strip and enter a shower. The exterior of the building deceived its interior. The shower room was small, awkward and appeared to be as old as the hill itself. I could not get any hot water for my shower and in my attempt to do so by turning the faucet, received my first reprimand and order there from another inmate who, as I later discovered possessed the title of *monitor*. 'Get in under that shower and hurry it up,' he shouted. I inquired of him as to where the hot water faucet was and he replied, 'Where in the hell do you think you're at? There ain't no hot water. Just get in there, you hear me!' During my shower, which was ice cold, he gave me a lecture which ended up in a sneering phrase, 'You'll learn.'

"From here I was ushered over to a cottage which was quarantine. Not five minutes had elapsed since I had come in the door than I found an inmate cutting off all my hair. For a month following I felt ashamed of my bald head and came to grow more and more proud of my hair as it grew out. After I had been in quarantine for a week I began to realize how miserable the place was. In all my twenty-six months or so there, and in every hour of the day, regardless what you done, you done it in a military fashion. When you went to eat, you marched. When you sat down or stood up it was everybody together and by orders and numbers. Whenever you were seated you had to have your arms folded and when you stood up you definitely had to be at attention. There was no ease, not even in bed. You were forced to sleep facing in one direction with both hands above the covers regardless of the cold air of the dormitory in the middle of winter. Before going to bed each night you were compelled to enter into a small room where the walls were lined with hooks, each boy having a numbered hook. There you strip off your clothing. The cottage officer stands at the door leading from the clothing room into the dormitory. Stripped naked, you raise both hands, spread your fingers, open your mouth, stick out your tongue and pass by for inspection, on your toes. Any time at all, while inside the cottage, dressed or not you are made to walk on your toes. A scrape of the foot or a normal pace would send you to court. Inside the dormitory you are given 1 minute to make your bed up and put on a nightgown. Then come the prayers. They are also ordered to be said 'by the numbers.' You bow your head at the count of one and raise it at the count of two. In the dormitory's first row of beds was what was called the 'wet row' better known to the inmates as 'piss row.' This row was feared by all the inmates. If you should make even the slightest spot upon your bed, accident or not, you were 'sentenced' by the family officer to several weeks in the 'wet row.' Every two hours through the night you were poked with a cane by the night man in a brutal fashion and ordered into the toilet, whether you needed to go or not. While in bed you were not allowed to have your eyes open, nor were you permitted to snore. If you talked in your sleep it meant court and you were therefore charged with 'running your mouth' in the dormitory which was considered a serious offense. You were awakened each morning by the family officer with a loud 'Attention!' You then had to jump to attention; then the order 'make beds!' would come. You dressed the same way. Then marched down stairs in the basement you were made to sit in silence for a half hour or so with arms folded until breakfast time. If you were 'on the line' you stood at all times throughout the day. 'On the line' is a punishment for minor offenses like turning your head in line, getting out of step in marching, turning your eyes, smiling, talking and a dozen other things. You marched to breakfast in a column of fours and at strict attention. There was no talking at the table, smiling or turning about. When you wanted salt, you put out two fingers, for the 'chow bowl' four fingers and so on. The eyes of the officers were on you constantly. From the time I entered quarantine until the time I was assigned to a regular family cottage I had never been told the rules of the institution and cannot recall to this day one time in which what I could and could not do was explained to me. The family cottage I was in had a reputation of being for 'desperados only' and its officer Mr. F., who had a crippled foot, was one of the meanest men of the institution. It would seem to hurt him if he were to see the inmates having a few minutes of peace and rest.

Quite frequently he would go into a rage and shouting hysterically he would make the entire family stand on the line sometimes for an entire week for what someone did which he could not find out but it was seldom that he never found out because most of the inmates would turn informer in an attempt to be on the officer's side, and they were not ashamed of this. Some of them would stand before the whole family and tell the officer what he saw another inmate do. The *monitors* did this every day, reporting sometimes 35 or 40 boys for minor offenses. This was their job while in the family. Many times the monitor would hear someone whisper while in the cottage basement. If he was unable to detect the guilty party he would take 7–8 or more boys out of line from the place where the whisper came, and they would subsequently all be punished for it. The entire institution was run on the basis of 'dog eat dog.' The inmates did all the work in the school and even were made to do the housework of the wives of the officers there.

"At almost any time one could enter my family and find at least half of it 'standing on the line.' When on the line one was not permitted to turn head or eyes, shoulders had to be back, head up, arms down, heels together, and thumbs even with the seams of one's trousers. One was not permitted to move unless ordered to do so. On Sundays one would stand the entire days (excepting meals) from six in the morning until ten o'clock at night. Many times new inmates would pass out in a faint only to be recovered with some water and placed back on the line. If they should pass out again they would be sent to court for 'scheming on the line.' On going to court one had to be at strict attention as he stood packed like sardines inside a small room. I have seen as high as 60 and 70 boys packed into this waiting room. While standing in this line, a monitor would stand on a bench agitating for more silence and to stand straighter even though a pin could be heard if dropped. Often he would take his fist and beat heavily upon some helpless inmate's head and then he would laugh about it. An inmate seldom knew when he was going to court, as the officer would hand his court charge in without the inmate knowing about it. The code there was 'the officer is always right.'

"From breakfast we were marched to the detail hall by monitors always outside and alongside the line. Once inside each family lined up on each side of the hall facing the center at strict attention. The family officers would count the boys in their families while the institution assistant keeper would stand arrogantly in the center of the hall surrounded by work detail officers. After count the assistant keeper would call court line, sick call, and then the work details in order. The kitchen boys had to work 14 hours a day and all the while put up with the most severe discipline. After the morning's work was done at 11 A.M. everyone was returned to the detail hall by their work officers, counted again, marched back to their cottages and lined up for 'wash.' There was no tooth powder of any sort for us and if you was unfortunate in not having a tooth brush you were forced to use your right hand forefinger. Each man was permitted one minute in which to wash his face and hands. One minute to use the toilet and only four sheets of toilet paper. All my time there the only physical inspection I ever received was the second day after my arrival and the week before my release. The hospital was a nightmare in itself. Nearly all of the doctoring that was done was by other inmates. They handed out pills and bandaged cuts and sores. To be admitted to the hospital one had to be down and unable to walk or work. All during the summer we only fell out to play (able to talk freely) about five times for thirty or forty-five minutes, each time.

"During the summer we were made to drill with nine pound Springfield rifles every morning until breakfast except Sundays. The drilling we done was without ease. Many times boys passed out from exhaustion. Giving commands did not seem to be as exerting. No Army unit in the U. S. Army, Navy or Marines could have competed with us for precision in drilling. We had it drilled into our heads by force. Almost every evening immediately following our supper we were made to drill for several hours. The only Godsend to the boys at K. school was sleep. On Sunday evenings we were ushered outside of the cottage and were made to listen to a band concert. This would have been quite a luxury had we been permitted to sit down. On Sunday afternoons we had to change from overalls to our uniforms. Each boy who was a non-com or officer wore chevrons. On the drill field they were the law over the other boys, and most of them knew it, and took full advantage of their authority. Monitors, also inmates, had the authority personally bestowed upon them to inform the family or work officer of any infraction of rules. They informed—and nearly everything was an infraction of the rules there. I remember a boy standing near me one day who actually got five days on the line for breathing too loud. The monitor had reported him as making impudent noises.

"After donning our almost embarrassing looking uniforms we would line up outside the cottage on the avenue and sometimes for a solid hour stand at attention with those stuffy hot uniforms on awaiting church call. When the call was given we were marched in complete military fashion to the chapel. We even had to keep perfect step every inch of the way going inside the chapel, removing our hats with the right hand on entering the door and placing them over our hearts. The only consolation of going to church there was the pleasure of being able to sit down. I remember one preacher there who hardly ever missed a Sunday without referring to us as sinners and telling us that if we tried it would be so easy to be like him. The rest of the time he would talk over most of our heads. One Sunday in particular, I remember hearing him say that we all had great opportunities awaiting us. He emphasized the possibility of every one of us as becoming soldiers some day, saying that then we would not regret so much the training which we were receiving there and adding that it was all for our own good. I truly wonder if he's thinking of those words today.

"Once a year the school has a military day. Each family would dress in their uniforms and would take turns on the field at drilling. All year they were rehearsed for this day. The reward was a pennant to the best drilling family. The drilling judges on Military Day were always several United States Army Officers with pad and pencils in hand.

"*Dining Room:* When each family was marched into the dining room each boy removed his hat holding it up with his left hand to his breast. When the line closed up he had to keep marking time. If he did not keep step when marching and was seen by one of the monitors or officers he would be punished. The officer of our cottage on several occasions issued a statement to the whole family that if any inmate marching in front of you should get out of step, you who were behind him should step on his heels in such a way as to make him get his step.

"The dining room had a strict silent system, talking was completely out of the question, except on Christmas. Then they per-

mitted you to talk for twenty minutes only. Anyone making a
spot on the table, accident or not, would be written up and sent
to court. That was a standing order.

"*Recreation:* Recreation? There was little. There was no base-
ball or football games. Basketball was played in teams for about
ten nights out of the year. That was all. The drill hall was our
recreation. They had a swimming pool there in which I got to
swim in only once. There was a lasting rumor that the reason
for it not being available to the inmates so much was because it
was being used by the institution staff and their children most
of the time. Most of our so-called recreation was consumed in
drilling half a day each week every evening and morning except
Sunday. There were no movies there. No amusements of any
nature.

"*Disciplinary Court:* Boys were packed like sardines in one
small room. The disciplinarian would call them individually into
his office where two clerks would sit taking down notes for him.
The average trial lasted one minute, sometimes thirty seconds.
No inmate was permitted to make any statement declaring the
officer who wrote him up as wrong: that was a crime in itself.
You would generally be asked 'Guilty or Not Guilty.' The best
you could do was say guilty but that the charge was an accident.
Sentencing consisted of the following.

"1. For escape—One year added, a spanking, forty days in the
Discipline Squad, the most feared punishment of the school.

"2. Smoking, first offense—spanking, second offense—spanking
and anywhere from thirty to ninety days added time, third offense
usually spanking, ten or twenty days in D. S., and time added.

"3. Table spot—either an S. S. (suspended spanking) or five
days added. Second offense—ten added and so on. There are many
more that I could add, but this should give some idea of the
system.

"After one would stand the entire afternoon or morning awaiting trial—some passed out from the heat while waiting. A spanking consisted of being taken into a small and dingy little room of
which the windows had been boarded up. Once inside you was
made to face the wall, drop your pants, raise your shirttail, and
draw your underwear tight about your buttocks. The paddle by
which you were beaten was about two feet long with a leather
handle for a grip, the striking part about seven inches wide and

was a little over one-quarter inch thick. Sometimes there was anywhere from one to eight and ten boys lined up against the wall at once. The spanking usually lasted about 15 minutes, according to the nature of the offense you were charged with or number of boys to be beaten. You would be beat on the buttocks, the back of your legs, the calves, back and shoulders, each strike leaving a red mark which later turned black. On several occasions, one of which I witnessed, boys were accidentally struck in the face because the paddle hurt them so terribly they had to turn around. But this was as a rule an accident. When a boy received a spanking for escape, planning to escape, smoking or sodomy it was generally a bad one, escape in particular. On some of these occasions the assistant keeper of the school would have his car parked just outside the door of the court room. In the back of his car he would have a white sheet thrown over the seat, because after the spanking the boy would be taken to the school's hospital for treatment. It is a rather bloody mess to see.

"I received a number of spankings but did not bleed too bad. Where blood had been drawn it quickly healed, although standing up was a pleasure for a few weeks afterward.

"*Discipline Squad:* The officer commanding the discipline squad was one of the most cruel and heartless men I have ever known. In the discipline squad as well as on the spanking line, boys ranging in age from eight years old to eighteen were all treated alike, like animals. The population of D. S. was around 40 or 50 most of the time, excluding the monitors who were the disciplinary overseers. They were chosen by disciplinarians or the officer in charge of D. S., and were always the biggest boys in the institution. Their authority had no limit when it came to punishment. They would strike another inmate as easy as not and get away with it. When they ordered a boy to get on the 'step out line,' the boy was always punished generally with several slaps in the face, but the piece of rubber hose the D. S. officer carried was his most used weapon, a two and a half foot piece of garden hose. During the day almost every day the boys worked in the filter beds near the school. In these beds was human waste and the boys took their turns, two at a time, while the remainder stood at attention awaiting their turn. They would load it into boxes, handles on each end. They loaded it with their hands. The odor was almost unbearable but worrying about the rubber hose almost eliminated the smell. This work was done out in the hot sun and drinking water could not be gotten.

"The routine on D. S. is as follows.

"1. Rise in the morning at 5:30 A.M. Jump to your feet at attention. By numbers 'one' you removed your nightshirt, 'two' you folded it, 'three' make bed. You had to make your bed in such a difficult and complicated manner that I will not even attempt to explain it here. You had only two minutes in which to make your bed and constantly as you were making it three monitors would shout, 'Hurry it up, make it snappy, lets move it up!' and so on in gruff voices. This shouting went on all day long. By the numbers you also dressed. If any-one made the very lightest ruffle of their clothing, dropped a shoe, scraped the floor, breathed too heavy, or any very minor noise, he was promptly barked at and told to get on the step out line for making a racket. One had to go up and down a very old pair of rickety stairs which squeaked terribly. You had to go up and down in close lock step, very slow and easy, make one noise, miss step and you was doomed to a face beating or a hosing. Everyone once down stairs in a very grim old gray walled room was made to face the wall each morning at strict attention, hands at side, thumbs even with trouser seams, head up, shoulders back, stomach in, heels together, eyes straight ahead, no scratching or putting hand up to face, no moving the fingers or head. In fact you had to be like a statue. After a half hour you would be ordered to do a left face. This done, you would get ready for breakfast.

"The first time I saw K. school I conceived it as a very beautiful school. I thought as I was being driven up to the front entrance that I would not perhaps mind my stay there so much, although I shuddered every time I thought of spending a whole year isolated from my home town and the rest of the world. My optimistic conception of the school was shattered not thirty minutes after my arrival.

"The weeks and months that followed caused me to become more and more embittered toward the school's officers. I had not thought of hating society, only those who were master over me at the school.

"I found it to be more difficult than any task I had had in my life to adjust myself to the rules, regulations and routines of the school. Every time I was made to do something I could not understand why it had to be done, because most of what I did do was in no respect beneficial to anyone or to any purpose. For example, marching at rigid attention, prohibited to talk, smile, turn your head or ask questions of your officer. I could see no reason for this. Only punishment.

"I had been told before my arrival at the school that I would be given an opportunity to learn a trade and receive a good education, and that I would learn most of all how to get along with other people, that I was not being sent there for punishment but for education, to learn right from wrong, to learn about God etc. Well, to begin with, the entire issue proved to be a complete failure. I never learned a trade there, not in the least. I was never permitted to discuss things of any nature. Most of the time, I was afraid even to ask. I did not learn how to get along with people. I only learned how to hate them. And God was out of the question. The chapel sermons were more or less on what's right and what's wrong, shameful criticism directed bluntly at the boys and myself and how fine it is to grow up doing what's right and becoming a good soldier. Today as I think about these things it sickens me. The philosophy of most of the boys in the school soon became my philosophy also. To look out for number one man, yourself, because if you didn't no one else would. The thing which would arouse my hatred more than most things was the way boys would deliberately tell officers about the misdemeanors that their fellow inmates had committed. There was no trust in the entire school. It was all based on a 'dog eat dog' system.

"I had been sent to court a number of times, although never for any really serious offense. I received several spankings from the disciplinarian, time added, and two terms in the D. S., which was the most brutal and irritating of all the punishments I have ever in all my life received. I cannot begin to remember the number of times I was beaten with a rubber hose across the buttocks and slapped mercilessly across the face. During the entire two sentences in the D. S. I never once from 5:30 in the morning till 10 P.M. at night sat down, excepting at meal times. They never deprived one of his food, but they would make him so utterly disgusted and sick that he would lose his appetite. The food was nothing to praise. Dispite the fact that the institution has a poultry and dairy farm, we received skim milk every morning and chicken once a year.

"I had no idea that the D. S. was as bad as I had heard it was before I went into it. I was actually astonished my first day in it. One cannot begin to understand precisely how strict and thoroughly enforced it was. The best way I can think of it in depicting it is that when you go in you become a robot and a statue combined and you remain that way until you get released from it. While in D. S. (for smoking) I was in constant state of fear. I was almost afraid to breathe. Even in bed at night I could not keep myself from being afraid. In the dormitory the lights were kept burning all night and every boy was compelled to sleep on his side facing a glass window where the night man would set reading and watching us. If a boy accidentally turned over in his sleep, he would be promptly roused out of his bed by the night man and would receive five lashes on the buttocks with a long wooden cane. On many occasions I would get an urge to burst out in tears and scream my resentment out. I would curse to myself, swear I would someday get these officers and beat them mercilessly. If ever I needed protection, help, or a kind friend it was during those days. What little belief I had had in God soon evaporated, and as the year wore on I began regarding religion as a farce.

"Standing on the line was another punishment which I found almost unbearable. More than once I have become sick and passed out while standing in my bare feet hours on end. Several times I have vomited and subsequently was forced to clean it up and afterwards was beaten for it. Once I became so utterly worn out that I faked a faint. I was only reprimanded for this, but I never tried it again. Everywhere one walked inside of a cottage he was compelled to walk on his toes and very silently. When marching in the D. S. it was absolutely compulsory for one to stamp his feet down on the brick avenue as hard as possible, keeping in step while doing so.

"The language used by the officers to the inmates there was in no way decent. . . . The monitors were devoted advocates of their masters' language and methods.

"The spankings given by the disciplinarian were brutal. I feared that and the court room as I would death itself. Even while a boy was in D. S. he was sent to court for the slightest infraction of rules. It was an impossibility for any human being to go even two days without breaking one of those rules. They were rules that practically forbid you to breathe and live.

"When writing letters from the institution, one was practically told what to write. In D. S. each boy was given a form letter in which he was made to copy upon his own word for word. If you received a visit you were fully warned that if you uttered so much as one crack about the institution it would cost you a spanking and very possibly thirty days in the D. S. Even after I had been released I was told by a parole officer that if I told any *lies* about the school it would be a violation and I would have to come back.

"About three months before my release, I was picked out in the line one morning by the disciplinarian. He told me that I was to be a monitor. I retained this job until my release. I liked this job as I was not picked on by officers so much afterwards. I regret that I was not a good monitor to the boys. I too became arrogant and began exercising my authority which to this day I regret, although not once did I ever report or tell on another inmate. That was my only virtue of which I am still proud.

"All of the twenty-five months I spent there was lived in constant agony, mostly mental but often physical. I was afraid of the officers and felt weak, stupid and inferior. But at times I would swear that I would get revenge, personal revenge. I actually used to daydream about coming back after my release and beating up one of the officers in town.

"I do know this, that school taught me to be an excellent liar, thief, and a hateful person. It taught me to think only for myself and to disregard whatever harm I may inflict upon someone else. I would willingly steal from another boy, as he would from me so I thought, but never would I tell on him. Sex in the school did not affect me too much. . . . There was always some threat, worry or something eating at me which substituted, although I did masturbate without making it a habit.

"I used to constantly tell myself that when I was released, I would tell everybody about the way boys was treated there, but I never did. When I was released I was on parole and I was so afraid of my parole officer that I would not so much as say 'boo' about the school although I did tell my parents and sister the whole story. My sister could not believe me, later on when I told others, I was told, 'You wouldn't be stretching the story a little, would you?'

"I shall never forget that place. I don't hate the men who treated me as they did any more, I pity them for their ignorance.

I forgive them for what they did to me when I was a child. I can understand grown men being able to stand some of that hell. They, grown men, would revolt, they would kill. But those children who are helpless are not being rehabilitated, they are being tortured. They are being made helpless to go out and meet life as it really is."

Apart from adventitious delinquency, which constitutes the bulk of offenses of youths and children, it cannot be denied that true criminosis exists in this age group. Moreover, it would seem that, if anything, those youths who are criminotics incline toward a more virulent form of the disorder than their adult colleagues. Their behavior is unchecked by physical limitations, they are suitable for more daring escapades, and they lack the cautiousness which only time and a certain amount of maturity can grant. Many of them are psychopaths with symptoms that are exacerbated by appearing in the time of ripening appetite and the full-flowering of biological potentialities. They and their criminotic but non-psychopathic fellows are recognized by the viciousness of their depredations.

It has been noted that a clustering of delinquency occurs in the age range associated with puberty, and some writers have assumed that this period is the most productive for overt criminality. This notion grows out of the old and by now somewhat discredited view of pubescence as a harrowing episode, a time of *Sturm und Drang* when life is chaotic and youth in constant turmoil. On investigation, however, this does not appear to be so, and as it applies to delinquency and crime, the most that can be credited to the effect of that time of life is a quality of daring and recklessness in the acts perpetrated. It is not, therefore, puberty which causes delinquency; puberty merely lends the delinquency a special quality and flavor.

Both for adventitious and basic delinquency the community must shoulder much of the blame. In the case of the former this is because it fails to provide sufficient outlets for the energies of youth, to meet the wants of children and young people for status, recognition, and wholesome participation in the life of the community. For basic delinquency it must answer for providing the plethora of precipitants of criminosis that have been stressed time and again. Consider for a moment the fact that much of delinquency, of both kinds, takes place not only with the knowledge but with the active participation and complicity of adults. Children do not own the moving pictures, the press, the radio, the shabby hotels, the bars, the vicious places of "amusement." Consider also the educational systems of even the best of our schools, and examine them for some evidence of an attempt to meet the moral and ethical confusions of the adolescent. When a governor of a state or a mayor of a city wants to economize, his or his advisor's first thought is to cut back the funds for education. The entire climate of our social life is glaringly opposed to the single guide-rule for successful living: the encouragement through education and training of the ability to wait, to wait for the satisfaction of desire and need which comes with the passing of time. On every hand the growing child is exposed to unhealthy influences, to attitudes which mirror the mentally unhygienic structure of our civilization.

The most we have been able to do about juvenile delinquency is to invent a legal procedure for the special handling of persons under sixteen years of age, thus salving our collective conscience by turning the problems over to others. From time to time, when the newspapers are in need of scareheads, editors inflate the toy balloon of a juvenile crime wave, raise excitement to a nervous pitch, carry it along until the desired circulation level is reached, and then turn to another kind of bait. Meanwhile, societies are founded, money is raised, and polite luncheons at the better hotels are given—all in the vain hope of finding solutions to the problem of juvenile crime. Sometimes these programs go so far as to induce the local government to add another judge to the juvenile court system, to hire a psychiatrist, to investigate a particularly "fragrant" institutional situation. There are all sorts of programs for countering and minimizing delinquency. Some of them are aimed at the schools and attempt to weed out the behaviorally disordered children, to give individualized attention to youngsters, to capitalize on visiting teachers and social workers. Another attack is through the police; this undertakes rigid supervision of vice-ridden areas, arrests adult fagins, watches for predelinquent children and recommends them to agencies and organizations. In some places communities undertake a coordinated program in a cooperative fashion in order to strengthen their internal harmony, to build upon their own assets, and to rid themselves of destructive and debasing elements. Private agencies and guidance programs abound, as do organizations such as the scouting groups, boys' clubs, and play centers. And yet, withal, delinquency goes on.

This writer has had no experience with juvenile delinquents directly and so is not competent to offer solutions. It would seem to him, however, that the problem must be placed on a research basis. The various programs and committees named above appear to employ "shotgun" techniques, founded on derived proposals and with the vain hope that this or that or something else will work. Institutionalization does not seem to be the answer, nor does the solution seem to lie in the activities of clubs and committees. The most baffling item of all in this complex field is the curious fact that the serious delinquents, the adolescent psychopath and the juvenile criminotic, are not the ones who challenge us. They can be treated by psychological techniques. It is the adventitious delinquent who vexes us.

A fundamental attack on juvenile crime must come from two directions. What is needed first is the separation of cases into those which are primarily adventitious and those which are criminotic. The juvenile court must eventually reconstitute itself into a center for diagnosis, and the entire community must undertake to accept its responsibility. The aim of the juvenile court must be to seek out the causes for the delinquency. If they rest with the community, then it must be induced to carry through the necessary internal reorganizations to do away with them. Where a real criminosis exists, however, immediate therapy of a penetrative and dynamic kind should be instituted. These two interdependent procedures offer the only present hope for even partially minimizing crime among juveniles. But the basic problem, that of the non-criminotic child whose adventitious excursion into delinquency does not come about through factors which can be remedied by community action, is beyond the ken of this writer. It is a problem for research in an area where solutions are needed as urgently as they are in cancer or tuberculosis.

Together with the resolution of the juvenile court into a clinically-oriented body, and the acceptance by the whole community of its responsibility, there must come about a general repatterning of our entire culture which will affect the individual moral and ethical codes of all citizens. So long as our present orientation obtains—the orientation already described in this volume—just so long will we continue to produce children and youths who work out their unrest and conflicts against the interests of the community at large.

# 18. Justice

WHEN one pauses to give the matter some thought, it is rather surprising and somewhat naïve of man to look for and expect justice. Certainly it has not been his habit to receive this quality in all his weary history. Regarded from the large viewpoint of the species, justice is the thing that has been rarest in its toilsome biography. When man was young, he contended with unfriendly elements and hostile creatures from which he could anticipate nothing but aggression and destruction beyond his puny powers to combat. In the rudimentary primeval family organization he could not expect to be dealt with fairly unless he asserted himself drastically and by brute force. Later he was buffeted by his rulers, his priests, his kings, and even his gods. And, paradoxically, he never— except in the most isolated instances—gave justice; for when *he* was patriarch or priest or king, that which he administered was likewise foreign to the concept of justice.

Even from the individual point of view he has no reason to expect fair dealing. Ripped from the dank somnolence, the warm-wet bliss of the uterine paradise, and exposed to the conspiracy of torture, denial, frustration, weaning, and pain that characterizes his first years, one would hardly expect him to look for justice. As a child, overtowered by patronizing adults, inwardly cleft by warring impulses and tensely conflicting segments of his psychological structure, surrounded by the indescribably inimical fixtures of the environment, and nakedly exposed to the infallible dictates of the culture, he receives none of the sought after impartiality, the equitable deserts. When he is grown, the incomprehensible forces to which he must submit, the vagaries of economics and politics, the hazards of his dangerous existence, war and the inequity of its instruments, disease and the tyranny of his own bodily structure, finally the sightless unfairness of death—all of these should have stifled the persistent want. And yet, hopefully, in all his ages and in all the times of his life, man expects justice.

This thing that man wants in spite of his history and which is opposed to his entire experience is an elusive quality of great criminological concern. To mete it out we have erected an elaborate edifice of rule and custom, agglutinated as law, with roots in an obscure and enshrouded past. As we have discovered, it is only fairly recently that judgment was confined to delegates and agents. Originally each man was his own dispenser of the quality. If another took his wife or his weapon, uprooted his garden, or expropriated his cave, he made a personal redress of the wrong. In later times the Blood Feud offered the channel through which the concept was executed, since organization was along kinship lines. The appearance of mediating figures between one man and another, between one man and the group, is a novelty when measured against the eons humans have inhabited earth. Guilt or innocence was established in some places, and as late as the first quarter of the Nineteenth Century, by such events as trials by combat and ordeal. In both of these the intercession of an unearthly, infallible power of determination was called upon for the exquisite decision.

The roots of our present manner of dispensing justice through the courts and their assorted personnel lie in the antiquity when king or high priest could no longer personally participate in ajudication. There were then set up several jurisdictions, operating in the name of this glorious figure and with his sanction, to rule upon the guilt of an offender, and to dispense the required mead of punishment. Laws as codes for behavior or as proclamations both secular and ecclesiastic provided the background against which decisions were made. The paramount object of each trial was to establish guilt or innocence, and at first there were no limits to the means employed for this end. Confession of guilt was the sole criterion—after ordeal and combat were done away with—and toward the extraction of this confession the energies of the court were directed. Only with the growth and spread of the pre-democratic idea was it admitted that the accused had certain so-called rights, and checks on trial procedure established to insure that such rights became incorporated into the legal framework. As the possibility for invasion of these presumed rights became more and more a matter of concern, procedural law took shape. Meanwhile, the archaic structure of the courts was maintained and continued. Law solidified even as it expanded to cover the growing function of the state and the complex variability of human life. The judge as the living personification of the state in English-speaking countries became limited in his power. His office came to resemble that of referee more than decider. In accord with the nebulosities of the democratic ambition and in an attempt to place a limit on the judge, the jury of peers was introduced. Because the business had grown so complicated, an individual could no longer be expected to find his own way through the maze of edict and procedure; and the lawyer came upon the scene. On the other hand, the prosecutor appeared to take the ancient role of accuser and of the conscience of the community which was personified by the judge.

Such is the bald history of the evolution of the system perpetuated to our day for the implementation of the quality called justice, that quality which the history of man gives him no cause to expect, but for which he continually yearns.

When crimes and criminals are considered from the point

of view we have been stressing, it becomes obvious that no satisfactory mechanism for the administration of justice can ever be constructed. As with food, so with justice, one man's taste is as good as another's and quite as unique. Only on a mass basis can it be defined, and from the point of view of the mass. Regarded individually, it is elusive and indefinable. The criminotic who is motivated by a need for punishment does not obtain justice before the bar unless the amount and quality of the punishment doled out or the conditions imposed sate his needs. Otherwise motivated individuals will similarly contend against any administrative situation, no matter how designed or with what safeguards, which does not meet their peculiar requirements. So at the same time that justice calls for defining in a mass way, it is obviously important that its administration be individual.

That the present-day organization and methods for administering justice are open to considerable criticism is beyond questioning. Investigators, writers, students of law and of criminology have inveighed against almost everything connected with our courts from their governing philosophy of law to their personnel. Muck-rakers have exposed corrupt judges and the political double-dealing behind their appointment or election. The roles of graft, prestige, and political favor have become common knowledge. It is universally recognized that the bail system is a veritable cesspool, that the sentencing procedure is unfair, that the office of prosecutor is usually regarded as particularly suited to unscrupulous incumbents with a disrespect for anything excepting power. Every aspect of the judicial procedure from the apprehension of suspects through sentencing to appeal to higher courts has been thoroughly and roundly criticized, and there is no need here to go into matters which have been expertly surveyed in the criminological texts of, for example, Barnes and Teeters,

Sutherland, Taft, or Reckless. Our concern is with matters that are more purely psychological, since crime, as we have shown, is essentially a psychological affair.

Examined from this point of view, it at once appears that the total orientation of our judicial system is such as to encourage crime and to interfere with the treatment of criminotics. Human values have become obscured by a Talmudic preoccupation with procedural law to a point where, on occasion, sight is lost of the chief function of law as protection not only of the accused but of those who are offended against. It is here that, sometimes, even the moral and ethical ambitions of justice founder, as in the following instance.

A colleague of this writer was once called to examine a girl at the request of the court. The question involved pertained to the competence of the girl to testify. She had been impregnated by someone, and the accused party had retained the best legal counselors, men who were well-versed and experienced in the law. They at once recognized that the girl was intellectually subnormal, and set about to offer proof of this fact in court. On examination, their suspicion proved correct; she had the intelligence of a four- or five-year old child, although she was at least nineteen and otherwise well-equipped for motherhood. The examination revealed that the girl was the child of good parents, farmers, who had realized the inherent danger in having a physically sound but feeble-minded daughter, and who had provided for her in every way possible so that she would not become a burden to the community. They had saved money against their deaths, and had entrusted the keeping of the girl to an older child. Meanwhile, she was useful and happy on the farm. This terrible catastrophe had been tormenting them in anticipation since they had first discovered her deficiency, and they had tried to guard against it. As they sat now in the examining room, the illegitimate child in the mother's arms, they were tearful and overwhelmed that their years of hard work and decent citizenship had yielded this shame and trouble. When the examiner concluded, he had sufficient scientific evidence at hand to prove the incompetence of the girl as a witness. She did not "know the meaning of the oath" she would have to take, was unable to distinguish the "meaning and quality of her acts," was not capable of deciding "right from wrong," except in a childish way. And, yet, the examiner was tortured by the lurking suspicion that the accused party was, indeed, the father of the child. This man, it seems, was a local resident who had a fair reputation. His demeanor in the courtroom was somewhat supercilious: he postured a good bit and seemed very apprehensive. But the examiner had been cautioned that his function was solely to reach a decision about the girl's competence. Accordingly, after the examination he reported his findings. The judge listened to his opinion, and summarily threw the case out of court, to the joy and relief of the accused and to the utter dejection of the girl's parents.

The writer's colleague, to whom courtroom work was no novelty, and who had been hardened in the crucible of long practice, was considerably upset by what had happened. He later declared that the action of the court was unfair to the complainant. A violation had taken place—the presence in the courtroom of the child was evidence of that—a person had been identified as the suspected violator, but because the complainant was feeble-minded, she had no means of redress. He did not necessarily want the man to be punished, and he thought that every possible protection against misidentification and misaccusation should be granted the defendant. At the same time, he saw the callous disregard in this case for the rights of the complainant—because she happened to be a feeble-minded girl—and the sheer unconcern of the court for the moral problem involved. He was later made even more bitter.

In a subsequent conversation with the defense attorney, the examiner asked what recourse the girl and her family had. The lawyer smiled and stated, in effect: "It's funny you should ask that. As a matter of fact, they have an opportunity for recourse which, I am sure, only their own lawyer's stupidity will prevent them from using. You see, the trial we just went through was completely out of order. The venue was wrong and because of this the decision of Judge C. to throw the case out of court is meaningless. In cases of this kind our state has a law that the county where the child was born determines the site of trial. In this case the trial was held where the offense was committed, and not where the child was born. So the decision has no value and they can easily obtain a new trial. Our client now has to sit tight and pray they don't find this out."

This tale is not by any means unique; the writer can supplement it from his own experience. What it proves is that the law has somehow become separated from its function, has become a ritualistic mumbo jumbo, almost a game. The individuality of the people who come before it, their problems, their needs, are lost, sacrificed to a devious and punctilious routine. The intimate structure of the courts is such that the law-breaker, the casual violator, and the inadequate in endowment, prestige, or finances are prejudicially handled. True criminotics and those with the purse to pay for talented representation are favored. There is little equality before the bar. Even if there existed the practice of undifferentiated treatment, if rich and poor were provided with similar legal talent, and appeared in an equal light to the court, still the situation would be flagrantly unjust. The personality of the accused is almost wholly left out of account in the sentencing procedure. Judges arbitrarily fix sentence "by guess and by God." Written law may provide limits to the amount of time to be served for a particular offense, but this varies not only from state to state but within each state and even within the legal compass of the Federal court system. Agencies of rehabilitation, such as prisons, are hamstrung by the imperious and peremptory judgments of the courts, which from nowhere and by no one knows what magic "decide" on the length of a sentence, daring by this to do what no physician of worth would attempt—prognosticate *to the day* the time needed for cure. Moreover, this inequality of sentencing, depending as it does wholly on the airy biases or the protean moods of judges, leads to bitterness among those on the receiving end and increases the already gargantuan task of rehabilitation. To illustrate sentencing disparity a prisoner once constructed for the author a chart to show how different judges in the Federal system had disposed of cases similar to his. For the same offense among individuals with a like criminaloid history, there was a variation of eighteen years in time to be served.

It must eventually be recognized that most judges simply do not have the training or the equipment to act in their present role. In spite of their medieval garb, their ornate chambers, and the veneration in which they have been used to basking, they are in dire need of help. They need help from experts in human behavior to understand the personalities who come before them, to decide on the motivation behind their offenses, and to determine the kind of treatment they must have in order to deal fairly, scientifically, and yet humanely with them. Either the judge must himself be psychologically trained, or he must be assisted by psychologically trained individuals. A thoroughgoing study of an accused person is the *sine qua non* of justice. For this, pre-trial investigation and examination are essential. It must be decided whether the bar is confronted with a case of law-breaking or criminosis. The proper form of treatment must be established by rigid techniques of diagnosis and by the utilization of available knowledge. Realism and an awareness of the wastefulness of our present procedures from an economic point of view should settle the sentencing procedure. If guilt is established and confinement and treatment are necessary, there is no alternative: the amount of time to be served in an institution of treatment or detention must rest with that institution. The personnel entrusted with the custody and therapy of the offender is the only proper source of determination for the length such confinement and treatment should consume. As it is, hostile, vengeful, and vicious persons are released from our prisons at the expiration of their court-appointed sentences with the certain knowledge of all who have been in touch with them throughout their incarceration that they will return; while prisoners who may have been thoroughly retrained, transformed, reformed, and rehabilitated are forced to continue serving time beyond the optimal point for release.

As for the establishment of guilt, here again is an area where the total inadequacy of our accustomed and venerable procedures is pointed up. It has been our habit to go to extremes. On the one hand, there is the inescapable fact of police brutality, of confession extracted under refined or direct forms of coercion which would blanch the ruddy features of an Inquisitorial monk; on the other, there is the farce of the trial by jury.

The jury trial was originally purposed as a protective device to function in the service of the defendant, to assure him a judgment which would not be prejudiced because of his rank and social status, and to aid in reaching sober decisions based upon unanimity of opinion. Although it was well-intended by the English barons who forced a reluctant John to acquiesce in its inception, in practice it has proved a barrier to justice. Apparently the facts of psychology were unknown to these august gentry, and for their enthusiastic error the public has been paying ever since. We know now that it is almost impossible to assemble twelve good men (or women) and true who will constitute the peers of the defendant. Equality is more than a matter of social rank and background. And even if a jury of true peers were available, certainly the present methods of selection would never permit it to sit. The process of selection has degenerated to a contest between lawyers which has as its end the packing of the jury box with as many characters as possible who will be manipulable by one or the other side. The interminable "challenges" by the contending representatives seems, to an observer, to be designed to choose either the most unstable, pliable, and impressionable members of the populace, or the most phlegmatic, stoical, and inert. The great Clarence Darrow was able to predict almost with certainty the outcome of a trial by studying the inhabitants of the jury box. And because of this, because the issue depends on the attributes of the jury rather than on the central problem of innocence or guilt, the criminotic is favored and blameless persons sometimes are punished.

The spectacle of the jury-room is appalling. Anyone who has ever partaken in such sanctified deliberations, or who has talked with jurors after a trial, can testify to the absolute stupidity of the system. The carefully selected jurors are usually bewildered by the professional terminology of the contesting lawyers, awed and overwhelmed by the emotion-laden appeals of either side, dazzled by the involved logic and pettifogging obscurantism of the judge's final summary and its resounding legalisms, blindly prejudiced for or against the defendant by irrational and preconceived factors having nothing to do with the matter at hand, and anxious only to put a swift termination to an uncomfortable episode and go home. The issues of the trial, its significance, the fact that a human life or its destiny hangs heavily on its hands, means little to the jury.

The time is rapidly approaching when the jury trial will be as extinct as the dodo, when it will be looked upon with that same smiling contempt with which we now regard the curious fixtures of the medieval dungeon. And, in the same way, it will be thought to have been an evil.

As matters stand, there is a wide-spread reluctance to utilize the tools which science has placed at our disposal for the ascertainment of guilt or innocence. While the last words have not been written on the photopolygraph (lie detector) and chemical or psychological techniques for determination, the horror with which these are regarded foretells a long struggle for their acceptance in courts of law. One wonders whether the hysterical protestations against the employment of scientific tools for guilt-fixing are not based on the same type of mechanism which motivates, let us say, anti-vivisectionists who were animal-torturers as children and who now nourish a secret sadism.

It is the lawyers who are to blame for the poor state of our system for the administration of justice. They have taken a high calling, that of intercessor and interpreter to the people, and have made of it, so far at least as it concerns crime, a shambles. Their tradition of honor and dignity has been lost in a hectic scuffle for money and influence. The measuring rod in our day for criminal lawyers is prestige and political influence—not knowledge of law and integrity. People in difficulty seek out only a lawyer who they have every reason to believe can "put in the fix," "make a deal," who "knows the judge personally," or "has plenty of pull." It is known that some criminotic organizations retain lawyers on a permanent salary basis in anticipation of being apprehended in a deed, that such lawyers are expected to spend their time cultivating judges and political connections against their need of them. These and others like them have made of their profession another marginal pursuit on the thin border of the permissible. All sense of moral responsibility to the community is gone from such individuals. They have neither the respect of their own colleagues (see Rodell's *Woe Unto You, Lawyers!*) nor the regard of those whom they pretend to serve. The word "pretend" is here used deliberately. Especially in the case of the miserable law-breaker is it painfully obvious how they have dealt. Prison inmates characteristically reserve their hatred and animosity not for the judge or the anonymous faces of jurors or even for the prosecutor, but for the attorneys who defended them. Caught in the unrelenting grip of the State, they have exhausted their funds to retain a lawyer who can get them off entirely or at least with a small sentence. Many of them have acted on the lawyer's advice to plead guilty—because "the fix is in," "I've made a deal," or "I know the Judge well." This procedure means no work for the lawyer, although his fee is assured. That the suspect is guilty or not doesn't matter. Much of the lawyer's supposed effort on a defendant's behalf is mythical.

It is staggering to realize that almost the entire legal profession is employed not in supporting the law or serving the victim, but in finding ways of evasion. The most competent evaders are the most successful—and expensive—practitioners. These, characteristically, are at the service of the criminaloid and the rich. The poor man and the haphazard law-breaker take what they can get, either the inexperienced junior or one of those shabby vultures who batten upon misery and grief, who practically take up residence in the courtroom and fawn upon the judge's entourage as it enters the courthouse each morning and exits each night.

It has been suggested that the Public Defender system will go far toward eliminating the evils we have only lightly touched upon. If such an institution could be maintained at a non-political level, it would undoubtedly provide the only presently visible means of bringing decorum, dignity, and honesty to the practice of criminal law. It must further be remembered that not all criminal lawyers are as we have depicted the majority. One need only look at men such as Clarence Darrow, or observe that Legal Aid Societies and Voluntary Defenders' groups flourish and promise an eventual house cleaning in the respects outlined.

Our entire organization for the administration of justice stands in need of re-examination and reorientation. In this chapter we have indicated only a few of the inconsistencies, inadequacies, and downright faults of our present techniques in the criminal courts. Nothing has been said of the pernicious bail system, the antiquated formalism of certain aspects of procedure, the cumbersome and prejudicial system of appeal which often asks defendants virtually to mortgage themselves in order to provide the next highest court with a printed document that will spare some dignitary's eyesight, of the motley galaxy of characters that infest any court, of the ridiculous pretense of the oath, of the shame of the "expert" witness, of the validity of most testimony as a function of the question, of the dictatorial office of prosecutor, and a host of other matters. Each of these deserves separate and lengthy consideration. But what we have discussed leads to inescapable conclusions. Procedural law must not be allowed to stand in the way of the true administration of justice by affecting the rights of accused or society, or to obscure the moral issues involved in any given case. The judge must either be replaced by or given the aid of psychologically trained and aware assistants, if he is not himself so trained or made aware. The jury system must be condemned as a barrier to justice and eliminated wholesale, as it has been in the Juvenile Court. The legal profession must somehow obtain a new and more healthful orientation to recapture its high purpose. Only by making such changes can we approach this goal of justice which has forever and so mysteriously evaded man.

# 19. Punishment

IT is likely that very few persons question why we punish. Certainly the general public takes it for granted that crime entails punishment; the two words are, indeed, almost an ideational unit, one inevitably evoking the other. As for workers in the field of criminology, most point to punishment as an ancient practice and trace it to the emotional response evoked by an act which threatened the security of the group, imperiling it in the esteem of its gods and calling for measures of propitiation. Behind this (as we shall soon understand) derivative notion only the dynamically persuaded investigators have gone. From their studies of criminotics, of normal individuals and groups, and of primitive societies, they have been able to see through and beyond the curtain which time and a reluctant and rationalizing but understandable human pretense has dropped to obscure and prevent an embarrassing self-awareness.

For an understanding of punishment, its meaning and its function, it is necessary to go back again through time to the day of the patriarch. It will be recalled that he it was who ironhandedly ruled the primeval roost. It was his unhappy fate to maintain his awesome power until challenged by the sons (or other males) for the possession of the females, the choicest cuts of meat, or the other tokens of his status. If, in this contest, he was defeated, his place was usurped and his body made the *pièce de resistance* of a feast during which his virtues and attributes were immolated and his magnificence shared in gory mouthfuls by his vanquishers. If, however, he was successful, he either killed or castrated the vanquished. When the first modicum of control and restraint was established by such methods, its obvious design was to impress the id, to place a curb upon it, to bridle the impulsions toward parricide and incest. As patriarchate yielded to totemism—the sacred animal inheriting the symbolic value of the immolated father—and family organization gave way to kinships and tribes, the representatives of the group continued to exercise the prerogatives. Yet the essential motivant persisted: everywhere and always there was a desire for the forbidden, the id exerting itself toward the fulfillment of its two paramount wants. The offender, then, became and remained a symbol. The inheritors of the patriarchal mantle, the priests and kings and the delegates of the people, all performed a service the purpose of which was *to re-enforce the egos* of every individual in the group. They, severally and together, insisted on punishment of the evildoer primarily to quell their own inward desires to do exactly as he had done. Each execution, each mutilation, each banishment, served the function of acting for a time as a prop to ego, lending to it a strength otherwise unobtainable in repressing intimate, even unconscious wishes. Moreover, like the scapegoat which, loaded with the sins of a repentant populace, was driven into the wilderness, the offender also functioned to expiate the "sins" of the entire community for doing what they, in their very hearts, longed to do.

Down to this day, the unconscious, hidden, unacknowledged—and, by some, bitterly resented and therefore scorned—primary reason for punishment remains. Each time our apparatus of justice pronounces a punishment, it is seized upon as an ally of ego in the eternal rebellion of the unconscious, re-enforcing it against the swarming and delicious temptations of id. This is why the struggle to reduce penalties, to "humanize" punishment, to mitigate suffering among the convicted is so bitterly fought and so tenaciously resented; for there is a hazy and fearful perception that one of the main supports of ego will collapse if these things are accomplished. The offender, in short, is punished for the forbidden "criminal" impulses of all of us, and in his punishment he bears a collective guilt.

We punish also for revenge. Every offense constitutes not only a fortuitous assumption of social guilt and a way of re-enforcing ego against criminalistic id, but it offers a threat to security. In order for living to proceed with a minimal amount of anxiety, a certain stasis or fixity of its organic and inorganic attributes must obtain. The disappearance of familiar and accustomed landmarks awakens the primitive dread of annihilation, the archaic fear of being left defenseless in a hostile and forbidden environment. Such a fear is expressed by striking out, by a blind but defensive vengeance. The deed of the offender, no matter how trivial, destroys one or many of our pillars of security and, Samson-like, threatens to bring ruin upon all of us. It exposes us, as a community, to the anger of the patriarch's descendants—for what he had done we want to do—and it reveals our nakedness which millenniums of the trappings of civilization have barely covered. So we lash back at the culprit.

Finally, we punish as a socially approved and acceptable way of working out our own aggressivity, our own sadism. The offender in the dock is the perfect target, the most suitable receptacle for the sadistic wishes and desires we have stored. He is weaponless, outnumbered. From our earliest days we have been checked in our aggressions by both tangible and intangible influences. Here, at last, is an object upon whom can be vented an almost unlimited amount of spleen. If we are not any longer permitted to throw spears at him, shower him with stones, crucify him, gouge out his eyes, or follow his expiring agony in the arena, we can at least demand his confinement in a place of mental if not physical torture, lash at him lingually in conversation and oratory in public places, avidly follow his torment in newspapers and pulp magazines, or—if we are very fortunate—participate ourselves in a lynching or witness an execution.

It is characteristic of men that they have rationalized the reasons for punishment. They have said that they punish in order to deter criminals, to prevent recidivism, or to correct or reform offenders. Such widely advertised rationalizations deserve examination, first to determine whether they work or not, and why they succeed or fail. Part of this work is already done. No reader needs convincing that persons are not deterred from crime by the example furnished by apprehended, tried, and punished offenders; even our unreliable crime-rate statistics make this plain. Nor is it necessary to offer proof that recidivism is and ever has been unaffected by punishment, even when it entails torture. As for reformation and correction, nothing more is required than a single glance at the simple arithmetic of recidivism or a nodding acquaintance with the bold fact that no matter how whitewashed the press releases of governors, directors of penal systems, or wardens are, there is no honest criminologist or worker in any of the allied fields of study who can state that our punitive apparatus does anything but brutalize, stigmatize, and discourage reformation in the vast majority of persons entrusted to it.

Punishment does not work, either for deterrent or reformative purposes, chiefly because its instruments and methods do not affect the predisposing conditions in criminosis; while for the law-breaker it is usually unnecessary and uncalled for. It must be realized that the only portion of the personality any variety of punishment affects is the ego, and because the ego of the criminotic is so permeated with id, so responsive to its demands and urgings, and so much a part of every criminotic action, it is completely unimpressed by stimuli from the techniques traditionally employed. No punishment yet devised can operate in the face of an ego shot through with and absorbent of id-urgings; it may, through the superego, bring about an awareness of guilt, but it cannot influence the behavior of a criminotic. There is about crime, as we have indicated, a drivenness, a compulsional element, which derives from the inexhaustible propensity of the persistent, unconscious wishes for besieging ego. To be effective, any punishment would have to possess not only the same continuous and quantitative value, but also would have to equal if not surpass such basal desires in quality. This is utterly impossible, and so humankind's attempt to make the punishment fit the crime is a witless ambition, resulting in a failure-strewn road marked by every device from the rack and the guillotine to the lethal gas chamber.

The immediate incentive in a criminal deed, the physical and psychological equilibrium that is achieved by the act in itself, inevitably must outweigh any misty prospect of punishment. The attractiveness of an act is its immediacy, its guarantee of basic satisfaction of desires which have rent and twisted the personality: punishment is something for the future if at all. The criminotic before and at the moment of crime is under strain, taut with tension. His discomfort is immediate, the promise of relief imminent. This is what takes precedence, not —as George Devereux has correctly labelled it—the "remote stimuli of the life-space," the prospect of future punishment. Characteristically, the possibility of punishment rarely if ever enters into the act of the criminotic. Unless he is driven by a need for punishment, the ego protects the act from detection only because its satisfaction does not include detection. If he "thinks" of punishment at all, he is responding to it more often than not on a purely fantasy and even wish-fulfilling level.

He is always aware that the probability of the full penalty being exacted is almost non-existent, and he deals with this negligible likelihood by imagination colored with what he hopes and wishes. Thus he fantasies either escaping detection, or escaping custody, or being released by the court, or making an immediate parole, or any one of an uncountable number of pleasing prospects. But the point is that (1) what *may* happen to him is less important than what *is* happening to him, and (2) what *may* happen to him is also robbed of any effectiveness with him because *now* is reality and *then* is futurity, a shadow either to be shrugged off or to be minimized by fantastic thinking. In short, the urge and promise of the present takes precedence over the uncertainties of the future, even though this future holds a prospect of punishment, which is robbed of its effectiveness anyhow by wish-fulfilling imaginings.

To illustrate what has just been noted, the following is extracted from a recorded interview with a criminotic prisoner. He had been serving his third sentence for theft and forgery, was non-psychopathic, and at the time of the conversation thirty-two years of age.

"Tell me; I assume that you've committed a few more crimes than the three on your record."

"Oh, yes. I guess I must have committed upwards of two or three dozen."

"All the same kind?"

"Well, mainly."

"How come you've only been caught three times?"

"Oh, I've been caught lots of times more."

"How did you get out of the others?"

"Various ways. Once I bribed a cop; once I got caught but escaped from a village stockade; a few times I got probated or suspended sentences under different names and so on."

"I'd like to know something. Some criminologists say that fellows like you weigh your chances of being caught before you do something. Is that true?"

"Well, it is and it isn't. I've heard fellows, other guys in jail, say that. But for me it ain't so. What I mean is you know that you might get caught, but it doesn't seem very important."

"What do you mean?"

"Well, look at me. I bet I done maybe 20–30 jobs of one kind or another. And I only been caught three times that amount to anything. I mean, three times I did any time for."

"Do you think that if the police were more efficient and your chances of getting caught greater you would stop doing this sort of thing?"

"Frankly?"

"Frankly."

"Well, there's two answers to that too. In the first place, cops can't be everywhere; and in the second place, I don't think that would stop me."

"Why?"

"That's what I'd like to know too."

"Well, I wonder if you would mind telling me something else?"

"Shoot!"

"What do you think of while you're doing something?"

"You mean while I'm committing a crime?"

"Yes."

"Well, I think of lots of things. Mainly about what I'm doing."

"Do you ever think of what might happen to you if you should be caught?"

"Yes. Sometimes."

"Well, what do you think of, exactly?"

"Oh, I see what you mean. Well, I think of how I'm going to get out of it."

"How are you going to get out of it?"

"Well, by making an excuse or running away from the cop, or something like that."

"Anything else?"

"Oh, crazy things."

"Like what?"

"Well, once I had it all planned out. I was going to get caught and then come to trial and in the courtroom I would tell the judge that if he didn't dismiss the case he would drop dead. Then I thought that he dropped dead in the middle of the case and no other judge would try me and so they had to let me go."

"Do you really believe anything like that?"

"I guess that's crazy, but I really had it all planned out that way."

"What about the other times?"

"Oh, I'd think about going to the can and there'd be a fire and I'd save one of the hack's kids or the Warden or something and I'd get a pardon; or that I'd escape or maybe I'd write a great book inside. Goofy stuff like that. I guess you think I'm blowing my top."

"Not at all. Tell me, do you think everyone is like that? Like you've just explained?"

"Yes, I think so. As a matter of fact, I'm sure of it from what I've heard fellows say."

In order to be effective in any of the directions toward which it aims, punishment would have to provide the same satisfactions and unconscious benefits the criminal deed includes; it would have to be certain and inexorable; it would have to be free from the fantastic elements human thinking offers as a response to its threatening possibilities. Chiefly, it would have to invade the dream-populated, figmental, impatient, half-world of unreality in which the criminotic exists. These things it cannot be, and these aims it cannot realize. Even the threat of the death penalty is emasculated by a feature of human psychology which calls for elaboration.

Man is utterly incapable of comprehending his own demise. He can think of dying but not of death. No conception of death is possible since the condition demands definition in terms of nonexperience; while all the material for thought which man has at hand is the datum of perception, derived from the various senses and interpreted through their special characteristics. This simple psychological truism robs the death penalty of any effect as a restraining agent. Taken together with the unalterable and unavoidable implications of the fictional character future punishment assumes, it is evident that the most dire threats, the most horrible promises, mean little to the performing criminotic organism. There is, really, no "harsh" punishment from the point of view of the person committing a proscribed act. It simply doesn't exist. Either it is distorted by anticipatory fictionalizing—as in the case of the inmate with whom a conversation about such matters was recorded—or else it is beyond the performer's ability to conceive.

What is more, punishment involves a tenuous, ponderous, oft-failing mediating social apparatus that can be controlled by bribery, dealing, or other techniques; that is unstable and uncertain, even manipulable. And if this were not so, there still remains to be reckoned with another factor which sociologists and psychologists have come to recognize as prepotent in human relationships.

Such controls as are established on the behavior of the criminotic result from inner pressures, it is true, but at the same time, the superego, as has been stated, becomes altered. Because it is our cultural tendency to put the criminal beyond the pale, to build around him a fence, to quarantine him to the extent that even our churches (which, like the more radical political groups, reach only those who are already convinced and "saved") view him with misgiving; because of this, any attempt to change his behavior comes from afar and over a social distance too great to be meaningful. Criminal action is condemned by classes and individuals beyond the ken of the usual criminotic. It is, in a very real sense, an activity undertaken by an enemy. Primitives have always known that punishments are harshest when administered by the in-group; but the penalties which Western civilization carries through originate and are overseen by a foreign social element, by an array of entitled and privileged segments of society which lack the basic community with the offender so necessary if the sanctions and penalties are to be meaningful. In our practice of—literally—mustering the offender out of society with a ceremonial as moving as the military practice of drumming an officer out of an army, we are setting up a circumstance which effectively reduces the meaning of any punishment. Moreover, this social distance, this unbridgeable gap between offender and agents of society, is one of the prime factors in producing punishments more severe than many offenses warrant, granting for a moment all the rationalizations supporting usual punishment practices. Contrary to public "opinion" or popular impression, the investigations of anthropological researchers reveal that primitive modes of punishment are not especially severe or barbarous. They are, on the contrary, rather mild compared with the practices of "civilized" societies. This is because the offender, in spite of his offense, is a part of the in-group, and hostility is reserved for the out-group; because such simple societies are characterized by close fellow-feeling, by a community consciousness based upon mutual personal relationships. Societies such as our own, on the other hand, are stratified, torn by conflicting interests, complex and impersonal. It is easier, therefore, under such circumstances as obtain among us, to deal harshly and more formally with those who transgress. They are distant from us psychologically, and their sufferings are both unperceived and unappreciated. And, yet, such are the fear and guilt of man that even in our heterogeneous, segmented, conflicting civilization, when punishment becomes too severe, we rebel and refuse to exact full penalties. Executioners are hard to find, fourth offender laws calling for life imprisonment are invoked only under unusual circumstances, widespread reaction against capital punishment is rife, people—even judges—recoil from imposing maximum penalties. This is no more than a protective device, based upon the unconscious recognition that the shocking deed of the culprit is really one of the secret ambitions even of those who try him. Like a bank account or a charitable donation, the exercise of mercy is a form of insurance, a deposit against a future which may include a similar act, and which needs to be insured against.

Although punishment does not achieve the aims posited for it, nevertheless it does have an effect. It does something to the offender, and it does something to its administrators. For the latter it re-enforces ego, satisfies the revenge motive, permits aggressiveness to be exhausted in a limited but approved manner. For these it also—depending upon the form it takes and the extent to which it goes—allows of a displacement of guilt (scapegoating) and a storing of "good works" against a time of need. But it also hardens them, makes them callous and indifferent, and increases the social distance between themselves and those to whom they minister.

As for the effect of punishment upon the offender himself, this depends upon his underlying nature, on whether he is essentially a law-breaker or a criminotic. For the law-breaker, punishment lacks meaning, and is unnecessary. Regardless of the form of the punishment, such is the nature of our society that he is stigmatized and degraded. His excursion into crime was, in any case, a matter essentially apart from his personality. Very little of him was involved in the act, and nothing done to him can have enough of real meaning to his personality in this respect. Yet, the social situation which he encounters at trial, during punishment, and after, may cause profound alterations. It may, and indeed it sometimes does, bring into focus a hidden criminotic element, acting thus as a catalyst, or a precipitant. On the other hand, it may lead to a neurosis, because of its traumatic impact. But so far as accomplishing a rehabilitative function is concerned, it is senseless. Punishment to the law-breaker is an ordeal for him and, usually, a waste of the State's time and money. The individual, at the very least, remains totally unaffected—because there was nothing in him to be affected—or, at the most, the experience serves only to lead to circumstances individually unhygienic.

F. L. was a law-breaker who had been sentenced to a short term in Federal custody. Since he was a trained professional, he was assigned to the Hospital to aid in his field of work. Until he had committed this offense, he was a model citizen. He sang in the church choir, raised a family, paid his debts, and was well regarded socially. His crime was a typical instance of law-breaking: not a shred of his personality was involved in it.

Until he came to the penitentiary at forty, he had lived a sober and productive life with his wife and children. Although he had a tendency to over-sentimentality and romanticism, and was given to sometimes purple expression of his feelings, he had an abiding attachment to his home. He was somewhat of a dependent type, but he had made a fortunate marriage and his wife was a forceful individual who cared for him and relieved him of much that would otherwise have caused grave problems.

In the penitentiary, F. developed a severe psychoneurosis. He first complained of dizziness, then reported excessive accumulation of gas, distention, heaviness of the gut, chronic fatigue, and other vague complaints. On several occasions he fainted without provocation, and he seemed to be continually depressed. Crying spells were frequent, and every conversation with him ended in tears. Yet he was physically well, and exhaustive psychiatric examination disclosed no basis whatsoever for considering him psychotic. After study, it appeared that he was a psychoneurotic whose main symptom was air swallowing.

When he was finally released, F. was still in need of psychiatric attention.

There are other instances in the writer's files of cases where punishment led, not to a psychoneurosis or—as is occasionally observed, a psychosis—but to a behavioral change the dynamics of which rest with the flowering under punishment of a personality characteristic until then successfully hidden or masked.

**C. G.** was thirty-seven when he was apprehended for a violation. He was a successful business man who had inherited a small fortune and by diligence and good luck had managed to increase it to rather impressive proportions. In his home community he was liked and respected. Somewhat of a Babbitt, he was the mirror of American suburban life. His crime was the result of a drastic financial crisis, precipitated by the death in an accident of a girl with whom he had been carrying on an illicit flirtation. In an attempt to meet the heavy penalties imposed by the courts in this matter, and a "shakedown" by the girl's husband, he ventured into a shady business deal.

When C. arrived at the prison where he was to be confined, he found himself without the comforts to which he had become accustomed, friendless, taking instead of giving orders, and severely limited in what he could do. In order to obtain small articles and luxuries the purchase of which had never concerned him before, he discovered the secretive way in which these things have to be gotten under confinement. He learned about "connections," and about other matters familiar to even the best-run prison. In time he made his peace with these procedures, learned to play the game, absorbed the typical inmates' philosophy, became embittered and resentful. He identified himself so thoroughly with the "inside" that he came literally to hate the "outside." On his release, he got what he expected: social rejection, limited opportunity, police interference with his movements, suspicion, and mistrust. His letters have been filled with recrimination and gall. In his extra-mural life, he seems to be dealing exactly as he dealt in prison, and this even now, after some years, remains the psychological pattern of his life.

For the majority of law-breakers, the hot humiliation of apprehension and trial is sufficient punishment. The social identification and rejection alone accomplish whatever effect more drastic measures might have. And if they survive the punitive experience, if they do not succumb to the atmosphere and develop either a neurosis or a deformity of character brought to fruition by the punitive precipitant, they remain totally unaffected anyhow. It is a truism among those who work in or are confined to prisons that the families of the inmates are far more touched by their incarceration than the offenders themselves; and this is particularly apt in the case of the law-breaker.

However, the effect on the criminotic personality is different. Usually, the punitive experience—again independent of its form and excepting cases motivated by a drive for punishment—serves solely to carry over the personality from one criminal action to another, meanwhile allowing time for the motivational urges to accumulate and flourish in an atmosphere peculiarly adapted to the nourishment of such underlying desires. The thing to be stressed here is that the situation of punishment is representative in the highest degree of those predisposing circumstances which themselves built the criminotic personality, gave it its special orientation and character. The individual, if anything, is even further encouraged toward continued exertions toward satisfaction of id-urges, especially because of the resemblance between punishment and those circumstances which originally and historically *made him a criminal*. This is why places of confinement are so suited to the planning of further crime, and to the projection of future efforts for obtaining basic satisfaction of criminotic designs.

For the ones who seek punishment, of course, the punishment is at hand, and the experience is ameliorative. Unfortunately, unless it is of the quality and quantity desired, it is effective only for the term of its duration.

We have discussed the meaning and effect of punishment, and have indicated why it does not accomplish deterrence, prevent recidivism, or encourage reform. It may well be asked now what is to be done. The answer, while simple, raises a host of problems and will undoubtedly be regarded as yet another fancy (impracticable, some will say) foible of the psychologist. Nevertheless, it is toward such a program that science and our own good common sense is inevitably leading us.

With the courtroom remade into a diagnostic clinic, the battle is half won. Here the offenders should be separated, the law-breakers from the criminotics, the salvageable criminotics from the relentless, uncompromising, untractable types. For the law-breakers, techniques of redress based upon fines, exaction in kind, and restitution should be resorted to, for apart from the hardships of these methods (such as they may be) the mere fact of apprehension and social identification is enough. They make up the bulk of offenders, and they are composed of individuals who offend usually only once. The salvageable criminotics should be *treated*, not in the wasteful and hopelessly ineffectual manner of the present time, where they are literally placed before a cannon loaded with all the empirical detritus of fancy rehabilitative techniques—shops, libraries, schools, social case work, and the other gaudy trappings of the modern "institution"—but treated in order to recover the motivations of their deeds, reoriented with respect to their manifold distortions, misrepresentations, and misconceptions, and the energies formerly exploited by the pathological criminotic process now redirected and recanalized into useful, hygienic, and productive pathways. But for the unsalvageable, those whom therapy cannot reach either because they are completely beyond its pale for reasons intimate to them, or because we do not yet know enough about therapy and its techniques—these should be segregated and retained for study and research. They should be available for every kind and variety of scientific endeavor necessary to the populace at large. And perhaps, under such conditions, we will eventually learn how to treat them, too.

This last sounds cruel and heartless, doesn't it? But, consider. Now these persons are beyond everything that can be done with them. They are fated to spend much of their lives under restraint anyhow, and for the rest of the time they are incorrigibly predatory. They are a small group, yet with them really lies the only hope of ever solving crime and wiping it from the earth as one of the most malignant and baleful of all plagues.

# 20. Prisons, I

WRITING of prisons has always been a sort of favorite indoor sport, characteristically popular especially with people who have been privileged to make abridged Cook's tours of such institutions. Like writing about one's trip to Russia, it has become almost a requirement, even a duty, for every college instructor who takes his class through the local jail or reformatory to worry words from his typewriter almost immediately upon his return from such a voyage. The graphic impressions thus achieved and recorded are duly foisted upon a public—fortunately limited—and the writer then either acclaimed or damned according to the preconceived prejudices of his reviewers, themselves "experts" by the same process. This produces one kind of chapter or book—the kind that either oozes sentimentality over the plight of confined inmates, or stoutly congratulates the forward-looking personnel for the clean cells and corridors he has observed. The sentimentalists tend toward dire comparisons with medieval times; the enthusiasts toward glowing prophecy. The former reveal an evangelical fervor and use the word "Bastille"; the latter hard-headedly prefer such expressions as "The New Prison," or "The New Penology."

Then there is another type of chapter or book written about prisons. This is the one prepared either by apologetic (and retired) prison wardens and administrators, suitably and ably ghosted by aspiring graduate students or free-lancing and glib magazine writers. These are reminiscent, rambling accounts that impress one with the basic good nature of the luminary whose name is on the title page, with his good-humored rendition of types and characters he knew in prison, and his amazing calm in quelling riots and demonstrations. The perpendicular pronoun is the word he prefers.

There is the third kind of account. This one is written by a bright and unhappy young man with scientific pretensions, envy of his superiors, and deep frustrations about his salary. He is bitter about the small-mindedness of the regime which keeps him chained to an interviewing desk or behind a stack of papers. He knows inmates well from having passed them in hallways, from "bull-sessions" engaged upon in good-fellow-ship with inmate secretarial aids, from august councils in classi-fication committees and clinics. He sends questionnaires to prisoners, has decided opinions on the solution to the sex problem in prisons, and a penchant for statistics.

Finally, there is the book written by the former inmate. This never quite comes off because he tries too hard and, within recent years, has had his ear cocked for an offer from Holly-wood whose siren-call drowns out the echo of the protest he formulated when his world had bars for a horizon. Only Fallada and Wilde (and possibly Koestler) have managed this sort of thing successfully.

It is presumption for anyone who is himself not a prison inmate to write about prisons, and in this sense the present ac-count is as erroneous and blind as any other. To describe what it means to be a prisoner, how one feels to be confined, the agonies of "the long moment of suffering," is impossible to one who has not, in the words of Fallada, "eaten out of the tin plate." What it must mean to be always under scrutiny, to be poked about and observed, to be subject to whims and de-cisions, to be eternally at the mercy of infallible powers, to be suspect and degraded, to live apart, dictated to, patronized, denied—of all this the writer cannot tell. He can only reveal what he knows at second hand from many depth analyses of inmates, what he has observed about the effects of all this on personality, what he regards as justifiably admissible to criminology from some years of living the major part of every day in prisons and with prisoners.

Let it first be stated that everything herein applies to what has been called "the new prison." These are architecturally sterling places, with clean corridors and well-ventilated cells. They are usually overseen by social-minded warders and directed by sometimes very earnest organizers who try, terribly hard, to "do something for the inmate," and who believe in a piece of verbal tyranny called "rehabilitation." The modern prison is humane, "scientifically" run, tender, protective. To be sure, there are extant remnants of former days. Some of the institutions this writer has himself seen are archaic in structure, contain virtual torture chambers, rely on brutality for discipline. But, on the whole, this kind of place is rapidly being superseded by structurally more satisfactory institutions, and by methods of management more in keeping with the humanitarianism we have inherited from the French Revolution.

No, it is not the structure, brick upon brick, of detentional and rehabilitative places which needs to be examined or criticized—although the senseless arguments between proponents of cottage-system *vs.* single housing unit still waste paper and words—nor is it the way in which prisoners are handled today, despite the sadism of the mobile chain gang, the barbaric whipping post, the thumb racks, the "hole," the bread-and-water diet, the filth, the abomination of water cures, the silent system, the lock step, and the countless other hellish vestiges that persist here and there that need exposure and examination; it is, rather, the self-delusion of modern penology, its sham, and its complete failure.

The Federal prison system of this country might well be the

architectural and organizational model for the world. Many of its institutions are almost unrecognizable as prisons. They are staffed by trained and technically adept personnel. There is little of graft, little of politics in them. Under the progressive policies of its past and present directors, Sanford Bates and James V. Bennett, they have become shining examples of humanitarianism, matters for pride to which citizens can point. They do not subscribe to the "mad-dog" theory of crime so popular in an allied bureau of government, nor do they "coddle" inmates as some of our columnists suggest. And yet, they, along with other prisons, are failures.

The failure of prisons to prevent crime or to rehabilitate prisoners cannot, of course, be separated from the things we have already indicated about our culture, about justice, and about punishment. But it is possible to fix them, for a moment, *in vacuo*, and to regard them objectively for purposes of examination.

Perhaps the most significant reason for the failure of the modern prison, or for that of any prison, is self-delusion. Somewhere, somehow, the idea that the noble endeavors and modern innovations—the provision of cleanly surroundings, the outside cells, the carefully compiled case studies, the expert medical services, the classrooms, the movies, the orchestras, the intramural newspapers, the athletic fields, the disciplinary courts, the sterile dining halls, the neat lawns, the frequent changes of laundry—the idea that these things *are* rehabilitation, *are* treatment, *are* curatives for criminosis and preventives of recidivism took hold. By some devious mechanic of mind the energies of all the bright young men, all the topnotch administrators, were thus diverted into little paths leading everywhere and nowhere. With our remarkable American talent for invention and organization, and with our shining zeal for remaking the world into an image of ourselves, we have placed the gilded stamp of "progress" upon everything that gives off a bright light, and we have characteristically proclaimed it the Absolute, the answer, because it both glitters and costs money. Rehabilitation, the cure or alleviation of law-breaking and of criminosis, is not a change of socks every day for all prisoners; it is not a new organ in the choir loft; it is not a balanced diet and a dietician's printed menu; it is not ice cream on Thursday nights and a ball-game on Sunday; it is not art classes, the number of license plates made in the in-dustrial shops, the gleam of surgical instruments in the hospital, the new type of lock on a cell door. *But the great penological delusion is that it is.*

Textbooks in criminology will become enthusiastic about these and many more things. They will speak trippingly and at great length about all the trappings of the modern prison and refer to them in phrases which use the word "progress" at least twice. But they are only encysting the delusion more deeply into the fabric of penology, insuring further against any real steps being taken to do what needs to be done. It is as if a conscious attempt were being made by some coalition of weird powers to nourish this great hoax. In conferences, in committees, in the resolutions of penal groups and societies, one notes always the malevolent fallacy that is basic to this delusion. It makes of the modern prison a kind of beautiful façade, a place gadget-filled and costly; but it robs it of the chance to fulfill its purpose.

From this great delusion comes the sham of the modern prison. These little things, it seems, achieve towering propor-tions when they are so blindly viewed as ultimates. Piddling routines, raised by a sightless logic to the level of treatment, reach an impressive arithmetic behind which they can hide. So the *number* of men who, let us say, attend school classes in a penal education department, the *number* of inmates who visit the prison dentist, the *number* of prisoners who come to chapel, the *number* of shirts washed in the laundry—these are taken as indices to therapy. More than this, since these things are held as the goals, and the real aims of the prison subverted by and lost among them, there is a tendency to treat even these with that adulation for large numbers so characteristic of Americans that to show our respect for them we make them even greater. This is dishonesty, but of a specious variety. Every department of an institution is guilty of it. The laundry launders between thirty and forty thousand pounds of wash each month; on the reports it appears as between sixty and eighty thousand pounds. Of a population of twelve hundred men in an institution, three hundred attend classes; reports claim five and six hundred. This falsification is evident from top to bottom of every correctional system in the land. It leads to the most amazing demonstrations of self-satisfaction, and all because of a delusion that things-in-quantity reflect basic processes having to do with the rehabilitation of human personality. Moreover, from this initial sham come others; the pretty but dishonest reports of committees of investigation, of wardens' surveys, even of bodies presumably above this trifling crookery. Recently the writer was present at a meeting where the report of a committee to which he had been appointed was requested. The chairman of the committee was absent but, nothing daunted, the secretary of the meeting made the bland statement, "I know personally that this committee has been hard at work and will soon have some interesting and significant findings to report." This astonished your author, because he knew that the committee had not met even once during its entire lifetime.

These ludicrous side lights are in themselves inconsequential; they function, however, to indicate what has been wrought by slavery to the delusion that the side shows are on the midway. This is why prisons fail, why they do not rehabilitate, why they do not treat.

Basic to the failure of the modern prison, and allied to the great delusion, is the miserable spectacle of what passes for classification in almost all penal institutions. The classification idea was undoubtedly a stroke of genius, and originally offered the single hope for rescuing penology. What it called for was to utilize all available knowledge to achieve an estimate of the individual inmate, his assets and liabilities, his needs and wants, the precipitating and predisposing factors in his offense; and on the basis of knowledge so gathered, on the diagnosis thus achieved, to plan for him a course of *treatment* aimed at restoring him to the community and preventing his return to custody. How this idea came to degenerate into the farce classification procedure has become another one of those insoluable mysteries. But become degenerate it has, and only a complete reorientation of penal philosophy can hope to turn it from what it is to what it should be.

Rather than analyze, point by point, what has happened to the classification idea, how its high purpose has been perverted, and to what its intended functions have become subservient, the following two illustrations are presented. These skits have been composed by the writer out of a store of experiences including service on such a committee for more than two years, visits to many prisons, both State and Federal, where he was permitted to observe the functioning of such bodies, and endless reports of members and inmates. They are not illustrations that have been reduced to the absurd; they are actual transactions, such as occur daily all over the land. The two chosen are representatives of separate types.

Time: *One O'clock This Afternoon.*
Place: *The Committee Room of a Penitentiary.*
Persons: *The Classification Supervisor, The Education Supervisor, The Industrial Supervisor, The Social Service Supervisor, The Warden, The Asst. Warden, The Chaplain, The Other Chaplain, The Doctor, The Captain of the Guard, A Stenographer, An Inmate.*

## I

*In this smoke-filled, talk-filled, paper-filled room, all of the characters are seated around a giant oak table. All, that is, except The Inmate, who is chewing his nails in the corridor under the watchful eyes of a Guard. The Classification Supervisor is mumbling to the Stenographer as he nervously fumbles through a large pile of file-folders on the table before him.*

CLASSIFICATION SUPERVISOR: [*Mumbling.*] Where the hell is the jacket on Jones, 00654? Oh, here it is. [*Aloud.*] A little order, gentlemen. The next case is Jones, 00654. [*Thumbing through the Jones file.*] This is a man of thirty-two, married, has two small children. Offense is forging government check. Third-time loser. Previously incarcerated in Singville and Villesing. Institutional records from both places indicate fair conduct. Got into this trouble as a result of unemployment and a little too much alky. Born in Z. in 1913, attended school to sixth grade. Parents both alive and well. No delinquency in family. Owns his own home, has two thousand dollar insurance policy. Marriage seems O. K., wife apparently supporting herself and children by working in a department store. No particular problems noted. Not a dangerous type. Doctor reports some need for dental attention, possibility of hernia, suitable for moderate labor only until hernia condition clarified. Blood negative, admits gonorrhea twice with treatment. Psychiatric shows tendency toward chronic alcoholism, some nomadic behavior in past, nothing of special significance, intelligence slightly below average. Educational tests indicate third grade although claims attendance to sixth. Recommend further schooling. Work history includes messenger boy, truck driver, shoe repair, factory worker. Protestant, good religious background. Recommend close custody in view of possible detainer. Looks like a natural for the laundry.

WARDEN: [*Grandly.*] Hold on a minute. Where'd you say he's from? Z.? I know it well. Nobody sends things to laundries there. Farming community. Not a laundry in fifty miles. Looks like he'd be better off in the shoe repair shop.

ASST. WARDEN: I think so too, Warden. Besides, the laundry's full up. Anyway, the shoe shop has closer custody.

DOCTOR: Will he have to do much heavy lifting there?

CAPTAIN: Hell, no! It's a soft job. [*Turning to* ASST. WARDEN.] What about the kitchen? Mr. Y. is running kind of close to the belt and can use all we can send him.

DOCTOR: Well, anything that doesn't involve heavy lifting.

ASST. WARDEN: What's the status of that detainer?

CLASS. SUPVR.: [*Fumbling.*] Wait a minute. Here it is. [*Reads.*] Well, I don't know. Parole violation from Villesing. Probably they'll come for him. [*To* STENOG.] Make a note of that. Jones 00654, check detainer Villesing.

WARDEN: Well, gentlemen, are we agreed?

CHAPLAIN: [*Looking up from his notes for next week's sermon.*] What's the story?

WARDEN: Tell the man, Pete.

CLASS. SUPVR.: Lemme see. He goes to the shoe repair. Close custody. Check family situation and detainer. I guess we ought to speak to him about some schooling, too. And attendance at chapel. [*To* DOCTOR.] Doc, you'll let us know about that hernia business? [DOCTOR *nods.*] [*To* EDUCATION SUPERVISOR.] You talk to him, Fred, O. K.? [*To* STENOG.] Press the buzzer.

[*The noise of a buzzer sounding in the corridor is heard. The door opens and* AN INMATE *walks into the room.* THE OTHER CHAPLAIN *motions him into a chair.* THE INMATE *sits, looking around the table apprehensively.*]

EDUCATION SUPERVISOR: [*Genially.*] How're you today, Jones?

INMATE: [*Nervously.*] Fine, sir.

ED. SUPVR.: Bill, this is the Classification Committee. We've been going over your case pretty carefully and we've called you in to discuss it with you. Understand?

INMATE: Yes, sir.

ED. SUPVR.: For the time being, you'll go to the shoe repair shop. We need some men of experience down there. Got to get around on leather, you know. [*Laughs.*] How does that suit you?

INMATE: Well, sir, I don't know. I never did anything like that before.

INDUSTRIAL SUPERVISOR: [*Annoyed.*] Hold on. Why, you told me you'd done shoe repair work in Singville for two years.

INMATE: [*Apologetically.*] Well, sir, I mean, I think I told you, sir, that I repaired shoe machines in Singville. That's what I meant.

IND. SUPVR.: [*Accepting the apology.*] Oh, well; it doesn't matter. Guess I misunderstood you.

ED. SUPVR.: Well, Bill, that's your program. Shoe repair shop. You'll like it down there. Mr. K. is a good man to work under.

INMATE: Yes, sir.

ED. SUPVR.: Any questions, Bill?

INMATE: Well, I-er-I. . . .

ED. SUPVR.: [*Magnanimously.*] Go ahead, Bill. This is the place to speak out! We're here to help you, you know.

INMATE: [*Hopefully.*] Well, sir . . . I just wondered if I couldn't get some help for my family. A job in the paying industries, I mean. You know, there are two kids and the missus. . . .

WARDEN: We understand, Bill, but right now that's out of the question. We want to see you make a real adjustment to the institution. Maybe in sixty or ninety days, after we get to know you better. . . .

INMATE: [*Weakly.*] Yes, sir. Is that all?

ED. SUPVR.: Yes. [*As* INMATE *rises to go.*] By the way, you ought to get up to school too. Your tests weren't too good. What do you say?

INMATE: Yes, sir.

ED. SUPVR.: [*Pleased at his salesmanship.*] Fine! Fine! Never regret it. Mr. T. will be getting in touch with you about it during the week. That's all!

CLASS. SUPVR.: [*As the door shuts behind* INMATE.] The next case is . . .

## II

*This action takes place in a different institution, but the characters are the same. They only belong to a slightly different school of penology, and their way of managing the meeting is somewhat distinctive.*

CLASSIFICATION SUPERVISOR: [*Mumbling.*] Where the hell is that Shultz jacket? Oh, here it is. [*Aloud.*] Let's have order, gents. We have a heavy schedule, so let's get along. This next case is Shultz, 00432. He's a white man of twenty-three, serving five years for robbery. Record dates back to 1930, picked up in San Antonio as a runaway from his home in Chicago. Runaway again in 1932, picked up in Knoxville. Committed to the Industrial

School in Illinois as an incorrigible, served three years. In 1937 arrested on a Dyer Act charge, served eighteen months in the Federal Reformatory at Chillicothe, Ohio. Released and picked up again for auto theft in Denver. Skipped bond. In 1938 arrested in Erie for investigation. On current charge he broke into a home on the West Side. Sticker lodged against him by the Federal Government for Conditional Release Violation, also wanted in Denver. Impresses quarantine as a young, unstable, irresponsible individual who will cause trouble. Has had poor institutional records in other places. Recommend close custody. Next!

SOCIAL SERVICE SUPERVISOR: [*Reading.*] This is a twenty-three year old, married, white man from Chicago, guilty of robbery, serving five years. The product of a broken home and poor economic circumstances. Inclined to be evasive and misleading. Seemed to be unable to assume the proper attitude for the interview situation. Has a very poor work history, spotted with unemployment and discharges. Wife appears to be satisfied with their marriage, although she knows he's been chasing around. No close family ties can be established. Parents dead. He's the third of four siblings, all males. Readily admits his guilt and is not remorseful. Wife has good job. No special family need. Close custody, poor behavior prognosis. Next!

DOCTOR: [*Reading.*] A twenty-three year old white male, 5 feet 8¾ inches, weight 154 pounds. Good posture, firm musculature. Vision corrected by glasses in right eye to 20/30, left 20/40 with near vision normal. Calculus deposits on teeth. Fractured nose in 1936, successfully operated 1937. Diphtheria 1931, no sequelae. Admits gonorrhea 1939, denies syphilis, serology negative. Suitable for arduous labor. Psychologist reports superior intelligence. Psychiatric shows him emotionally immature, indifferent, showing no desire to understand himself. Is well oriented but shows poor insight and judgment. On the whole, a cool, immature psychopath. So diagnosed. Close custody. Poor prognosis. Next!

EDUCATIONAL SUPERVISOR: [*Reading.*] Average grade status 7 point 6. Man claims to have finished eighth grade with normal progress. Rating indicates deficiency in arithmetic. Professes an interest in clerical work, including typing, but unable to register a rating on a standard five-minute test. Recommend close custody, enroll in Bookkeeping, Typing, Arithmetic, Shorthand. Next!

INDUSTRIAL SUPERVISOR: [*Reading.*] Subject was typesetter for twenty months in Industrial School. Worked as truck driver one year. Secured relief job in Chicago, operating adding machines. Was filing clerk for W. P. A. When confined did laundering, barbering. Odd jobs have included chauffeuring, restaurant work, porter. Recommend close custody, clerical assignment. Next!

CHAPLAIN: [*Reading.*] Weak religious type. No attendance at Mass before present sentence. Recommend attendance at Mass, close custody.

WARDEN: Quite a customer! Looks like he belongs on construction. Too smart and no control. Construction No. 6? Any objections? [*A moment of silence as the* WARDEN *surveys the table.*] No? All right, let's have him. Gimme that jacket.

[*The far sound of the buzzer is heard as* THE INMATE *enters and looks nervously about.*]

WARDEN: [*Loudly.*] You Shultz, 00432?

INMATE: Yes, sir.

WARDEN: All right. Sit down. [INMATE *sits.*] You're here on a five year sentence. What for?

INMATE: Robbery, sir.

WARDEN: That's right. And before that you were in the Industrial School and Federal Reformatory. You've been bumming around all your life. Ran away from home, stole here and there, raised hell in every institution you've ever been in. But you're in a different kind of place now, get it?

INMATE: [*Weakly.*] Yes, sir.

WARDEN: Behave yourself and do what you're told or we'll know how to take care of you. Understand?

INMATE: [*More weakly.*] Yes, sir.

WARDEN: That's fine. There'll be none of your monkeyshines here, and the sooner you find that out and get it through your head, the better off you'll be. Understand?

INMATE: [*Even more weakly.*] Yes, sir.

WARDEN: Good! Now we understand each other. You'll be assigned to a construction gang. That's all! [*As* INMATE *leaves.*] All right, Sid, let's get on to the next case. . . .

Classification must eventually establish itself on a firm foundation, recognizing its function to be that of diagnosis and prescription. To do this, it must free itself, or anyhow become free, of the shackling influence of the great delusion. It must learn to distinguish between law-breaker and criminal, and how to prescribe for each. It must, in short, adopt a dynamic philosophy founded upon the recognition of the basic propositions of criminology as we have uncovered them in our way through this volume.

It seems to this writer that the first step in classification should concern itself with the separation of law-breaker from criminotic. If society persists in sending law-breakers to prison, at the time of initial classification they should be carefully weeded out from their fellow prisoners, assigned perhaps to aid in the operation and maintenance of the institution, and managed humanely. To bring to bear upon them the exertions of specialized personnel and techniques is to waste time. They don't need it. For the criminotics, the function of classification should be to separate the salvageable and treatable from the unregenerate and unamenable. Although the latter should not, ideally, be retained in the same institution, if they are, they should also be utilized for maintenance purposes. As for the others, for those who are criminotics *and* salvageable, these should be exposed not to the grapeshot charge of a rehabilitative cannon based on happy thoughts, bright ideas, and borrowed but untested hypotheses from the fields of education, guidance, philosophy, and other disciplines, but to treatment.

Knowledge is immediately available to classification bodies for the accomplishment of this sorting task. Psychiatry and psychology have yielded techniques which can at once be utilized. The salvation of the criminotic *is* possible, so long as he is properly diagnosed as such, and so long as his personality structure contains elementary requisites for therapy. Present practices distribute the energies of expert penal personnel in a wholesale fashion. Everyone who comes to prison has thrust upon him expensive and time-consuming ministrations whether he needs them or not, whether he can absorb them or not. This is another, and an important, reason why prisons fail.

The usual excuse to which every member of a classification committee resorts when he is confronted with the charge that his beloved and restful sojourn of an afternoon is a farce runs to the effect that, "Institutions have to run, you know. There are other considerations: custody, detainers, the separation of co-defendants, all sorts of things." These rationalizations (for such they are) do not bear any weight when it is considered that each of these items can be strictly accounted for and yet the job can be done as it should.

Correct and adequate classification must take into account every possible facet of personality and environment for each prisoner. The job, as it is being done now, is only half done. Some years ago this writer made an analysis of the assignments made by a classification committee in a large institution. These were then compared with the isolated factor of intelligence in each case for more than twelve hundred inmates. For every job assignment the optimal level of intelligence demanded by the work was held as a constant, based on the psychologically tested proposition that satisfactory performance of work is possible only when an individual has neither too much nor too little intelligence for a given job of work. When the optimal standards were correlated with the assignments made by the classification committee, it was found that "greater success could have been achieved had assignments been made on a purely chance basis, selecting men for jobs by lot." If classification committees can do not better than this, they should be dispensed with, and in their place we should substitute an old hat from which decisions could be drawn with greater expectation of success and far less expense.

The real job of classification is to distinguish among those who come to prison, make selections for treatment, and not only prescribe but oversee the carrying-through of therapy.

As the situation stands, the latter is another place where it founders. All administrators undoubtedly are happy and content in the fiction that because a program for an inmate "has been worked out"—in what fashion we just observed in our illustrations—even these paltry and frequently inadequate steps are being taken by the remainder of the personnel. This is another delusion, masked by the prepossessing and over-blown figures that pour in a bimonthly avalanche over executive desks. The sorry truth of the matter is this: *in almost every prison*—and we are being kind—*nothing real is being done toward rehabilitation, except in isolated instances where a courageous psychiatrist, psychologist, or educator is striking out on his own.* Perhaps it is believed that fancy shops, ornate grillwork, and reports are doing the job; or maybe it is believed that rehabilitation is a heaven-sent thing, falling like rain and governed by superior powers, and that we have only to await its coming. Whatever the belief is, the sorry truth is that nothing real is being done. The brass hats of the prison business, classification officials, and department heads are resting comfortably in the misguided expectation that the number of eyeglasses provided, dentures made, classes attended, meals cooked, tests given, flower beds attended, and rows of corn planted have something to do with treatment for crime. They do not. Inmates of prisons mark time between one escapade and the next if they are criminals, resign themselves to a gray limbo relieved only by imagination if they are law-breakers. The things that are thrust upon them—things which pass for rehabilitation and that are really only hollow tedium-relievers—pass over them like the Avenger over the Children of Bondage, without touching them, without affecting them. A function of the classification committee should be to see that treatment is carried out, that its recommendations and its programs are at least given a chance. As a matter of fact, the committee itself should consist only of people who are capable of doing the job themselves. Administrators should have, like the flowers of spring, nothing to do with the case.

In a prison that will not suffer from the great delusion and that will have a classification system of the kind we have sketched, this body must be the final arbiter of release. To entrust the job of determining whether an inmate is suitable for return to the community to the courts with their senseless sentencing procedures, their lack of understanding of the dynamics of criminosis, and their hidebound Talmudism, defeats the purposes of rehabilitation. To entrust the job to an appointed Parole Board, often politically conscious but more importantly completely outside the therapeutic situation and untrained in evaluation of personality change, is to place an unwarranted trust in its judgment and knowledge and to continue the present error. The job belongs in the institution itself, in the hands of the expert members of classification groups provided that their composition is functional and not administrative.

# 21. Prisons, II

UNDER existing circumstances rehabilitation occasionally takes place in prisons, but this is not due to the operation of factors provided by the prisons as such in terms of fixtures and procedures. Instead, criminosis in such instances is cured because the recent offense has met and satisfied unconscious needs, which therefore no longer predispose toward criminosis, or because there transpires during incarceration an internal change which diminishes if it does not altogether disintegrate the internal pressures. This last has been sometimes known as maturation; and it does take place. If the impetus to it is not provided by therapy, it comes from a feature of institutions that operates upon all its incumbents for good or ill.

The *climate* of an institution can be defined only as its atmosphere, its temper, its essence, in brief, as the characteristic impact it makes on those for whom it cares. A reason why most prisons fail is that they do not provide a rehabilitative climate, despite the size of their budgets or the amount of chrome-plated hardware they have on display. Climate has nothing to do with the appurtenances of an institution: whether its cells are arranged in tiers, its inmates housed in dormitories, or the presence or absence of a wall. The writer knows institutions of the open type, the wall-less variety, that are more nefarious in their impact than others surrounded by thirty-feet high and five-feet thick slabs of concrete reenforced with sheet steel. Perhaps the chief element in good institutional climate is personnel. And here we invade a difficult field of discussion.

Unquestionably, prisons are the sinkholes of society. Most citizens know about them only through their newspapers, which regard them with eyes blinded by circulation figures. Citizens don't want to know about prisons; in their view, they are necessary buildings which the State provides in return for taxes and operates for their protection or holds ready to receive them should they do something they are not supposed to do. Their curious attitude extends similarly to people who work in prisons, and consequently the social status of the prison worker is not very high. As a matter of fact, the very idea of working in a prison is somewhat repugnant to most, and only under dire stress does it ever occur to citizens to seek prison jobs. When unemployment is rife, institutions are fully staffed; in good times it is hard to find any personnel. It will also be conceded by the average citizen that "such places" are fine for wounded veterans, for failures, or for unfortunates "waiting for something else to turn up." What results, then, is either the use of prisons for the minor spoils of a State's regnant political machine, or their employment as a place of refuge for persons who have been bowled over by adverse economic winds.

The selection of the prison officer, from guard to warden, should be one of the most serious businesses of the State, and is certainly as worthy of careful deliberation and study as the choosing of any other public servant. The job that prisons have to do demands training and education. (The reader will perhaps be surprised to learn that in one prison known to this writer, more than seventeen per cent of the custodial force are illiterates, twenty per cent never got beyond third grade, and only a bare ten per cent went to high school.) To be a successful prison officer requires understanding and judgment, and an intimate knowledge of personality and social relationships. These qualities are, however, non-existent in most modern prisons, where a guard's job is patroling a corridor and turning a key, and where most other functionaries shuffle endless papers.

From the inmate's point of view, most prison guards are "hacks" and "screws," persons to be resented and distrustfully regarded. And, in truth, much of this appraisal is correct. If they are not fearful creatures who have little ability to fill other jobs and are consequently racked by insecurity, they are time-marchers who have their eyes fixed both on the clock and on the prospects of getting another job.

The fault lies at the top and with the citizenry. In all except Federal institutions, salaries are pitiful and working conditions are poor. The jobs prison guards are given to do permit them no freedom, no room for thought. They are regimented as surely and as completely as their charges. The work is soul-destroying and, in large part, without a future. They have reason to be gruff, to work out their terrible frustration in brutality, to be perennially disgruntled. The morale of the best run prison is poorer among its personnel than among the inmates. In the climate resulting from this bitterness, treatment is out of the question. Workers in prison are there, as inmates are there, under duress. Only a very few are there because they conceive of the work as an interesting and promising career; only a very few are there from motives of service. They cannot help but reflect the futility of their lives and their hatred of this veritable exile in their performances. Prisons must be recognized as special places of work, selection of employees must be based upon the particular qualities the jobs demand, conditions of work must be made attractive. Above all, the citizenry must be taught that if it wants prisons to fulfill their function, its conception of them must change, and it must be willing to pay for what it hopes to receive.

In a climate where the personnel is chosen in the fashion in which most prison employees are picked, where conditions of work are poor, wages miserable, social status lacking, advancement impossible, and services unappreciated, therapy cannot take place. The truth is, as every one who has tried to do something pertinent about intramural treatment knows, treatment efforts are derided first by the personnel, and from them the attitude is communicated rapidly to the inmates. This primarily affects the efforts of professionals—psychologists, physicians, educators—who find themselves thwarted, and who eventually lose heart. Men who start out in the prison business with high hopes for rendering a service in a place where the need is most acute, soon find themselves also slipping into the prevalent attitudes. They cease to care as they tire of butting their heads against ineptness and stupidity —and, like the inmates, they await deliverance. There is further to be considered the fact that, by some gymnastic of bureaucratic mentality, there has become common the notion that prisons must be placed in isolated areas and relatively inaccessible places. This means imprisonment for the personnel not only for the eight working hours of the day, but for the other sixteen as well. In short, if more attention were paid to the morale of prison workers, prisons would be less likely to fail.

In this chapter we could, among other things, tell of the plethora of rules that characterize institutions, of the major and minor rituals and observances, and of the petty adjuncts to prison existence which plague prison officer and inmate alike. Fortunately, other books have tirelessly dwelt upon such boresome stuff. But our attention is directed now to a consideration to which such volumes rarely yield space.

It is fashionable for criminology text writers to take pot shots at prisons and the way they are operated, and we have done some of this ourselves. Yet there is another side to the story that these gentry do not appreciate because they have not lived with it. In presenting the custodial point of view we do not necessarily abandon our therapeutic arguments.

All institutions are custody-minded: the first requirement of them is that they should *hold* what the courts turn over to them. Under present conditions they cannot do otherwise. All else is secondary and derivative. As the prevailing form of punishment, they are deputized by the public through the courts to remove certain people from the community and to keep them for lengths predetermined. This is their trust, and if they fail in it they are abusing the confidence of the commonwealth. Such a simple fact must be the starting point for any evaluation of prisons. And in this particular they are eminently successful. The number of escapes from prison is very small, almost negligible, despite the lurid screechings of the press.

*The custodial point of view*, on the other hand, is a reason for the failure of prisons. With security the paramount consideration, administrators cannot be blamed for subordinating all else to this single fact. When they are charged by writers with lacking appreciation for the rehabilitative point of view, with lacking courage to try new procedures, these charges must be weighed against their vulnerability.

To operate a prison is not an easy assignment. Administrative problems beyond the ken of the most well-informed citizens crop up every day. The maintenance of a huge plant alone is a terrific job, and this is but one phase of the work. Prisons are social constellations crossed and crisscrossed by a multitude of currents created by the special attributes of an environment that is necessarily restrictive and punitive. What morale there is must be created out of whole cloth. They are places where people do not want to be, where they are held against their wishes. Tensions exist from the moment of admission and are aggravated by events and situations which ordinarily would mean little. There is nothing positive about the circumstances of prison life: all is negation, denial, frustration, and prohibition. Therefore, many things about institutions which at first blush and to an outsider, and even to inmates, appear senseless—things like mailing regulations, inspections, daily counts, and others—are forced upon officials. The horror of all this is that eventually these minutiae obscure the real issues and come gradually to dominate the picture. The position of prison administrator is not an enviable one. Because of pressure from press and public, he mistrusts and fears the encroachments into his domain and the urgings of professional workers who plead for a chance to test the only kind of hypothesis that offers the remotest possibility of solving the riddles of crime and criminosis: persistent and deep therapy.

What happens to a man or woman in prison, the effect the experience has upon him, depends more upon the kind of person he is than it does upon the kind of institution in which his time is spent. In general, one of three changes takes place. If the atmosphere, the climate, is therapeutic, and if his internal needs diminish through simple chronology or by direct effort, an inmate may mature. The period of literal exile may bring with it a relaxation of internal pressures, permit a redirectioning of the life course, and allow a reorientation of the style of life to take place as regards goals and attitudes. But this happens so rarely that it is more than likely a phenomenon applying chiefly to the law-breakers, character deviates, and criminotics who are motivated especially by a need for punishment.

A second effect of incarceration is retardation in maturity. It is as if all were held in abeyance and suspension. The same wants persist, the identical predisposants remain static, the potentiality for certain precipitants to ignite active criminotic behavior is undiminished. The period of imprisonment is a limbo, a state of consciousness approaching the trance of hypnosis, where stimuli are received and responded to but where they do not involve the whole organism. The condition is a variety of schizophrenia; to be exact, it is a withdrawn, beclouded, semiawareness. The routine obligations, both physical and psychological, are assumed and performed, but as in a haze of unreality and disbelief. They are somehow not cogent, not applicable, and the seasons roll in an endless tedium. All responses are automatic, and the adjustments made from moment to moment are on a sort of reflexive level that does not involve more than a segment of the total personality. Occasionally this comatose existence is broken into by illness or pain, or by an acute heightening of experience, or by situations demanding choices. Instances which produce a hiatus in this unbroken twilight state are, too, those crux-like episodes of anxiety such as parole hearings, appearances before officials, certain visits, notifications of further legal action to be taken, and other events. Such apathy and indifference is the most common of penal effects. By some, it is misinterpreted as evidence of reform and the effectiveness of the delusional "rehabilitative program." And it is a condition which is highly regarded by prison officials, for the more inmates who experience it, the quieter will be the institutional scene.

The third effect of incarceration is to cause the prisoner to regress in his developmental course. This comes about as a result of the fact that the total penal situation is a replica of the state of infancy. When an individual enters upon a term of imprisonment, he loses what has been attained in the struggle toward adulthood. In a very real sense he is thrust back to a time when decisions were made for him, when choice was infrequently demanded by the environment, when it was not his to determine his destiny. He is clothed, housed, fed, cared for, told where to go and what to do. His life is governed by routine and tradition, departure from which is fraught with hazard. Every least act is directed and supervised. Protection, of a sort, is guaranteed him against everything from illness to the weather. He does not even have to decide what to wear, or to choose between items on a menu. In effect, he is robbed of maturity, and he becomes habituated rapidly to a regressive mode of life. And the ridiculous, paradoxical assumption is made that this is designed to "prepare him for useful citizenship." Moreover, when he then behaves regressively within the prison, he is punished by techniques his supervisors would never recommend even for a child, despite the fact that such is the inadequate, dependent being he has actually become.

The regressive effect is often brought sharply to the attention of penal personnel, especially psychologists and psychiatrists, by a common phenomenon, vernacularly and with rare insight called "short-term-itis." As the end of the term of incarceration approaches, it can be observed that those who have responded regressively go through a period of emotional turmoil and upset: they report sleeplessness and tension, loss of appetite and diffuse somatic signs, seem markedly apprehensive and often require hospitalization. This complex of symptoms has been interpreted as the result of anxious anticipation, as a kind of inability to await the day of release. On the contrary, it is instead a result of fear, an index that the individual is haunted by anxiety because he correctly if dimly apprehends the removal from him of all the props and supports prison provides. He is not eager for the moment of release; he dreads it. From that time on he will have to make choices, to care for his own interests. But the effect upon him is quite as it must be upon the fledgling who is routed from his nest, and the generalized symptoms of apprehension overwhelm the total organism.

Unique among all forms of experience, incarceration in a prison is a continually frustrating circumstance. The pervading awareness, no matter what the *total* effect upon the personality, is one of helplessness. As one prisoner put it: "You may not *feel* anything, you may be completely dead to your surroundings, but you are always aware of things happening to you, and of your inability to control them or modify them or change them." The prisoner can do nothing concrete about his fate; family relationships necessarily deteriorate because direct communication is impossible. Events wash over the inmate, unprecedented things transpire—and he can only roll with them or, if he opposes, break against their irresistibility.

In prison, one has to "take it." There is nothing he can do about it. Explanation is improbable, the alteration of the past impossible, planning for the future a guessing game. This is why there is so much unreality about the situation, and why the thoughts of incarcerated men turn so frequently to the past. Their conversation is filled with, "If I had only. . . . What I should have done was to. . . ." And much time is spent in reconstituting the past in imagination, reviewing mistakes.

The utter futility of effort is not helped by the desertion of wives, their infidelity, the loss of friends, the threat of further legal action, the expectation of the hostile community reception which they know so well must be anticipated. The true criminal, however, absorbs these things and adds further (often unconscious) fuel to inner fires. The law-breaker, on the other hand, is more apt to strain hopelessly against them, to become exhausted emotionally about them, or to deal with them fantastically.

What the prisoner thinks about prisons will be presented in the next chapter. But here it is necessary to dwell for a moment on some misconceptions about prisons that prisoners themselves nourish. Law-breakers, on the whole, consider themselves either above the prison situation or regard it and all its attributes as something into which they have been thrust by a malign fate. In general, they do not resent the authority they see everywhere about them, and they attempt to make common cause with their keepers. Although they may deride custodial and administrative personnel, they feel a social kinship with them. True criminotics and psychopaths project upon the prison and those who have them in charge all their own base motivants. For example, they cannot conceive that anyone—from warden to turnkey and including the entire professional staff—can possibly be in the work for idealistic reasons. Their misconceptions, in other words, which date to infancy and childhood, carry over without alteration to the place and time of imprisonment. The hated and resented characters of the historical life-drama are here reconstructed, and they behave toward the latter-day surrogates as if they were mirror-images of ancient types. Such misconceptions and mis-identifications are important barriers to treatment.

In the last two chapters an attempt has been made to disclose the chief reasons for the failure of the modern prison. The approach was through the survey and analysis of factors ordinarily overlooked in evaluating such institutions, both from the point of view of the personnel and its procedures, and from that of the inmate. For actual penological data relating to physical details of prisons, for their historical and architectural development, the reader must look elsewhere. What we have discussed are the constants of those psychological and social monuments to man's inhumanity to man.

# 22. The Inmate Tells His Story

IN introducing the two documents which follow, it is necessary to point out only that neither is wholly representative; each depicts a peculiar constellation of ideas and opinions achieved by way of particular experiences. At the same time, each deserves study.

The documents were prepared for the writer by inmates of his acquaintance. The first has already appeared in print in *The American Mercury*, in an abbreviated form, where it attracted wide attention and caused extensive comment. It was written by a middle-aged law breaker who was highly literate and sensitive. His views are colored by recognizable features of character formation and a previous enviable social status. They should be read with this in mind. The second document was put together by a psychopathically inclined youth of twenty-six who had been embittered by his life experiences. The reader is asked to view both of these in the light of the past two chapters.

. Behind the first document lies an interesting story. About three years ago, the author of this book was teaching a course in criminology at Bucknell University. It was his practice not only to present firsthand material, such as case reports, histories, phonograph recordings and other materials of enlivement, but also to invite to the classroom guest lecturers of note in the field. Toward the close of the semester, after all the material had been presented and each speaker had had his say, it was felt that the course would lack completeness unless a prison inmate was permitted to present *his* views on imprisonment. The available literature was carefully searched for such stuff, but everything found was either terribly self-conscious or apologetic. The best plan would have been to have a prison inmate come into the classroom and give direct expression to his opinions. This was impossible for many and very obvious reasons (although the writer still thinks it a good idea). A compromise was, however, made. The writer asked this sensitive, perceptive, highly vocal man to write a lecture for him, one in which he would say what needed saying, and in which he would be unsparing. What resulted was the following letter:

Dear Doc:

You have asked me to do an impossible job. If the prisoner's look at prison life is to have any authenticity, any validity applicable to others as well as himself, I am probably the last man who could give you the right answers. By the grace of Providence I am, for better or for worse, far different from the general run of my fellow convicts—different not only in the less important aspect of social status (I am a pretty good democrat), but especially with regard to my esthetic and intellectual prejudices. So, if what I say here does not seem to you either objective or even fair, you have brought it on yourself. The rasping sound in the middle distance is No. ooooo grinding his own personal axe.

One of the most untrue and stupid old saws is the one frequently declaimed with feeling by the dramatic high school student to the effect that "Stone walls do not a prison make—." It is precisely they, which *do* make a prison. I, at least, remember the cold apprehension with which I looked at the grey walls surrounding the penitentiary when I first arrived here in the company of a slightly drunk and hence highly sympathetic marshal. If prison authorities had any creative imagination, they might think of hiring someone like Diego Rivera or even John Stuart Curry to cover the frosty, unpleasant, no-color surface of these walls with fresco paintings. Dante and I could give them some excellent suggestions on composition.

And that isn't just a first impression. All through your life here the consciousness of the wall runs through the stolid symphony of your days and nights like an ever-present discord. In summer, when some parts of it are covered with creeper, you can fool yourself for a brief while. From the main corridor, the large windows on the South side give on fair-sized plots of meticulously groomed lawn, framed on both sides by the dull red brick of the buildings and by vividly-colored flower beds. The white walk, the catalpa trees and the vine-clad wall close the vista; and what you look at might well be an English garden, particularly in the cool of an early summer morning, when the dew is still on the grass. But if, like John Donne, you see "the bone beneath the skin," the illusion doesn't last long.

The admission formalities are simple and thorough enough. You are examined physically as completely as you have ever been in your life: they look under the bridge work in your mouth and even through your hair to see if you have any "dope" on you; then, after a shower, you are clad in the dun uniform of Quarantine and relegated to a white-washed cell containing a cot, a chair, a locker, toilet facilities, and a wash stand. All your belongings—I mean quite literally all—are taken from you and sent to your people, and a provident Government furnishes you with a comb, toothbrush and powder, a safety razor and blades, and a shaving brush (shaving twice a week at least is obligatory). During all that time, you are conscious only of a dull and hopeless indifference. The door, which has just shut behind you, bears in invisible letters Dante's famous inscription over the gates of Hell: *Voi qu'entrate, lasciate ogni speranza!*—you, who enter here, leave all hope outside!

And then, curiously, comes relief. You are alone, undisturbed, in your cell. It is clean, aseptically, painfully clean and unmarked, like a room in a hospital, an army barracks, or a monastery. They show you how to make your bed in accordance with regulations—it becomes a deft, automatic chore in the weeks that follow. And you lie down on it, and for the first time in months you feel something like peace stealing over you. The confused solemnity of the court room, the hot humiliation of the finger printing and "mugging"—("lift your head there now, buddy, and look straight at me!")—the clanking of your handcuffs, the unspeakable filth and misery of the county jail, the noisy rush of your railroad trip—all these are far behind you, and you know that you have entered upon a new phase of your life.

The first week in Quarantine is not hard to bear. Every day you are called for some investigation or examination. They take your blood pressure, your pulse beat, your I. Q., your parole application; they pump blood out of you and typhoid bacilli into you—there is never a dull moment. In the intervals, the Prison Library sends you some books—a curious enough selection: next to a blood-and-thunder Western there reposes the pale and yet vivid ghosts of Balzac's "Père Goriot," and Mr. Lin's charmingly formal and urbane prose makes an incongruous bedfellow for the stilted and uncouth accents of some lurid detective story. And you read them all; it is the only escape left open to you; you read again with the insatiable curiosity of your youth, and you seem never to get enough. There are no newspapers or periodicals in Quarantine—not because they are forbidden, but because it takes a month to make your subscription effective. The result is that you live as on an island, utterly and completely divorced from all that goes on in the world, thrown upon your own intellectual and emotional resources, such as a monk or a lay brother might be in some ecclesiastic retreat of medieval times, and the illusion is heightened by the austere simplicity of your cell and your clothing. Fortunately, you can be clean; there is ample opportunity (and in fact compulsion) for bathing, and an abundance of hot water available in your cell, so that the daily shave and grooming is no chore but a ceremonious luxury.

Sometime during your first day the Quarantine officer's shrill whistle reminds you of eating, and you line up with your fellows to march, in a silent, shuffling procession of twos, to the dining room. Through interminable, tortuously winding corridors, down an incline, up some steps, you march into an immense vault of a hall, large enough to seat and feed fifteen hundred men at one time, constructed in severe prison Gothic—probably the most loathsome and depressing architectural style in all history. Of course, it is meticulously clean, as all things are clean in this place—it is being washed and scrubbed and mopped a dozen times a day—but not with the fresh and wind-swept cleanliness of a house inhabited by self-respecting people. There is about it the self-conscious sterility of an operating room, or a white-tiled Child's restaurant. The fragrance of cabbage and hot grease is fighting a brave but losing battle with the acrid smell of strong laundry soap, which reigns uncontested everywhere in the institution. The food is served, cafeteria-style, on flat, chromium-plated trays; it is surprisingly good, the materials of obviously sound quality, and there is plenty of it; but it is, as the Spaniards say, somewhat *desabrido*—flat in taste, without pleasant surprises, and of a deadening monotony. If you don't want to consult a calendar, you can always tell by the food at dinner just what day of the week it is. Most of it is boiled or stewed; there are of course practical reasons for that: you can't bake or broil or roast conveniently for so many people, but you can build a steam-kettle as big as an automobile. And the coffee—I have often regretfully contemplated the dispassionate sobriety of the English language when looking at that coffee. You could say proper—or rather, improper things about it in Arabic, or in Spanish, or even in French. The only word suitable for the chaste ears of your class which occurs to me—"foul"—is a masterpiece of gentle understatement.

Yet you drink it and you eat the food, and you get so that you even dislike any break in the routine. Men will get used to anything—let that be a consolation to those feminine members of your—or rather, my—audience, to whom a stern Providence has denied a feeling for decent food, and who will therefore spread large gobs of factory-made mayonnaise on the salads they will set before their resentful but uncomplaining husbands.

At meals, and during the brief rest periods after meals, you first learn to know your fellow inmates. You can spot the first offenders among them right off, not only because, like decent people with Anglo-Saxon inhibitions, they show a reasonable reserve, but because the stigma of their sudden and drastic removal from genteel society is plainly on them. There are doctors among them, and ministers, lawyers, bankers, a university teacher or two; almost all of the professions and trades are included. In Quarantine they keep to themselves and form little cliques, to which one or the other young psychopath occasionally attaches himself—he thinks he can learn something from them, or that he can get a job from them or through them. Later on, when they have passed through the purgatory of Quarantine, the differences in manner, in speech and in apartness tend to disappear. Prison is a very democratizing institution: soon the psychopaths talk like the lawyers, and the lawyers like the psychopaths.

This place, I believe, was originally intended to accommodate chiefly first offenders. But all of the laws of your New Deal notwithstanding, there just aren't enough of them; so there has been and continues to be a steady infiltration of habituals until now they form a large majority. It is they who give the prison its tone and color. Even in Quarantine, they know their way around. They get messages through to old "rap partners" or friends who are in blue, and the friends respond by sending them cigarettes or candy. You can buy these at the Commissary; but the first week or so in Quarantine you have no commissary book, and so you are denied the wonted comfort of smoking. Somewhat gingerly, you begin rolling your own with the issue tobacco, of which the Government supplies you with one small sack a week (it is known in prison parlance as "rip"), and you find you like its rank and biting taste better than you thought you would. "Tailor-mades," just the same, are at a premium, and the old-timers know it and make good use of it. They make a quick adjustment, and you stand enviously by while they run, pitch horseshoes and play baseball noisily, when the quarantined men are taken out to "stockade"—an immense, ochre-colored, barren parade ground given over to that regulated recreation which is a dour substitute for what you used to know as out-of-doors.

If you have the misfortune of being able to listen to the troubles of mankind in four languages, you are soon sought after. You observe the Quarantine officer trying to explain some of the more abstruse intricacies of daily routine to a Brazilian seaman, who doesn't know yet why these crazy *Yanquis* put him into a lovely place like this, where you get three enormous meals daily, and don't have to either pay or really work for them—a rare people that! He looks at the officer questioningly, uncomprehendingly, out of ox-like, round eyes. The officer gets desperate; he raises his voice and gesticulates wildly, interpolating, ever so often, an encouraging "savvy?"; but the man—dark-skinned, immobile, imperturbably courteous—doesn't savvy in the least, until finally you can't resist stepping in and helping out a little. His gratitude is out of proportion, and highly articulate; he begins sending you customers, and presently you find yourself translating and writing letters for Italians, French-Canadians, Puerto Ricans to waiting Micaelas, Helenes, and Mercedeses. One Italian, in particular, is extraordinarily persistent; he harbors the most passionate and uninhibited feelings for his soulmate, and insists on having you put them on paper in plain English, until you explain to him with some difficulty, that the *Inglese-Americani* are quite stupid and priggish people, and that you cannot get a letter past the censor if it refers with approval to certain qualities in your woman which, in Anglo-Saxon countries, are highly appreciated, but not much talked of. Fortunately, the total number of letters a man may write is two a week (though he may receive seven); if it were more, you would have to neglect your own correspondence. At first, your own letters to your people are restrained, brief, somewhat embarrassed; it takes time for you to lose the self-consciousness which comes from your knowledge that the censor reads all the things you have entrusted to the bland privacy of white letter paper.

After you are over the effects of your typhoid antitoxin shots, and the insensate curiosity of the bureaucrats has transposed all of your record and qualifications on neatly-numbered and orderly-filed cards, Quarantine life begins to pall on you. You don't get out into the fresh air often enough; you can't possibly read all the time; you are bored. So when the call comes for some quarantine men to help out in the kitchen, where they are short of hands, you half-hope that the lightning will strike you. Eight of you are presently picked out at random, and under the guidance of a guard you march over into the kitchen, where with soapsuds and steel wool you work for a couple of hours scrubbing pewter cups, butter dishes, cereal mugs and pots and pans generally. The work varies—sometimes they take you out on the kitchen porch, where you join a large group of morose, elderly men (they are known as the "grand jury") in peeling onions, beets, and potatoes.

Finally, all too slowly, dawns the day when you are released into the "population." You turn in your khaki and receive a set of "blues"—a blue shirt, and trousers of a lighter blue—the uniform and comfortable garb of all inmates save those working in the hospital, who dress in pristine whites. For thirty days or so, you haven't been able to go to church, to see a movie, or to do any regular work; all of these are privileges reserved for the "blues." Now your life in prison begins in earnest.

In the beginning everything is a little confused. You pack all your belongings into one of your grey bed blankets (it is an operation with which you become familiar as you get moved around from quarters to quarters) and lug them over into a dormitory—a large, oblong, crowded room, bed on bed in military precision, filled with smoke and men's talk and laughter. While you are arranging your things in the locker assigned to you, and making up your bed, you begin to get acquainted. One or two of your immediate neighbors—you don't know them in the least, but they are as friendly as puppy dogs—offer to help you. Afterwards they show you around and volunteer some sage counsel as to your future conduct in the institution. From the officer in charge (who treats you with a great deal less of the stern condescension to which you have become used in Quarantine) you learn with dismay that your background, your talents, and your education have obtained employment for you in the kitchen; you will serve coffee, tea, water and rarely cocoa to the "main line." The next morning at five someone rudely pulls your feet, and while the rest of the dormitory keeps on sleeping until the whistle, you slip into your clothes, get over to the kitchen and, after a hasty breakfast, start the day's work by getting the dining room ready for the first meal of the day. Cups have to be set out, silver to be laid; butter dishes and syrup flasks must be on each table, and all of it must be in the strictest military array or the mess hall officer will unpleasantly want to know why. Then you slip on a white smock, put a white forage cap on your head, fill the four large cans assigned to your section with the morning coffee, and wait.

And, pretty soon, the bugle sounds the call to mess: *Tah de dah de dah dah—dah de dum*—and from cell blocks and dormitories, from honor rooms, from everywhere, through the wide open doors of the dining room a stream of blue-clad humanity pours itself. They advance with measured steps; there is nothing precipitate about it; they simply come to be fed another meal. But they march in the indescribably sad rhythm of the jail house. Day after day, three times a day, they make this trip: advance to the steam tables, get their victuals, walk back to their tables, sit down and begin to eat. Ordinarily, prisoners have faces, even as you and I have faces—they look vivacious, melancholy, intelligent, stupid, lively or slow-witted. But when they march in this aggregation, they are reminiscent of nothing so much as the characters in O'Neill's *Great God Brown;* they wear the vacuous and sullen masks of prison, and they all look alike. You cannot imagine a more spirit-destroying, depressing spectacle. It would take a William Blake to do it full justice. When you think of the sum of human misery, the thousands of years of wasted living, the urgent and repressed desires for freedom, for light, for air, for love, the amount of human energy laid barren, which is represented by this mass of men, shuffling in dispirited regimentation to get their sustenance, you shudder, and your own troubles seem insignificant enough by comparison.

Otherwise, the kitchen is not too bad. True, the working hours are badly arranged; but the work is spaced, and there are long intervals when you have nothing to do. That isn't any longer the liability it used to be in Quarantine, for now you can go out on stockade for two hours at a time; and you can also go to the library at stated periods and select your own books. The library is a charming room, well appointed and simply decorated, and it is unquestionably the best-run department with which the average inmate comes in contact. The librarian is a slight young man who is brief, courteous, reserved and helpful; the joker is that you may not stay in the library for more than fifteen minutes at a time. Letting a man browse would be a token of deplorable inefficiency; and the fleeting happiness he might experience exploring unknown books by leafing through them at leisure would be highly unbecoming in a prisoner, who must never be allowed to forget his place.

In your new job you do have to know how to get along with people. Most of your fellow workers are confirmed psychopathic cases; transfer to the kitchen is supposed to be a form of punishment for men who don't do well in other jobs. Often enough the atmosphere is tense with resentment, likely to flare up into a fight, sometimes with fists, rarely with a "shiv," which in the kitchen, despite the eternal vigilance of the officers, is perhaps a little more easily available than elsewhere. But if you mind your own business, and display a reasonable amount of unruffled courtesy to everyone, you won't run into any trouble.

Soon you are moved again, this time to one of the kitchen dormitories. Here your neighbors are more lively; many of them are Southern boys, and in the evenings the twanging of their guitars, mandolins, and jew's-harps is counterpointed by the soft drawl of their hushed singing voices. I like them when they sing the songs, at once ribald and melancholy, of prison—say, the *Brown's Ferry Blues*, or the one about *Willie the Weeper:*

> "Ah'll sing you a song of Willie the Weeper
> He had a job as a Chimney Sweeper—
> He had the dope habit and he had it bad—
> Leave me tell you 'bout a dream he had—"

But when they whine about their lost loves in one of Mr. Berlin's or Mr. Kern's potboilers, they are pretty awful. The advantage you have in a dormitory is that you don't have to listen to them; you may play checkers, occasionally a good game of chess, and you can almost always get into a surprisingly competent bridge game.

After you have worked in the kitchen for about a week, one day early in the morning your officer (in prison speech always referred to as "the hack") hands you matter-of-factly a pass: at eleven you are to appear before the Classification Committee which will assign you to a permanent job. This is a matter of great moment; for days it has been the subject of concerned and tortuous discussions among the newly arrived. "Where are them guys goin' to put me—I can't make my time in some screwy place like the laundry issue—I'm liable to blow my top!" As for yourself, you keep hoping. You want to get into the hospital—your narcissism will be compensated to some extent by wearing "whites"—and through the grapevine you have learned that you stand a good chance. The Psychologist's office is going to lose a man—he is going out soon, and they have to break in a successor. This Psychologist—let's see—Dr. what was his name again, Linder—no, Lindner—looks like a good egg—and since psychology has been the hobby horse you have been riding (with more enthusiasm than skill) since your college days, you feel qualified enough. Besides, there are the unforgotten achievements of your youth: shorthand and typing—blessed days when you got paid for your work, instead of your judgment; you had nothing to worry about then. So you join the long line of fellows sitting dispiritedly on a long, long bench in the center hall of the main corridor, which is known as the Captain's Court; waiting with that dull patience which is the first prison virtue, for the pleasure of the Board which will decide on your fate.

Finally your call comes, and, with some trepidation, you step into a large room completely filled with brass hats. They all stare at you; for a moment you feel as if you were a mannequin in Macy's window. Without much ado, someone tells you presently that you have been assigned to the one job you coveted, and that you are to begin working as soon as it is practicable to transfer you. You can hardly believe your good luck—you've heard so much about the ludicrous stupidity with which other assignments have been made; there is actually a feeble-minded clerk, and a man with one of the highest I. Q.'s in the institution is working on a labor detail. Before they have a chance to change their mind, you slip out in a state of high enthusiasm.

The first chill on your delight materializes right away. Naïvely, you have been taking it for granted, that that's all there is to it, and that perhaps that same afternoon you are to assume your new duties. But it appears that the kitchen is too short-handed to spare you; you suddenly assume the proportions of a valuable asset. Reducing it to factual analysis, which is less flattering, they are damn well sick and tired of breaking in a new man every ten days. The ensuing two weeks are the hardest in your whole prison career. Every day, every hour, you hope your transfer will come through; every day you are disappointed. Finally, with the help of a loudly protesting medical department, you make it. You get yourself a set of white clothes—after that you get three of them a week—and present yourself to your doctor.

But the kitchen gets a parting shot. There are wheels within wheels, and they begin grinding; this place is as full of petty politics as Congress. Instead of going to one of the more elegant dormitories, where most of the older first offenders go, and where your neighbor is as likely as not an ex-bank president or an airplane manufacturer in for income-tax trouble, you receive orders to move to a certain cell-block, notoriously the worst location in the institution. It is full of psychopaths, youths of twenty-two or -three with anti-social records an ell long, overt or suspected homosexuals, boys who are continuous disciplinary problems and who spend half their time in the "hole." Your cell is no worse, though perhaps a little more shopworn, than the one you had in Quarantine, but you enter it full of misgivings. You are pleasantly surprised, however. Your reputation as an interpreter has preceded you from Quarantine and the kitchen, and while the psychopath nervously shies away from the dusty and weary processes of learning, he has the abject respect of the ill-bred for what seems to him a man of education. You are treated with great consideration, and after a brief while, one or the other of the boys comes up to you with some very special problem of his own, on which he wants your advice. You get some strange glimpses into the motive springs of human behavior; more importantly, you make some exceedingly useful friends. They stand you in good stead later on.

Meanwhile, your work begins to absorb your interest. Every week, the newly arrived men come up from Quarantine for intelligence tests and behavior analyses. It will be your job to help give the former, and fill in on the latter. It seems ludicrously easy, but you soon discover that it isn't; there is a knack to it that you have to learn. Aside from the technical angle, your temper has to be equable and unruffled; and you have to have a reasonable amount of human sympathy and understanding. The miseries of a thousand people—rich man, poor man, beggar man, thief—unfold before you, as you see these men, week after week; you must know how to keep discipline in a room full of mischievous boys, to whom the group I. Q. test seems like a lot of esoteric nonsense—they have a much stronger, monosyllabic word for it—and how to give an encouraging and consoling word to the troubled in heart, who come in pride, and leave in tears.

On other days, you help out on experiments. So you check film graphs until your eyes smart, and make beautiful looking plates and graphs of your own on patient white paper with india ink; and you begin to lose your resentful indifference, because you feel that you are doing useful work. Intermittently, you argue with Doc about music—the music you love and miss horribly—and pretty soon, by way of illustrating a motif, you and Doc get to whistling Mozart's *Kleine Nachtmusik*, or the second movement of Tschaikowsky's *String Quartet opus #11*, with occasional violent disagreement as to whether it goes like this: *ta teee*—or like this: *ta taaa*. The beautiful part of it is that the argument is never settled. You know contentedly that you will have something to fight over for a year at least.

With the help of a little gumshoe politics, you are soon moving again; this time to a coveted dormitory, where you settle down for a more or less permanent stay. There your neighbors are less confiding, more reserved; their prejudices and notions are more specifically middle-class and respectable. There are some interesting people among them; but on the whole they are a dull lot. Still, there are advantages to living with them; they bathe and shave more regularly than your recent chums.

While you are in the hospital, you are thrown into contact with the rest of the staff. Most of them are very decent and nice people, particularly the doctors, who are uniformly softies (all doctors are), and who hide the tenderness of their hearts beneath the weary profanity which is the customary affectation of their ilk. The special reason why inmates like to work in the hospital is probably the fact that the human relations between the medical and administrative staff and themselves are very much more friendly than they are elsewhere in the institution. If you are even reasonably competent, you soon assume the dignity of a fellow-worker, and the feeling of social degradation, with which you were infected when you first came here, disappears almost completely. If rehabilitation is the end and purpose of institutional imprisonment, the other departments of the penitentiary might well take a leaf out of the hospital's book. To rehabilitate a man, long before you try to teach him a trade, or a sense of responsibility, or that vague something which is known as "social adjustment," you must give him back his belief in himself; and you cannot do that if you shout at him, order him around senselessly, make him feel with every word and gesture that he is an outcast and a man without rights other than that to the sullen resentment which is the keynote of prison life.

Even the officers assigned to maintain order and discipline in the hospital wing have a tendency to relax somewhat in its mellow atmosphere. As a matter of fact, most of the hacks are not at all what your imagination (based on the movies) has pictured them to be. The large majority of them strike you as rather good-natured, slightly bewildered men, somewhat underprivileged as to intelligence, who are trying hard to do their best. When they first get into their uniforms, they are as scared as the men in Quarantine; after a while some of them develop the arrogance typical of the military mind and begin to order you around. These are the ones who love beyond all other things to blow their whistles, the sole outward token of their authority. But most of them learn, sooner or later, by practical experience that an overbearing attitude does not get them anywhere in particular. In the hospital we have tamed some pretty wild ones.

Soon you are established in your routine, and the even tenor of your days goes on and on. You have weeks when the work is all-absorbingly interesting—as when you get some special cases (the psychiatrist ghoulishly speaks of a "beautiful" paranoia). There are other times when your days and nights drip, like water-drops from a leaky faucet, into the vast sink of time, and when you have to muster all the resources of your brain and spirit just to keep on living. Those are the days when you pick quarrels with anybody who gets in your way; with Doc, for instance, and you say harsh and cutting things, for which you are suitably sorry the day after. Doc is very nice about it—he knows what's wrong with you, and that there isn't much that anyone can do about it.

Not that there aren't any diversions. In the evening you have your bridge game; once a week, on Saturdays or Sundays, you go to see a movie; most importantly, there are constant excuses for laying off work, if it isn't too important, because of the one or the other of the men furtively coming into the office to ask you to write a letter, advise them on some problem, or intercede for them in one or the other direction. For, by now, you are known as a "right guy," and a valuable "connection." There is hardly a word in the language which is more extensively used than that word "connection." If you need a new pair of shoes or a coat—if one of your shirts is torn and you would like to have a brand new one issued to you on clothes-changing day—you establish a "connection" with the inmate who is the key man in that department. For the truth is that, in fact, the institution is run by the inmates—the civilians and officers only give the orders. From the Warden's office on down, the whole penitentiary would be a shambles of confusion, if for some reason or other the inmate clerks or attendants would not or could not function. Small wonder! Many of these men are outstandingly competent and capable, used to serious responsibilities in the outside world; not a few of them have commanded and will again command salaries of substantial size. No intelligent civilian or department head would refuse his key man a small favor—not unless he isn't smart enough to come in out of the rain. And there are so many stupid, pettifogging, illogical, and meaningless little rules and regulations that it would be utterly impossible to live in the place unless you could occasionally soften their impact by some means. Sometimes, these connections are on a very simple mercenary basis; a "pack" (that is a pack of cigarettes) will fix you up. More often, it is not a question of paying off, *manus manum lavat*, and if your friend in the laundry has provided you with a new shirt in place of the disgraceful-looking one you had to wear last week, it is no more than fair that you should help him out with a small bottle of mineral oil, which—contrary to the rules and regulations as made and provided in the book—he puts to the deplorable use of slicking his hair down.

As a matter of fact, while they officially frown on the practice, the more intelligent of the administrative officers wink at it with both eyes. At least, some of them do so in the cases of men who belong in the lower social and intelligence groups, and whom an all-knowing Classification Committee (and perhaps a connection) occasionally and disastrously assigns to places of trust and responsibility. Against the high I. Q. men, the first offenders, the men who have occupied a somewhat superior position in their outside life, there reigns a scarcely disguised dislike and distrust on the part of many of the civilian and custodial employees. That, of course, is merely the natural working out of a persistent inferiority complex; some of them will treat the most unruly, undisciplined and incorrigible pimp with more courtesy, decency and consideration than some of the men whose shoes they are not fit to shine, and whose intelligence, honesty and earning power they could not begin to match.

Even the Parole Board seems to hold that general attitude. Their coming (four times a year) is an occasion similar to that first Classification Board meeting. The hopes and fears of the men who go up to be examined with you are so intense that they are almost like a tangible pall that hangs over their heads. The great day dawns; you get your pass; once again you interminably await your turn. This time it isn't so hard; by now you are used to waiting. When you go in, you cannot possibly judge your examiner's reaction; he doesn't give you enough time. To be fair to him, he hasn't enough time to give you. In the limited period at his disposal he must see fifty or more men a day. Each of these people represents a special, particular, individual problem; it would take the memory of a Caesar, the mind of a Socrates and the judicial qualifications of a Solomon to do them justice. You will never find out whether your Parole Board member has these qualities. After a few minutes, you are curtly dismissed. Then you wait for the final decision. Some make it; some don't; why and wherefore no one appears ever to have discovered. You see men with three previous convictions go out on parole; you see others with a life-long record of decent living, recommended by the prosecuting attorney and the sentencing judge, refused without reasons or explanations being given. Being a pessimist, you don't really expect to make it; Doc, being honest, opines you won't either. So, when the verdict comes down: "Denied!"—you only feel a momentary pang of hot bitterness. Then you settle down to pull your time. By now you are an old-timer. When you first came in your principal emotion was a bitter resentment against your fate, and it expressed itself, when you did anything articulate at all, in such sonnets as this:

> The prisoner is guilty—Let no doubt
> Arise of his pretended innocence!
> He did, feloniously and with malice prepense
> Transport this whiskey—rob that bank—go out
> And buy his girl a ring—get drunk, and shout
> And so get taken. He has no defense—
> And let no silly, maudlin sentiments
> Obstruct the law! Go, fingerprint the lout
> And send him up!
>                         Thus, now, he counts his time
> And whilst slow days and slower nights distill
> The bitter drops of justice from his crime
> He does his chores—and sleeps—and eats his fill
> And damns a world, into which, without rhyme
> And reason he was born—and then is still.

But now your attitude has changed into a sort of resolute melancholy. You have done a year (I wonder, Doc, if even you quite realize what that means. For a year there has been no woman to embrace, no baby's cry or laugh to listen to, no animal to fondle or even to look at, not a real friend to commune with) so another seven months will not be too hard to do. Besides, you have got your teeth solidly into a piece of work that needs to be done and which, by a sort of intuition, you have the inner certainty you can do better than anyone else; and a kind of intellectual lockjaw (also known as a good workman's conscience) keeps you from thinking too much about your own troubles.

I could drone on like this for quite a while, but I think your hour is up. Don't forget, we've got that case this afternoon—you know, that French boy who wants to be a statistician? I know you'd forgotten it; that's why I'm telling you.

And now tell me more about that Sibelius Second that Barbirolli was playing yesterday. . . .

#ooooo

## POLICE AND COUNTY JAIL

"In 1936, at the age of 17, I was arrested for the first time for Highway Robbery. During the summer of that year the police of F——, and the State Police in that area were rather busily engaged in rounding up a number of gangs, who all summer long engaged in one holdup after another until the city was virtually 'wide open.' During that summer one gang in particular became quite famous for their daring 'jobs.' I mention this particular group because of the fact that I was indirectly connected with them, insofar as some of my 'work' was credited to them. There were 6 in this mob operating on State liquor stores principally; the other half of the crime wave was me.

"In the section of town where I lived, there also lived most of the city police force, politicians of both city and state, firemen, and even the most of the streetcar conductors—all Irish. My success in eluding the police for most of the summer was largely due to the fact that they all knew me personally—none ever thought that I would ever engage in holdups—all of them talked freely in my presence, and therefore I usually knew their plans just as quickly as those plans were made. I was never identified in any of the holdups I 'pulled.' Towards the end of summer I was caught in the act by city and state police who happened to be a part of a 'net' spread to catch the gang of six who were operating too. My arrest more or less exploded the local police force. Being blood-suckers at heart, they felt sure that my name could very easily carry the weight of all unsolved crimes throughout the county, and so they proceeded to 'persuade' me to 're-member' committing numerous crimes I had never heard about. The night of my arrest I was taken to the city detective headquarters. There I was 'introduced' to the cream of the local crop! These were in the form of 4 city detectives, headed by a neighbor of mine and a certain Detective C——, another jerk. Also present were four State Police, who thought that my arrest had ended all crime waves. At any rate, I received quite a beating at the hands of all 8 of them, even going so far as attempting to rupture me. I was beaten quite carefully, though, because a bruise or cut doesn't register well in a court room. The usual method of beating a prisoner is to use rubber blackjacks and heavily gloved fists on a person's body and head—neither leaves a mark externally. The main reasons for my getting the 3rd degree on that occasion was simply because the local police were embarrassed to find the man they were looking for all summer was really a neighbor to most of them, and also because they had to have someone plead guilty to a long list of unsolved crimes which they themselves were too stupid to solve.

"It was a Sat. night when my arrest took place. For approximately 3 hours or a little more I was questioned and beaten in the city police station. I refused to admit any crime except the one I was actually caught in. After the first session I was thrown in a cell—'put on ice.' No one was allowed to see me—no one was even notified as to my whereabouts. When my family visited the police station to see me they were told that I had been transferred elsewhere. Early Sunday morning I was hustled from the police station and taken to the Barracks, famous as the most brutal of all State Police Barracks. I was questioned there for a short while in the most polite and genteel way possible for a cop to produce —their questions weren't even answered, because I felt like I had just been released from a rack of torture. Following the easy questions I was taken to the basement where two of the force 'went to work on me' for about an hour. When they finished I didn't even know what year it was. Then I was taken upstairs to the showers and while bathing was examined by the same two (one was also a neighbor of mine) for cuts or bruises. I suppose they didn't see any but I certainly felt them—from there back to the city detective headquarters and lodged 'on ice' for four days. These four days without receiving a hearing are illegal in G. By law a prisoner is entitled to a hearing before a magistrate within 24 hours after arrest, and either sentenced, dismissed, or held for jury trial. I waited four days without anything. On the fifth day I received what they called a hearing. I had been unable to get counsel. The magistrate was told by two detectives that I had confessed to a number of unsolved crimes and that it would be advisable to hold me for court! There was no confession presented to the magistrate. I was not allowed to speak for myself. There were no spectators present, no lawyers, no prosecuting attorney even. The only persons in the court room were a few city detectives, the magistrate, two State Police and me. Following that procedure I was thrown in a cell. That afternoon I was taken to the County Courthouse and into the judge's chambers. There was nothing formal about this 'highly formal' procedure either. No trial whatsoever. The charges were read by the District Attorney, and they included at least 3 or 4 crimes that I had never heard of, besides the holdup I had been caught in. Again I was denied the chance to defend myself, I still had no lawyer. The judge gave me a sermon on how much he would like to send me to the penitentiary for a very long term, but decided to let me off 'easy.' So he gave me 2 to 5 years in the County Prison. My age was 17—in G. that is considered being a minor—what consideration is supposed to be given a minor I don't know but I do know I didn't get any at that stage of the game anyway.

"From Court I was hustled to the County Prison and there my 'luck' changed quickly. I was met there by the Prison Warden, who happens to be a very good friend of my mother. He voiced his sorrow at my treatment and told me all would be well. My mother was called in immediately and there developed a 'council of war among the Irish.' I was granted every privilege in the book by the Warden, and some that weren't in the book. I was given a job in the prison commissary, the privilege of receiving private visits from anyone, the right to walk in and out of the prison at will. Practically the only restriction that was placed on me was this: I had to be in the prison at exactly 9:30 each night to answer for count.

"The following day I received a visit from a young lady who at one time was my next-door neighbor. She was County Parole and Probation Officer and also private secretary to the judge who had just sentenced me! She brought with her a promise that I would be home before Thanksgiving day of that year (three months from then). In this particular County Prison there seemed to be everything but discipline! Cards and dice were allowed—

whiskey was smuggled in continuously—all supervision was lax to say the least. A few of us had the privilege of leaving the prison during most of the day and night, and it was not uncommon to see one or two of the trusties appearing at the front door very, very drunk. Next door to the Prison there lived a 'retired' prostitute. She was 'retired' insofar as only one other man and myself were granted her 'favors'! I was considered a favorite, mainly I think because I was practically keeping the whole family (3 children and a husband) with the supplies from the prison commissary! I paid quite a few visits to this young lady and my time went by very smoothly. Shortly after beginning my job in the commissary I discovered another source of pleasure. The Warden's apartment was above the prison itself and he employed two women from the Women's Detention Quarters to act as housemaids in his home. During the day and early evening while the Warden was busy elsewhere I would pay the girls a visit for an hour or two, usually bringing them a quart or two of whiskey to smuggle back to their own quarters. For such favors as this, and seeing they had spending money, I was rather well thought of!

"I spent approximately three months in that prison, until the day before Thanksgiving. On that morning I was taken to the sentencing judge and he paroled me, parole rules to be worked out by his secretary and the warden of the county prison. From the judge's chambers his secretary and I went to her office. She told me I should come to see her at least twice each month and that I should visit the Warden at least twice each week. This was an attempt on their part to insure my not getting into more trouble. I paid each one a single visit and then discontinued the practice. The 5 year parole that I was under was never enforced and I was never questioned as to why I didn't report.

"After being released from this sentence I found myself quite popular with the local police, insofar as they thought it was their privilege to stop me no matter where or when they saw me. These times were numerous and often proved embarrassing to some of my friends. I would be stopped on the street and questioned as to my whereabouts and actions almost every time a holdup was committed in town. Several times I was taken to the police station, not placed under arrest for any specific charge because I wasn't guilty of any, but merely for questioning in an attempt to have me plead guilty to a few unsolved crimes. This is a practice that is going on throughout the country regardless of laws.

"Shortly after my release from my first sentence I moved from home and began living on my own, or maybe I should say on other people, because I again engaged in robberies and holdups. Six months later I was arrested and charged with Armed Robbery of a local silk company. I was quite guilty of this charge, but the night watchman claimed there were two men instead of just one, and as I refused to plead guilty or sign a confession, also because the police could not find the other man (there really wasn't any accomplice), I subsequently 'beat the rap.' Just about two weeks later I was again arrested and charged with the same crime, this time they decided there wasn't any accomplice and I was tried and found guilty. I was sentenced to the Reformatory for a maximum sentence of 3 years. (Under G.'s law a person cannot be sent to a reformatory with a minimum sentence—the sentencing judge has only the power to give the max. for the charge found guilty on) I arrived with the 3 year maximum, the Clinic (similar to the Class. Committee) having power to give exact sentence, up to the maximum. There I was given a job as secretary to the Assistant Superintendent, and with the job came a lot of privileges. This was in 1937, just one year after the institution had received a thorough 'house cleaning' by the governor's office. Prior to 1937 every officer stationed there carried on his person some sort of a weapon, usually a riot club. There was no talking allowed, no smoking at all, each inmate was placed in a certain 'class' depending upon the number of infractions charged against him and these classes were designated by colors (Red, Blue and Black squares on the shirt). The old lock step was used, and for any infraction the usual procedure was for the officer in charge to just walk up to the guilty one, or whoever he thought was guilty, and beat him with the riot club. The only recreation was short periods in the yard each day—no movies were allowed and the inmates received no pay for their work. Their heads were shaved upon entrance to the institution. Whenever an infraction of rules took place, and after the officer in charge used his club, the inmate was taken to 'court.' There he had no chance at all to speak, was immediately sentenced to either segregation or loss of time or both. The Clinic had the power to extend the inmate's sentence at will, up to the maximum given by the sentencing court. For instance if a boy stole a car and was arrested for it the court gave him 10 years. From then on the Clinic in the institution could either take away or add to his time until he finished all of the ten years.

"In 1936 the institution was cleaned out thoroughly. New officers were installed and all rules were changed. The name 'Reformatory' was removed and from then on the official title was 'Industrial School.' The new superintendent was a gentleman in most ways and just a bit careless in a few instances. He was also Secretary of Welfare and in that position managed to gain quite a number of privileges and benefits for the inmates in his institution. He put every inmate on a paying basis, installed visiting privileges, built a new library, built an auditorium and introduced movies every week (twice a week during winter); he also provided for plenty of time in the yard every day during summer, and in the winter the gymnasium was used. He kept one eye on his Clinic to see that additional time was not handed out carelessly. He was and is very well thought of by most men who have served time during his regime.

"As mentioned above I was assigned as secretary to the Asst. Superintendent. He, too, was a real man. In this position I handled most of the confidential material in the institution and had access to all confidential files, including those on each officer. There were still quite a lot of inmates who had been serving time there during the old regime and quite naturally had learned to hate anything with a uniform on. This of course resulted in a lot of trouble throughout the institution, such as numerous attempts to escape, riots and 'gang warfare.' Rackets of all kinds were flourishing also, and as a result most of the inmates carried a weapon of some kind at all times. The new officers were usually chosen from young college graduates, and these proved to be both wild and tough. Instead of the usual 'write-up' for an infraction, the young officer would rather fight, and such fights were a common occurrence. A rule was made in the institution that any inmate who professed hatred or ill-feeling for a certain officer would be granted the privilege of 'taking him in the ring.' I believe the Superintendent made this rule in an attempt to prove to the inmate population that the officers were really superior. Unfortunately for the officers it proved just the opposite, and it wasn't a bit uncommon to see a half-dozen officers making their tour of duty with black eyes and cuts from some inmate's fists. In the case where some small inmate would have trouble with an officer much bigger than he, and knowing that he himself could never stand a chance with the officer, he would find himself a friend who really knew how to fight, and have him pick an argument with that particular officer. The result, of course, was the officer didn't stand a chance himself. After a few months this practice was barred.

"I had been in the institution for some time when a cold-blooded murder took place. A young colored boy refused to leave his cell one morning for work. He had fashioned a knife from a metal spoon and threatened any officer who dared to enter his cell. This was the procedure. The officer in charge of that cell-block notified the Captain of the Guard. The Captain in turn notified the Assistant Superintendent. The Asst. Supt. notified the Superintendent, but the Supt. told his assistant to handle the matter quickly and effectively. So, the Asst. Supt. knowing that his superior was referring to tear gas, ordered the Capt. of the Guard to subdue the inmate. The Captain then appointed two of his biggest officers to handle the matter. They first fired tear gas into the boy's cell until he was thoroughly subdued. They then entered the cell and dragged the inmate through the quarters to the punishment block. There they gassed him again and beat him with flashlights (a common and useful weapon in all institutions). Following the beating he was gassed again, and then dragged to an old punishment section which had been condemned years before as not fit for human use. In this section the inmate was beaten again and again gassed. There he was left, without food or water, no medical attention, and no air. The following morning the door to this unit was opened and it was found that the inmate was dead. He was then taken to the hospital and the prison physician pronounced him dead of heart failure. For 3 days he was left in the hospital, no one was notified of his death, not even his family. After 3 days the coroner from town was called in. He performed his examination but pronounced the boy dead from gas and severe head wounds—he had found the gas still in the boy's lungs. The boy's family received word of the crime and appealed to a Negro Society. This society hired lawyers and demanded an investigation from the governor's office. The State Police were coming in, but before they could get there the entire institution was emptied of all tear gas, blackjacks and other weapons. The State Police searched the institution but found nothing, not even the names of the two officers who committed the crime. The investigation went on for months, in the meantime the two guilty officers were given a 'vacation.' The Superintendent claimed he was in L. on the days of the crime and therefore knew nothing about it. The Captain of the Guard claimed the Assistant Superintendent had passed out all the orders governing the situation. As a result the Assistant Superintendent was made the sucker. He went on trial for manslaughter, was acquitted but lost his job and barred from holding any state position for the rest of his life. That supposedly cleared the institution of all 'carelessness.'

"Approximately three months later an inmate in the punishment unit set fire to his mattress. Several officers with fire fighting equipment arrived at the cell and unlocked the barred grill. One young officer, a sergeant, had a large fire axe in his hands. He rushed in when the door to the cell opened—there was a great deal of smoke in the cell. When he came out he was dragging the inmate with him. The axe was buried in the inmate's back and he was quite dead. In this case there was merely a routine investigation with no results at all. The sergeant remained on the job and nothing was said, but the inmate population were most curious. They wanted to know just why this Sergeant was carrying an axe and what he was supposed to be doing with it on the scene—there was nothing at all for an axe to be used on in the unit—the door to the cell opened with a key, and if it hadn't opened with a key, a fire axe would be useless on it simply because the doors were made with solid pig iron at least 2 inches thick. Inside the cell there was only a mattress and a toilet, no other furnishings whatsoever. There was still nothing said about the affair among the officers, but a few weeks later the inmates had their say-so. A riot was started in the dining room one evening when the Sergeant was present. The lights in the dining room went out and everything in the place was thrown. When the lights came on a short time later and the inmates were brought under control the Sergeant was found laying on the floor with a knife in his back, but not dead. The guilty person or persons were not found, and the Sergeant recovered but never turned his back on an inmate again."

## THE PENITENTIARY

"In 1940 I was sentenced to the Penitentiary for from 1 to 2 years. This Pen is in two branches, one in the city and the other outside. The city branch of the Pen is over 100 years old. It has officially been condemned at least a dozen times. All prisoners sentenced to the Pen must be committed initially to the city branch. First comes quarantine, which is approximately 9 weeks. Nine weeks without movies, library privileges or yard privileges. Nothing to do but sit around in a cell that looks more like a tomb than a tomb does, and wait for the prison officials to get around to seeing that routine is carried out. Following quarantine period the inmate is assigned to either the city branch or the country branch. In the city branch the entire prison setup, buildings, and most of the rules are just as old as the city. The clothing is of the old style, wide stripes on the trousers, blue work shirts, striped coats and blue caps. The furnishings are old and worn, obsolete to say the least. It seems that with the growth of the prison population since the day the institution was opened, each new building to be added was just thrown haphazardly together in an available spot. Prison records show that the institution started with less than one hundred men. On the very same plot of ground there are now two thousand men. Throughout the prison are evidences of the old days, the days when torture chambers were used regularly. In the prison dining room are large iron rings hanging from the walls where prisoners of yesteryear were fastened as punishment. The 'yard' in the prison is nothing but a driveway. Two thousand inmates are supposed to have sufficient space here for exercise and games. The games consist of dice and cards. There is football allowed here but unfortunately the game must be played on this very same driveway—cobblestones it is made of, and one side line consists of the prison wall, and the regulation football is played here every week between the colored inmates and the whites.

"The cells in this branch are of different sizes. Some house only one man. Others house as many as 8 or 10 men. The windows are approximately one foot wide by about two feet long, set so high up on the wall that one can see nothing but sky outside. Even with such small windows someone found time and reason to put bars on them. The dining room in this prison is still the very same room that has been used for years and years, same furniture; the men eat on long hard benches. They are fed cafeteria style and file into the dining room from the steam tables set up outside. In going to and coming from the dining room all inmates must either have the top button of their shirt fastened, or if not must hold it together with one hand while marching through the 'circle.' The circle is the center of all activity in the prison, and it is here the Captain has his desk and all business is usually done here. During the winter it is a prison rule here that all men must wear both coat and cap to and from the dining room. Food becomes cold before one can eat it because it is necessary to walk across a courtyard to the actual place of eating. This is probably the reason why all must wear their coats during cold weather. Another institution rule from other years but still in effect is shaving the inmate's head upon admission. His entire head is sheared then shaved, but only on admission. When it grows in he is allowed to then have it cut any way desired. All in all the city branch of the Pen is indeed obsolete yet it has never been closed.

"The country branch of this penitentiary is some miles from the city. The inmates there, of which there are 2000, are transferred from the city branch after quarantine and classification. It is indeed quite a change after being in the other half of the prison. It is 'new' insofar as it was opened in 1932. It is clean and bright, scrubbed down completely every day. There are 5 cell blocks there, each one housing 400 men, all in single cells, and every cell has a large window facing outside. Each cell has a sliding door, the bottom half is sheet steel and the top half is composed of panes of glass, without bars. The cells are well lighted and each one contains a small radiator set on the wall, also a modern toilet built in the wall, and a wash stand built into the wall. Every cell contains a reception unit for radio use and the first privilege given to every man who arrives is a set of radio earphones. The price of these is usually $2.50. If the inmate is with sufficient funds to pay this it is collected immediately, but if he is without funds, the set is furnished free of charge until his time is finished and he receives the $10.00 release fund furnished by the State, then the $2.50 is deducted from that. Each cell block has its own inside dining room and the food is considered good, better than average for a penitentiary. The entire prison is 'streamlined' and has a very good reputation. Altho, just as in the city branch, there are not enough jobs to keep the entire population at work, this has never created a difficult situation for either prison officials or inmates. The inmate has the right to refuse a job offered to him, and to spend his time in any one of a number of things. The prison yard is very large and well set up. Athletic equipment is rather plentiful and teams in many sports are organized and carried through a regular schedule with teams of the same sport from the outside world. In the prison yard there is a football field, a baseball diamond (and neither overlaps the other), volleyball and outdoor basketball courts, horseshoes, boccie ball, with the entire wall surrounding the yard lined off and separated into handball courts. Along the edge of the yard are benches for lounging. The peculiar difference this place has from other large prisons is this: the majority of long time prisoners there will not accept a job to keep themselves busy. Instead they spend their time doing the things they enjoy most, indulging in sports, lounging around the yard in summer, or listening to the radio. That fact in itself proves that it isn't necessary to keep an inmate engaged in work in order to send him out a better man. There is no 'pressure' on the inmate body because there everything is done directly with no red tape. The inmate is told what the rules are when he enters and from then on he is left alone. Supervision and watchfulness are always present but he is not pushed all around.

"There is in the Penitentiary a racket flourishing, supposedly for the benefit of the inmate being released, but in reality just another 'legalized racket' benefiting certain officials. First of all let me say here that all prisoners in that penitentiary who appear for parole must have a job to go to and a sponsor who will maintain a friendly contact with them outside. These must be gotten before the prisoner is released, yet he may be granted parole without them, with the understanding, of course, between himself and the parole board, that he get both job and sponsor before leaving the institution. In the city there is a certain man, ———, who for years has professed a 'friendly' interest in men leaving such institutions. *He* has quite a number of political connections in the state. *He* is allowed to come and go in the Pen as he pleases. *He* is allowed to look through all inmate files, using the information there to his own advantage. *His* first interest when 'helping' a prisoner is to look at the man's cash account in the institution. For instance, a man is granted parole but he has no job to go to and no sponsor. He must wait in the institution until he gets both. This has happened in my own case. The man may, through working in the institution and through gambling, have acquired a few hundred dollars, yet he has no job and no sponsor to go to. This is where *He* comes in on the scene. *He* will act as sponsor for the inmate and guarantee him a 'job' plus a 'home' upon release. Indeed by doing this kindness *He* is actually securing the man's release for him. So *He* interviews the inmate and they decide that *He* is the man's sponsor and the man will live where *He* designates. The necessary parole forms are filled out and the man is paroled to *Him*. Before leaving the institution, however, usually on the very day the inmate is to be released, *He* being present to insure smoothness, the inmate is informed by *Him* that his personal cash will be held and 'protected' by *Himself*. This, *He* says, is done so that the inmate will not spend foolishly upon release. Of course *He* adds that the inmate can have so much at a time until his money is exhausted. And so all is well, the inmate is released from the institution and *He* takes him directly to the 'home.' There the ex-convict finds a small home. Inside there are usually 10 or 15 other ex-convicts in the same boat. In charge of the 'Home' is another ex-convict who happens to be in on the profits. The sucker receives a job in a small building next-door owned and operated by *Him*. Here the men saw wood and make the pieces into small bundles. Each bundle sells for 30 cents and the bundles are prepared by the truck loads and sold immediately. The wood is bought for $3.00 a truck load, and each truck load contains (after cutting and bundling) approximately 3 or 4 truck loads of bundles. The men in *His* shop are paid $2.50 per week, working 6 days every week for 8 hours each day. They live in the 'home' on almost nothing at all, they sleep on cots, no clothing is furnished them and they must be in bed at 10 each night. If a man happens to be out later than 10 he is locked out for the night. Any clothing or other expenses for personal use needed must be gotten by some other means, and the only other way left open is to steal it. In the case of the man with the few hundred dollars that he had when he left the pen, he may draw on it, but in doing so he must first explain to *Him* just what he wants it for. He must show damned good reason why he can't be satisfied with less than what he wants. He must wait at least a week or two after requesting some of his own money before *He* will give it to him. If he came from the Pen with more than a hundred or two he is very lucky if he ever gets all of it. *He* has a very bad memory concerning other people's money.

"In this racket there is just one escape or maybe two. The ex-convict can either return voluntarily to the Pen for parole violation, or he can break his parole and leave town. There are no complaints to be made simply because *He* has the power to have a man returned to the Pen for violation. *He* is the man's sponsor and 'friend' and until the man's parole is ended he is stuck with *Him*. If the ex-convict wants to look for another job, he can do so—on Sundays. If he gets another job it must be approved by *Him*, or better still, *He* will get the man a job *Himself: He* has more irons in the fire than one. Upon request *He* will get the man a job with a contractor, a building contractor. The man will be paid 20 or 25 cents an hour on the same job other men receive 50 and 55 cents per hour. Actually the contractor is putting out the 50 or 55 cents for the ex-convict's work, but about half of that is going to *Him*, the ex-convict gets the other half. *He* is able to get by with that practice simply because *He* has the power to condemn the contractor's work if so desired. Instead *He* allows the contractor to use material of any kind in his work, *He* will inspect the building officially and okay it, and in doing so *He* gets another 'cut' from the contractor from the money saved by using defective and cheap material. And that is *Him*, the friend of ex-convicts, but to ex-convicts who have seen *His* 'work' *He* is just another thief. . . .

# 23. Sex in Prison

IT should come as no surprise to anyone to learn that the sex problem in prison is perhaps the most important one of all for inmates and officials alike. For the former it represents an issue to be dealt with by techniques which, contrary to common belief, arise not from deliberate choice but from the intimate mechanics of personality; for the latter it is an aspect of custodial care and management which is an intrinsic element in the total penal situation.

Most of the books that have been written on this subject, and most of the papers that have been presented, hold the viewpoint that the problem is essentially one of homosexuality. This is misleading. True sexual deviation is more evident among prisoners than elsewhere, it is true, because the group is smaller and the abnormal stands out like the proverbial sore thumb; but the proportion of deviation of the basic or essential type is no greater within than without prisons. What are proportionately greater in number are the haphazard, experimental, tentative excursions into perversity.

The whole thing is a matter of definition, as we shall see. Yet before we reach the point where definitions are apt, a ground for understanding must be cleared. The reader is again warned against his own prejudices and biases. Particularly in this field is he likely to be more sensitive and hence more resistive.

Sigmund Freud was among the first to overturn the comfortable applecart atop which Western civilization had been

innocently riding in the assurance that all its acts were motivated by principles and ideals originating, generally, from
above the belt. He and those of resounding names that preceded and followed him rudely awakened the culture to a
recognition of the intensive strivings and wants which,
depending upon innumerable and interlocking features of
heredity, development, and environment, and the ways in
which these are managed both collectively and individually,
are the wellsprings of behavior. For the first time in the history of the species, the mask of innocence was dropped, the
scales of pious pretense literally torn away. After a generation
of investigation and discussion, the fundamental thesis that
sexual energy—its amount, direction, goal, and quality—is at
least one of the chief considerations in the behavior of humans,
and in what results from this behavior, remains valid. In this
very volume we have seen the potency of sexual energy in
motivating toward crime and producing criminosis; with respect to other human phenomena this energy has similar
dynamic significance.

It appears certain that the sexual characteristics with which
a child is born have but little causal relationship to the type of
sexual behavior he will later demonstrate, apart from exceptional cases. That is to say, the presence of male genitalia
is no guarantee at all that a child will, in fact, be a male. What
happens to him following birth is what determines his actual
sex. Although equipped with male organs, his cultural circumstances, his experiences, the impact upon him of parents,
nurses, friends, relatives—in short, a multitude of conditioning
influences—may result in his possessing the psychology of
the female. Often this will transpire without the knowledge
even of the subject himself. And it is likewise true that in
every female there is a male component just as in every male
there is a female component. These are the propositions from
which the treatment of our present subject must originate.

Prisons provide the germinal soil in which heretofore un-recognized sexual propensities achieve full-flowering. They are not only places where the normal expressions of sexuality are beyond hope of realization, but they encompass circum-stances and effects which act to draw upon unconscious proclivities. The main thing to be recognized is that places of detention and segregation are prohibitive chiefly in the sexual sphere. In the modern prison, almost everything except free sexual expression and movement outside circumscribed limits is provided. The essential wants and needs, even the basic rights (if there are such things) are satisfied. Food, clothing, shelter, books, movies, theater, recreation, employment—the list is never-ending and always on the increase—are obtainable. Only sex is not—that is, opportunity for heterosexuality. And at the same time, that which is not provided achieves a value which is wholly disproportionate to its real one. Philip Wylie, in his *Generation of Vipers* and other pieces, has expertly pointed out how sexuality has come to invade every province of Western civilization. With an ironic finger he traces the outlines of our prim denial of sex juxtaposed against its veritable flood in press, radio, and entertainment. These things —even were it possible or correct to do so—cannot be kept from imprisoned men or women. Almost every advertisement, every story, every play, every song, is pointed toward the boudoir, the bedroom and its drama are almost ever-present, thrusting themselves on our consciousness continuously. The culture, therefore, is a titillating one, made even more so as it strikes against prison walls.

In the free world the urge for sex and sex experience is ex-pressed through channels respectfully regarded. One can, if he so desires, engage in overt heterosexual activity, usually without conflict or even anxiety. Or, if the opportunity is by some chance or circumstance lacking, there is the resort to daydreaming and the minor aberrations, such as masturbation in its myriad forms. Under conditions of confinement, however, the outlet of greatest satisfaction is denied. The prisoner can only daydream, perform aberratively in a chronic and intense fashion, or indulge in perversity and homoerotism. To require an imprisoned man or woman to forego all sexual expression, leaving him meanwhile in a riptide of sexuality, is sheer madness. To insist also that he deny the agonizing call of his biology to the extent of punishing him for indulgence in the chronic aberrations of the drive is to impose a torture unwarranted by anything he may have done. And yet, so tight-corseted are we despite our wholesale flaunting of sexuality in every medium of interchange and communication, that this denial seems to be what we demand from the inmate.

It was stated that true homosexuality is more obvious but less widespread in prisons than we have been led to believe. This calls for a defining of what it is that one actually finds within institutions. For the most part, essential homosexuality is of two kinds, the physiological and the psychological. In the one, the biology of the individual is involved in a manner that is obvious upon examination. Such a person may lack normally-sized or normally-functioning generative organs; he may lack certain secondary characteristics, such as the expected distribution or texture of hair; he may be physically proportioned like a member of the opposite sex. With the essential psychological variety, however, the strivings and attitudes, occasionally even the habits, are more like those of the opposite sex. His preferences, tastes, inclinations, and wishes are opposed to his visible biology. And these are the individuals who, despite popular opinion, are not so readily distinguishable.

Like the confusion of alcoholism and crime, there is a similar confusion of homosexuality and crime. Homosexuality is not crime and has nothing whatsoever to do with it. Just as some alcoholics may be criminotics, so some homosexuals may be criminotics. Homosexual behavior has, however, been raised to the legal status of a statutory criminal act, in the same way as drunkenness has achieved such a distinction. *But homosexuals in prison are not necessarily criminals.* They are far more likely to be law-breakers.

When the true or essential homosexual comes to prison, he plays therein the same role as he did on the outside, depending upon his passive or active inclinations. Indeed, prison is often a relatively happy place for him to be, since therein he has less competition from females (or from males in the institutions for women), his services are in greater demand and his worth is immeasurably increased. It may even be that his operationally effective field is broadened considerably, for in the restricted, prohibited environment his contacts do not have to stop with the essential types who heretofore responded most readily to him. Under the frustrative and deprivative situation of prison life the ordinarily effective checks on the latent sexual component disappear in a surprisingly large number of cases, and erotic behavior between individuals of the same sex is common. But this does not mean that all who indulge are themselves homosexual; it does mean that the situation has forced a regression to a phallic level, to a level where the urge and not the object is the paramount concern. So we have in places of segregation the curious phenomenon of men and women behaving erotically toward and with members of their own sex, yet themselves not being homosexual. They are merely satisfying a powerful and normal urge in an expedient way, using what material the environment provides.

What also should not be overlooked in all this is the fact that criminotics are generally persons whose developmental course has been fixated frequently at levels *before* the wholesome and adequate resolution of the oedipal struggle. This means that a normal psychosexual maturation was made impossible for them, and at best they are in a state of ambivalence as regards sexuality, and their unconscious trends are readily mobilized under deprivative conditions. Psychopaths notoriously betray a perversive sexuality and are, in this sphere as in all others, inconsistent, diffuse, and confused. Since they experience great difficulty in achieving emotional rapport with other persons, and since it is impossible for them to maintain permanent emotional or intellective ties with anyone, their sex history is non-selective, transient, and adventitious. Any sex act in which they do indulge is a purely biological expression, lacking sophistication and without the preliminaries our culture demands. It is as if they are continuously experimenting, seeking, and for this reason the sex of the passing love-object matters little, and the psychopath's role in the act may be either active or passive, aggressive or submissive, dominant or dominated. In attitude, however, the psychopath ordinarily maintains that of his own sex.

Perverted sexuality is not a criminological problem, although an attempt has been made to bring it within the compass of that field. Apart from the biological types of homosexuality, it is primarily a problem of the education of children. The prevention of homosexuality rests with proper psychological education, the isolation of extreme cases not only from the community but even from the prisons, and finally the toleration of those homosexual adults who have achieved a satisfactory adjustment on their own level in free society and who lack predatory and aggressive characteristics. At the same time, prison officials must be brought to the realization that homosexuality is not the problem they must attack: their problem is homoerotism, the transient sexual exchange among members of the same sex who are confined together under a situation of heterosexual starvation, and who are more readily brought to such behavior because of their basically ambivalent sexual natures, and overstimulated by omnipresent aphrodisiacs.

The sensible approaches toward elimination or, at the very least, mitigation of the sexual problem in prison are well-known in this country and have been tried abroad with enough success to warrant experimentation with them here. While it is not believed that the employment of such techniques—things like granting furloughs, allowing visits from wives, permitting prostitutes to call on unattached males who express such desires—would eradicate all of the present evils, they would at least drain off enough tension and anxiety to curtail the spread of the homoerotic infection. As matters now stand, sex is unquestionably the most pertinent issue in the inmate's life behind bars. Much of the chaos, the upset, the querulousness, the electric-charged atmosphere of any prison is due to this denial. Most of the psychiatric casualties of prison life can be traced to acute panic episodes resulting from conflict about homoerotism. Men (and women) from all walks of life are generally imbued with strong feelings against indulgence in homoerotic, perversive behavior, but they find themselves in a situation suffused with it; their bodies yearn for some expression of sexuality and for the relief of accumulated sex tensions. At some point they discover that their thoughts and dreams contain foreign elements which they have been taught to deny. To these they react violently and fearfully, and they strive for the repression of such forbidden elements. With most, repression is incomplete and unsuccessful. In disguised form they crop up either physically as complaints referable to any part of the body, or as more direct psychological signs of the neurotic designation. Yet some succumb to the temptations offered, and when they do they are often overwhelmed with terrible and unbearable guilt, manifesting itself also in psychosomatic or neurotic ways.

Not always, of course, is the sexual thwarting of prison life expressed in homoerotism. Onanism is, if anything, far more prevalent. And here, as well, everything that pertains to other forms of gratification or indulgence applies. Despite the assurances of medical and psychological authorities that the practice is not of itself harmful, so great is the burden of the culture that it yields a comparable harvest of guilt and inner turmoil. It cannot be ignored that every man in prison and every woman in prison masturbates in one or another fashion. Even elderly inmates are impelled toward the practice, not out of need ofttimes, but merely because life without some form of contact, however casual, with persons of another sex is denied, and self-manipulation functions to evoke the image that life now lacks. Moreover, in view of the prevalence of this type of activity and the reasons therefor, one would like to believe that a tolerant officialdom would not condemn the act. And yet there are penal institutions in this country where discovery in the act of masturbation or evidence that the practice has been indulged in is warrant for sometimes severe punishment.

There has been some glib talk and writing that homoerotic behavior, onanism, or other forms of both aberrative and perversive sex activity in prison have a lasting effect on individuals who have been exposed to them or have partaken of such satisfaction as they offer. This moralizing, however, is simply misleading. If there has pre-existed a trend toward homosexualism or bisexualism it is very likely that the penal catalyst will have brought it into focus. But, lacking predisposition, prisons no more *turn out* sex deviates (maniacs, if we are to believe the howling press), perverts, despoilers, rapists, and homosexuals, than they do criminals. Homosexuals and perverts *come* to prison, as do criminotics. Prisons do not make them, although they may mobilize them and teach them new techniques; it is life itself which has made them. Obviously, the error here is of the same family as the error obtaining in the field of criminology at large; the only effect of association is mobilization; and it cannot affect things which are not already in the personality. That a man in prison acquires a taste for erotic relationships with nice, fresh-faced youngsters or for some other mode of sex pleasure—a taste which he will carry over beyond the date of his release—means only that he was already predisposed toward such extravagant appetites and that they have been precipitated by confinement. In other words, he was essentially and already whatever it is he is now— pederast, fetishist, voyeur, onanist, or what not.

That prisons precipitate latent homosexuality is undeniable. While this feature may, in and of itself, be a tragic one, it can be argued that in a few cases it may serve to increase the social and psychological adjustment of the personality so affected. This is rare, yet it occasionally transpires that a criminotic loses his criminosis by finding himself in homosexuality. On the whole, however, the salvation of the rare case is no excuse for the disillusionment wrought, the lives ruined, and the shame descending upon the bulk of prisoners who are exposed to the miserable, frustrated unwholesomeness of prison sex life.

The homoerotic and homosexual romances that blossom and bloom in prisons are interesting to observe. They usually are little dramas that, at first, involve only two people, later three, and finally more. They have their counterpart in the courtship episode of the free world, except for special characteristics provided by confinement and the fact that the parties are of the same sex. There are also all kinds of variations on the main theme.

A characteristic approach is that of the "wolf" who is already in the general population and who baits his line for new fish. Either through a "connection" in quarantine, or by direct observation, he fixes on a "lamb," who may or may not be homosexual or homoerotic. He may then use one of alternate means to put the new man in his debt and begin the pursuit. One way is to walk up to the neophyte in the mess hall or some other place and to deposit some cigarettes, toilet articles, and candy before him with a casual, "Here, kid, you'll need these. No, don't thank me now. I'll be seeing you later. My name is Jones. If you need anything else, just give me the high-sign or tell my friend Smitty." A less obvious technique is represented by the following letter which a new inmate had thrust into his hand as he was leaving the prison hospital after an examination.

Dear Jim:

I was looking through the papers on the desk and notice you come from Brooklyn. I sure am glad to see another fellow from "God's country" here. I also see you come from F——— Street and this was a real surprise because that's where I lived for a while too. I am writing this letter to you to tell you you got a friend in here and thats me. Us F——— Street guys have to stick together. I'll bet we'll have a lot to talk about when you get out of Quarantine. Meanwhile just take it easy and leave everything to me. You know how a Brooklyn guy can operate, ha, ha. I got things pretty well lined up in this joint and its not a bad go. Just leave it to a F——— Street flash.

I'm sending you some soap and candy and cigarettes today through my pal Roy. You don't have to smoke that lousy Rip. These are tailor-mades and you can have all you want. If you need anything just tell Roy. In case you don't know who I am I'm the fellow that was sitting behind the long reception desk. I have blond hair, about 6 ft. tall and weight 184 pounds, stripped. You can recognize me by an eagle tatooed on the back of my left hand. I cell in ———.

So long and don't take any wooden nickels, ha, ha. Be seeing you. Remember you Pal from F——— Street.

Yours truly
Charles Carroll
#00012

Another mode of approach is somewhat more direct. The old hand fixates a new arrival, manages to get near him, and says, "Look, Bud, you're the kind of guy that needs protection, and I'm the baby that can give it to you. You know what I mean? Anybody bothers you just let me know. Don't take nothing from nobody. You can take it easy and if anyone gets rough just let me know."

In all of these cases the newcomer is placed in a debtor's position. There is no room or time for refusal, and he little suspects—unless he has been "educated" in a reformatory or a private school—the price he will be called upon to pay for favors received. Often a "crush" and then a real love affair burgeons from these small beginnings. But more often the initiate will find himself trapped beyond hope of redemption. When the showdown arrives and payment is demanded, he may be unwilling to come across. Then a startling transformation comes over his benefactor and erstwhile friend, and the harassed neophyte finds himself backed against a wall with a knife pressed to his stomach, and he hears the demand to "f—— or fight."

The aggressive homosexual or homoerotic inmate is not the only "operator" in this situation. There are also the homosexuals who play the field, flaunt their charms, flirt, bargain, and actually seek out a loving protector, a "Daddy." These are often innocent looking but extremely clever artists, who know just how to behave in such a way as to get the most from their affairs and to excite the passions of those whom they desire. A person of this kind is probably the most dangerous of all institutional types, for his role is exactly that of a stray female who has somehow found her way into the prison. Over him there are jealous brawls, knifings, and other serious breaches of institutional peace.

To convey the essence of homosexualism and homoerotism in prison is beyond the scope of this work. No published ac-

counting has yet given it the attention it deserves, and only
one who has been in daily contact with it for years can hope
to grasp the enormity and monstrosity of the situation. The
processes of seduction in themselves are variable, culturally-
toned and influenced, and individualized. Only through the
medium of the case history and the illustrative abstract can
even the faint beginnings of understanding be transmitted.

*From the diary of a "wolf":*

Aug. 14—I guess I grasp at life in a very selfish way. Why? Because I love to live. I take what pleasures I can find from life and
accept troubles that can't be averted. Do I think more of one
person than another? Truthly, No. I think more of myself than
any Person alive.

Aug. 15—There is one Person I enjoy talking to very much. I
feel we have *quite* a bit in common, and Mutually understand
Human Problems. Why the sudden interest? Too soon after my
other affair? Better watch your step Kitty, I'm after you. With
three to choose from I know not what One to take. Life rapidly
grows more interesting.

Aug. 16—This morning I have scored again. It should pay off.
Had a talk with that *most* Interesting Person. Learned quite a
bit. Enjoyed it very much. Life is certainly a happy affair.
Wouldn't miss it for the world. And *He* doesn't know what its
all about. Some fun.

Aug. 19—Talks continue every day grows much more Interesting. What gives?

Aug. 21—A very interesting Subject. Apparently *It* hasn't the
slightest notion of what's in the Wind. Still it seems a bit shy.
Could I have scared him? Better be careful.

Aug. 22—No progress today. Spent a pleasant two hours but
didn't get Very far.

Aug. 23—No success. Subject seems scared. Maybe I'm on the
Wrong Track? We'll see.

Aug. 26—Oh, ho. I have another hot number who is now on
the brink of self-destruction. His emotions seem to overweigh his
Better judgment. His approach is very crude, at the same time
he is *quite* Frank. Should I play him along too? No I really

shouldn't yet I don't know. My Victim has just taken another step into my hands but he doesn't Know it. He'll never know until too Late what Happened. I wonder what makes me such a vandel. I don't know or care but I thrive on fleshly Pleasure. Its a Shame to put simple children among knowing Wolves. But that's not my Problem. I hereby discount the New eliment and go to work once more on the Present Problem. This will be interesting to me.

Aug. 27—I find I'm making real Progress. Its really cruel but I enjoy the whole Thing. Subject is at the Puppy stage and doesn't know it has even Fallen.

Sept. 4—Well I'm quite successful. I have the subject on my list. Subject is now at the stage where It will succumb to any Idea.

Sept. 6—Still going O. K. Asking advice and loving it. Has a good mind but is far behind in Worldly affairs. Maybe will improve in time. Certainly has Plenty.

Sept. 9—Like shooting Fish in a Barrel. Fresh and clean. There won't be any more starvation in this house Mother. What a Dish for rainy days. . . .

*A letter from a "wolf" to an unwilling "lamb":*

Dear Bob:

If you think you are getting away with something your wrong. I got my back up now and anyone will tell you that ain't good. Running into the hosp. won't do you no good. You come across or I'll eat your heart for breakfast. All that dough I spent on you wasn't for you to run out on me. You better learn that this ain't a free world, babe. Your my cookie and there's work for you to do if you want to go on combing that curly hair of yours anymore. I'm beginning to get peeved and thats not good so baby stop dancing and come on home.

Your friend<br>Jack

*From one homosexual to another:*

My daddy,

I'm perfectly contented with our marriage and am willing to accept your terms with pleasure. As for loving you my sweet,

I'll wait until you ask me to, which wont be too long in the future! You think that is a strange bold statement, dont you? But who can tell what the future may bring forth? Anyway, I only want to say that I'm in perfect agreement with you child and am willing to share my body with you as everything else. So, I'm certain we shall be very happy together, but darling, we must learn to hide our feelings in public in the future so as to assure no unnecessary complications that may cause us to be busted apart. You are mine and I am yours, *forever*. Well, my love, I'll ring off for tonight wishing I was ——— you and loving you right now.

To my man and wife, your<br>Obedient Slave<br>Chuck

*From an unrequited lover to his love:*

Dear Sam: if I make no mistake this is four time I have Wrote you Asking could we be More than friend sam you Know I love you way down deep in my Heart and there nothing in the Worl sam that I wooden do for you an you Know it Sunday when you come in side and lef me and give me that Look that way I come in behind you. sam if you only Know how I feel to you you would not do like you do. Because you know it hurt so bad to love some one and they Pay you no mind at all sam please believe me you dont have to spen your money What you got save it. If you Will just let me do with you anytime you see fit I get you a ten dollar every mont sam if you tink I lying to you wait til Satday And I will prove it to you sam if you will just be with me when you can I will do the same For you if you want me and give you anything I got sam. I really mean it from my heart an you Know I Do After all sam We have a long while in Here and we Could make ourself happy if you are Willing to sam Please give me just One chance to prove What I am Saying be true You know yourself I have done without cigarettes for you cause you Said you could not smoke rip. I did not want see you beging for smokes and I still Wont long as I got Money An listen if I am saying anything in this letter to make you angry with me please sam for give me cause I love you an always will. I dont want to Lose your friendship but you know How it is I love you an cant help myself sam I look at you an feel like it Something Broke in my Head sam please ans this letter this afternoon Whatever your ans be let it be yes sam I am beging you all I know how in the worl sam say yes I will close with all my Love.

Chester

*From a passive feminine type homosexual to the lover who has spurned him:*

Ted:

I hope that you are satisfied now that you have plunged me into the depths of hell. You will not be troubled with me any longer. I know when I'm not wanted. You certainly can dish it out and maybe I can't take it, but on tonight of all nights you make me miserable. For the first time in my whole life I am away from home on Christmas and *you* wish me a Merry Christmas by call- ing me a ———— bum. I must send back this candy for I am sure your people would not like their gift to you to come to a bum like me. I do not blame you entirely for I am partly to blame. Smart me, I was the only one of our crowd who could not be hurt by a man or by love, and then I had to come here and let a boy not much older than me do to me what no one has been able to do before. I fell in love but I can't take it. Oh! I will always love you but I know now that you don't want any ties or strings attached to you. I must try to pick up the broken pieces of my heart and it will be a struggle for me. You are free but I am not. I am sorry if I have offended you, but all week you have shown what you feel. If I can ever be of any *use* or *service* to you I am at your call for I do not love lightly. Thank you for all you have done to me and for me. There shall be no other and I shall cease to have sex affairs with any other. Sometime you may find use for me when no one else is at hand. As I have said, my body is yours to possess. Don't think too badly of me for I was true to you, which you seem to doubt, contrary to what you think. May you have the best of luck. Adieu.

F.

One of the prime causes for disaffection in prisons is the sexually frustrative and deprivative regime it imposes. This leads to homosexuality and homoerotism, to degradation and demoralization, to chaos and resentment. It is a powerful impediment as well to rehabilitation. With the temper of our society what it is—titillating yet prudish, aphrodisiac yet puritanical—a solution in the visible future is improbable. As with so much else, not only about prisons but about many other aspects of American culture, our attitude is ostrich-like. It is not true to say that prison administrators are unaware of the awful situation: they are alive to it and live with it and agonize over it daily. But they, too, are under cultural pressures and, since as a group they are generally untrained psychologically, they have a stock approach to the problem. They are, moreover, aware that something should be done about it, and they are similarly aware that the public, our American public, would oust them summarily from their jobs if they made the most tentative steps in any of the directions leading toward solutions. So that what we have depicted will, like so much we have encountered in this survey, go on and on. . . .

# 24. After Prison

ROMANTIC literature, the motion pictures, and the daily press have stuffed the public at large with a gross misapprehension about the release from custody of men and women who have been imprisoned. The stereotype we have absorbed is that of a former inmate, the prison gate swung wide before him, his hands outstretched toward a demure but attractive wife shepherding a bevy of children beyond the barrier, himself smilingly conscious of this dramatic moment and very obviously dedicated to the highest ideals of the community. As the scene fades upon the surety that he will never again return, there is the trick shot of the slowly closing prison gate, the affable guard, the embrace, and the sunset which—particularly in technicolor—conveys a bright promise of tomorrow. Or if this is not our sweet fiction, the alternate one is of the surly, embittered, reckless character who, as the gates clang behind him, indicates by the stiffening of his back, his casual glance over the shoulder at the penitentiary, and the way he draws on his cigarette, that he is ready again to plunge into the underworld.

The moment of release is neither of these things. Instead, it is a time of apprehension and self-examination, of acute discomfort and questioning, of vivid consciousness, of self-doubt and torturing convictions of inadequacy and inferiority for most prisoners.

This writer has been party to the release of countless men; he has observed them at the moment of release; he has accompanied them to their destinations; he has met them on trains and busses carrying them away from prisons. In addition, he has received many letters from discharged prisoners who, knowing of his interest, attempted to describe not only what happened to them but how they felt. The following letter, one of many that vary only as regards specific instances, is considered typical.

Dear Doc:

When you asked me how I felt just as I was leaving I couldn't think of anything except how different it was between us and I didn't have time to tell you then. There you were with your hat on the back of your head and a book under your arm, talking to Dr. R. and just going home after another working day while for me it was something I was looking forward to without a minute's rest for six years. You seemed so confident that the gate would open and you would go out but with me I couldn't be sure. Another thing was that you wanted to leave that night while me, in spite of the fact that I had been looking forward to that minute for six years, I was not so sure I wanted to go. Does this seem strange to you? Abnormal? Well, there it is. Not that I wanted to stay in prison. I had plenty of that, thank you. Only that I was afraid, afraid to go back again. You knew what was waiting for you and so did I. You were going home, maybe play with the kids, eat your supper, read a little or visit friends. I was going home too but to something different.

I've been let out before and its always the same thing. The first time I was scared because I heard from others what to expect. All the other times I knew from experience. I knew first of all that people would know I was a convict. Maybe my cheap suit and shoes and new hat wouldn't give it away but I still knew inside of me that everybody on the train and in the street would know. It was a *feeling* and whether they really knew or not I knew and thought they knew and so they knew. Is this what you mean by paranoia? Anyhow, the train trip wasn't bad except for that. I felt self-conscious. When a woman sat down on the seat beside me I felt like running away. I stared out of the window and tried to act unconcerned not about her being a woman but about her being anyone. When the conductor came to punch the ticket it was easy to see that he knew. Just that little pause before he pressed the gadget told me he just said it to himself.

You would think I would spend the train ride making plans wouldn't you? I guess you would think how I would be working out what I was going to do, how I would change things and stuff like that. Well, I didn't. All I did was stare out of the window. Maybe I was free but I didn't feel free (and still don't). Nothing had a free meaning to me. I thought that when I saw the highways with the cars running along them and the open fields and girls and kids and got the feeling of moving that I would know I was free, but it didn't work.

I didn't know what I was going to do. You'll say, "What about your job?" Well, Doc, that was a lot of crap. I never had a job. My wife just made the arrangements with some guy who got a fifty for answering letters and promised to carry me on his pay-roll if anyone should ask. Most parole or C. R. [conditional release] jobs are like that. I tried to figure out something but I couldn't. So I gave up and tried to read but that was no good either.

When we got into the station Alice and the kid were there. They were all dressed up and it only made me feel worse. Alice said she was taking me to a restaurant for a real dinner before we went home. The meal was good but I hardly tasted it. Both of them jabbered away and I tried to act gay and hopeful but I didn't feel that way. That night was a disappointment too and someday I'll tell you about that but not now.

Nothing else I have to say would be unfamiliar to you. It's the same old story. It was a struggle to land a job and if it wasn't for the war I suppose I'd still be looking. After a while I got the point. At first I was hoping it would be different but it wasn't. They still don't want ex-cons unless their business is shady or they want labor spies. I ran into the same thing before. Remember how I told you about the —— who made a deal with me when I got out of the reformatory? My parole officer at that time told me to go up to this place and I went. The job was a pretty mean one. At the end of the week I found out that he was paying me about 50¢ a day and I asked him about it. He said it was enough for a convict and if I started any trouble he'd have me sent back to the can. That was the manager and I know he was pocketing the rest of the so-called wages. Then there was the time of that elevator strike when practically every ex-con in the city got a job for a few weeks. Personally I'm finished with telling about my record. It's better to deny it and eat for a few days than to admit it and starve.

Anyway I landed a job and its like it always was, talk behind your back all the time and you worried sick about whether the auditor will find a penny missing and they land you for it. Of course there's the cops too. Every time someone spits in the subway you get dragged in, and you can't get away from the feeling that you're branded like a steer on a ranch. And in addition to this there is that sort of butterfly feeling inside you all the time. Our talks [this man had been under analytic therapy for a while] showed me how I got into trouble and I don't think I'll ever do those things again because of them, but that fluttering inside is hard to live with. Its like being scared all the time. I guess I'll get over it.

So that's the story and that's the way it is. I'm keeping in touch with the parole officer. He's a good guy but doesn't know the score and I think he looks at me every time I see him as if I'm a newcomer. He deals me out the same crap each time. When I go to him I get jumpy for no reason at all and I'm awful glad to get away. As for my advisor, the minister, well that's a real joke too.

Is this what you wanted?

Yours,

Ned.

Release is, in a very real sense, a more trying, more crucial experience than imprisonment. If it resembles anything, it resembles the first moments of incarceration. There is the same need to alter habits and conform with existing practices, the same trepidation and insecurity, the same fears of inadequacy in the face of an overwhelming rush of novel impressions. It may even be more drastic in the sense that, on coming to prison, one is usually prepared for what he will encounter, whereas on being released he cannot know the mood and temper or even the details of the physical and psychological facts awaiting him. Some say that prison is rarely so bad as one expects it to be; while release is usually worse.

In general, prisons prepare a man poorly against his release.

For a given length of time he has been robbed of initiative, made subservient and docile insofar as it was possible to mould him; the controls over his own behavior which he heretofore had to exercise have been taken from him; his diet has been regulated both physically and mentally. Now, of a sudden, he is literally pushed into a world which is completely rejecting, which actually does not want him. If he has been a law-breaker he can often take up, after a time, the threads of the life he had been forced to drop. But if he is essentially criminotic and has not received the therapy which is the only excuse for imprisonment, that hostility which he meets will only serve more rapidly to precipitate another criminotic deed.

In all too few jurisdictions is an inmate given even marginal preparation against the day of his release. Certain Federal units have been conducting rather half-hearted and extremely tentative experiments in this direction, and their success seems to call for an extension of such attempts. In the main, they are limited by physical facilities. If an institution happens to have a farm or a camp attached to it, or within reasonable distance, as the time of release comes near an inmate may be privileged to leave the institution proper and to spend the remainder of his time in an environment that is somewhat less penal. Here he has something of an opportunity to recapture the "feel" of extra-mural living, to become accustomed to a less restrictive and prohibitive atmosphere. His areal limits are wider and he is, psychologically at least, slightly more independent. These crude beginnings point the way toward a time when— if insistence on imprisonment does not abate—the main unit of a penitentiary will be utilized therapeutically, and other units will provide intermediate steps on the road to complete freedom within the community. There is no reason why an inmate, after the completion of his sentence, should be catapulted into a world for which he has not been readied with care. There is every reason for progressing him steadily toward the goal of release by providing successive stages-in-release after treatment. It would seem far more important to construct housing units approximating those in the world outside and to grant opportunities for absorption by the prisoner of prevailing standards and attitudes while he is yet under guidance than to throw money into the quicksand of decorative but non-rewarding machinery and personnel. We can readily envision a program of measured return to civil life based on the principle that one does not bathe in an obviously hot tub without testing the water by preliminary and segmental immersion. An ideal would be for an institution to be so arranged that more and more liberty is granted as the release date approaches. This writer is heartily in favor of permitting more than "free" but somewhat limited access to the community as some systems do in the form of furloughs or visits. He would even advocate a system of allowing families to live with prisoners in the final stage of the progression. Here would be a splendid opportunity for marital knots to become unravelled and adjustments to be made with the expert guidance and counsel available.

The great delusion, which we have done our best to shatter, has as one of its bases the unspeakably naïve notion that people who commit offenses often do so because they "have no trade" or "are idle," or some such drivel. In keeping with our hypocritical puritan heritage we have attempted to foist an ideal of endless work, work at all costs and without regard for anything but work, on everybody else. So we have filled the prisons and penitentiaries with equipment ranging from raffia strands to looms and punch presses, and we sit back in the fond comfort that the supportive slogans on the wall about industry and honest toil and habits of occupation will remake the twisted personality that the criminotic is into a "useful" citizen. We pride ourselves, both as taxpayers and interested overseers, that we are "giving" a man or woman a trade, that we are encouraging irreversible habits of employment. Yet the truth of the matter is that a very pitiful few are so affected and of those who are, almost all are law-breakers.

If we are so completely deluded as to entertain even for a moment the idea that the rehabilitation of an offender takes place at the work bench, we are indeed in a sorry predicament, but even this inanity is no excuse for the rest of the tale. The stated aim of rehabilitative philosophy is to return a former prisoner to civil life, now equipped with the means for adjusting more satisfactorily. But in blithe unconcern with the economic world, we invest fortunes in "training" more and more men and women for occupations and trades already glutted. Even assuming that prisons do rehabilitate men through industry, that they do teach and encourage habits of work, that they "train" men and women; what are they training them for? The trade training programs consist of the following: the culinary arts and their derivatives—cooks, bakers, waiters, dishwashers, butchers, handlers, canners, etc.; the skilled trades —carpenters, electricians, painters, plumbers, bricklayers, floor finishers, etc.; the industrial skills—toolmakers, designers, draftsmen, and the lesser technical lights such as welders, operators, etc.; the semi-professional ranges—nursing assistants, clerks, stenographers, etc.; and others, such as tailors, cutters, pressmen, truckdrivers, porters, etc. Merely a glance over this incomplete list reveals immediately that institutional training programs function to turn out workers in economic areas already surfeited. If they are going to prepare men for jobs, one would think a careful survey of areas where workers are needed would be the first consideration. Instead, apparently unconscious of such a rudimentary requisite, they set free men who are not wanted to places where they are not needed. There are many situations in our economy where there exist drastic shortages, places capable of absorbing workers as fast as they are released. These opportunities should be exploited.

It must be considered that persons who have been in prisons, particularly criminotics, are more rapidly and more readily responsive to adverse economic winds. They are like people who are allergic to certain pollens or to some kinds of infection: unless they have been immunized against the catastrophic effect of unemployment, let us say, they will succumb to it by criminosis. If, therefore, it be objected that special measures such as those suggested are too elaborate for them, that they are undeserving, our only answer must be that the time and money now being invested is wasted, and that only by some such practice can criminosis be brought under control.

To follow the suggestion made above about preparing prison inmates for employment not in the over-crowded economic areas but in places of need would require a continual shifting and, from time to time, a realigning of the training program. This in itself would be a good thing. But, more importantly, it would mean that the intramural program would have to be concerned with providing basic skills and be necessarily introductory rather than finished, otherwise it would be essential to re-equip our places of detention periodically. Moreover, it would further necessitate an outright program of propagandizing to change the current attitudes of industry toward the ex-prisoner. While most business men pay lip service to the idea of hiring former inmates, as our correspondent has stated they are used mainly as a source of cheap labor or for degrading work such as strike-breaking, agitation, and spying.

The entire program of preparing a man against release is a complex one. At the time of this writing, with prevailing sentencing, detention, management, and release procedures, the situation is tragic. If the sentencing process were different, *if* prison inmates were treated during incarceration, *if* release were not such a critical episode, *if* the community had a more humane and rational attitude, the proper kind of training would be possible. This would not be in-service training but would take place in the community, during therapy, and be based on true classification, itself predicated on the examination of the total personality.

A figure of central importance in the entire process of readaptation to extramural life is the parole or probation officer. It is this person on whom, in the final analysis, the burden of rehabilitation falls. For this reason, one would expect him to be chosen with the greatest of care, to be a person of training and talent and tact, with an inclusive view of his work and a professional orientation toward it. Yet this is so only in a small number of cases, most of which fall in the Federal system. For the most part, they are harassed men of small abilities, doing a haphazard job and, like everyone else, attempting to justify their work by impressive figures or stacks of reports. Or if they are not this, they are bombastic politicos for whom the atmosphere of the courtroom is a stage on which they perform in the self-delusion that their role is one of importance. The position of parole or probation officer is a grand repository for party spoils to be distributed to minor ward organizers and vote-getters, and membership in the Kiwanis, the Rotary, the Elks, and the Masons is a more important qualification than training in social case work or a degree from a university.

Yet, if the parole and probation systems are ever to work, the salvaging of the ideas on which they are founded rests with the deliberate selection and training of personnel. In a very basic sense, a parole officer should have a psychological orientation toward his job, which in essence is that of a therapist. Since it will be his task to guide and direct the lives of his charges, he must himself be a stable and well-adjusted person. This is not to advocate the ideal that he undergo analysis, but his selection should certainly be guided by psychiatric principles and made as a result of intimate and prolonged survey. Too often, even among those with higher academic training, one finds such public servants to be themselves bowed down with strong inadequacies and to be using their jobs either as refuges or as compensatory situations wherein anxiety, insecurity, and inferiority can be worked out against their petitioners.

The technique utilized by such officials can be criticized almost endlessly, but many of their adversely criticized actions are performed because of factors for which they are not wholly responsible. They are provided with raw material released from the prisons and it is their job to assist in the prisoner's return to a community which is, at the very least, unfriendly to him. The case load they bear is tremendous. The most they can do is see the releasee once or twice, review the reports he sends to their desks and, if he is in trouble, either to return him to prison or make minor situational readjustments to stave off for a while such a catastrophe. They are beaten at the outset, of course, by the inescapable fact that the ex-prisoners who come to them are products of the system we have already depicted, are thrust without preparation into extra mural life, and are fundamentally the same personality types who entered the prison in the first place. They are also defeated by the haphazard paroling systems, and by the failure of adequate intramural classification. If their charge happens to be a law-breaker, fortune is smiling on them; for then they can rest happily in the assurance that only under the most unusual or accidental circumstances will they "have trouble" with him. But if their client is a criminotic, aspirin or alcohol is their fate.

A little thought will lead to the acceptance of the proposition that the position of parole or probation officer is analogous to that of the psychotherapist. In the same way as the therapist capitalizes on the relationship with a patient, so should the probation or parole official exploit the situation that brings the client into his orbit. Parolees and probationers will approach the officer with certain attitudes. The first task is the discovery of such attitudes and the estimation of the parts they will play in achieving or impeding the aims of the relationship. Proceeding on the basis of this knowledge, it is the official's task to know his charge, to comprehend his motives, and particularly—if he has not been treated for criminosis— to estimate the kind and quality of precipitants which must be avoided. His role becomes that of a father, a guide, and because of this there becomes fixed upon him the exact same kind of regard in which a therapist is held. He must, therefore, learn to handle the *transference*, the energy provided by the accord between himself and his client. In the manipulation of this rapport or relationship, in its exploitation for adjustment purposes, the parole or probation official must become efficient, for only by its proper handling will he ever be able to function as he should.

Current practice is to set a limit on parole and probation, but nothing could be more absurd unless it is the pompous assumption of parole boards that they can predict exactly the moment of rehabilitation. To set limits to the period of guidance and supervision which is parole and probation is like declaring to an ill patient that he will be healthy again on two weeks from Wednesday at high noon. The period of probation and parole should be indefinite, its termination left entirely at the discretion of the officer charged with it. He alone will know when he is no longer needed, when it is safe both for the ex-prisoner or probationer and the community for the reins to be dropped. And in dismissing his charge, he must eventually come to the realization that this is a most delicate task. The relationship has to be dissolved with a finesse almost surgical, and its energies redistributed proportionately and properly.

Under existing circumstances, parole and probation officers have to take what they get. Only in probation work is it possible for the official to exercise some choice in the cases he receives from the courts. Parole authorities, on the other hand, merely take what prisons turn out—law-breakers, psychopaths, and criminotics. They have to deal, in many cases, with unregenerate, hostile men and women who have had added to their already supercharged personalities all the gorge and mistrustfulness that is the usual bequest of prisons. If the classification process within the prisons were true to its trust, this burden could be minimized. Law-breakers, first of all, do not require the same intense aftercare by parole officers as other releasees. If they are indeed such, this ministry is almost superfluous. Advanced, unamenable, and unresponsive criminotics should also not be permitted to swell the case-loads of these over-burdened functionaries; they should not be released. Only those who offer prospects of reassimilation within the community, the hopeful and therapy-absorbing cases, should be placed in their charge. But now, with classification a veritable comedy, with sentencing anybody's game, and with prisons intent on custody or blinded by the great delusion, parole and probation are the stepchildren of penology, tolerated and supported for reasons of conscience and as a sop to the "new penology."

Parole boards and authorities, those vague and distant figures which come from afar and in a mysterious and magical way deal a secondary justice from on high, deserve all that has been said against them and more. They owe their jobs to a fallacy of thought: one which assigns to them a Jovian infallibility of judgment. In a sense they are atavistic hangovers from a day when many men believed that character and personality were betrayed by physiognomy.

The men who comprise parole boards are generally political appointees often with legal training but rarely with psychological schooling or even experience with prisoners except from the towering heights of a judicial bench. They rely, in the main, on their own intuitively derived snap judgments, make little if any use of the laboriously collected information about an offender which some prisons maintain—except, of course, the man's or woman's record, the current offense, and perhaps the institutional "disciplinary" adjustment—and perform as their prejudices dictate. With a horrible ease they grant or deny parole applications, and one of their cutest tricks is the pat determination of a date of parole to become effective months or even years ahead, in the facile assurance that on that date a prisoner will be more suitable for release than he is now. These Olympians, moreover, have decided prejudices against certain offenses, and are not above biases in other directions. In some places, it is believed, they can be approached politically or with hard cash.

Parole hearings, these so crucial events on which the future of men and women hang, are spectacles that could be enjoyed were it not for the feeling a sensitive observer has that he is in a Roman coliseum where the casual wave of a bored dictator's thumb can dispense with a life. Only rarely does it transpire that the parole judge does not retry the case for which the sentence is being served, and when this does not take place, there is usually a recital of the past record. Little if any attempt is made to draw upon available scientific data. Prediction tables of the kind proposed by the Gluecks in their monumental studies are ignored. The average parole judge is thoroughly ignorant of the psychological studies in the field of criminology and has a rather uneasy contempt for the psychiatric and sociological counsel that is available to him almost everywhere he performs.

A typical parole hearing which led to a denial was the following. On the basis of this interview alone did the official pretend to grasp the intimate psychology of the offender, to estimate his likelihood of success on release, and to gauge the extent and depth of his rehabilitation.

"During the course of these hearings, while the Judge is leafing through your jacket, you get the impression that everything is against you and that whatever you say isn't going to help you in any way. Most of the Judges have a certain demeanor which right away leads you to believe that no matter what you say it isn't going to be taken seriously, and that the judge is just going through a formality because he has to. The hearing I had went like this:

'Your name is Edward C. McGeorge?'

'That's right, sir.'

'You were sentenced to four years in the —— court of —— by Judge ——?'

'Yes, sir.'

'I see by the record that you've done quite a bit of travelling.'

'That's right, sir.'

'You were in the Army in 1936?'

'That's right, sir.'

'Why did you leave the Army?'

'I don't know, sir, I just suppose I didn't like the discipline.'

'There was a woman involved in your case. Is that right?'

'Yes, sir. I had a girl with me when I was arrested.'

'Well, have you anything to say, now?'

'Yes, sir. I think that I have changed considerably since I've been in this institution. I have always been led to understand that the object of the institution was to rehabilitate men or prepare them for leading a better life on their release from the institution. I have tried to better myself educationally and have tried to learn a vocation. I have done quite well on my job assignment and feel I can hold down a similar job on my release. And I therefore would like to have another chance, sir.'

'O. K. That's all. We'll see what we can do for you.' "

The further pursuit of this topic of release is a fruitless one. By this time the reader well knows the philosophy governing this work and the recommendations that naturally proceed from it. Not until the determination of sentence length is taken from the judiciary and given to therapeutically-minded penal authorities can a constructive program become operative. Not until probation and parole officials are chosen with a care to their training and suitability can these areas of criminology hope to function satisfactorily. Not until release procedures are more segmented can the anxiety and insecurity of the period following release be removed from the list of especially dangerous times for the released prisoner. Not until institutions themselves take advantage of their potentialities for true classification can the determination of who should be released be made. And not until the public learns that crime is an illness like any other sickness, and loses its hypocrisy while increasing its understanding, will the release of prisoners from penal custody be the return to health it should be.

# 25. In Summary

WE have traversed a long road through a region of man's behavior and the techniques evolved to check and control a form of chronic internal warfare arising from it. We have seen that this behavior is an inspired thing, resulting from a sickness in the culture of our times. Now is the moment for a summing up and a prescription.

The treatment of the individual criminotic can be accomplished by depth psychology. By utilizing the dynamic concepts which form the very marrow of the new orientation in psychological science it is possible, in many cases, to penetrate behind the veil of criminosis and to reach into the dank substrata of the unconscious, to probe forth for examination and appraisal the secrets of the criminal deed, actually to reconstruct the personality. This is an arduous task, but a rewarding one, and with the passage of every day we are gathering new knowledge on how to go about it with more ease and surety of success.

Of all the approaches to treatment the dynamic ones offer the greatest promise of success, and in spite of their patent limitations the area of their effectiveness is being extended through research. But there are other avenues of approach through the application of medical art and science, through physiology and biology, which are applicable in certain special instances. Here, one need look only to the investigations of Wilder, for example, with those episodic and violent outbursts of criminal deed precipitated by the hypoglycemic states; to the patient experimentation and research of the brain physiologists; to the hormonal studies.

Yet it cannot be denied that all the analytical mining and construction work, all the exquisite application of laboratory science and correctional medicine, are but nibblings at the odoriferous mass of the crime problem. True, the workers in these fields salvage some of the salvageable, they cure some of the curable, and they reclaim some of the reclaimable, but they are a small band of devotees and they are pitifully limited by the boundaries of human endurance and the inexorability of time. The curing of individual criminosis creates only a small ripple in the immense ocean of crime. And, yet, in spite of this, it is the *one* productive and hopeful fact of the present.

Prisons have failed. They have been distracted by a delusion that they can cure criminosis and reduce crime by keeping people in air-conditioned zoos furnished with distracting toys. Moreover, they are subverted by the courts and the public which little know or care for anything beyond an assurance that there exists a kind of social graveyard in which society's mistakes can be buried. Even with the reforms we have suggested, even with the conversion of prisons from places of mere detention to the treatment centers which they *must* become, there would still be crime.

Crime prevention programs and projects have failed and must continue to fail. Their delusion, in the words of Edwin Lukas, is that they are attempting to prevent crime where they should be preventing criminals. Were they to bend their efforts to this ideal, some success would be theirs; but it would be a mean one, a thin one, like the unit triumphs of the psychotherapists. These programs cannot prevent crime any more than can the lone therapist in an institution or the massive walls of the penitentiary.

Where, then, is a solution?

The answer to the crime problem is similar to the answer to every other social problem. It calls for an attack in concert on the predisposants and precipitants of the illness. The assault on both requires the devoted efforts of the community as a whole and must proceed from the same philosophy and with the same enthusiasm that urges toward a better world.

The knowledge and the skills are at hand. We *know* what predisposes toward crime: the haphazard breeding between psychological and physical mismates that produces both social and biological abortions, that stacks the cards against the growing child by making the home a demon-ridden wilderness; the economic harvest of denial and want, of privation and frustration, affecting parents and children, perverting life to a struggle for mere existence; and the shoddy culture of withheld promises and shams, of prejudice, of tinsel and counterfeit. We *know* what precipitates crime: the touchstones of the culture and the economy. And we know what to do about these evils. In short, the criminological problem is the social problem.

*Not education of parents alone, not the psychoeugenics of mating alone, not slum clearance alone, not the psychotherapy of the individual criminal alone, not the reorganization of social institutions from courts to prisons alone, not any separate phase or aspect or portion or part of our total social configuration by itself will prevent crime, but all of these together and at once.*

# Index

# Index